THE UNFATHOMABLE ASCENT

ALSO BY PETER ROSS RANGE

1924: The Year That Made Hitler

THE UNFATHOMABLE ASCENT

HOW HITLER CAME TO POWER

PETER ROSS RANGE

LITTLE, BROWN AND COMPANY

New York Boston London

Little, Brown and Company
Hachette Book Group
1290 Avenue of the Americas, New York, NY 10104
littlebrown.com

First Edition: May 2020

ISBN 978-0-316-43512-3
LCCN 2019952533

10 9 8 7 6 5 4 3 2 1

LSC-C

Printed in the United States of America

For

Franklin and Caroline

CONTENTS

PART TWO
RESET
(1928–1929)

PART THREE
TURNING POINT
(1930–1931)

PART FOUR
GRASPING FOR POWER
(1932)

THE UNFATHOMABLE ASCENT

DENMARK
NORTH SEA
Kiel
SCHLESWIG HOLSTEIN
Stralsund
Hamburg
Elbe R.
NETHERLANDS
PRUSSIA
BERLIN
Braunschweig
RUHR REGION
Göttingen
Rhine R.
Essen
Düsseldorf
Cologne
Leipzig
Weimar
Dresden
Chemnitz
THURINGIA
SAXONY
BELGIUM
GERMANY
HESSE
Frankfurt
Main R.
LUXEMBOURG
Bayreuth
Wagner's home
Nuremberg
Nazi Party conventions
BAVARIA
FRANCE
Rhine R.
MUNICH
Nazi Party headquarters and Hitler's home
Obersalzberg/ Berchtesgaden
Hitler's Alpine retreat
SWITZERLAND

Germany
During the
Weimar Republic,
1919–1933
BALTIC
SEA
LITHUANIA
Tilsit
Königsberg
Danzig
EAST
PRUSSIA
Oder R.
Breslau
SILESIA
POLAND
Vistula R.
CZECHOSLOVAKIA
AUSTRIA
Danube R.
HUNGARY
0
100 Miles

TIMELINE

1889: Hitler is born in Braunau am Inn, Austria.

1908: Hitler moves to Vienna, Austria's capital, where he fails the arts academy admissions exam. He falls on hard times, living in a homeless shelter for men.

1913: Dodging the Austrian draft, Hitler moves to Munich, Germany.

1914: Hitler enlists in the First World War, serving as a battlefield messenger.

1918: The war ends in Germany's defeat. Revolution transforms the country from a monarchy into a democracy that becomes known as the Weimar Republic.

1919: Hitler joins the tiny German Workers' Party in Munich.

1920–21: Hitler takes over the party, renaming it the National Socialist German Workers' Party: the Nazi Party.

1923: Hitler attempts a coup d'état called the Beer Hall Putsch. It fails, and he is thrown in prison for more than a year.

1925: Released from prison, Hitler reestablishes the Nazi Party.

1928: In his first attempt at national politics, Hitler fails. The Nazi Party wins only 2.6 percent of the vote in a national parliamentary election.

1930: Hitler stuns Germany and the world by winning 18.3 percent of the national parliamentary vote, making the Nazi Party the country's second-largest party.

1932: In early spring, Hitler runs for president against incumbent Paul von Hindenburg. Hindenburg is reelected, but Hitler captures 37 percent of the vote.

1932: In late April, the Nazi Party wins an average of 37 percent of the vote in a series of state elections involving 80 percent of the country's voters.

1932: In July, Hitler again wins 37 percent of the vote in the year's most important contest: the national parliamentary election. The Nazi Party is now uncontestably Germany's strongest party.

1932: In November, the votes won by Hitler's Nazis fall to 33 percent in yet another national parliamentary election. Though still the strongest party, the Nazis and their leader are considered to have peaked and to be in gradual decline.

1933: On January 4, Hitler's fortunes are revived in a secret meeting with former chancellor Franz von Papen, who wants to use Hitler's popularity for his revenge-seeking goal of becoming chancellor again.

1933: Throughout January, a series of secret meetings reverses the power constellation. Papen agrees to become vice-chancellor in a cabinet with Hitler as chancellor.

1933: On January 30, Hitler is made chancellor of Germany.

LIST OF CHARACTERS

Max Amann. Hitler's company sergeant during the First World War, Amann later became head of the Nazi Party publishing enterprise, Franz Eher Nachfolger.

Edwin and Helene Bechstein. Heir to a piano-making fortune, Edwin supported his wife's habit of donating funds to Hitler and hosting him at their villas in Berlin and Bayreuth.

Otto von Bismarck. A Prussian aristocrat and chancellor of Germany from 1871 to 1890, Bismarck is credited with achieving victory in the Franco-Prussian War (1870–71) and with uniting the fragmented German lands into a single country.

Eva Braun. A Munich shopgirl, Braun became Hitler's girlfriend, mistress, and—just before their joint suicide, in 1945—his wife.

Aristide Briand. A French prime minister and foreign minister, Briand formed a friendship with German foreign minister Gustav Stresemann. Briand, Stresemann, and Austen Chamberlain, the British foreign secretary, earned Nobel Peace Prizes.

Hugo and Elsa Bruckmann. A conservative Munich publisher, Hugo indulged his wife's penchant for making financial gifts to Hitler and connecting him with influential people. Elsa advanced Hitler's social standing by often inviting him to her weekly salon in the couple's Munich mansion.

Heinrich Brüning. A technocratic financial expert and austere Roman Catholic, Brüning earned the nickname the Hunger Chancellor for his harsh deflationary policies as chancellor during the Depression.

Houston Stewart Chamberlain. A British-born political philosopher, Chamberlain became a German, married Richard Wagner's daughter, Eva, and wrote (in German) a two-volume racist tome entitled *The Foundations of the Nineteenth Century.*

Bruno Czarnowski. A rabidly anti-Semitic Storm Trooper, Czarnowski created scurrilous slide shows for Hitler's grassroots political campaigns.

Charles G. Dawes. A banker and US vice president under Calvin Coolidge, Dawes in 1923 led a commission to devise a viable reparations plan to help stabilize the turbulent German economy—the Dawes Plan.

Theodor Duesterberg. Duesterberg was a leader of the 250,000-strong Steel Helmet veterans' association.

Friedrich Ebert. Weimar Germany's first president, Ebert was a workingman who rose to the chairmanship of the Social Democratic Party (SPD).

Dietrich Eckart. Playwright, publisher, right-wing roué, and coffeehouse philosopher, Eckart held radical views on nationalism, Jews, and German destiny that profoundly influenced Hitler.

Hermann Esser. Esser was an early Nazi Party member who belonged to Hitler's "Munich clique," a group that relished beer-hall brawls and virulent anti-Semitism.

Hans Frank. Hitler's lawyer and sometime confidant, Frank became governor-general of occupied Poland during the Third Reich. Sentenced to death during the Nuremberg trials, he hastily wrote a memoir that included his own wonderment at Hitler's "unfathomable ascent."

Wilhelm Frick. A lawyer and Munich police official, Frick was part of Hitler's inner circle during the final climb to power. He became the head of the German internal security forces in Hitler's government.

Joseph Goebbels. Riveted by Hitler's forceful speeches, Goebbels dedicated his own propagandistic talents to boosting his leader's political cause. As a near-daily diarist, Goebbels created a detailed insider's account of Hitler's ascent.

Hermann Göring. A First World War flying ace, the socially adept Göring joined the little Nazi Party in 1922. Badly wounded during the 1923 coup d'état, he fled Germany and became a morphine addict. In 1928, he returned to Germany and became part of Hitler's brain trust.

Ernst Hanfstaengl. The scion of a wealthy German art book publishing family, Hanfstaengl grew up in Bavaria but went to college at Harvard, in the United States. In Munich, he traveled in high society and introduced Hitler to the city's conservative elite. Especially well connected to the Anglo-American press, Hanfstaengl became Hitler's walk-around pal and international press secretary.

Konrad Heiden. Heiden was a German journalist who chronicled Hitler's rise from the beginning. Writing for the *Frankfurter Zeitung* and the *Vossische Zeitung*, he recognized Hitler's unique emotional appeal early on but pronounced him "a falling comet" just weeks before he took power.

Heinrich Held. The governor of Bavaria, Held allowed reinstatement of the Nazi Party after Hitler was released from prison but imposed a speaking ban on the Nazi leader when he resorted to violent language. Held firmly opposed Hitler, alerting Germany's leaders to his extreme leanings.

Rudolf Hess. Another well-born former pilot, Hess marched in the 1923 putsch attempt and spent six months with Hitler in prison. Upon release, he became Hitler's private secretary and traveling associate. His letters to his fiancée and his parents are useful sources of details about the Nazi rise to power.

Heinrich Himmler. A trained agronomist, Himmler helped organize and discipline the Nazi Party. He played a key role in shaping Hitler's successful 1930 election campaign and was appointed head of the SS (Schutzstaffel), a branch of the Storm Troopers.

Paul von Hindenburg. A First World War field marshal who vanquished the Russian army in 1914, Hindenburg was Germany's most respected national hero. In 1925, he was elected the Weimar Republic's second president. Reelected in 1932, he overcame his distaste for Hitler, the former foot soldier, and yielded to his advisers' pleas that the Nazi leader be appointed chancellor in January of 1933.

Adolf Hitler. A nobody from nowhere, Hitler became Germany's chancellor, dictator, and warlord. Born in 1889 in a small Austrian town, he quit school at the age of sixteen, moved to Vienna at eighteen, and at twenty-four ended up in Munich, where he soon enlisted as a soldier in the First World War. Entering politics in 1919, Hitler took over the tiny German Workers' Party—renamed the National Socialist German

Workers' Party (Nazi Party)—and became a main attraction on Munich's boiling right-wing political circuit. In 1923, he mounted a coup d'état that failed spectacularly. Following a year in prison, he refounded his party, beginning the long march to power. Eight years of zigzag struggle and strife followed, with near-death experiences and surprise triumphs. Hitler climbed to within grasping distance of the German chancellorship in 1932. But his star began fading. He seemed in decline, dropping four percentage points in a national election, when an improbable series of events in January of 1933 saved him—and made him Germany's chancellor.

Wilhelm Hoegner. A Social Democratic Bavarian politician, Hoegner tried in vain to warn Germans of Hitler's vicious intentions.

Heinrich Hoffmann. Hoffmann, a jolly and bibulous Munich photographer, developed a unique relationship with Hitler. Gaining exclusive access to the rising politician, he covered all Hitler's dramatic election campaigns as well as his informal moments away from politics.

Alfred Hugenberg. Born in 1865, the thick-girthed, mustachioed Hugenberg was a fervent nationalist, business baron, and newspaper mogul turned politician. Temperamentally at odds with Hitler, even when they agreed on policy, Hugenberg became the linchpin in Hitler's hopes for the chancellorship. At the last minute in 1933, Hugenberg reluctantly agreed to serve in Hitler's cabinet, enabling the Nazi leader's ascension to power.

Karl Kaufmann. Kaufmann was a Nazi activist in northwest Germany who became Hamburg gauleiter.

Harry Kessler. A member of the German nobility and a former soldier, diplomat, and patron of the arts, Count Kessler was a well-met man-about-Germany, especially in Berlin. His voluminous diary entries written during the Weimar Republic offer acerbic insights into the political and social life of the period.

Karl Liebknecht. A leader of the Spartacist League, which became the German Communist Party, Liebknecht tried in vain to declare Germany a soviet republic in November of 1918. He was murdered during the violent upheavals in January of 1919.

Erich Ludendorff. A hero of the First World War, Ludendorff promoted the legend that German armed forces had been stabbed in the back by home-front shirkers. The retired general allied himself with Hitler in his failed 1923 putsch attempt. In 1925, Ludendorff ran for president and lost badly.

Rosa Luxemburg. A coleader of the Communists and a far-left theorist, Luxemburg was assassinated in January of 1919 by right-wing Free Corps units that were defending the government of Friedrich Ebert.

Melita Maschmann. Maschmann was a Berlin teenager drawn to Hitler's promise of a classless "national community" and a return to German greatness.

Karl Mayr. Hitler's commanding officer after the First World War, Captain Mayr sent the Nazi leader to a one-week training course in political history—a turning point in Hitler's life. Assigned by Mayr to teach nationalistic doctrine to new recruits, Hitler discovered his talent as an orator.

Hermann Müller. Germany's last Social Democratic chancellor during the Weimar Republic, Müller and his five-party coalition collapsed in March of 1930, ushering in an era of "presidential cabinets" that ruled more by decree than parliamentary legitimacy. This was the beginning of the end of German democracy.

Carl von Ossietzky. Editor of the renowned left-liberal weekly *Die Weltbühne* (The World Stage), Ossietzky ridiculed Hitler as a rube with no future. His dismissive essays were emblematic of elite thinking during Hitler's rise.

Franz von Papen. A Catholic aristocrat from Westphalia, Papen was a lightweight politician tapped by Kurt von Schleicher as Germany's chancellor in 1932. When Schleicher eased Papen out five months later, the nobleman sought revenge by making common cause with Hitler. Papen's maneuverings—and special influence with President Hindenburg—made Hitler chancellor in January of 1933.

Franz Pfeffer von Salomon. A First World War veteran and Free Corps fighter with a penchant for brutality and discipline, Pfeffer was commander of the Storm Troopers from 1926 to 1930.

Walther Rathenau. A leading businessman who served as Germany's foreign minister, Rathenau in 1922 initiated the Treaty of Rapallo, declaring a final peace between Germany and Russia. A moderate liberal and a Jew, Rathenau was assassinated by a right-wing hit squad.

Angela Raubal. Hitler's half sister, Angela was the mother of Geli Raubal, arguably the love of Hitler's life. Angela sometimes traveled with her daughter on Hitler's trips and became his housekeeper when he acquired a mountain house in the German Alps above Berchtesgaden.

Geli Raubal. Born in 1908, Geli moved into Hitler's spacious Munich apartment in 1929. She and "Uncle Alf"—he was nineteen years her senior—became a couple around town, leading to speculation about the real nature of their relationship. In 1931, at age twenty-three, Geli was found dead in her room under suspicious circumstances that could have derailed Hitler's career.

Fritz Reinhardt. A Bavarian Nazi gauleiter who developed a correspondence course for Nazi Party public speakers, Reinhardt (no kin to Max) had turned out several thousand trained orators by the time of the crucial 1930 election.

Max Reinhardt. Austrian-born Reinhardt was the most celebrated German-language theater director of the 1920s, overseeing eleven different stages in Berlin alone. As a Jew, he was vilified by the Nazis.

Ernst Röhm. A scar-faced First World War captain, Röhm took part in the 1923 putsch attempt but later split with Hitler. After several years in exile in Bolivia, Röhm returned to the Nazi fold, taking command of the Storm Troopers and assisting Hitler during his final negotiations for power. Hitler had him murdered in 1934.

Alfred Rosenberg. An ethnic German from Estonia, Rosenberg became a Nazi Party ideologue and editor of the *Völkischer Beobachter*. Rosenberg's massive tract *The Myth of the Twentieth Century* was overshadowed by Hitler's own book *Mein Kampf*.

Hjalmar Horace Greeley Schacht. The son of pro-American parents, Schacht became a leading banker and nationalist politician who supported Hitler. He lent economic gravitas to the Nazi movement as it was rising to national prominence after the 1930 elections, influencing other businessmen to support Hitler.

Philipp Scheidemann. A Social Democratic politician, Scheidemann earned his place in history by single-handedly proclaiming, on November 9, 1918, the end of monarchy and the beginning of republican democracy in Germany.

Kurt von Schleicher. An armchair general who rose high in the military through his political connections, Schleicher became part of the influential camarilla around President Hindenburg. Though appointed chancellor in late 1932, Schleicher lasted only fifty-seven days in the job. Hitler had him murdered in 1934.

Walter Stennes. A Storm Trooper commander, Stennes twice rebelled, denouncing Hitler as an "un-Germanic" despot and stirring fears of a general uprising. Hitler had him purged.

Gregor Strasser. An artillery officer during the First World War, Strasser was trained as a pharmacist but soon entered Hitler's orbit. The big Bavarian with the hearty laugh became the Nazi Party's most energetic organizer and recruiter, building a grassroots network that drove the Nazis' nationwide electoral successes. With administrative skills and a common touch, Strasser became the second-most-powerful man in the party. Yet he never quite accepted Hitler's self-deification, and at the eleventh hour of their long struggle together, he deserted Hitler.

Otto Strasser. The younger and brainier brother of Gregor Strasser, Otto was a left-leaning Nazi whose Marxist writings in the newspaper he owned with Gregor led to a break with Hitler.

Gustav Stresemann. The son of a beer distributor, Stresemann rose to become Germany's foreign minister during the Weimar Republic. The only politician to serve in eight successive cabinets, Stresemann succumbed to a stroke at the age of fifty-one, in 1929, depriving Germany of one of its most skilled moderate politicians.

Cosima Wagner. Cosima was Richard Wagner's widow and the matriarch of the Wagner clan in Bayreuth.

Richard Wagner. Born in 1813, Wagner became the reigning genius of German musical composition and was renowned for his complex themes and dramatic orchestration. Best known for operas based on Norse mythology, he had a profound influence on German nationalist politics. To Hitler, Wagner was a hero on par with Frederick the Great and Martin Luther.

Winifred Wagner. Married to Richard Wagner's son, Siegfried, Winifred was born in England but raised in Berlin. She became an early supporter of Hitler, sending him gifts in prison and inviting him to the family mansion in Bayreuth.

Bernhard Weiss. The Jewish deputy police chief of Berlin, Weiss was the butt of vicious anti-Semitic satirizing in Goebbels's newspaper. Goebbels peremptorily gave Weiss the nickname Isidor—and it stuck in the popular imagination.

Wilhelm II. The last of the Hohenzollern kings of Germany and Prussia, Kaiser Wilhelm assumed power in 1888. The erratic monarch fired Otto von Bismarck and began a turbulent reign that in 1914 helped plunge Germany into the First World War. When Germany capitulated, in 1918, Wilhelm fled Berlin for the Netherlands and within days abdicated the throne.

August Wilhelm of Prussia (Auwi). One of six sons of Wilhelm II, Prince Auwi was an early supporter of the Nazis. Auwi surrounded himself with artists and scholars and was rumored among the Nazis to be gay. Though they sometimes ridiculed him, the Nazis welcomed the whiff of royal approval that Auwi lent to their movement.

Owen D. Young. Founder of the Radio Corporation of America (RCA), Young in 1929 led a second reparations commission to further reduce and extend Germany's post–First World War reparations payments. It was called the Young Plan.

A NOTE ABOUT STORM TROOPERS

The term *Storm Troopers* refers to the Sturmabteilung, or "storm detachment," of the Nazi Party. Often abbreviated SA, the Storm Troopers began as a security detachment to maintain order at Nazi rallies. The brown-shirted paramilitary group later morphed into the party's street-fighting force and grew to more than a million members—as many as in the rest of the civilian Nazi Party. Though forbidden to bear firearms, violence-minded Storm Troopers often carried blackjacks, brass knuckles, and other concealable weapons and became a key element in Hitler's rise to power. The Sturmabteilung (SA) is referred to throughout this book as the Storm Troopers.

A NOTE ABOUT PHOTOGRAPHS

The photograph of Adolf Hitler on the following page, and on the pages separating this book's five parts, are the work of Hitler's photographer, Heinrich Hoffmann. Hoffmann began photographing Hitler in Munich in the early 1920s. He often used glass-plate negatives for posed studio pictures. After the Second World War, Hoffmann's sometimes cracked or broken glass plates ended up in the U.S. National Archives Collection of Foreign Records Seized. In recent years, Archives preservationist Richard E. Schneider painstakingly reassembled many of the damaged plates and digitized 1,270 of them. The six images in this book stem from that work.

A NOTE ABOUT MAPS

The map of Germany during the Weimar Republic on pages 2–3 is by David Lambert. The map of the Berlin Government District in January 1933 on page 339 is by Shannon K'doah Range.

Prologue

It was a stunning turn of events. On a bitterly cold Monday night, Berlin blazed with torchlights and thundered with the cadence of martial drums. It was January 30, 1933, and Nazi Storm Troopers by the tens of thousands, and civilians in nearly equal numbers, were marching through the historic Brandenburg Gate. An excited German radio announcer described the march as "a human river" and "a historic moment whose full meaning is not yet clear to us." To an American journalist, the scene was the "greatest torchlight procession in German history."[1] Turning up Wilhelmstrasse, the German capital's main corridor of power, the marchers belted out their national anthem ("Germany, Germany, above all!"), raising their right arms and cheering as they passed the chancellery. In an open second-story window, a man in a dark suit extended his right arm in return. It was Adolf Hitler's moment of triumph.

Seven hours earlier, President Paul von Hindenburg had sworn in forty-three-year-old Hitler as chancellor of Germany. The installation of a former First World War foot soldier into Germany's highest government office came as a shock even to those in the capital who closely watched the baffling political churn of a country in free fall. Of all the speculations swirling through Berlin during the past month of uncertainty, the least likely was the emergence of a government led by the radical Nazi Party chief. Secretive behind-the-scenes negotiations had left Germany's leading newspapers and prognosticators grasping at straws—and guessing wrong. Yet Hitler's ascent momentarily solved the urgent conundrum of who was to run a nation that had become effectively leaderless. The appointment of a Nazi-led cabinet was a desperate stab at finding a way out of an economic depression that had left six million Germans unemployed and the country on the brink of civil unrest.

Still, the portentous choice of Hitler, the leader of an authoritarian movement bent on dictatorship and conquest, augured a political shift so profound that few could imagine the totalitarian calamities that lay ahead. In the coming twelve years, Hitler would launch the most destructive war in history, murder eight million Jews and other allegedly inferior people, subjugate most of Europe, and come close to adding both Russia and Great Britain to that stunned and abject list. When his perverse crusade ended in the hellfire of 1945, much of Germany would lie in ashes and ruins. Hitler's ten-minute swearing-in ceremony, on a cloudy winter day in 1933, would have greater impact on the planet than any other single administrative act in history.

Those horrific events still lay in the future. As Hitler's jubilant supporters tromped past on this night in Berlin, the Nazi leader's beaming presence in the spotlit window was the improbable culmination of a circuitous, often quixotic, and very nearly unsuccessful march to power. After thirteen years in public life; after eight years of electoral politics; after frequent setbacks and restarts; after detours, disappointments, and party purges; after nonstop electioneering and Nazi Party activism; after the sensational defection of his top lieutenant only weeks before; after being dismissed, ridiculed, and frequently left for politically dead—and after surprise successes that brought fully one-third of German voters into his camp—Hitler had reached his goal. The Nazis, finally, were at the pinnacle of power.

Watching over Hitler's shoulder as the torches and drums streamed down Wilhelmstrasse, propaganda meister Joseph Goebbels felt it was "like a fairy tale."[2]

Hitler's ascension indeed seemed like a magical salvation to many in a country buffeted since 1918 by wartime defeat, national revolution, fractured politics, and grinding economic crisis. To Hitler's supporters, a rebirth seemed at hand. To others, it was a moment of shock. Even during Hitler's quasicoronation, on this frenetic night in Berlin, many in the educated upper middle class already feared the implications of Nazi rule. Among those watching the torchlight parade were the parents of fifteen-year-old Melita Maschmann, a Berlin schoolgirl standing with her family on the fringe of the procession. Melita knew that her father and mother, though staunch nationalists, disapproved of Hitler's paramilitary Storm

Troopers and their rough tactics; they rejected the Nazis. Yet Melita, who listened to her parents read the newspapers aloud every day, thrilled to Hitler's promise of a new "national community" of all Germans, regardless of class or background. The teenager had picked up her reformist ideas from her mother's seamstress, a limping, hunchbacked woman who saw hope in Hitler's message. As Melita stood on the sidewalk watching the bright-faced torchbearers—many of them teenagers, like her—she envied the Nazis in the parade. She saw in their optimism a future she wanted to be part of. Without telling her parents, Melita secretly "longed to hurl myself into this current, to be submerged and borne along by it." The young Berliner would soon join millions of other idealistic teenagers in the Hitler Youth and League of German Girls organizations. After that, she became a committed cog in the Nazi machine.[3]

Today the question still looms: how did an unknown failed painter from Austria weave his way through the dense thickets of post–First World War politics to become the last man standing when Germany's democracy crumbled?

A nobody from nowhere, Hitler had none of the makings of a public figure. He was not a working-class activist who rose through the ranks of Germany's Social Democratic Party (SPD)—as did Friedrich Ebert, the Weimar Republic's first president.* The Nazi leader was no schooled intellectual—as were Marxists Karl Liebknecht and Rosa Luxemburg, leaders of the Spartacist League, which morphed into Germany's Communist Party (both were murdered during violent upheavals in 1919). Hitler had nothing in common with university-trained businessmen such as Walther Rathenau and Gustav Stresemann, who became the Weimar Republic's revered foreign ministers. The unsophisticated Austrian was hardly a captain of industry—as was Alfred Hugenberg, who shouldered his way into politics by building a newspaper empire. Hitler didn't spring

* The German president was in theory the head of state—the holder of a ceremonial post like the British monarch's but invested with key powers that would, in time, prove fateful. The German chancellor was the head of government, analogous to the British prime minister.

from the elite officer corps, as did General Erich Ludendorff and Field Marshal Paul von Hindenburg, who rose to the top of the military before entering politics—Ludendorff as a right-wing reactionary and Hindenburg as Germany's second president. The highest military rank Hitler attained during his four and a half years in uniform in the First World War was private first class.*

For decades we have struggled to understand the rise to power of Hitler, the accidental politician. Yet the facts, the events, and the politics of his climb are available for examination and telling. They reveal Hitler's nearly unbelievable journey from beer-hall rabble-rouser to national leader between 1925 and 1933. His serpentine path during the eight years that really mattered shows that, despite his obsessive self-belief, his ascension to power was far from foreordained. His climb was, politically and historically, a concatenation of bluster, accidents, and a train wreck of epic proportions laced with flashes of political skill. These latter included dogged organizing, a brilliant political ground game, and an exceptional rhetorical gift.[4] Hitler's lawyer and confidant, Hans Frank, later governor-general of occupied Poland, called the Nazi leader's rise an "unfathomable ascent."[5]

Hitler's journey is a political cliff-hanger of unexpected twists, turns, and near-death experiences from which the protagonist always recovered through political savvy, astonishing tenacity, raw brutality, and, often enough, pure luck. Hitler was saved by his fanatical self-assurance (his "will"), his native oratorical talent, his instinctive propagandistic skills, an uncanny feel for the mood of the masses, and the choice of a gifted number two man with keen administrative skills. The Nazi leader profited from a nearly perfect storm of constitutional weaknesses in Germany's virgin democracy, the profound splintering of the German body politic, the untimely deaths of statesmen who might have thwarted his climb, the onset of the Great Depression, continual underestimation by the political establishment, the woeful incompetence of contemporaneous players on

---

* Hitler's rank was *Gefreiter,* which has been erroneously translated for decades as "corporal." Unlike an American corporal, a *Gefreiter* was not a noncommissioned officer; a *Gefreiter* had no command over anyone. He was merely a buck private promoted to private first class.

Germany's political stage, and the craven motives of others at a critical moment.

Despite all that, Hitler had frequent close brushes with political obscurity. But for an unlikely sequence of events in January of 1933, Hitler would quite possibly have remained only a footnote to history. During the last four weeks of his political odyssey, Hitler outmaneuvered his political competitors with tactics that were alternately Machiavellian and melodramatic. Throughout that period, his moves were opaque and confusing even to his closest confidants. Like the protagonist in a bedroom farce, Hitler was constantly opening and slamming doors, appearing and disappearing without warning, engaging and rejecting, making outrageous demands, then suddenly leaving the stage. The play unfolded in late-night meetings at posh secret venues and did not reach its denouement until the very day Hitler was sworn in as chancellor. His chancellorship was in doubt up until the last fifteen minutes before he took the oath.

But that gets ahead of the mind-boggling story.

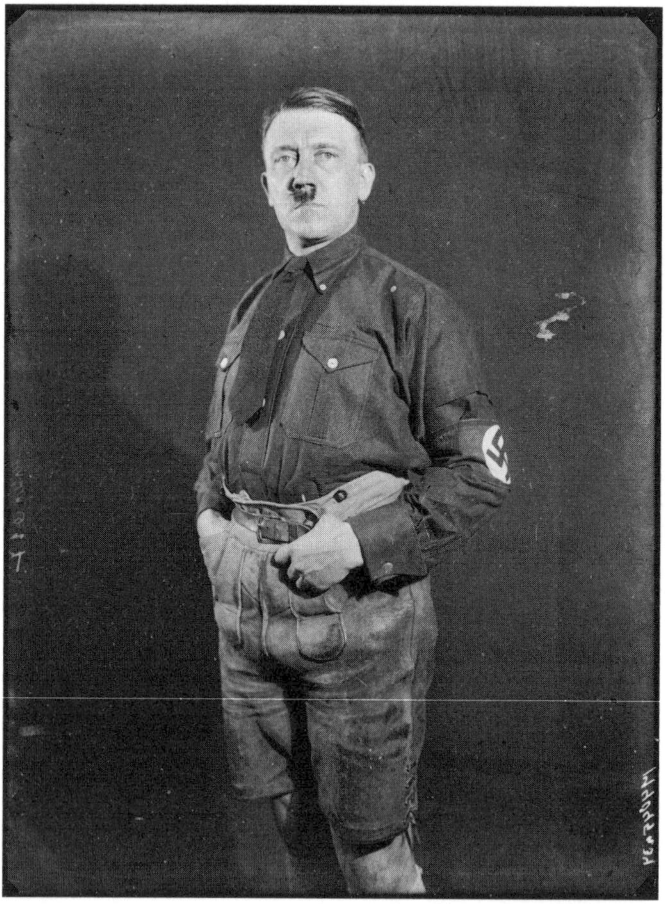

Part One

REBIRTH AND REBUILDING

(1925–1928)

Scarcely a week passed, but a huge procession of starving excitable men would march through the streets. There was a constant tension in the air. One government followed another. The Marxists held huge mass meetings. The population was split up into tiny parties. The atmosphere was teeming with all sorts of plans. There was no unity of purpose anywhere.

—*A government clerk who joined the Nazi Party, 1926*[1]

This horrible sense of insecurity kills people. You get trained in a skill, and afterward you are out on the street.... You have a horrible feeling of uselessness.

—*Paul R., a twenty-year-old cabinetmaker*[2]

1

BACKSTORY

Herr Hitler is, if I may say so, a born popular speaker.

— German army recruit, 1919

It was the unlikeliest moment in the unlikeliest of venues. On a winter night in 1925, a convicted traitor was mounting a political comeback in the same beer hall where he had committed treason only sixteen months before. Surrounded by delirious supporters, welcomed by a Bavarian band blasting his favorite marching tunes, and protected by a massive turnout of Munich's finest—one of Germany's largest police forces—Adolf Hitler, at thirty-five, was serving notice that he was back.

The fiery-eyed Nazi leader had been written off in 1923 when he attempted a coup d'état that failed. Now, improbably, he was staging his own rebirth. It was just the kind of bold stroke that had appealed to the dreamy Austrian throughout his checkered and ill-directed life.

Adolf Hitler was born in 1889 in the tiny Austrian burg of Braunau am Inn. He was the fourth child of the third wife of a local customs official, Alois Hitler, who drank heavily and often beat his sons and his wife. While taking his morning wine one day at the local pub, Alois keeled over, dead at the age of sixty-five; Adolf was only thirteen. Released from his father's dominance, the restless teenager quit school three years later, at sixteen, and declared himself an artist who also had an interest in architecture. For two years, he drew and painted everything in sight, and redesigned (in his head) every major building in Linz, the town where his father had relocated the family when Hitler was nine years old. Then, at eighteen, young Hitler migrated to the bright lights of Vienna, Austria's capital. There the headstrong youth met his comeuppance: he was summarily rejected for admission to the renowned Academy of Fine Arts. "Test drawing unsatisfactory—few heads," noted the examiners.[1] Without a high school diploma, he dared not follow the examiners' suggestion that he might apply to architecture school instead.

Devastated, Hitler was soon homeless. After several months of uncertain living arrangements, including at least a few nights on park benches, the vagrant young man fetched up in a men's shelter, where he earned a meager living by drawing postcard-style paintings of Viennese landmarks for the tourist trade. In his spare time, he became a voracious reader of history, architecture, and politics, often picking up free pamphlets in all-night cafés or spending long hours in a small bookstore. He began lecturing his hapless housemates on the evils of international political movements such as socialism.

By the age of twenty-four, Hitler was on the lam from his draft board. He was due for service in the army of the Austro-Hungarian Empire, an enlistment that could last for years. Hopping a train to Germany, he stepped down in the first big city he came to: Munich. The capital of Germany's southernmost state, Bavaria, Munich gleamed with monuments, museums, and stately architecture; Hitler fell in love. Yet he was penurious, aimless, and stuck in a rut, still peddling watercolors and sketches of city sights. After little more than a year, however, the draft dodger was rescued by the unlikeliest of events: war.

The First World War broke out in the summer of 1914. Like many Austrians and Germans, Hitler was caught up in war fever. Bitterly rejecting the multicultural Austro-Hungarian Empire of his birth as a misbegotten political construct, he eagerly embraced a sense of German ethnicity. He joined excited mobs on a Munich square, loudly welcoming the coming war. He eagerly enlisted in a Bavarian regiment that did not reject him because of his Austrian origins. He shared what Ernst Simon, a German Jew, referred to as the "intoxicating joy" of going to fight for his homeland.[2] The young Hitler, who had constantly played war games on the meadows near his boyhood home, was soon on his way to fight the real thing on the fields of Flanders and in northern France. Soldiering was Hitler's first actual job. War became the primal transformative experience of his life, giving shape, purpose, and discipline to a chaotic existence.

Hitler began to grow up. The foot soldier showed skill in improvisation and self-preservation. Following several harrowing months on the front lines, he cadged a relatively safe and cushy job as staff courier at regimental headquarters far behind the trenches. While his messenger's job gave him a "warm, lice-free stretcher" to sleep on, his forays to the front put him often, though briefly, in mortal danger. He was wounded twice. Promoted from buck private to private first class, Hitler was awarded an Iron Cross Second Class and an Iron Cross First Class. The value of his medals is uncertain: sixty other men from his regiment received the First Class award on the same day.

Hit by a gas attack in 1918, Hitler lay recovering in a hospital north of Berlin when news arrived that Germany had surrendered to the Allied powers. After five years of slaughter, with almost two million German soldiers killed, the fatherland was defeated. Adding to the tragedy—at least in Hitler's eyes—was the fact that the long-reigning monarchy of Wilhelm II had been deposed. A Social Democratic–led revolution had turned Germany into a democratic republic.

Germans were shocked by their generals' capitulation, a prospect about which they had not been warned. Like many Germans, Hitler was stunned and angered by the news of the country's defeat. He later claimed that Germany's loss and its conversion into a democracy had persuaded him on that very day to enter politics. Yet he showed no immediate signs of seeking a profession in public life. Half a year after hostilities ended, the rifle-toting soldier was still in the army while six million other German servicemen demobilized. With no training, no skills, and no prospects, the uneducated Hitler's only hope for a roof, a cot, and three meals a day was the military.

Luck was on Hitler's side. After he returned to Munich, the thirty-year-old was eventually attached to a new training and propaganda unit. Its job was to combat the rampant Marxist ideas circulating among recruits in the new, slimmed-down army—the Reichswehr. The unit's commander, Captain Karl Mayr, regarded Hitler as a "tired stray dog looking for a master."[3] But Mayr needed lecturers for his propaganda program, so he sent Hitler to a one-week course in political history at the University of Munich. This serendipitous assignment unlocked Hitler's talents as a declaimer and debater. His fierce argumentative skills surfaced in after-class discussions in the hallways, which were noted by his professor. Captain Mayr dispatched Hitler to harangue new troops about German nationalism and the perfidy of Marxists (including Communists and Social Democrats) at a military camp outside Munich. Strident and full of examples drawn from his own casual but wide reading of history, Hitler enthralled his young students with patriotic and unabashedly anti-Semitic arguments. "Herr Hitler is, if I may say so, a born popular speaker," wrote one soldier in a postcourse evaluation."[4]

Hitler was again transformed. Through a week of talking, he had discovered his singular gift. "I could 'speak,'" he noted with astonishment.[5] The unpromoted private with the big mouth and bigger ego had stumbled into his life's work.

In another fortuitous turn, a month later, Hitler's path into politics opened. Curious about the burgeoning right-wing political scene, which was dominated by rejection of the parliamentary republic, he attended a meeting of the fledgling German Workers' Party. He claimed that, at a gathering of several dozen attendees in a dim Munich pub, he stood up and demolished the argument of a speaker who favored Bavarian separation from Germany. Hitler, on the other hand, fiercely embraced pan-German unification, including Austria. The other man was haplessly driven from the room "like a wet poodle," insisted Hitler—a possibly invented or embellished story.[6] Whether the account is true or not, there is no question that Hitler was drawn to the little political group. A watershed was reached when Hitler decided to join the party. It was autumn of 1919.

The freshly minted new member of the German Workers' Party wasted no time in asserting his rhetorical skill and authoritarian muscle. Though a neophyte, Hitler became the party's chief stump speaker within five months. His maiden outing, in the capacious Hofbräuhaus, in February of 1920, turned into an uproarious melee. With his fiery orations, he was the attraction who could draw listeners and money to the party (in those days, people paid to hear a speech). As its rising star, Hitler gained control and elbowed aside the group's cofounders. He added two words to the party's name, restyling it the National Socialist German Workers' Party.

It was quickly nicknamed the Nazi Party (*Nazi* derives from *National-sozialistisch*, the German word for "national socialist").

On a Munich political stage filled with right-wing groups vying for attention, Hitler's high-flown rants attracted notice. Quickly regarded as the most dynamic speaker on the local beer-hall circuit, he became an act that people wanted to see. His rabid confidence, edgy ideas about race, politics, and foreign conquest, and theatrical speaking style often left him drenched in sweat. Women, in particular, were fascinated by the unmarried ex-soldier with the apocalyptic pronouncements ("Marxism... will overrun the rotten edifice of our national life")[7] and undiluted sense of messianic mission ("A new German Reich will rise again!").[8] Hitler rejected accommodation of the humiliations and burdens imposed by the 1919 Treaty of Versailles—including its "sole war guilt" clause and heavy reparations requirements. To listeners who despaired over Germany's economic and political plight, his message was both sizzling and inspirational. His was a combative voice for frustrated and angry people.

Speaking in beer halls and even in private drawing rooms, the sharp-voiced Nazi leader turned his party into a fast-growing upstart "movement," as he liked to call it. By early 1923, the Nazi Party could count twenty thousand members. After a busy spring and summer, membership nearly tripled, to fifty-five thousand.* The Nazi Party's appeal was soaring in a time of turmoil.

Postwar conditions had led to food shortages and hunger riots. German police were firing on starving Germans. "As I came home," remembered one former frontline soldier, "I saw hungry, dispirited faces, a people to whom nothing mattered any longer. The most anybody could wish for was a square meal and being left in peace."[9] Hyperinflation meant that there were four *trillion* marks to the US dollar. People were desperate. "Rice, 80,000 marks a pound yesterday, costs 160,000 marks today," reported one newspaper. "The day after, the man behind the counter will shrug his shoulders, 'No more rice.' Well then, noodles! 'No more noodles.'... Somewhere patience explodes.... then comes the umbrella

---

* Though large, fifty-five thousand was an insignificant number on the national scene, where the Social Democrats had more than one million members. Even the Communists boasted three hundred thousand members.

handle...crashing through the glass cover on the cream cheese. And the cop standing watch outside pulls a sobbing woman from the store."[10]

Germans bitterly watched French and Belgian troops march into the industrial Ruhr region four years after the end of the First World War in retaliation for Germany's unpaid war reparations. By autumn of 1923, Germany seemed headed toward civil war. Bavaria was in a state of near rebellion against the national army. Hitler sensed a chance to steal a march on history. He made the most foolish decision of his political life.

The Nazi leader's near-fatal mistake occurred on November 8, 1923, when he staged a coup d'état. For four years Hitler had agitated for an authoritarian government to replace Germany's unwieldy parliamentary republic—and for the "criminal" leaders of the 1918 revolution to "hang from lampposts." Now he decided impulsively to move against the government of Bavaria and the national government in Berlin. While people on other parts of the German political spectrum advocated a form of authoritarian government, none was as passionate or impetuous about it as Hitler and his Nazis were. With three thousand armed men at his disposal—and the windfall of finding Bavaria's key leaders gathered under a single roof on a single night—Hitler staged a putsch in Munich's packed Bürgerbräukeller beer hall. Bursting through the doors with a platoon of insurrectionists in helmets and battle gear, Hitler bounded onto a chair and fired his Browning pistol into the drinking establishment's coffered and chandeliered ceiling. "The national revolution has begun!" he shouted in his best caudillo style, stunning an audience of several thousand and stupefying Bavaria's ruling triumvirate—the state commissioner, state police chief, and divisional army commander.

The entire beer hall was now Hitler's hostage. With his combat units seizing other key points around Munich, he appeared to have succeeded in deposing the leadership of one of Germany's most important states, Bavaria. In the coming days the wild-eyed revolutionary planned to march on Berlin, where he would unseat the hated Weimar Republic along with its Social Democratic president, Friedrich Ebert.

But Hitler's hasty putsch was poorly organized and soon crumbled. Within seventeen hours, a hail of gunfire by government troops brought down his march through the center of Munich, intended to stir up support for his revolution. Fifteen of Hitler's followers were killed, along with one bystander and four government riflemen. The Nazi firebrand escaped death only by inches; the man marching arm in arm with him in the parade's front row was struck by a fatal police bullet. Other shots hit Ulrich Graf, Hitler's bulky bodyguard, as he fell atop Hitler in the melee. Fleeing the scene, the lightly injured Nazi leader (he suffered only a dislocated shoulder) hid for two days in a friend's villa south of Munich. When police surrounded his hideout, Hitler pulled out his pistol and threatened to take his own life (he had already mentioned suicide twice as his coup attempt crumbled).[11] But his host, Helene Hanfstaengl, yanked the firearm out of his hand and tossed it into a nearby flour barrel. Hitler was captured and thrown into the slammer.

At age thirty-four, Hitler seemed finished. "The Munich putsch definitely eliminates Hitler and his National Socialist followers," opined the *New York Times*.[12]

But his burning ambitions were not so easily quelled. Sentenced to a wrist-slap prison term of five years for high treason with the possibility of early parole, the Nazi leader spent just over a year behind bars. After a bout of depression—and another brief suicide attempt, via hunger strike—he underwent a revitalization and reorientation of his political plans. He restyled himself as a political savant and Germany's redeemer. With a head full of grand plans and mythic notions of greatness, Hitler in his jail cell drafted a political memoir that bulged with megalomania and certitude. The self-assured Nazi put himself in the company of Prussian king Frederick the Great, Reformation leader Martin Luther, and opera composer Richard Wagner. Sprung from prison just before Christmas in 1924, Hitler could think of only one thing: starting over.

2

RESURRECTION

Either the enemy will walk over our dead bodies or we will walk over his![1]

—*Adolf Hitler, Bürgerbräukeller speech, 1925*

Released from Landsberg Prison on December 20, 1924, a contrite Hitler played the reformed revolutionary. The newly liberated Nazi announced that he intended to forsake armed revolt in favor of the ballot box. "We must follow a new line of action," he told a supporter. "Instead of working to achieve power by an armed coup, we shall have to hold our noses and enter the [parliament].... If out-voting them takes longer than out-shooting them, at least the results will be guaranteed by their own constitution."[2]

Hitler's hope now lay in long-haul politics, not the quick fix of revolution. In a meeting with Bavarian governor Heinrich Held, the seemingly penitent Nazi promised that he would attempt no more putsches if the government would lift the ban on his party and his public speaking. He would seek power only by political campaigning, not by the gun.

"The wild beast is checked," Held told his aides. "We can afford to loosen the chain."[3]

With his political resurrection scheduled in the same Bürgerbräukeller where he had overreached in 1923, Hitler was now certain that he could go all the way, no matter how long it took. Among Munich's large drinking venues, the Bürgerbräukeller—an upscale establishment on the slope of the Isar River, which bisected Munich—was special. Its atmosphere was more banquet hall than beer brawl: its guests were often pillars of the bourgeoisie, not just cloth-cap workers or mountaineers in lederhosen. By choosing the Bürgerbräukeller for his political revival, Hitler was sending a message: his aborted mini coup had not been wrong in purpose, just mistaken in method—and certainly premature in timing. This time he would do it right.

At quarter past eight on the evening of February 27, 1925, the Nazi leader's Mercedes touring car—a gift from a rich supporter—pulled up in front of a seemingly besieged beer hall. Munich police had blocked off streets for several blocks and set up a triple security cordon. More than a thousand ticket-waving Hitler supporters clamored to get inside, but the doors had been slammed shut. Three thousand attendees had already overfilled a hall that seated only two thousand; the Nazis had oversold Hitler's stagy "second coming." One desperate Hitler fan shouted to a reporter passing through the police checkpoint: "One hundred marks to temporarily 'borrow' your press credentials!"

Inside, the journalist had to declare that he was "not a Jew" before being led to the press seats. A loud band stirred the agitated crowd with Bavarian tunes and military music, including Hitler's favorite, "The Badenweiler March." A gaggle of young women who had arrived at 9:00 a.m. in the Bierstüberl (a side room) cadged good seats when the main hall opened at 4:30 p.m. Hall monitors wearing Nazi armbands handed out little swastika flags. Finally, on a cue from a Nazi floor manager, the band ended its blaring with a great cymbal crash, the hall filled with roars, and people climbed onto their chairs to cheer the man they had waited for months to see again. Through a double phalanx of Storm Troopers with raised arms strode the unprepossessing politician with the smudge mustache, staring sternly ahead.[4]

"He passed by me quite close, and I saw a different person from the one I had met now and then in private homes," recalled an observer of Hitler's entrance ritual in another beer hall on another night. "His gaunt, pale features contorted as if by inward rage, cold flames darting from his protruding eyes, which seemed to be searching out foes to be conquered." The observer wondered if Hitler was possessed of "fanatical, hysterical romanticism with a brutal core of willpower."[5]

So it was on this night at the Bürgerbräukeller. The Nazi leader's unerring sense of theatrics—the emotional appeal of uniforms, martial music, flags, colors, the stiff-armed Nazi salute, a delayed entrance—infused the political show. The boisterous crowd waved their Nazi banners and craned their necks toward the grim-faced man with the penetrating blue eyes. Their cheering and *heiling* went on for a full ten minutes. "Hitler still knows how to make hearts race a little faster," noted one newspaper. "When Hitler shows up, people want to have been there."[6]

After sixteen months away from the beer-hall circuit, Hitler had lost none of his demagogic skills. During four years as a political speaker, he had taught himself a thespian's repertoire of gestures, imprecations, and throaty barks. Waving his arms and wagging a reproachful finger toward invisible enemies, Hitler rolled his *r*'s in an exaggerated growl that gave an aggressive edge to his words (he never talked that way conversationally, said his secretary). In perorations that lasted up to three hours, he had learned to rivet his audiences with punitive rhetoric, populist sentiments, lurid anti-Semitism, mocking put-downs, and sly irony. His voice rumbling low before rising into whole-body invective, he mesmerized audiences with elaborate historical theorizing followed by sweeping utopian visions. He constantly repeated catchphrases such as "the November criminals" to denigrate the democratic leaders of the Weimar Republic as perpetrators of an illegitimate enterprise.

Tonight, the practiced firebrand evoked his favorite bugaboos, conspiracy theories, and nationalist fixations.[7] Giving his eager followers the political red meat they had come to hear, Hitler stroked their emotional chords, thrumming anger at real or perceived insults to national pride. The Nazi speaker invoked the themes and tropes that would constantly recur in the 692 speeches he would make in the coming eight years. These included Germany's loss of its "racial consciousness"; its broken sense of nationhood; its false belief in its own war guilt, as prescribed by the loathed Treaty of Versailles; the importance of "perpetual struggle" as the permanent condition of mankind, implying the inevitability of another war; the need to create a *Volksgemeinschaft*—a national community—that would unite all Germans, regardless of class, religious denomination, or profession. (Hitler claimed that his was the only movement untethered to any existing economic or class interests such as the industrialists, the landowners, the bourgeoisie, or the working class.)[8] Only by elevating the state to primacy over the person, argued Hitler, could Germany reclaim its inherent greatness. Preaching with the fervor of a zealot, he promoted his radical gospel with the faux sophistication of a self-taught historical scholar.

In his political ramble, Hitler saved special venom for Jews. German Jews were a tiny minority—about 550,000 in a nation of sixty-three million, or less than 1 percent of the population. Yet since Jewish Germans were often prominent in science, business, banking, and publishing—as well as in critical areas of rural life, such as livestock trading—they were perceived by some as ubiquitous, all-powerful, and far more numerous than they were. In the German countryside, Jewish cattle merchants were sometimes demonized as oversexed predators whose religion allowed them to prey on Gentile women.[9] Given the underlying anti-Semitism that had been latent throughout the fifteen-hundred-year presence of Jews in Germany, it was easy for Jews to be scapegoated as devious string pullers on the political left who had "stabbed Germany in the back" near the end of the First World War.[10]

Many Germans' resentment of "the other" was triggered by the arrival since the 1880s of "Eastern Jews" driven from their homelands by pogroms in Russia and Poland. Sometimes wearing traditional Orthodox clothing or shtetl garb and working as Yiddish-speaking peddlers on the streets, the strange-looking new arrivals were demonized as drags on a depressed economy and as potential criminals—and even negatively stereotyped by long-settled, upper-middle-class German Jews who felt their assimilationist strivings were harmed by the *Ostjuden* (Eastern Jews). Walther Rathenau, an assimilated Jew, leading industrialist, and, briefly, Germany's foreign minister, took the view that Eastern Jews were an "Asiatic horde" and an "exotic tribe."[11] To Theodor Wolff, a Jew who for twenty-seven years was the acclaimed editor of the highly respected *Berliner Tageblatt* newspaper, the self-segregating Easterners were "unpleasant haggler types."[12]

Hitler seized on the virulent anti-Jewish sentiment that had burbled and stewed in Germany's radical-right nationalist movements for the previous two decades—a revival of anti-Semitism that had begun in the mid-nineteenth century in France, Austria, and Germany. The First World War had only heightened latent anti-Semitism, leading to an official army census in 1916, intended to measure the number of Jews serving on the front lines. Designed to prove that Jews were underrepresented in combat and thus unpatriotic shirkers, the *Judenzählung*—Jewish count—in fact showed that Jews were *overrepresented* in combat relative to the percentage of them in the population. In all, more than eighty-five thousand German Jews served in the war, and 70 percent of them saw frontline duty. Thirty-five thousand were decorated for bravery, and at least ten thousand died.[13] Those inconvenient facts, at first suppressed by the military but later publicized by Jewish groups, did little to dampen the growing anti-Semitism.

In Hitler's telling, Jews had embarked on a plan of world domination through business success, sly cunning, and the promotion of communism. Flinging out unfounded generalizations, half-truths, and distortions, Hitler argued that Jews were an unlanded people with no country to call their own. They were parasites on their host nations with a pernicious internationalist rather than nationalist outlook. Punctuating the air with his raised finger, hurling his voice into the banquet hall, Hitler declared that Germany's Jews were part of a "satanic power" whose goal was "to destroy the backbone of the nation-state, destroy the national economy, eliminate the racial foundations [of a country], and establish their own dictatorship."

Combining his animus for Jews and Marxists into the term "Jewish Bolshevism," the Nazi leader argued that Jews contaminated the blood of the German race. Jews were a "culture-destroying" people who weakened the German gene pool and would lead to the nation's downfall. "Purity of blood" was Hitler's first commandment. "The greatest danger for us is the foreign 'racial poison' in our bodies," he declaimed. Turning graphic, Hitler declared that, in the fleshpot that was Berlin, one constantly saw "Jewish boy after Jewish boy with a German girl on his arm" strolling along Friedrichstrasse, the famous shopping mecca. This could only mean that "night after night, thousands and thousands of times, our blood is destroyed for eternity in a single instant. Children and grandchildren are lost to us forever.... Once poisoned, our blood can never be changed, and... it takes us further and further downward every year."

The self-styled political serologist was dancing close to political pornography; evoking scenes of copulating couples was daring stuff in 1925. Yet the Bürgerbräukeller crowd loved it, giving Hitler's words "loud agreement," noted a stenographer.

Fanning his audience into a state of hatred for a perceived enemy—the most powerful of emotions—Hitler worked himself into a lather. Fighting the Jewish-Marxist "pestilence" could not be done "in a respectable style that inflicts no pain," he foamed. Taking on the Communists had to be done with ruthless brutality: "Either the enemy will walk over our dead bodies or we will walk over his!"[14]

A gasp must have rippled through the plainclothes police spies and journalists in the audience as they scribbled "dead bodies" into their notebooks. Hitler had just crossed a line, possibly violating his promise to Governor Held not to seek power through violence. Making matters worse, Hitler insisted that his revived Nazi Party needed committed "fighters," not educated parliamentarians.[15] He would rather have a small party of passionate warriors than a large one made up of men not really "ready to die" for the cause. The true fighters, he claimed, could be found only "in the broad masses"—the sole source of men prepared to "use any means" to reach their goals.

Any means? Hitler had crossed another line.

Finally, Hitler got down to the real business of the evening: refounding the Nazi Party. His challenge was to reunify the warring splinters of the National Socialist and *völkisch* movements behind his sole leadership.* For two months since leaving prison, Hitler had reached out to the squabbling rivals. While some felt it was time to drop their independent strivings, others resisted Hitler's appeal to join him in a show of unity in Munich. Alfred Rosenberg, a little-loved Nazi Party intellectual, rejected the idea of artificial "brother kissing" at Hitler's opening-night comeback

* *Völkisch* is almost untranslatable. Sometimes called a German offshoot of Romantic nature mysticism, *völkisch* can mean "racist," "populist," "ethnic-chauvinist," "nationalist," "conservative," "traditional," "Nordic," "romantic," and various combinations of these. Politically, the *völkisch* movement harbored a belief in German ethnic superiority as well as a nostalgic longing for the supposedly purer values of the preindustrial age.

rally. Ernst Röhm, the scar-faced former army captain who tried to start his own new militia while Hitler sat behind bars, also stayed away. Gregor Strasser, a bluff Bavarian who would soon rise to the number two spot in the party, also demurred.

Yet with six other Nazi leaders from two opposing factions on the podium with him, Hitler was able to stage a scene that was, as Rosenberg had predicted, a teary-eyed show of fraternal fealty. The tableau of seven men on the stage was a replica of the 1923 Beer Hall Putsch, when Hitler had temporarily persuaded men from conflicting camps to join in his ill-starred coup. Tonight, Hitler was trying to take up where that act had left off. "The fighting is over," Hitler said, because "today all of Germany is watching us."

As it did in 1923, the spectacle ended with nearly all four thousand people in the Bürgerbräukeller singing the Weimar Republic's national anthem, "Song of Germany": "Deutschland, Deutschland über alles...."*

Hitler departed the beer hall immediately, striding through the buoyant crowd. The unsmiling leader never lingered for questions or even congratulations; he scorned mingling with his followers at staged events. Such sentimental gestures would tarnish his sheen of infallibility, he felt. His business finished for the evening, he left while the aura of hope and deliverance still hung over the crowd.

* "Song of Germany," originally written in 1841, was not, as many assume, a Nazi creation. The anthem's famous line, "Germany, Germany above all else...in the world," was not a call for German domination of the planet. It was rather a plea for national unification of a Germany that, in the nineteenth century, was fractured into three hundred separate kingdoms, principalities, duchies, and city-states. These were finally united into a single nation by Chancellor Otto von Bismarck in 1871. The Weimar Republic adopted "Song of Germany" as its national anthem in celebration of the new democracy. After 1933, the Nazis kept the anthem, and their aggressive singing of "Germany above all else" was interpreted to mean German conquest of the world. After the Second World War, the new Federal Republic of Germany (West Germany) kept the anthem but removed "Germany, Germany above all else" and began with the third stanza's "Unity and justice and freedom for the German fatherland!"

3

WAGNER'S GHOST

At a stroke you have transformed the state of my soul.

—Houston Stewart Chamberlain in a letter to Hitler, October 7, 1923

Hitler's car was speeding toward Bayreuth, the obscure Franconian town in the hills of northern Bavaria. It was the middle of the night on February 27, 1925. In the back seat of the chauffeured Mercedes, Hitler was in conversation with a tall, striking twenty-seven-year-old woman named Winifred Wagner. Winifred was the daughter-in-law of Richard Wagner, the long-deceased king of German opera and the most controversial musical talent the country had ever produced. Though the composer had died in 1883, his operatic legacy still animated audiences all over the world, nowhere more than in Germany—and nowhere in Germany more than in little Bayreuth, where the master had built a remarkable monument to himself, an opera house that performed only his works. At the center of the Wagner cult stood the maestro's living heirs, headed by his widow, Cosima Wagner. The clan resided in or near Wahnfried, the villa that Wagner had built for himself in Bayreuth. Tonight, Hitler and Winifred were headed for the boxy mansion.

Hitler was already a figure in the Wagners' world. When the Nazi leader paid a political visit to Bayreuth two years earlier, Winifred (an Englishwoman who grew up in Berlin) had been so taken by Hitler's speech and personality that she invited him to breakfast the next day at Wahnfried. There Hitler met the eighty-four-year-old Cosima Wagner and struck up a relationship with Wagner's son-in-law, Houston Stewart Chamberlain. An Englishman who had adopted Germany as his home, Chamberlain was the renowned writer of the two-volume racist tome *The Foundations of the Nineteenth Century.* A pan-German polemic riddled with racial constructs and justifications of Aryan superiority, the book was the bible of anti-Semites throughout Europe. Hitler worshipped Chamberlain, and, following their meeting, Chamberlain proclaimed himself deeply impressed by Hitler. Sixty-eight and ailing, the old agitator wrote Hitler a mash note calling him an "awakener of souls from sleep and lethargy.... At a stroke you have transformed the state of my soul."[1]

Richard Wagner's influence on Hitler's thinking, on his concept of Teutonic nationalism and racial identity, cannot be overestimated. Hitler had been a fervent fan and student of Wagner since his youth. Beginning with *Rienzi* and *Lohengrin,* he had imbibed the Wagner oeuvre as if it were strong wine. *Rienzi*—based on the life of Cola di Rienzi, a fourteenth-century Italian populist who championed the oppressed people of Rome—appealed to Hitler's budding Napoleonic instincts.[2] The Nazi leader's theatrical presentation of his political persona—the fields of flags, the pulsing fanfares, the uniforms, the solemn marches—were derivative of Wagner's operatic grandiosity.[3]

After his 1923 breakfast with Winifred and the family, Hitler had been allowed to ruminate in reverential silence at Richard Wagner's grave in the sanctumlike circle of shrubs behind Wahnfried. In this one-man cemetery, he seemed to commune with his hero. While Hitler was no doubt enamored of the anti-Semitism in Wagner's infamous 1850 tract, "Jewishness in Music," it was the master's burning Germanic nationalism and reach for a higher aesthetic plane that most enthralled him. The firebrand politician planned to become one of the greatest Germans, too.

After the long drive from Munich following the Bürgerbräukeller speech, Hitler and Winifred arrived in Bayreuth after midnight. The next morning, they set out for Plauen to attend the premiere of an opera composed by Siegfried. But during the drive, the traveling party received shocking news: Friedrich Ebert, the president of Germany, had died in Berlin. Only fifty-four, he had succumbed to complications of an appendectomy following a bout of poor health—or to long-standing gallbladder disease, depending on the source.

Ebert had been the only president Germany had ever had. The nation went into mourning. Operas and other entertainments throughout the country were canceled. Depositing Winifred back in Bayreuth, Hitler and his driver raced toward Munich.[4] Hitler's new car could hit eighty-four miles per hour on a straight stretch but was constantly slowed by the highway's winding path through the nineteen Bavarian towns along the route. Still, he wanted to return to his political world as fast as possible. He understood that Germany had lurched into a moment of uncertainty.

Ebert's death raised critical questions of succession. Though the president was the head of state, not the head of government, the Weimar constitution stipulated that he be elected "by the entire German people."[5] The document gave the president no direct policy-making power, but it did assign him a monarchlike gatekeeping role by giving him the authority to decide who could form a government following elections. His veto over government formation, especially in the unstable Weimar era, gave the president enormous extrapolitical influence, regardless of what the voters may have said. He also had crucial emergency powers that could make or break a government.

For the first time in their history, Germans would cast a popular vote for a president. Like almost everything else in the Weimar Republic, a presidential election would be a new and untested experience for a nation still finding its way into democracy.

4

EBERT TO HINDENBURG

The German revolution, having been made on order, was no true revolution at all.

—*Edgar Ansel Mowrer,* Triumph and Turmoil: A Personal History of Our Time, *1968*

Hitler faced a threshold political question: What should the barely reborn Nazi Party do about the presidential election? Was a national political campaign an opportunity or a threat to Hitler's fledgling operation? If the Nazi leader took the party into the race on behalf of one candidate or another, it could generate windfall publicity for his renascent movement—or it could bring him ridicule if he chose the wrong horse. Now an avowed participant in the messy business of democracy, Hitler was facing a classic political quandary sooner than he expected.

But nobody else had been through such an experience, either. After all, Friedrich Ebert had been a nearly accidental president; the German republic had been an inadvertent democracy. At lunchtime on November 9, 1918, Germany had abruptly made the transition from monarchy to republic. A Social Democratic parliamentary leader, Philipp Scheidemann, had proclaimed Germany a republic from a balcony of the Reichstag, Germany's parliament. It had been a precipitate and desperate act. Only a day before, the country's forces had capitulated to the Allies, ending the First World War. Wilhelm II had fled Berlin for the Netherlands. A Socialist revolt in Munich had deposed the Bavarian monarchy; a sailor's mutiny had taken over the naval port of Kiel; leftist uprisings had sprung up in other German cities. On the morning of November 9, Scheidemann learned that the kaiser's abandoned Berlin palace had been occupied by

German Communists under the leadership of Karl Liebknecht. The Communist leader was preparing to turn Germany into a Soviet republic.

On the greenswards outside the Reichstag, Scheidemann saw a restless and growing crowd of Berliners demanding to know Germany's fate. The country's future hung by a thread, he felt. Consulting no one, possessing no authority, but determined to avert a plunge into Bolshevist madness, Scheidemann stepped onto a balcony and shouted: "The old and rotten, the monarchy, has collapsed. The Hohenzollern monarchs have abdicated. Long live the German republic!"[1] Thus was German democracy born.

"You had no right to proclaim a republic!" scolded the stumpy, mustachioed Friedrich Ebert when Scheidemann returned to the parliamentary dining room.[2] Though a man of the working class who had risen to become head of the Social Democratic Party, Ebert had envisioned a parliamentary monarchy for Germany at war's end rather than a pure republic. Even a democratic Germany needed a kaiser, just as democratic Britain needed a king, he felt. It was too late: parliamentarian Scheidemann had stolen a march on the Marxist insurgency and gotten ahead of the unrest breaking out around the country. By Scheidemann's act, Ebert—as the head of Germany's largest political party—became the provisional head of government.

Two hours later, Communist leader Liebknecht made good on his promise, proclaiming Germany a "free Socialist German Republic" from a balcony of the Royal Palace, in the center of Berlin. But Liebknecht's effort to communize Germany would fail after several months of bloody civil war in the capital. A heavily armed insurrection by the Communists and other leftists nearly toppled the republic. To save it, Ebert had to make a devil's bargain with the defeated German military and the newly formed Free Corps militias, made up of nationalistic right-wing war veterans. These units crushed the insurgents, especially in Berlin and Munich, where street battles raged for weeks.

Scheidemann's hasty decision to create a democratic German republic had worked, and so had Ebert's strategy to rescue it. But the birth pains were terrific and necessarily left Germany with an unreconstructed, elitist military establishment that could contribute to the country's instability. The new democracy's rough beginnings created the conditions for an ongoing struggle between its defenders and its rejectors, loudest among them the Nazis. All parties were bent on Germany's salvation from war, from humiliation, from economic misery, from political uncertainty—but each according to its own very different lights.

Berlin became too dangerous for the government to function. Even the Reichstag was occupied by Free Corps soldiers, who squalidly camped out in its rooms and hallways. "Soldiers and sailors stood and lay about on the enormous red carpet and among the pillars of the lobby," noted Count Harry Kessler, a diarist and man-about-town. "A multitude swarmed among the seats."[3] When they finally departed, in May of 1919, the squatters left behind an infestation of lice.

Friedrich Ebert's provisional government had to get out of town. Along with a newly elected National Assembly, he and his cabinet decamped 207 miles south, to the small Thuringian town of Weimar, where it could write Germany's new constitution in relative calm. With 181 articles, the constitution was hailed as one of the most democratic and progressive founding documents ever produced. It enshrined freedom of the press and freedom of assembly. It guaranteed the right to vote to every German over twenty, male or female, thus establishing women's suffrage a full year before women in the United States attained the right to vote.

But the constitution had two key flaws. The first lay in the parliament's system of proportional representation without a minimum percentage of votes required for a party to gain entry into the Reichstag.* Any party that could muster enough votes for *one* seat in the roughly six-hundred-seat parliament would be admitted. With more than a dozen parties in the parliament all the time, this caused severe splintering, weak coalitions, and frequent governmental turnover. The second constitutional defect was article 48, which gave the president emergency powers to suspend parliament temporarily and rule by decree. While the so-called emergency article could be useful in averting chaos, the provision would also

* To counter this flaw, the modern German parliament requires a party to win at least 5 percent of the national popular vote to enter the Bundestag.

become a dangerous default that paved the way for an authoritarian takeover.

In August of 1919, Ebert was installed as the country's first president. He and the new democracy were plunged into unsettled politics, poverty, and unemployment. They were saddled with a nearly unpayable war reparations bill of more than $33 billion worth of gold marks—a financial burden that economist John Maynard Keynes labeled "abhorrent and detestable" and that could "sow the decay of the whole civilized life of Europe."[4] Germany became a flailing beast, with six million demobilized soldiers among its sixty-two million citizens. In early 1920, disgruntled right-wing militias mounted a coup d'état that drove the Ebert regime out of Berlin for three days before the insurrection failed. In 1922, Ebert's respected foreign minister, Walther Rathenau, was assassinated by a right-wing hit squad—one of more than 350 politically motivated murders by rightist groups in three years. In early 1923, the French and Belgian invasion of the Ruhr region triggered work stoppages, spiraling inflation, and violent insurgency. Hunger strikes broke out; German police in some cases shot enraged demonstrators. By late 1923, Communists had attempted two coups that failed, as did Hitler with his Munich Beer Hall Putsch. In six years, President Ebert administered the oath of office to twelve different chancellors.

By 1925, things were improving. A new currency, the Rentenmark, halted inflation. Support from American banks gave a boost to the technologically advanced German industrial machine. A reparations-relief plan organized by US banker Charles G. Dawes created a more manageable payment schedule. The Dawes Plan opened new opportunities in Germany for American investors while promising withdrawal of occupying troops from the Ruhr region. With support from Ebert, Germany's creative foreign minister, Gustav Stresemann, skillfully guided Germany back into the community of nations and a standing of equal among equals.

And then Ebert died.

Almost immediately, Hitler knew he would join the fray of the presidential election. If the Nazi Party had no stated preference among the presidential candidates, Hitler reckoned, it would allow his detractors to claim the Nazis were not even in the game. He decided to throw his support behind a man he had come to hate, General Erich Ludendorff. Though Ludendorff, a First World War hero, had marched with Hitler in the 1923 coup d'état, the Nazi chief no longer wanted the old general feeding off his political base. The sooner he could help usher Ludendorff off the political stage, the better. Yet with his 100 percent name recognition and authoritarian stature as a grim-faced soldier with a chestful of medals, Ludendorff as a presidential candidate stood to win two million out of thirty million votes cast, reckoned Hitler. The Nazi leader calculated that supporting Ludendorff in the election's first round would give the Nazis bargaining chips for the probable runoff election (seven men had declared for the presidency, with no one likely to win a majority outright).

Hitler made a big show of supporting Ludendorff's candidacy. The *Völkischer Beobachter* ran front-page articles and exhortations demanding that every true Nazi—there were now about fifteen thousand party members—vote for Ludendorff. "I expect blind obedience from all members of the party," Hitler wrote, making good on his promise to run the Nazi Party with an iron hand.[5] At the same time, Hitler privately admitted that Ludendorff was just a placeholder: his candidacy was "hopeless," he told political intimates. "He need not and should not give speeches," Hitler told his backroom confederates.

In the election, held on March 29, Ludendorff, the celebrated military leader and embodiment of Prussian rectitude, won only 285,793 votes out of nearly twenty-seven million cast, or 1.1 percent of the total.[6] It was laughably short of Hitler's predicted two million votes. Clearly the Ludendorff name had lost its appeal. If he had not been politically dead already, he was in rigor mortis now. Though he would agitate on the fringes for years to come, he was politically finished and never recovered. For Hitler the debacle was only a minor embarrassment. Having Ludendorff eliminated politically was the far greater gain. "Now we've finished him off," Hitler gleefully remarked to his party comrade Hermann Esser.[7]

Some observers believed that Hitler and his comrades in Germany's *völkisch* movement were also finished. As had happened before, and would happen often again, observers on the intellectual left argued that Hitler's Nazis and their lunatic undertaking had, with their endorsement of a failed candidate, passed their peak. "The patient is dead," wrote Berlin journalist Heinz Pol in the left-liberal weekly *Die Weltbühne*. "The survivors... are already wrangling. They will never be unified."[8]

In the runoff election of April 26, 1925, Germany elected as its second president a man who had not even run in the first round. The nation's other First World War hero, Field Marshal Paul von Hindenburg, had been persuaded to run only in the second round. Already seventy-seven years old and retired for six years, Hindenburg had tried to stay aloof from politics. But beneath his pose of neutrality and his preference for country estate life in East Prussia, the old aristocrat was, like so many old-school officers, deeply opposed to the Ebert-led Weimar Republic. He feared a possible Communist uprising and longed to see Germany swing back toward the Bismarckian and Wilhelmine world that he had known and served—and that had served him so well.

The field marshal's full name was Paul Ludwig Hans Anton von Beneckendorff und von Hindenburg. Born into a titled East Prussian family in 1847, the future commander had spent his life in the military, starting as an eleven-year-old cadet. After a long career, Hindenburg retired in 1911 but was recalled in 1914 to save Germany from Russian forces when the First World War broke out. His success in the Battle of Tannenberg, on the eastern front (with Ludendorff as his deputy and tactical genius), led to his appointment as head of the German army. In 1915, he was honored with a forty-foot-high wooden statue nicknamed the Iron Hindenburg. It was imposingly erected next to Berlin's 219-foot brightly gilded Victory Column—a memorialization of Germany's 1871 victory in the Franco-Prussian War. As was the custom during the First World War, Germans paid for the right to drive a nail into the wooden edifice—a form of fundraising for the war effort.

Though many in 1925 thought the septuagenarian Hindenburg could never live out a seven-year term as president,[9] they pleaded with him, for the sake of Germany, to come out of retirement and take his rightful place on the throne as an *Ersatzkaiser.* With his six-foot-five-inch frame, impressive walrus mustache, and unsmiling gaze, the old field marshal certainly looked regal. In the runoff election, without even campaigning, he won the presidency with 48.3 percent of the vote (a plurality was sufficient for victory in the runoff).

To many on the left, Hindenburg's victory was a dismaying expression of Germans' latent longing for authoritarian rule. Diarist Harry Kessler saw Hindenburg as "the god of all those who long for the return of philistinism." The election of a Prussian officer meant "farewell progress, farewell vision of a new world."[10] Putting an old monarchist on the republican throne proved to American journalist Edgar Mowrer, the *Chicago Daily News* correspondent in Berlin, that "the German revolution, having been made on order, was no true revolution at all."[11]

5

ALWAYS ON THE RUN

It's a signal honor to be the only person out of sixty million [Germans] who is banned from speaking. Heil!

—*Adolf Hitler, 1925*

Hitler's political comeback had begun with his flashy February 1925 rally in Munich's Bürgerbräukeller. It continued three days later with a splash in Nuremberg, Bavaria's second-largest city, where Hitler spoke to three sold-out arenas in a single night. Charged-up Hitler fans treated their leader like a returning messiah, mobbing his car "so tightly... that we could move only at a crawl," remembered Rudolf Hess, the Nazi leader's private secretary and traveling companion. People were beside themselves, sometimes knocking over policemen in the car's path.[1]

Yet within a week, Hitler's crusade hit a wall. On March 9, 1925, he was deprived of his chief recruiting tool, his stentorian voice. His intemperate remarks in his opening-night speech about running over "dead bodies" had come back to bite him. The quotation had appeared in all the newspapers; so had Hitler's vow to use "any means" to achieve his political goals. Bavarian governor Held decided to put the beast back on the leash. Five Nazi rallies scheduled for a single day in Munich were banned. A speech in the town of Bamberg was canceled for fear Hitler would "whip up violence among the masses." The state of Bavaria dropped a complete public speaking ban on Hitler for an indefinite period.

Without Hitler, the Nazi movement was just a bunch of guys in brown uniforms handing out flyers. Now they could no longer plaster a Bavarian city with their favorite red posters announcing a *Massenversammlung*—a mass rally. The party needed Hitler as its star speaker for fireworks, for content, and even for money. Ticket sales to Hitler's speeches—usually one mark apiece—were the party's primary source of income.

Brought up short by the public speaking ban, Hitler flew into high dudgeon. Only he, out of sixty-two million Germans, was denied free speech, he howled. Yet he wore the prohibition as a badge of honor.[2] Allowed to address only closed-door gatherings, not open rallies, Hitler gleefully asserted that the ban showed how much the ruling powers "fear my words."[3] He said: "Since every bum, every vagabond, every pimp, even every Frenchman in Germany can speak publicly, it's an honor to be banned from speaking."[4] At a closed meeting of 120 Nazis—covered by a police spy—Hitler brazenly bared his teeth: "Whoever wants battle will get it! Whoever attacks us will be stabbed from all sides! I will lead the German people victoriously to the end of this battle for freedom, if not on a peaceful path, then with force! I'm repeating this line expressly for the police spies so that they won't fabricate anything!"[5]*

Unable to stage mass rallies, Hitler threw himself into small Nazi meetings around Munich. His goal was party building: no group was too obscure or too far away from the center of the city for the Nazi revivalist's nighttime attentions. Wearing a brown trench coat and a floppy-brimmed slouch hat, and often carrying a dog whip or cane—the quasi-gangster look he favored—Hitler darted about the suburbs, never missing a chance to press the flesh at a local chapter gathering, even if only for a few minutes. One night he arrived after 9:00 p.m. at the Franziskaner beer hall in the tiny exurb of Giesing, on Munich's fringe, for a gathering of sixty Nazis. Carrying a knobbed walking stick and not even removing his trench coat, he sat quietly for a while, listening as the local leader droned on. To the police spy in attendance, Hitler "seemed subdued." But when he finally talked, he made short work of it: "Friends, you know I am not allowed to speak. But you all know what I would say: stick together and stay true to me.... Heil!" Hitler was lustily cheered. The men lined up so their hero could give every man a deep-in-the-eyes gaze and a firm handshake. According to the police report, he did not miss a single hand.[6]

* The Munich police department, like that of all German cities, had an intelligence-gathering section that sent undercover agents to report on political meetings all over town.

"No time for anything; he's always on the run," complained Hess.

There was a loophole in the public speaking ban: it applied only in Bavaria, Germany's second-largest state after Prussia. None of Germany's sixteen other states had so far prohibited the Nazi declaimer from addressing the hordes.[7] Hitler could carry his crusade outside the borders of Bavaria, connecting with a ready pool of devoted followers and others willing to be converted to the Nazi cause. One of the richest lodes of support was in Thuringia, the state just to Bavaria's north. Thuringia's capital, Weimar, would play a key role in Hitler's future trajectory. He loved the classical city for its architecture and history and saw it as a stepping-stone to Berlin. Weimar was a suitable complement to Hitler's other favorite burg, Bayreuth. Both were small towns; both lay in the alluring foothills of the dark-forested German countryside; both were redolent of German high culture and achievement. With their traditional ocher-colored houses, each town was a model of Hitler's idea of Germanness. While Wagner's personal opera house was the cultural anchor of Bayreuth, the stately German National Theater was the heart of Weimar. Though the theater had been the venue of the Weimar Republic's official founding, the classical building would also become a platform for Hitler's preachings.

Hitler glommed on to Weimar's reputation as the home of Johann Wolfgang von Goethe (1749–1832) and Friedrich Schiller (1759–1805), literary giants of the German Enlightenment. In the center of Weimar lay a picture-perfect market square—called simply *der Markt*. On the square stood the curiously named Hotel Elephant, a comfortable establishment with a convenient second-story balcony where Hitler could speak or wave to crowds below. Hitler's suite there would become his home away from home, the site of many critical strategy sessions.

Because it lay beyond the reach of the Bavarian public speaking ban, Weimar was the ideal spot for Hitler to hold public rallies. On March 22, 1925, a springtime Sunday, Hitler spoke four times in two different halls, each with a capacity of one thousand seats—hardly enough to accommodate the Nazis who wanted to hear their hero's words. Hundreds of listeners were left out on the streets, peering through doors and windows to get a glimpse of their resurrected leader. One reporter noted that the crowds were heavily female.[8]

But there were still divisions in a Nazi movement that had fractured during Hitler's year in prison. Some of those fissures sprang to the surface in Weimar. A local Nazi leader who had his own detractors was constantly heckled and interrupted. Hitler did not miss a beat, resorting to a technique that became his signature method of burying internal dissent—a mass oath-swearing. It was Hitler's psychological ploy for converting a quibbling mob into an evangelical horde. He called upon all who believed in his cause to raise their right arms and swear fealty to the movement. Arms shot up; his unexpected gesture seemed to work. "We are all fighting and bleeding for a common ideal," he told his followers. "Let the quarreling be over, so that I may leave this city knowing that the [Nazi] movement has also struck deep roots here."

Nazism would indeed become deeply rooted in Weimar and Thuringia, giving Hitler a base outside Bavaria as he painstakingly and doggedly built a following for his cause—and himself.

6

MEIN KAMPF

After this confessional work, Hitler is utterly finished.

— Frankfurter Zeitung, *1925*

Hitler was the ultimate political animal. In the five years since discovering his rhetorical gift and igniting Nazism, he had been consumed by politics. Public declamation had become his métier, his preferred form of communication, his identity. Banned from the public podium in Bavaria—oxygen deprivation to a compulsive talker like him—Hitler had to find other outlets for his busy mind. If he could not talk, he concluded, he would write. Though he always extolled the "magical power of the spoken word," he prized the written word when it suited his purposes. "The less I can speak, the more I can write for hundreds of thousands of people," he told fellow Nazis.

Hitler's biggest writing project—the manuscript he had drafted in prison—was constantly talked about in the media. Even before he had been paroled, Nazi-friendly newspapers announced his forthcoming book. Its original title was a jawbreaker: *Four and a Half Years of Struggle Against Lies, Stupidity, and Cowardice: A Reckoning.* The title was later changed to, simply, *Mein Kampf: Eine Abrechnung* (My Struggle: A Reckoning).

Legend has it that Hitler dictated *Mein Kampf* to fellow prisoner Rudolf Hess. That is incorrect. The Nazi boss typed his manuscript on a brand-new American-made Remington portable typewriter—most likely a gift from his benefactress, Helene Bechstein, wife of the renowned Berlin piano manufacturer, Edwin Bechstein.[1] The ardent prison author worked long hours. "At five o'clock in the morning, I make a cup of tea for Hitler," noted Hess in a letter to his father.[2]

Mein Kampf was the Nazi leader's attempt to lay out "for all time" the fundamentals of National Socialism as he intended for his followers to understand them.[3] He wanted to establish himself as the unchallengeable chief intellectual and ideologue of the movement. In thrall to his own messianism, the fanatical party leader needed to create the catechism and write the scripture himself. By owning the doctrine, Hitler could thwart rivals such as his own party comrade Alfred Rosenberg, who fancied himself a Nazi ideologue and who would write his own tome, *The Myth of the Twentieth Century*.

What Hitler produced was both memoir and manifesto. It was "the most comprehensive and, in some ways, most intimate statement of a [future] dictator whose policies and crimes completely changed the world," noted the editors of a massively annotated version of *Mein Kampf* that was released in 2016.[4] Usually at pains to shroud himself in a mysterious allure, Hitler, in his politically motivated autobiography, baldly disclosed his dark vision. He reshaped his ramshackle life into an imagined apprenticeship for greatness. He invented a Great Man whom Providence had chosen to lead the German people to redemption. Structured as a coming-of-age story—a bildungsroman—the book took readers from Hitler's days as a defiant schoolboy in provincial Austria to his emergence as a budding politician addressing revved-up crowds in Munich. The book was also a long-winded elucidation of Hitler's increasingly rigid worldview. Giving vent to his rabid anti-Semitism in a crucial chapter called "Nation and Race," he presented elaborate theories of racial struggle and racial degeneration using simplistic variations on social Darwinism—a pseudoscientific departure from Darwinism that used botanical principles to explain human evolution and typologies. He compared human ethnicities, which he always called races, to animal species such as storks, minks, wolves, and field mice.[5] Any mixing among any of the species—animal or human—would have a necessarily degenerative effect, wrote Hitler. Ventilating on the "iron logic of nature" that the strong should prevail over the weak, he justified war and the need for "permanent struggle" by the superior race, the Aryans.[6] Jews were described as both strong and weak: a cunning enemy that sought to overwhelm the brave, well-meaning Aryans; an unproductive "race" that sucked the blood of other groups and never produced anything of value to society.[7]

An intellectual magpie who picked up phrases and thoughts wherever he found them, Hitler wove random ideas into the fabric of his writing without attribution or sourcing them so that everything sounded as if it were original to him. His equation of field mice and minks with various human "races" sprang in part from Houston Stewart Chamberlain's false 1899 claim that human races were in fact different species.[8] Hitler's labeling of Jews as a plague and tuberculosis echoed philosopher and art historian Julius Langbehn's 1892 denigration of Jews as "a passing plague and cholera."[9] That view in turn followed historian Heinrich von Treitschke's notorious 1880 assertion that "the Jews are our misfortune!" Nearly thirty years earlier, French writer Arthur de Gobineau had put forth the argument that human races are fundamentally different, that nations come and go depending on their racial makeup, that the white race is superior, and that racial intermingling dooms a society to collapse.[10]

Ranging widely in his book, Hitler freely appropriated the anti-Jewish thinking of writer Theodor Fritsch, who insisted that "solving the Jewish question" was society's greatest challenge. Whoever accomplished the deed would become "the greatest hero of all time, a real dragon slayer, the true Siegfried," claimed Fritsch.[11] Hitler later wrote to Fritsch that as a young man in Vienna he had read Fritsch's famous 1893 bestseller, *Handbuch der Judenfrage* (The Handbook of the Jewish Question), and that it was instrumental "in laying the groundwork for the National Socialist anti-Semitic movement."[12] To Hitler, biological division was holy writ and rabid nationalism its natural antidote. The Nazi leader embraced the primacy of the *Volk*—the people, the nation—over the state and the preeminence of the state over the individual. His intolerance for minorities such as Jews became the foundation for his panacea, the *Volksgemeinschaft*—the national community.

In matters of war and peace, Hitler painted an exceptionally clear picture of what he had in mind if he took power: conquest of "living space" (*Lebensraum*) for Germans in Europe's east, which meant invading Russia. Hitler considered Germany the "embodiment of all human progress";

he decried its current pacifist-minded renunciation of land acquisition at the expense of "less worthy nations" such as Russia, which possessed "gigantic" surface area.[13] To act decisively, Germany required a strong "personality"—Hitler's euphemism for the notion of a Great Man, or dictator. His Great Man was both prophet and practitioner. He was uniquely endowed with a rare combination of philosophical insight and political pragmatism, both necessary to lead a nation to new heights. "At rare intervals in human history," he wrote, "it may occasionally happen that the practical politician and the political philosopher are one."[14] Such an interval had now arrived, and Hitler left no doubt as to who he thought possessed the twin talents needed for heroic leadership.

One of Hitler's gifts, he believed, was a preternatural instinct for reaching ordinary people, whom he considered inherently gullible. In *Mein Kampf,* he was astonishingly frank in his assessment of the untutored masses and how to manipulate them. "The great masses of the people in the very bottom of their hearts tend to be corrupted rather than consciously and purposely evil," he wrote. This insight could be exploited by a skillful leader, since most people fell more easily victim "to a big lie than to a little one, since they themselves lie in little things but would be ashamed of lies that were too big."[15]

Beyond its impact on readers, *Mein Kampf*'s greater importance lay in its impact on Hitler himself. Writing the book was a clarifying experience that dramatically boosted Hitler's self-estimation, sharpened his political philosophy, and hardened his strategic plan for conquering Germany and other countries. Even Hess, the fawning acolyte who served as Hitler's sounding board while reading drafts aloud in prison, was struck by Hitler's "enormous belief in himself."[16] Confidence intensified aggression, including Hitler's galloping anti-Semitism. "So far I've been too mild," Hitler told a visitor he received in prison. "Working on my book has made me realize that in the future, the harshest weapons" would have to be used against Jews. "This is an existential matter not only for our nation but also for all nations. Jewry is the pestilence of the world!"[17]

In the end, Hitler created a book that some dismissed as unreadable grandstanding but others embraced as stirring inspiration. It was a call to combat with a battle plan included. The Nazi leader claimed that he, like

Moses, had delivered a finished set of guidelines for himself and his movement. Researching and writing the book, he said, had convinced him that his earlier intuitions had been right all along. The facts, as he discovered them, supported all his theories. He had attained a belief in himself that "nothing could shake thereafter."[18]

Hitler's manuscript was finished by the end of September in 1924. Yet the 372-page work was far from ready to see the light of print. Though Hitler was released from prison before the end of that year, the book was still unpublished. The nettlesome *Münchener Post,* a Social Democratic newspaper always seeking ways to spite Hitler, taunted: "The book has not been written and will never be written."[19] In fact, Hitler's draft needed work. The prose resembled his speaking: one long shout. His hodgepodge ideas were sometimes hard to follow, out of order, overwrought. To get the book into shape, several hands pitched in, including Hess and his fiancée, Ilse Pröhl; Josef Stolzing-Czerny, a music critic at the *Völkischer Beobachter;* and Ernst Hanfstaengl, a tall, rich publishing scion and Hitler's sometime walk-around buddy. Some stylistic changes were designed to put a human touch back into the text to capture Hitler's speaking voice—his strength. Countless filler words were added—such as *now, but, since, once, in addition,* and so forth. As a piece of writing, the book became worse, but the diction and pace felt more like Hitler's.[20]

The book still did not appear in print. Hitler was hesitating, partly out of fear of deportation to his Austrian homeland if he stirred too much official ire with his polemics. He knew that banishment to Austria could sink his career. The terms of his early parole from prison after serving only eight months of a five-year sentence included expulsion from Germany if he veered close to his old ways of promoting violent revolution. Luckily for him, Austria had no interest in repatriating him. Austrian chancellor Ignaz Seipel gave Bavarian authorities a one-word answer to their queries about turning Hitler over to his native country: "No!" Thus Seipel preempted the Bavarians and effectively deported Hitler to Germany. That evening, when they received the news, Hitler and Hess celebrated with a rare glass of wine. Hitler felt German to the core and wanted no further truck with Austria—at least not until he could realize his dream of annexing the rump state left behind by the breakup of the Austro-Hungarian Empire after the First World War.

To finish work on *Mein Kampf,* Hitler needed to get away. He needed a respite from the political carnival, a retreat into his own head so he could finalize his book. He needed the mountains.

Hitler had already discovered his highland nirvana. The village of Berchtesgaden, one of the gems of the German Alps, was tucked into the southeastern corner of the country, 110 miles from Munich, near the Austrian border. The little town commanded views of the highest mountain entirely on German soil, the Watzmann (8,901 feet),[21] and looked down on the dreamy expanse of a fjordlike lake called the Königsee. Hitler had found this idyllic retreat when he traveled in 1923 to visit Dietrich Eckart.

A radical anti-Semite, Eckart was a writer and political intellectual, a publisher and an editor, a renowned roué and far-right seer—as well as an alcoholic and a morphine user. Drug-addicted though he was, Eckart had foreseen the coming of a character like Hitler. "We need a leader who isn't bothered by the clatter of a machine gun," Eckart said. "The best would be a worker who can also speak... and who does not run from somebody swinging a chair at him. He has to be a bachelor—then we'll get the women!"[22]

Eckart became Hitler's first and most important political mentor—a "polar star," in Hitler's eyes. Seeking Eckart's counsel in 1923, Hitler had to ascend the long slopes of the Obersalzberg, a mountain above Berchtesgaden, to reach the sage's guest lodge, the Pension Moritz. A flatlander from the Danube plain around Linz, Austria, Hitler was no outdoorsman. "Are you nuts?" he finally asked his guide. "Won't this trail ever end? Do you think I've turned into a mountain goat and we're climbing the Himalayas?"[23]

Hitler's whining stopped when he reached the Pension Moritz. The small guesthouse faced a dazzling range of Alpine peaks marching off into the distance. Having been without a real home since leaving Linz at the age of eighteen, the footloose thirty-four-year-old Hitler fell in love. The Obersalzberg would soon become his favorite spot on earth—his refuge in times of stress, the place where "all my great projects were conceived and ripened," he said.[24] His Nazi comrades took to calling the Obersalzberg Hitler's "magic mountain," echoing the title of Thomas Mann's bestselling novel *The Magic Mountain,* which appeared in 1924.

Returning in the late spring of 1925 to finalize *Mein Kampf,* Hitler was offered a small writing hut that stood a bit higher up the mountainside than the Pension Moritz. The *Häusl,* as a tiny cottage is called in Bavaria, had a single room and a low overhanging roof. Well back in the woods, it was just far enough from the main lodge without being too far. Hitler rechristened the hut *Kampfhäusl,* or combat cottage. There he finished his book, removing six possibly incendiary chapters on how he would run Germany as a dictatorship. These he would hold for a second volume.

On July 18, 1925, the first volume of *Mein Kampf* appeared in an edition of ten thousand copies. Hitler and his publisher, Max Amann, were thrilled finally to see copies of the book in print. But they could not have picked a worse time to publish—in the dead of the German vacation season. Worse still, three other prison memoirs had been published just weeks before—one based on a soldier's imprisonment in France during the First World War and two based on events close to Hitler's own story. But by the fall of 1925, *Mein Kampf* began to take off. Though its twelve-mark price made it a tough purchase for cash-strapped Nazi Party members, they were practically under orders to buy the book; it soon became known as the "Nazi Bible."[25] Even *Simplicissimus,* the bitingly satirical weekly magazine, printed on its cover a caricature of a Hitler look-alike peddling *Mein Kampf* in a crowded Munich pub. A paunchy drinker, ensconced before his tall beer mug, says in Bavarian dialect: "Twelve marks for this little book! A bit steep, neighbor. Say, have you got a match?"[26] Negative publicity, but publicity nonetheless.

In the coming months, nearly fifty publications would review Hitler's book with opinions that ranged from grudging respect to derisive dismissal. "His cramp!" ("Sein Krampf!") mocked a nationalist newspaper. The respected Swiss newspaper *Neue Zürcher Zeitung* derided his know-it-all style. "How ridiculous… [he] appears when he claims omniscience and then ventilates with equal self-assurance on matters of race, modern literature, education issues, Malthusianism, the nature of the state, and one hundred other subjects."

One essayist noted that Hitler's virulent excesses about Jews "raised doubts about the mental stability of the memoirist." Yet a leading Jewish publication, the *Abwehrblätter* (Defense Journal), saw in Hitler's rambling discourse little cause for alarm. The weekly magazine blithely dismissed the anti-Semitic outbursts as ignorant nonsense, reliant on the discredited *The Protocols of the Elders of Zion,* a fabricated anti-Semitic text first published in Russia in 1903: "One sets aside Hitler's book with the *comforting feeling* [italics added] that as long as the *völkisch* movement can't come up with other leaders, it will be a very long time before it conquers the nation of poets and thinkers."*[27] Such blithe dismissals of Hitler as a future political force were common. The *Frankfurter Zeitung,* one of Germany's most thoughtful newspapers, treated Hitler's book to a long, detailed review but ultimately discounted his political prospects: "After this confessional work, Hitler is utterly finished."[28]

The general reading public was less interested in Hitler's sweeping ideological pronouncements than in his war stories. Newspaper excerpts from the book favored narratives from the muck of the First World War.[29] Hitler's hair-raising, nearly elegiac description of entering the killing fields of Flanders was considered especially gripping ("As daylight began creeping out of the fog, a steel greeting ripped over our heads and loosed its edgy shrapnel into our ranks, digging up the wet earth"). Yet even this story was later shown to be a highly stylized account that compressed events and probably invented details.

To those who wanted to believe Hitler and find an intellectual framework for their hypernationalist and racist leanings, it did not matter that *Mein Kampf* was a work of overweening pomposity. The book appealed to desperate people in desperate times. Hitler, the high school dropout, had

* Because of Germany's literary achievements and high intellectual standards, the country has been known among the cultural cognoscenti since the nineteenth century as "the nation of poets and thinkers."

read (or partially read) scores of books while down and out in Vienna, while serving four years in the German army, and while in prison. His wide reading was superficial and selective and often came from the cheap newspapers and free pamphlets scattered everywhere in those days. A dazzling dilettante, Hitler admitted that he cherry-picked whatever confirmed his fixed beliefs. He retained just enough detail to make his extreme conclusions about Jews, Aryans, Marxists, biology, social struggle, military matters, and large historical topics sound credible. Just as he could sense crowd mood and rouse a beer-hall audience hungering for someone who would channel their frustrations and hopes, Hitler could also churn out a book that had something for almost anyone who could make the long march through its dense pages.

Rarely in history did a future tyrant lay out with such clarity what he intended to do if he seized power—and then go on to do it, noted one German historian.[30] Diarist Victor Klemperer described *Mein Kampf* as a propaganda textbook of "shameless openness."[31] But Hitler's virulence was widely discounted as the razzle-dazzle of a beer-hall pontificator. With only a few exceptions, his huffing and puffing was considered unrealistic, unattainable, and unthreatening.

7

BAYREUTH

I was thirty-six years old, and life was delightful. I had all the pleasures of popularity without any of the inconveniences.

—*Adolf Hitler, 1925*

Hitler loved the rush and roar of politics. The Nazi dervish threw himself into frenzied speech making. He traveled through the night for political meetings. He shouted himself hoarse when he had willing listeners, whether he was in a packed beer hall or in a back room with a dozen party intimates. He stayed up far past midnight debating, sermonizing, and always dominating the conversation. Upon leaving prison, in late 1924, Hitler had renounced alcohol; he could outlast anyone in a late-night discussion.

But he could not bear the constraints of a regular schedule or keep his appointments and obligations. As a political leader, he was more passion than executive function. One minute he was behind his desk acting like a party leader; the next he was out the door, headed for nobody knew where. "You could never keep him off the streets," bemoaned Hanfstaengl, who often accompanied the Nazi leader on his impromptu jaunts to a Munich café for a casual afternoon of newspaper reading, all prior commitments forgotten. A disorganized bohemian at heart, Hitler caromed among his favorite haunts: the Café Heck, beside Munich's Royal Garden; the cushy Carlton Tea Room, on Briennerstrasse; and, for lunch, the Osteria Bavaria, near the Nazi Party headquarters. He never ceased thinking of himself as a potentially great artist or architect; self-indulgence was second nature to him.

In late July and early August of 1925, Hitler's indulgence was opera; he attended the renowned Wagner opera festival in Bayreuth. There the longtime Wagner fanatic wallowed in the master's works. Hitler saw productions of *Die Meistersinger von Nürnberg, Parsifal, Götterdämmerung,* and other operas. It was only the second revival of the festival following its closure during the First World War. The German press followed Bayreuth's parade of singers and conductors, princes and potentates as if they were movie stars.

Hitler reveled. Bayreuth "exerted its full charm on me," he recalled. "I was thirty-six years old, and life was delightful. I had all the pleasures of popularity without any of the inconveniences. Everybody put himself out to be nice to me, and nobody asked anything of me. By day I'd go for a walk, in leather shorts. In the evening, I'd go to the [opera] in a dinner jacket or tails."[1]

After the performances, Hitler often sat up late with the singers. They schmoozed at the opera house or in the cozy Hotel Goldener Anker.[2] For the failed painter and would-be architect, these were blissful hours. His only complaint was that a Jew, Friedrich Schorr—the greatest bass-baritone of the era—was singing the preeminent role of Wotan, the king of the gods in the four-opera cycle *Der Ring des Nibelungen*. Hitler called it a "racial disgrace."[3]

Once again, Hitler was cosseted by his patrons, Helene and Edwin Bechstein. The wealthy Berlin couple offered him accommodation in their rented villa on Lisztstrasse, just around the corner from the Wagner compound, Wahnfried. Winifred Wagner was under orders from her husband, Siegfried, to give Hitler a wide berth, at least for a few days. Siegfried had gotten into a spot of trouble with important Jewish patrons of the festival because of his and Winifred's well-publicized friendship with the outspoken anti-Semite.

Keeping Winifred at bay was fine with Helene Bechstein. She wanted no competition for Hitler's attention and reflected glow.[4] Though the impetuous Winifred showed up at the Bechstein villa on the festival's second day with a bouquet of flowers for Hitler—"things got lively," he recalled—it was not until the second week that Winifred gave Hitler a personal tour of the famous hilltop Festspielhaus (Festival Theater). This was Wagner's personal opera house, built with unusual features such as rough flooring in the main seating area and a recessed orchestra pit, which forced the instrumentalists to play right underneath the opera stage.

Soon Hitler yearned for the mountains and his writing desk. He wanted to begin the second volume of *Mein Kampf.* "Herr Hitler is doing fine—he is withdrawing to Berchtesgaden to write the second volume of his book," wrote Hess to a fellow Nazi.[5] With only a few interruptions, Hitler spent the next five weeks in Berchtesgaden at the Hotel Deutsches Haus—he did not like the new owners of the Pension Moritz, on the Obersalzberg. There he worked on "the basic ideas of a German National Socialist foreign policy." Just as he had done while speed-writing the first volume of *Mein Kampf* in Landsberg Prison, Hitler put in long hours composing his draft—but now he was dictating to a secretary. He was working so hard that Josef Stolzing-Czerny, his sometime editor, predicted that the new book might appear before Christmas in 1925.[6] He was off by nearly a year.

8

STRASSER AND GOEBBELS

He was a man of the people in an entirely different sense from Hitler, who seemed so unapproachable to us.

—A Storm Trooper speaking of Gregor Strasser

While he was off in the mountains writing the second volume of *Mein Kampf,* Hitler was immersed in deep thoughts about large matters—alliances with England, tighter relations with Italy, grabbing *Lebensraum* from Russia. What he was not doing in the summer and fall of 1925 was paying attention to Gregor Strasser.

Gregor Strasser was a big man with a stentorian voice and a down-to-earth style. He was to become the most important Nazi whom history would later forget. Because Hitler was chronically disorganized, administratively hopeless, and often absent from party headquarters, it would be Strasser, not Hitler, who would build the smoothly running political machine that would, in a key moment, catapult the Nazi leader to national prominence. Strasser could arguably be called the man who made Hitler.

Strasser was an unlikely kingmaker. A pharmacist from the small Bavarian town of Landshut, he had been drawn to the Nazi cause through his intense nationalism after Germany's loss in the First World War. A decorated artillery officer who had been wounded in battle, Strasser had natural administrative gifts. He organized Nazi support in northern Bavaria and, while Hitler was in prison in 1924, got himself elected to the Reichstag on the National Socialist Freedom Movement ticket. Following Hitler's refounding of the Nazi Party, in 1925, Strasser threw in his lot with the group. Hitler soon tasked Strasser with building the party's network beyond its base in southern Germany.

Focusing on northern and western Germany—including the industrial

Ruhr region—Strasser busily worked the back roads, small burgs, and sprawling working-class neighborhoods of the far-flung regions outside Bavaria. The activist recruiter roared from town to town, meeting with Nazis or would-be Nazis, gaining their loyalty by his very physical presence. Though his looks were nothing special—he was oval-faced, nearly bald, and plain-featured—the big man was nimble-spirited and a good speaker with "a lion's voice and a bear's strength," according to journalist Konrad Heiden, who covered the Nazi Party's early years.[1] For pleasure, Strasser read Homer in Greek yet welcomed the occasional beer-hall brawl.[2] Compared to Strasser, wrote Heiden, Hitler was "just a bundle of nerves."

Strasser was also popular. He made ninety-one public speeches in 1925 (Hitler made only thirty-nine, mostly to closed Nazi gatherings). The peripatetic Bavarian identified leaders and set up local chapters.[3] He greeted everyone with "Whaddya say, neighbor?" in his slangy Bavarian dialect. "We instantly liked Strasser," said one Saxon Storm Trooper who met the roving politician. "Something paternal emanated from him.... He was a man of the people in an entirely different sense from Hitler, who seemed so unapproachable to us."[4]

With Strasser's activism, the Nazi Party was growing faster in his realm—northern and western Germany—than in Hitler's realm, Bavaria and the south.[5] Focused on himself and his self-assigned role as undisputed leader, Hitler was blind to Strasser's reach and success.

Another Nazi idealist who would soon play an outsize part in Nazi Party affairs was also active on the hustings—and had emerged as one of the busiest and most sought-after Nazi agitators in Germany's industrial northwest. Twenty-seven and energetic, Paul Joseph Goebbels was the well-educated son of a petty factory clerk in Rheydt, a small town in the Rhineland. Born in 1897 and raised Catholic, young Goebbels was beset by physical challenges. He had a weak constitution, a small stature, and a foreshortened clubfoot that caused a pronounced limp. First World War doctors pronounced him unfit to fight—a permanent humiliation and a political shortcoming in postwar right-wing politics.

But what the short, dark-haired Rhinelander lacked in brawn he made up in brains. After earning a doctorate in literature from Heidelberg University, he sought jobs at newspapers and began writing novels—but failed at both. Stuck in a bank clerking job that he hated, the self-absorbed Goebbels indulged in conflicted love affairs and an epic inner political struggle. The smart but disoriented young man was torn between a grand idealism that drew him to Soviet communism and strong nationalistic urges that connected him to Germany's reactionary political scene. Goebbels recorded all his struggles in a diary he started in late 1923 and filled with thousands of entries over the following twenty-two years.[6]

"Chaos inside me," he wrote regarding both art and politics. "Fermentation. Unconscious clarifying."[7]

Goebbels began reading daily newspaper reports about a sensational trial in Munich. A firebrand politician named Adolf Hitler was being prosecuted for treason, having staged a coup d'état against the government. "I am busying myself with Hitler and the national socialist movement," noted Goebbels. "Communism, the Jewish question, Christianity, the Germany of the future.... Hitler touches on many questions. But he makes the solution very simple."

From Hitler's trial speeches, the young Goebbels began envisioning what the leader must be like. "What is liberating about Hitler is the involvement of a really upright and truthful personality," he noted. "Hitler is an idealist... who is bringing new belief to the German people. I am reading his speeches; I am allowing myself to be inspired by him and carried to the stars.... Only Hitler continually concerns me. The man is indeed no intellectual. But his wonderful *élan,* his verve, his enthusiasm, his German feeling."[8]

Hitler's fierce belief in himself and his cause electrified Goebbels. In the Nazi agitator and his party, he felt he had found his new religion and its messiah. In August of 1924, he cofounded a local chapter of a Nazi-related political group. Like Hitler, he belatedly discovered he had a talent for blistering oratory. The little man had a big voice, with a hectoring style and biting anti-Semitic sarcasm that often led to tumult, sometimes fisticuffs. Goebbels loved taking on hecklers. Abandoning his plans to become a novelist, he began to succeed at his more natural métier:

political proselytizing and propagandizing. By 1925, he was even busier than Gregor Strasser, giving 189 "inflammatory speeches" around the Rhineland and northwestern Germany.[9] Because Goebbels, unlike most Nazis, was university educated and even had a doctorate, he soon became known in Nazi circles as "the little doctor."

In mid-July of 1925, Goebbels traveled to Weimar for a Nazi Party gathering. He met various Nazi bigwigs, including self-styled economist Gottfried Feder, Hitler's favorite. But when he finally had a chance to see and hear Hitler, Goebbels was transformed. "I'm a different person," he wrote in his journal. "Now I know that the man who leads was born to be a leader. I'm ready to sacrifice everything for him."[10]

The narcissistic Goebbels imagined that Hitler was falling in love with him, too. When they finally met personally for the first time, a few months later, in the town of Braunschweig, Hitler was eating dinner when Goebbels arrived. "He jumps up, stands there before us, shakes my hand like an old friend," noted Goebbels. "This man has everything it takes to be king. A born man of the people. The coming dictator."[11]

Two weeks later, after both men had spoken to a Nazi gathering in Plauen, north of Bayreuth, then spent a late evening in conversation, Goebbels wrote: "How I love him!"[12]

Despite his growing adulation for Hitler the man, Goebbels still had some reservations about Hitler the policy maker. Like Gregor Strasser, Goebbels harbored doubts about Hitler's commitment to the *socialism* part of National Socialism. Strasser and Goebbels also disagreed with Hitler's harsh views of Russia. In contrast to Hitler, both Strasser and Goebbels did not believe that the Soviet Union—or even the basic ideas behind Bolshevism—was necessarily a bad thing. They felt that a general overlap of interests between Russia and Germany might lead to a fruitful alliance.* Strasser argued in a *Völkischer Beobachter* article: "Russia is our ally, and it is a crime against Germany's future not to recognize this."[13]

Hitler had gone in the opposite direction. He had developed a strong animus for Russia, not just because of "Jewish Bolshevism" but also

---

* The Nazi leaders habitually said "Russia," even when they meant the Soviet Union. The terms are used interchangeably in this book.

because he had been deeply disappointed that the death of Russian leader Vladimir Ilyich Lenin, in 1924, did not lead to the overthrow of the rotten "Jewish-dominated" regime, an event that he and other Nazi intellectuals had confidently predicted.[14] Hitler now saw Russia only as an implacable enemy and a ripe target for German colonization.

Beyond policy differences with Hitler, both Strasser and Goebbels shared a strong distaste for the crowd of advisers around Hitler at Nazi Party headquarters in Munich—especially Hermann Esser, Julius Streicher, and Max Amann. Strasser considered them untrustworthy hustlers. Esser was regarded as an unsavory figure, partly for his reputation as a shameless skirt chaser. The "Esser clique," as Goebbels called the Munich group, was closest to Hitler all the time: they exercised a cynical influence on the leader, drawing him away from the ideals of National Socialism in favor of raw power politics. Though he was himself anti-Semitic, Strasser felt the Munich inner circle practiced a gratuitously virulent style of Jew baiting that led Hitler to extremes.[15]

Strasser was emboldened by his organizational successes in northern and northwestern Germany. At a meeting with Goebbels, he laid out a plan. He wanted to unify his fast-growing network of Nazi chapters into a centralized structure called the Northwestern Working Group.[16] The group would pull together the Nazi Party's northern and western district leaders, whom the party called gauleiters.* The gauleiters would promote information sharing, exchange of political speakers, and publication of an internal policy newsletter. Strasser had already secured Hitler's approval for such worthy but anodyne goals.

In reality Strasser had bigger ideas. He wanted to change the course of

* The German word *Gauleiter* means "*Gau* leader," or "district leader." *Gau* was an archaic term for "district," which the Nazis revived. Once it was fully organized, the party would divide Germany into thirty-five *gaus* (districts), corresponding to Germany's thirty-five electoral districts. Each of the thirty-five gauleiters led a district, making him a party potentate, like a state governor. The gauleiters were also part of the Nazi Party's leadership structure. Some gauleiters would eventually become members of the party elite. For ease of understanding, this book uses an *s* to pluralize *gauleiter,* though in German the word *Gauleiter* is both singular and plural—and always capitalized.

the Nazi Party. He hoped to reshape Hitler's juggernaut, bending its course toward his romantic vision of a collectivist society with a friendly stance toward Russia. He especially wanted to neutralize the Esser bunch in Munich. Strasser recruited Goebbels as his coconspirator by making him the editor of the Working Group's new bimonthly publication, *National Socialist Letters* (*Nationalsozialistische Briefe,* or *NS-Briefe* for short).[17] In Goebbels's eyes, the *National Socialist Letters* could be used as "a weapon against the ossified bosses in Munich," he confided to his diary. "We will make ourselves noticed by Hitler."[18] Later he added: "When the Working Group is large enough, we'll go on a general attack. It's all about National Socialism—nothing else!"[19]

Strasser's effort had all the makings of a party schism or, in the worst case, a coup against Hitler. The Working Group set about drafting a new constitutional foundation for the Nazi Party—a venture onto dangerous ground. The party already had a set of founding principles, known as the Twenty-Five Points, and Hitler viewed them as holy writ. Conceived in early 1920, just as Hitler was gaining influence in the German Workers' Party, the Twenty-Five Points were the little group's attempt to define itself and to draw a crowd by presenting a programmatic statement. Hitler announced the points in his first major appearance at a mass event. Though he was not listed among the evening's speakers, and though he appeared after all others, Hitler the budding propagandist turned a potentially boring recitation of the party's twenty-five-point manifesto into a provocative rant that had people jumping atop tables and shouting at one another.[20] It was the fledgling group's first lunge into beer-hall rabble-rousing on a large scale, and it set the tone for all future events. The explosive evening confirmed Hitler's claim that the little party had to start thinking big; it catapulted him to the forefront of Nazi Party agitation.

As a program, the Twenty-Five Points seemed extreme to some but were common currency in the right-wing *völkisch* political milieu of Munich. The platform envisioned a redefinition of Germany's place in the world plus sweeping social and economic reforms along with exclusionary citizenship laws. The document insisted, first, on a Greater Germany—a unification of Germany, Austria, and unnamed other German-speaking lands. Such a union would be a flat-out violation of the Treaty of Versailles, but the Points rejected the entire treaty as well. One point demanded "land and soil" for the feeding and resettlement of Germany's "excess population"—a preview of Hitler's future policy of grabbing *Lebensraum* from Russia. The Twenty-Five Points also envisioned nationalization of big trusts, expropriation of wealthy landowners, and the guarantee of a basic living for everyone—even at the cost of expelling every noncitizen from the Reich. The expulsion clause was aimed mainly at Jews, who would by definition not meet a requirement that every citizen be "of German blood." Included among the Twenty-Five Points was the creation of an exclusively "German press"—a direct shot at large Jewish-owned publishing houses such as Ullstein Verlag (*Vossische Zeitung, Berliner Morgenpost*), Rudolf Mosse Verlag (*Berliner Tageblatt*), and the *Frankfurter Zeitung*. Economically, the credo favored peasant farmers and small shop owners.

Once written and presented, though, the Twenty-Five Points received almost no attention from the outside world and were barely even noticed inside the Nazi Party. Even for Hitler, the Twenty-Five Points became party wallpaper: they were always there, but nobody ever talked about them. In his speeches over the ensuing eight years, Hitler seldom acknowledged the existence of a Nazi Party program. Instead, he made arguments like those in the platform but no mention of any "Twenty-Five Points."[21] Nonetheless, he insisted on treating the decree as political scripture if it came under attack.

To Strasser, Goebbels, and others in the Working Group, it made simple good sense that the original party platform, written five years earlier in haste and inexperience, needed to be updated. Over several months, they developed a draft that emphasized socialism over nationalism, beginning with the words: "A nation is a community of destiny, distress, and sustenance."[22] It was a measure of their wild idealism—and leftist utopianism—that they proposed a communitarian society with a corporatist political structure and an anticapitalist economy. It was to be based on state ownership and, unbelievably, on nearly medieval notions of barter. "Efforts will be made for [wages and salaries] to be paid largely in kind," read the document.[23] Rather than receiving a check or cash on payday, Germans would leave the steel mills, shipbuilding docks, government offices, and small shops with flour, butter, shirts, and shoes. To the men of the Working Group, this naive vision was the appropriate response to a deep-seated fear of hyperinflation, which had robbed many Germans of their worldly possessions and soured them on money as a medium of exchange. In their woolly wanderings, Strasser and his insurgent Nazis were playing to a renascent longing in the German lower middle classes for secure, ancient guild structures and stable social and economic conditions. Finally, in January of 1926, their draft was ready.

9

BAMBERG DEBACLE

We'll play the coy beauty and lure Hitler onto our turf.

—*Joseph Goebbels, 1926*

This is one of the greatest disappointments of my life. Which Hitler was this? A reactionary? . . . Horrible!

—*Joseph Goebbels, 1926*

There had been a leak. Strasser's Working Group platform draft had gotten into the hands of Gottfried Feder, one of the early Nazi Party founders and a coauthor of the Twenty-Five Points. A rabid anti-Marxist, Feder was a fervent loyalist in the Munich wing of the party. As one of only a handful of persons cited by name in *Mein Kampf*, he was intensely faithful to Hitler.

Strasser panicked. From his Reichstag office in Berlin, he rushed a letter out to Goebbels. Strasser wrote that he had just been confidentially informed "that Feder received the program draft and is furious over its dissemination without Hitler's knowledge. He's going to make a stink with Hitler."[1]

Like a schoolboy caught with his hand in the honey jar, Strasser proposed immediately sending Hitler a copy of the draft—"with a cover note from me explaining that I, as a private person, wanted to get a collection of opinions from various party comrades as the groundwork for the later creation of a definitive party program." He added, "I will make no mention of the fact that Feder knows about this."

Strasser needed to sandbag his flanks. He decided to send all the northwestern gauleiters a memo disingenuously declaring the Working Group draft "a nonbinding collection of points from party comrades interested in the topic"—as though the months-long wrangling had been a purely intellectual exercise. The gauleiters, therefore, should "use discretion."

When the gauleiters in the Working Group gathered again a few weeks later in Hannover to discuss the program draft, they had a surprise coming: Gottfried Feder showed up. With a head full of indignant steam, the Nazi economics maven was there to confront Strasser, Goebbels, and the others over their unauthorized foray into program writing. Feder represented the eyes and ears of Munich: the Working Group conspirators tried to bar him from their meeting, then relented but gave him no vote in their proceedings.

The discussion turned nasty, especially on matters of foreign policy. Goebbels was fiercely attacked for his views on relations with Russia; he retreated outdoors to calm down and smoke a cigarette. When he returned inside, he used his turn to speak to rip into his critics, at least in his own telling. "I let them have it with both barrels," he wrote. "Russia, Germany, Western capitalism, Bolshevism—I speak for a half hour, a whole hour. Everyone is silent with expectation. Finally, a storm of applause."

According to some reports, Goebbels—or perhaps another northern Nazi—even stood on a chair and proposed the expulsion from the Nazi Party of "the petit bourgeois Adolf Hitler."[2] If true, it had the ring of a Bolshevist accusation at a Russian show trial. Afterward, Goebbels claimed, Strasser came up and shook his hand. His tormentor, Feder, by contrast, had been rendered "small and ugly."[3]

Throughout the meeting, Feder scribbled notes and wrote down names.[4] He recognized what a threat the Working Group's discussion was to Hitler's hold on the party, especially in the northern wing. His report to Hitler the following day clearly jolted the Nazi leader, who finally recognized the Strasser initiative as a challenge to his leadership—or a possible breakaway movement.

Responding like a cornered animal, Hitler summoned all Nazi gauleiters to a general meeting three weeks later—to discuss "some important questions." The meeting was to be held on Sunday, February 14, 1926, in Bamberg, a charming Nazi-friendly town in northern Bavaria. Hitler effectively packed the house with his own supporters, inviting even low-level Nazi activists in Franconia, where Bamberg was located.[5] He also mobilized the local Storm Troopers to make a point about his power.[6] Strasser's and Goebbels's supporters were all in the north or northwest; they would have only ten members of the Working Group at the confab.[7]

In Bamberg, Goebbels and Strasser met for an early-morning strategy session. "[Strasser] in good spirits. Discussed our battle plan," Goebbels reported. Goebbels confided to his journal that "we'll play the coy beauty and lure Hitler onto our turf.... No one believes in Munich anymore. Elberfeld [Goebbels's regional headquarters] will become the Mecca of German socialism."

Goebbels and Strasser were strolling through old Bamberg when suddenly Hitler's big touring car roared past. The king had arrived. Little did the two men know that inside the car sat another man, Gottfried Feder, who had been prepping Hitler for his confrontation with the rebel faction.

At noontime in the Gasthof zum Stöhren, Hitler thrashed through the hopes and ideas of the insurgents with a broad rhetorical scythe. It took the Nazi leader between two and four hours (reports about the duration of the meeting vary) to destroy Strasser's and Goebbels's notion of making common cause with the Russians, denouncing Bolshevism as "Jewish handiwork."[8] Any sort of alliance with Russia was "national suicide." Germany needed "land and soil" that could only be obtained with an eastward-looking policy of colonization. As Strasser and Goebbels glumly listened, Hitler rejected any attempt to update, expand, or rewrite the Twenty-Five Points. "The [existing] program suffices; I am satisfied with it," said Hitler. With barely a flick of his rhetoric, Hitler annulled the program-writing work of six months.

"It pains my soul," noted Goebbels.

But the Munichers loved it. "Feder nods. Ley nods. Streicher nods. Esser nods."[9]

Only Gregor Strasser rose to defend the northern position. His presentation was feeble; he had no clearly defined concept to hold up against Hitler's. "Strasser is beside himself. Hesitant, trembling, unskilled—the good, honest Strasser," noted Goebbels. "Oh, God, how weak we are compared to these idiots from [Munich]."[10]

With his drumbeat invective, Hitler had batted away the challenge mounted by Strasser and Goebbels. The Nazi chief had once again, if belatedly, asserted his claim to sole leadership of the Nazi movement. Personality and oratory had trumped program and apostasy. There was only one Nazi orthodoxy, and it was whatever Hitler said it was.

Goebbels was devastated: "I am beaten down; I am dumbfounded.... This is one of the greatest disappointments of my life. Which Hitler was this? A reactionary?... Horrible!"

The Working Group was dissolved. Hitler had survived the first meaningful challenge to his exclusive hold on the Nazi movement. The denouement of the abortive uprising had been a withering display of Hitler's ferocious will and persuasive powers. And though Strasser had, in the end, been easily vanquished, tensions and troubles between the two leading Nazis were not over.[11]

10

BRUTAL WILLPOWER

The broad masses are blind and dumb and don't know what they are doing.... The masses don't think, they act.

—*Adolf Hitler, 1926*

Such a scintillating intellect—he can be my leader.... I love him.

—*Joseph Goebbels, 1926*

Crushing the Working Group's attempted uprising invigorated Hitler's fighting instincts. Yet victory in Bamberg did not mean the end of sniping and flank attacks from other upstarts. As soon as Hitler returned to Munich, he faced a challenge from Count Ernst zu Reventlow and Albrecht von Graefe, leaders of the northern-based German Völkisch Freedom Party, a competitor to the Nazi Party for the *völkisch* vote. The two northerners had been invited to speak in Munich by Anton Drexler, the disgruntled former head of the German Workers' Party, the predecessor to the Nazi Party. Drexler brazenly booked the northern politicians into the hallowed Hofbräuhaus. And he did it on a sacred date: February 24, 1926, the sixth anniversary of Hitler's first major Nazi Party speech.

On the night of Reventlow's and Graefe's appearance, Hitler decided to confront the interlopers head-on. He exhorted the party faithful to fill the beer hall early. By 8:00 p.m., the place was hopping with Hitlerites. When Reventlow rose to speak—"We assume he was speaking only because his lips were moving," wrote one journalist—the Hofbräuhaus broke into bedlam. With Hermann Esser leading the mayhem, Nazis scrambled onto chairs, waved their fists, and called the northerners "low-life traitors." Reventlow was denounced as a *Saupreis* (Prussian pig), the ultimate Bavarian insult. Women who supported Hitler joined in the catcalling. "The very well represented gentler sex were beside themselves with lung power that had to be heard to be believed," reported a Munich newspaper.[1]

As Reventlow was driven from the dais, Hitler—who had not said a word during the tumult—climbed onto his chair and took Charlie Chaplin–esque bows in all directions. The debacle was a classic disruption tactic—a practice at which the Nazis (and the Communists) would become masters. In the political carnival of 1920s Munich, such an uproar was all in a night's work.[2]

The battle did not stop there. After a series of insults, editorials, and counter-rallies, the northern challengers were beaten. Hitler cunningly used the rivalry to tout the Nazi Party's runaway success in its first year as a refounded party. In an "open letter," he claimed the Nazis had staged 2,700 meetings over the previous twelve months, held more than 3,500 discussion groups, and distributed millions of flyers, brochures, and pieces of propaganda. Even if the numbers were inflated, Hitler delighted yet another beer-hall audience with his braggadocio. Graefe and Reventlow were effectively driven out of town, and, within a year, Reventlow would strike his colors, admitting that Hitler's aggressive juggernaut had outflanked his faction-torn party. "I subordinate myself without further reservations to Adolf Hitler," he wrote. "He has proved that he can lead."[3]

To expand his base, Hitler carried his political crusade onto new turf outside the beer-hall bubble of Munich. He traveled to the rarefied haute-bourgeois world of the entrenched elite in Hamburg, Germany's preeminent port city. Invited to speak to a closed meeting of the prestigious National Club of 1919, Hitler was welcomed at the luxurious Hotel Atlantic by four hundred members of the city's former Wilhelmine ruling class—top civil servants, military officers, jurists, and businessmen.[4] In his Hamburg outing, Hitler appeared as the well-mannered political strategist rather than as the workingman's mischief maker. He wore a frock coat and tie, not the quasimilitary garb and swastika armband of a Nazi firebrand.

Yet in his speech the Nazi leader laid it on thick. Pandering to the presumed intellectual superiority of the lost empire's leadership class—men like those seated before him—Hitler painted an elitist picture of national life in which only "the best blood" should prevail. He pummeled the traitorous "lowlifes" who had undermined the First World War effort, fueling the stab-in-the-back legend of Germany's defeat so beloved by the nationalists. Current peacemaking efforts by the Berlin government only guaranteed Germany's "sorrowful end," intoned the Nazi orator. "Those who claim that a great people of sixty million cannot perish deceive themselves!"

Startlingly frank, Hitler revealed his cynical contempt for the very Germans he claimed were key to his insurgent movement. The least educated but largest group on the socioeconomic ladder—the working class—was the foundation of any effort to stop Marxism, said the Nazi leader. But brute force was the only thing the workers understood. "The broad masses are blind and dumb and don't know what they are doing," Hitler told the men in ties and tails. "The masses need to feel the triumph of their own strength.... The masses don't think, they act." As unthinking actors, Hitler continued, the masses provided "the primitive power of one-sidedness"—an essential ingredient for Hitler's kind of revolution.

Though addressing a genteel audience, Hitler was open in his cold-bloodedness. He used the word *brutal* sixteen times—brutal willpower, brutal force, brutal energy, and brutal strength. No one voiced any objection (in the stenographer's account) when Hitler characterized as weak any government that was not willing to "put its enemies in the noose."[5] During the First World War, defeatist Germans who promoted peace over conflict "should have been delivered without mercy to the gallows." The more radical Hitler's words, the greater the shouts of "Bravo!" and "Exactly right!" from his audience. Holding his listeners apparently spellbound for two and a half hours, Hitler concluded with an evocation of a coming Germany not just "of freedom" but also "of power." This earned him "stormy ovations and shouts of 'Heil!'" noted the stenographer.

Hitler's address to the National Club marked a turning point. The Nazi Party chief had shown his closest followers that his definition of a new pan-German community included even the ultraconservative ultracapitalists. Wealth was not a disqualifier, not even when one was wearing a bow tie and tuxedo. Tactical alacrity and crosscutting class inclusion were clearly among Hitler's movement-building tools.

Having thwarted his would-be challengers in the Northwestern Working Group in the dead of winter, Hitler chose the springtime of 1926 to draw the renegades back into the party fold. First, Hitler flattered Gregor Strasser with a surprise visit to his home in Landshut, where the Bavarian leader was laid up with injuries resulting from an automobile accident. Then Hitler began to court Joseph Goebbels.

Goebbels was still an uncertain factor, a free radical in the Nazi universe. Something about the wicked fire in Goebbels's eyes, the combination of a bent body with a booming voice, and the erstwhile rebel's coruscating wit had caught Hitler's attention. He needed to woo the feisty Rhinelander, who seemed loaded with energetic talent but had conspired against his own party chief. Goebbels had shown he was a disciple longing for a redeemer.

The mating dance reached new heights when the Nazi chief summoned Goebbels to Munich in April of 1926. Hitler disguised his invitation as a need to discuss matters of mutual interest and invited two other northern Nazis—Karl Kaufmann and Franz Pfeffer von Salomon—to accompany him. Hitler sweetened the summons with an invitation for Goebbels to make a speech at the Bürgerbräukeller, a celebrated speaking venue in the Nazi pantheon.

When the three men arrived at Munich's main train station, they found Hitler's personal Mercedes, along with its chauffeur, awaiting them. On the drive to their hotel, Goebbels saw his name plastered on "gigantic posters" advertising his speech the next night. Hitler gave the men his car for the afternoon: the driver sped them to nearby Lake Starnberg, one of Bavaria's bucolic gems. On the following evening, Goebbels spoke at the Bürgerbräukeller. He recalled, "My heart was jumping out of my chest.... I give it everything.... People roar, huge noise." Afterward, Hitler embraced Goebbels with tears in his eyes. But even as Goebbels edged closer to Hitler—and further from the northern wing—he was accused of apostasy by his fellow Nazis. Kaufmann and Pfeffer told him that his speech had been heretical, abandoning the firm principles established through the hard efforts of the Working Group.

Having wined and dined Goebbels, all but placing laurels on his head, the party boss the next day took the little doctor down several notches. He summoned the three men into his office and berated them for their perceived misdeeds in the Working Group. "Strasser and I come off badly," Goebbels recorded. "Every careless utterance is revisited."

Following his usual playbook, Hitler abruptly went from excoriating to magnanimous. Having first humbled his minions, he then stood and offered the ceremonial handshake—a pledge of forgiveness after an unmistakable warning. He sealed his charm offensive on Goebbels with a three-hour peroration on Italy, England, Russia, socialism, economic production, trusts, conglomerates—a classic Hitlerian sweep of the waterfront. The little doctor gushed: "New insights. He has thought through everything.... Such a scintillating intellect—he can be my leader.... I love him."[6]

Word reached the northern Nazis that Hitler had swept Goebbels off his feet. The little doctor's detractors began to mock the Munich lovefest as a "Damascus moment." And indeed, Goebbels had undergone a near-religious conversion that would rarely waver in the coming battles, defeats, and triumphs. Harnessing Goebbels's zeal, propagandistic skills, and slavish loyalty, Hitler had converted a potential source of trouble into a useful and nearly indispensable instrument for his own purposes.

11

WEIMAR PARTY CONVENTION

Whoever wasn't wearing a swastika was liable to be attacked.

—Berliner Tageblatt, *1926*

No sacrifice is too great.

—Adolf Hitler speaking to Storm Troopers, 1926

Hitler was ready to make a splash. His small party was little noticed outside *völkisch* circles; he wanted to put it on the national political map. To prove to the world, and to himself, that he was *somebody*, Hitler had to demonstrate that his tilt at the windmills of German politics was a real movement with a big heart and a loud mouth—that the one-man show had a real political base and the accoutrements of a grown-up political party. Hitler's far-flung followers needed a sense of national cohesion, a chance to see their leaders and flaunt their colors, a public affirmation of their new religion. Hitler convened a Nazi Party convention in Weimar.

The Weimar gathering in July of 1926 would surpass anything the Nazis had seen before. For a long weekend, Hitler would convert Weimar's revered German National Theater, where the statues of Goethe and Schiller stood out front and where the Weimar Republic had been founded, into a temple of Nazi speeches and cultish ceremony. He would turn the streets of Weimar into a Nazi stronghold.

Thousands of young Nazis and Storm Troopers streamed in from all over Germany. Weimar took on the feel of a convention town, with meetings and greetings, drinking and carousing, and high spirits everywhere. "The streets are crawling with our people. I have to shake a thousand hands," noted a delighted Joseph Goebbels after arriving on Market Square, in front of the Hotel Elephant.[1] A fellow Nazi pulled up on a motorcycle and offered Goebbels a quick pillion ride through the surrounding countryside. His name was Heinrich Himmler.

Himmler was the son of a Bavarian school principal and the holder of a university degree in agronomy; he was an unlikely soldier in the Nazi cause. Born in Bavaria in 1900, young Heinrich had longed for a life in the military. But he had been a sickly child and, though assigned to a reserve battalion, never made it to battle in the First World War. After the war, Himmler was more interested in fencing and right-wing politics at the University of Munich than in studying. He soon came under the spell of Captain Ernst Röhm, the rough-hewn army officer who was a secret supporter of Hitler's Nazis. When Hitler put out the call for a coup d'état in November of 1923, Himmler joined a Röhm-led unit that seized the Bavarian war ministry without firing a shot. He was a flag bearer. After the failure of the putsch, he returned to his studies and later made a brief go of farming. But he soon joined the Nazi movement full-time as deputy to Gregor Strasser. It was a felicitous pairing: Himmler was both obsequious and efficient, speedily executing the ambitious Strasser's organizational plans. By the time he arrived in Weimar for the party's big July weekend, he was a man on the way up.

Goebbels happily hopped onto the back of Himmler's motorcycle. The two men made a motorized ramble through the delights of the Thuringian countryside. Taking in the gentle slopes of the Ilm River valley and its dense forests, the men may well have visited the bucolic Ettersberg, a picturesque overlook located in a beech wood—a *Buchenwald*—three miles north of town. (It would be another fourteen years before Himmler would appropriate the word *Buchenwald,* turning the Ettersberg into a notorious concentration camp.)

Returning to bustling Market Square, Goebbels ran into Helene Bechstein, Hitler's Berlin benefactress, along with Austrian singer-actress Tini Senders, whose hand Goebbels gallantly kissed (perhaps unaware that she was Jewish).[2] The three were pleasantly gossiping when Hitler suddenly popped out of the hotel, wading through excited crowds. The Nazi Führer swept up Goebbels in his train, moving across the flagstones like a bona fide celebrity. Everywhere they turned, the two men seemed to be photographed. Hitler confided to the young Nazi his delight that "things are going so well."

Hitler was right: the July weekend would become an impressive display of his strength with both the foot soldiers and the leadership cadres of the party.[3] It would convince Hitler that he was making the right moves: he was firing passions among a small but growing following, including young men such as Erich Buhrow. An eighteen-year-old Storm Trooper from faraway Danzig, on the Baltic Sea, Buhrow was attending the Nazi Party convention and considered it the thrill of his life. The young Nazi had canvassed all his relatives for donations to pay for the long railroad journey "to go see the Führer."[4] Buhrow's small Storm Trooper unit donned their brown shirts on the train and gleefully disturbed the peace of other passengers by their very presence. Changing trains in Berlin, the "little shock troop," as Buhrow called it, was briefly arrested while marching the fourteen blocks from the Friedrichstrasse station to the Anhalter station. Since the Nazis were from the Free City of Danzig—then under League of Nations control—the cops decided to keep their hands out of international politics and let the Storm Troopers go. As gung-ho as they were, the young men from Danzig were shocked on the train to Weimar when a troop of Nazis from Berlin belted out bloodcurdling songs, including one that ended with, "We'll take an ax to Severing and to all his comrades."*

Hitler's Weimar convention became a preview of the clamorous, strutting, photogenic party congresses of later years in Nuremberg. Marching bands greeted chartered trains. Like a ringmaster at the center of everything, Hitler himself met the railroad cars bringing in Nazis from Bavaria. Young Buhrow was there: "The excitement was so great, the Führer so enthusiastically cheered... and tightly surrounded that he [must have] thought he would never escape with his life."[5]

As Hitler had hoped, the Nazi conclave—with speeches, committee meetings, and lusty, beer-drenched evenings—was turning into a moment of success for a minuscule movement that had been reborn only sixteen months earlier. The Hitler Youth organization, for fourteen- to eighteen-year-olds, created in 1922 but disbanded after the failed putsch, was called

* Carl Severing, a Social Democratic politician, was Prussia's hard-line interior minister, in charge of the state's huge police force.

back to life. Early on Sunday morning, Hitler presided over a general muster of the Storm Troopers and SS men. The SS (Schutzstaffel) was a subordinate unit of the Storm Troopers and was charged with Hitler's personal protection. Hitler was at pains to bind the paramilitary groups to himself and his vision. If not tightly tethered, the restless young men in the smart uniforms could veer onto their own violence-prone, impatient path, upsetting Hitler's climb to power. An improvident lunge toward revolution—like the one Hitler had taken in 1923—could set the Nazi movement back years, maybe to oblivion.

As they gathered in the German National Theater, Hitler reminded the Nazi militiamen that although they were unarmed, they were nonetheless the combat wing of the Nazi movement—the "fighting horde of the coming Germany." Unarmed, of course, meant only that Storm Troopers were not allowed to carry firearms; it did not mean they could not have such handy and concealable weapons as blackjacks and brass knuckles. Hitler's ambivalence toward violence showed when he told the Storm Troopers that their defining spirit was "hatred for all enemies of the fatherland" and that their job was breaking the "terrorism" (street fighting) of the opponents—Communists and Socialists.[6]

"No sacrifice is too great," Hitler proclaimed.

The pageantry and stagecraft on this Sunday morning included the solemn presentation of the sacred Nazi Blood Flag (*Blutfahne*) to a participant in the failed but now sanctified 1923 putsch. During that disaster, a large swastika banner, blood-soaked and crumpled, had been recovered from the melee that ended the hopeless coup attempt on a Munich square. The banner had been rechristened the Blood Flag and worshipped by Nazis as if it were the Shroud of Turin. Now, in the German National Theater, Hitler solemnly handed over the relic to Joseph Berchtold, a putsch veteran and commander of the SS. At Hitler's signal, all the men stood and raised their right hands with three fingers extended. Three thousand Storm Troopers rumbled: "I swear to you, Adolf Hitler, I will stand by my flag to the last drop of my blood."[7] The young zealots were initiated into the cult of death; they were sworn to fight to the end. Adolf Hitler was the man they were ready to die for.

Beyond such ceremonies, Hitler knew the Weimar convention was his best chance since refounding the party to lay out his political philosophy to the membership. In his Sunday afternoon address, he shifted from a pugnacious to a pensive tone, painting Nazism in existential terms.[8] "What is politics, really?" he began, elucidating his belief that a nation is an organism, just like a human body. Politics, he said, was "the searching and longing for the preservation of a people.... It is the most primitive manifestation of people's instinct for survival [and] the basis for the future existence of a people, of a race." The individual was but a single cell in the larger and more important body of the race. Without the subordination of each individual to the body, the race was doomed to extinction.

Like a traveling tent evangelist, the Nazi leader summoned the faithful into an idealized social construct. Once again, he evoked the racially defined German *Volksgemeinschaft,* or national community. Though the concept of a *Volksgemeinschaft* had been around in Germany for more than a century and had been invoked to arouse national unity during the First World War, Hitler presented it as an original idea. So that they could become part of the community, Hitler was asking each man in the Nazi Party and the Storm Troopers to remake himself by means of a kind of religious conversion. Choosing Nazism was an act of faith; it made the initiate a member of a mythic sect.[9] Only by making a commitment that was *fanatical*—a word Hitler used continually—could a follower survive the trials of self-doubt, ridicule, and violence that would no doubt befall Nazis even in their own towns.

Hitler's words were a strong tonic to men seeking purpose in an unmoored world. The cocoon of the Nazi Party and especially of the Storm Troopers, with its martial structure and hypermasculinized style, was an appealing substitute for a humdrum existence. By donning the Nazi raiment as Hitler described it, a man could go from a nobody to a somebody in his town or neighborhood. Hitler offered a parallel universe of certainty, social cohesion, and militant activism. Warming to his message as he addressed the Nazis in the German National Theater, he even seemed to endorse the violence that had been bubbling around Weimar over the weekend.

"We National Socialists are here as fighters for a new worldview—not just as preachers," he said.

There had already been fighting aplenty. Even as Weimar filled with Nazis, the Social Democratic Party decided it should not let Hitler's spectacle go unanswered. Social Democratic leaders encouraged members of their own militia, the Reichsbanner, to wear their uniforms and stroll the streets to confront the Nazis.[10] It was a losing move. Mocking the Reichsbanner name as "Reich Bananas," the Nazis attacked the Social Democrats on sight.[11] Two men were stabbed, one person was knifed in the throat, and a car was attacked with the passengers still inside. "Day and night, in the streets and in the pubs, [the Nazis] created a deafening roar and put the entire city under their [control]," complained the *Berliner Tageblatt.* "Whoever wasn't wearing a swastika was liable to be attacked."[12]

After his speech, Hitler led his thousands of followers on a long, winding march through Weimar—a demonstration of strength and aggressiveness. To the Nazi foot soldiers, their show of pomp and power in the streets of Germany's cultural mecca was the dramatic climax of the weekend. Incongruously dressed in his Alpine walking garb of lederhosen, white knee socks, belted jacket and tie, and wide-brimmed slouch hat, Hitler led the marchers onto Market Square. He climbed into his open car and, for the first time, repeatedly raised his right arm in what was fast becoming the official Nazi salute. It was an unabashed copy of the Roman salute, previously appropriated by Benito Mussolini and his Fascisti organization.[13] Hitler's salute was returned by the long columns of marching men, their right arms raised.

Jamming his disciples into the relatively tight space of Market Square demonstrated Hitler's flair for good optics and dramatic moments. With their forest of red-black-and-white banners, the Nazis looked like a gathering army. Fighting broke out on the fringes as Social Democratic hecklers and other protesters mocked the marchers. The weekend's violence gave the party a black eye in the national press, which reported on the events under headlines such as HITLER'S TERRORISM IN WEIMAR, NATIONAL SOCIALIST RIOTING, and SWASTIKA-WEARERS' TERROR IN WEIMAR.[14]

To Hitler and Goebbels, all publicity was good publicity. They seized on photographs showing the Nazi marchers filling the streets and jamming the squares of Weimar; they fed the pictures to Nazi publications all over Germany. On the cover of their new monthly photo magazine,

Illustrierter Beobachter, the Nazi Party plastered a large picture of Hitler in a leaderlike pose against a sea of men and flags in Weimar. The magazine quoted Hitler's prediction two years earlier during his treason trial: "The army that we are building is growing faster and faster, from day to day, from hour to hour."[15]

How fast Hitler's political army was really growing was open to question: party membership had still not climbed back to the fifty-five thousand it had reached before the misbegotten putsch attempt. Yet the flag-waving assemblage on Weimar's Market Square certainly evoked the beginnings of an energetic militant movement. It looked, walked, and sounded like an army. The question was whether an army was the appropriate tool for building a political movement.

12

CONQUERING THE WORLD

My head will not roll in the sand until my mission is fulfilled.

—*Adolf Hitler, 1926*

Hitler was back in the mountains. Comfortably ensconced in Berchtesgaden's Hotel Deutsches Haus, taking morning walks on the Obersalzberg slopes, dictating each afternoon to his secretaries, surrounded in the evening by his fawning followers, Hitler was in a kind of heaven. Through it all, he was writing his way toward the most important part of his ideology: a vision of the world as he intended to shape it.

On its face, vacation for Hitler seemed to be just another opportunity for speechifying—not in front of huge crowds but rather before a small audience of invited pals who came along on his sojourns in the Alps. Beginning in the latter half of July 1926, Hitler spent nine of the next fifteen weeks in the mountains. That summer's entourage included Joseph Goebbels; Gregor Strasser; Rudolf Hess; Hess's fiancée, Ilse Pröhl; Hannover gauleiter Bernhard Rust; former prison mate and chauffeur Emil Maurice; and the ever-present photographer, Heinrich Hoffmann. A jolly Municher, Hoffmann had ingratiated himself with Hitler years earlier by agreeing not to photograph the beer-hall orator until the politician said he was ready. At the time, no picture had ever been published of Hitler; he wanted to maintain his mysterious aura by remaining unseen except when making a speech. Finally, in 1923, the Associated Press broke the attempted embargo with a shot of Hitler during a parade in Nuremberg. After that, the pliant Hoffmann was granted unique and exclusive access to the Nazi leader, who took a liking to the bibulous Bavarian. Hoffmann was soon an intimate member of Hitler's traveling troupe, taking the kind of human-interest photographs—picnics, leisure-time interactions with common citizens—that would be used to soften the Nazi leader's image.

Even though he was cogitating constantly, Hitler liked being in the company of his minions and relishing the Berchtesgaden countryside. With Emil Maurice behind the wheel, Hitler and his crew made excursions to the Königsee, rambled the trails leading to the Hochlenzer Gasthof restaurant, and dined al fresco in the garden of the slopeside Marineheim Hotel, with its stunning view of the Watzmann peak. Through it all, the guests listened to Hitler's endless perorations. "The boss talks about race questions," Goebbels wrote after one such evening. "It's impossible to describe it. One had to be there. He is a genius."

Social issues, political revolution, seizing control of the state, drafting a new constitution, even the public architecture of a future Reich—these were the daily topics. Hitler was clearly liberated and stimulated during his Alpine forays. Later he declared that his most important decisions were made in the mountains because his imagination was stirred and he was spared the "small stuff" of everyday politics. "I see what's right, what's better, what will succeed," he said.[1] Goebbels, too, noticed Hitler's creative juices flowing as the Nazi leader expressed "thoughts that I've also had but never spoken." Hitler fairly bubbled over with "ideas that he had never developed in Munich.... This is what the creator of the Third Reich looks like," noted Goebbels.*

Goebbels was so carried away by Hitler's monologues that he imagined seeing a swastika formed by a passing cloud in the sky. "A sign of destiny?"[2] Hitler, too, was thinking of fate. One evening, as dinner broke up, he said: "My head will not roll in the sand until my mission is fulfilled."

* The concept of a Third Reich—a third German empire—stemmed from Arthur Moeller van den Bruck's 1923 book, *Das Dritte Reich* (The Third Reich). Moeller, a rabid German nationalist, envisioned a conservative, nationalistic (but not necessarily Nazi) empire rising from the mess of the postwar era. With visions of intellectual greatness in a harmonious social order, his Third Reich would be the logical successor to the "first empire" of Charlemagne during the Holy Roman Empire of the German nation (800–1806) and to the "second empire" created by Otto von Bismarck and Wilhelm II (1871–1918). The Nazis soon embraced Moeller's appellation but bent it to their own purposes.

Between his long rambles and his longer monologues, Hitler was developing his grand plans for conquest and laying them out in the second volume of *Mein Kampf.* Thinking aloud, pacing his hotel suite as he talked, he dictated passages for his book that gave form and voice to his vision of a future Germany. The loquacious author expounded on party philosophy, the internal struggle against Marxism, the purpose and uses of the Storm Troopers, the advantages of a single-party movement over a coalition. But he reserved his weightiest discourses for foreign policy. None was more important than his expansionist zeal toward Russia. "When we talk about [acquiring] land and soil in Europe, we can only consider Russia and its subject nations," he wrote.[3] (Even in the first volume, Hitler had written: "It cannot be God's plan to give one people fifty times more land than another.")[4]

Since writing the first volume of *Mein Kampf,* the self-styled Nazi philosopher had shifted from purely restorative foreign policy goals to a more radical view. Like most German politicians, Hitler had thus far simply espoused the reestablishment of Germany's pre-1914 status as a major power. That meant reclaiming the borders and holdings of the prewar period (under the 1919 Treaty of Versailles, Germany lost 13 percent of its land and 10 percent of its population as well as its overland connection to East Prussia).[5] Many politicians, like Hitler, accepted war with France as the necessary path to such an outcome. But Hitler now regarded such an irredentist plan as "political nonsense of such scale and consequence as to make it almost criminal."[6]

Hitler's new vision was grandiose and expansionist. Fighting France was no longer Germany's main mission but only a preparatory battle for the real goal: conquering Russia. When war came, as it must, neutralizing France, to Germany's west, would merely be "covering our rear flank" (*Rückendeckung*), he wrote.[7] The larger ambition lay to the east—a land grab for Germans on Russian soil. "Expanding the living space of our people in Europe" was Hitler's shorthand for seizing western Russia up to the Ural Mountains. He blithely believed that conquering the Russian colossus would be child's play—"The giant empire is ripe for collapse," he argued. Weakened by the Bolshevist destruction of the "Germanic" leadership dynasty initiated by German-born Catherine the Great in 1762, Russia's new Jewish-dominated Communist masters were racially fated to fail, he felt.

Germany had a right to sufficient agricultural space to feed its entire population, argued Hitler, but it currently had twenty million too many people for the land it lived on. The Nazi leader rejected food imports and modern agricultural advancements as viable solutions to this purported land-and-population dilemma.[8] His predatory intentions sprang from an apocalyptic vision of human affairs—along with a Darwinist conviction that politics was "nothing more than the struggle of a people for its existence."[9] To him, there was no such thing as a settled and inviolate national boundary. "State borders are created by man and are changed by man," he wrote.[10]

Stealing land from Russia would be consistent with a policy that Hitler labeled "continental colonization," or "land colonization"—in contrast to "overseas colonization," practiced by the European powers with their worldwide empires. Germany's pre–First World War attempts at overseas colonization in such places as Africa were foolish and misguided, in Hitler's view. Instead of seeking overseas dominions, Germans should "pick up where [our forefathers] left off six centuries ago," when the Teutonic knights conquered territory in Europe's east, pushing high up the Baltic coast. Their conquests created East Prussia and the boundaries of Germany, which had lasted ever since.[11] Only by rejecting "traditions and prejudices"—such as national borders and long-settled populations—could the German people "be freed from the danger of disappearing from this earth or living enslaved in the service of others," Hitler wrote.[12]

Composing his words at full speed in his rooms at the Hotel Deutsches Haus, Hitler also gave free rein to his anti-Semitic obsession. He even fantasized a mass killing of Jews, though not anything like what would come to pass fifteen years later. His fantasy was of a preemptive elimination of the Jews, who had become, in his fevered view, the backstabbing defeatists and profiteers who undermined the home front during the First World War. "If... twelve or fifteen thousand of these Hebrew corrupters of the people had been held under poison gas, as happened on the [First

World War] battleground to hundreds of thousands of our very best German workers, the sacrifice of millions at the front would not have been in vain [and] might have saved the lives of a million real Germans."[13] (Hitler's reference to poison gas evokes the genocidal gassings of the Holocaust, yet historians discount this as a direct harbinger of Hitler's later actions. Indeed, eliminationist language toward the Jews had been part of the *völkisch* vocabulary for at least two decades.)[14]

Hitler's only previous written declaration of his genocidal intentions was in a 1919 letter in which he forecast "removal" of the Jews from Germany without giving specifics. The Nazi leader also allegedly suggested extermination of all Jews in Germany in an interview he gave to a Catalonian journalist just a few hours before the 1923 Beer Hall Putsch. "Do you want to kill [the Jews] all in one night?" Hitler supposedly said to reporter Eugeni Xammar. "It would of course be the best solution, and if this could happen the salvation of Germany would be guaranteed. But I have studied it from all directions, and it is not possible. The world would be all over us instead of thanking us, as it should. The world has not understood the importance of the Jewish question for the very simple reason that the world is dominated by the Jews."*[15]

On December 11, 1926, the second volume of *Mein Kampf* appeared. The new book did not receive anything close to the attention accorded the first volume in 1925. More significant was the book's role in Hitler's personal and political evolution, augmenting his burning sense of mission. He even compared himself to Jesus Christ at a Nazi Christmas party a few days later. Since the Christian savior had been "the greatest early fighter against the Jewish world plague," insisted the Nazi leader, he would now follow right in Jesus's footsteps. Standing before two Christmas Tannenbaums dripping with tinsel, Hitler told the celebrants: "The work that Christ had begun but could not finish, I will conclude."

---

* Xammar's interview with Hitler was published on November 24, 1923, two weeks after Hitler's failed putsch, in the Catalonian newspaper *La Vue de Catalunya*. But the retrospectively sensational conversation—forecasting the Holocaust almost two decades before it happened—went unnoticed by historians and others until the journalist's memoirs were published, in 2000. Some Catalonian writers who knew Xammar well have cast doubt on the interview's veracity.

13

FALLING IN LOVE

You are now my wood sprite, my little fairy.

—*Adolf Hitler, Berchtesgaden, 1926*

On the ground floor of Hitler's Berchtesgaden hotel, the Deutsches Haus, stood a clothing store owned by a family named Reiter. Stopping to gaze in the shop windows one day, Hitler saw something he liked: a beautiful young woman. Hitler fell in love. Or at least in lust. Or at least into a feverish infatuation with a fresh beauty named Maria.

Hitler was thirty-seven, and Maria was merely sixteen—not even of legal age. But that did not bother the Nazi Party leader. Entering the shop, he invited the young teenager to meet him in a park during her lunch break for conversation. Even though she was turned off by Hitler's curious little mustache—"I always giggled," she recalled—Maria agreed. After all, Hitler, already famous in Berchtesgaden, was well dressed: he wore riding breeches and a velour hat, and he carried a little riding whip; he looked sharp to the shopgirl. She was charmed by Prinz, Hitler's German shepherd dog. Maria also had a German shepherd. Hitler used their common interest in dogs to initiate conversation.[1]

While formal and polite in their first park-bench chat, Hitler was also intense and rushed. He invited Maria—he nicknamed her Mimi, Mizzi, and Mizerl—to attend a speech he was to give on the very next night at the hotel. He had her seated at his own table. Within days, Hitler's pursuit of his newfound passion led to a striking scene in the mountains. He had his chauffeur, Maurice, drive the couple to a secluded copse of trees on an Alpine slope where he could admire Mizerl's beauty. "We came upon a gorgeously lit spot in the woods," she recalled. "Hitler stood me in front of a tall fir tree, turning me left and then right.... He stepped back and looked at me as a painter might.... I thought he'd gone crazy."

After beholding his prize as if she were a discovered treasure, Hitler finally said, "Do you know what you are now? You are now my wood sprite, my little fairy." Maria giggled.

Hitler suddenly put his arms around the teenager and began kissing her "wildly, passionately, with no inhibitions," she remembered. Maria was stunned, but by then she, too, was swept into the moment: "I wanted to die, that's how happy I was." Promising marriage and "blond" children some day in the future, Hitler also pleaded that he had no time at the moment even to consider such a fateful step. Indeed, he left half an hour later for business in Munich.

Although Hitler's brusque approach seemed odd to Mimi, she admitted that he had won her heart. The two had an off-and-on relationship that lasted, mostly in secret, for years, she claimed. Around Berchtesgaden, Hitler and Maurice sometimes picked up Maria blocks from her home to forestall gossip. Despite an ongoing exchange of affectionate letters, Hitler at one point cut off contact with Mimi when a notice appeared in a local newspaper accusing him of seducing young Berchtesgaden girls. When she thought Hitler had left her for good, Maria even attempted suicide. She put a noose around her neck, tying the rope to a doorknob and slamming the door. She almost succeeded, but her brother-in-law found her (unconscious) in time to save her.

Mimi asserted that she and Hitler had done some heavy necking and, five years after their first meeting, had had sex in Hitler's Munich apartment. Yet by that time Hitler was already involved with another woman—his half niece—who lived in the same apartment. In Mimi's telling of the incident, Hitler offered to make her his live-in mistress without marrying her—a prospect she summarily rejected. She wanted marriage and children. "All you women think about is having children!" Hitler screamed at her.

However far the relationship may have gone, Maria's story at least shows that Hitler sometimes felt an ardent desire for a fetching young woman and that he sometimes acted on his passions. His preference for a female much younger than he was followed a pattern set by his own father, who married three times, twice to much younger women. Maria was one of the first, but certainly not the last, of the very young women who captured Hitler's fancy.

14

GIRDING FOR BATTLE

We must show the Marxists that the future boss of the streets is National Socialism, just as one day National Socialism will be boss of the state.[1]

—*Adolf Hitler, November 1926*

Even when writing a book or chasing an underage girl in his Alpine paradise, Hitler was never entirely removed from the raw politics of the Nazi movement. The center of political gravity was wherever the Nazi leader happened to be; his mind was his office. From Berchtesgaden, even though it is 110 miles southeast of Munich, he made sorties into the political fray, darting in and out of the party's power game at will. And Hitler's will in late 1926 was to draw lessons from the challenges he had faced earlier in the year.

The men in the Northwestern Working Group who had given Hitler the greatest trouble had, at the least, shown themselves to be strong-willed leaders. They had ideas, and they took risks. To harness their energy and forestall future rebellion, Hitler decided to boost three of his main challengers—Gregor Strasser, Joseph Goebbels, and Franz Pfeffer von Salomon—into key positions of responsibility.

His first task was to neutralize Strasser's rebelliousness. Hitler gained the big pharmacist's loyalty by making a key concession: he would demote the much-loathed Hermann Esser. Though he would not expel Esser, his good friend and early supporter, from the party, he agreed to remove him from the national leadership and from his job as propaganda chief. Hitler asked Strasser to take over the propaganda portfolio, putting his chief potential adversary into the job that was key to the entire Nazi enterprise. Propaganda, to Hitler, was synonymous with politics. In each volume of

Mein Kampf, he devoted an entire chapter to the power and uses of propaganda. Appointing Strasser to lead that department effectively made him the number two man in the party. Shifting Strasser from his northern regional perspective and into the orbit of national operations in Munich turned out to be a masterstroke.

Hitler had also noticed the talents of another member of the northwestern cabal, Pfeffer. The original gauleiter of Westphalia, the industrial region along the Rhine River, Pfeffer was a tough disciplinarian with the look of a hardened Prussian soldier—close-cropped hair, a blank stare, and a short mustache thicker than Hitler's. Pfeffer had been an officer in the war, had joined a right-wing Free Corps militia afterward, and had participated in the ill-fated 1920 putsch that deposed the German government for three days before the rebellion fell apart. He had also organized resistance to the 1923 French military occupation of the Ruhr region—an audacious action that led to shootings, sabotage, and executions.[2] Such boldness suited Hitler's taste for daring, defiance, and passion. Pfeffer seemed to be the right man to take over the restive Storm Troopers. Not only was he a good organizer and leader of uniformed men, he also would be beholden to Hitler, not to an agenda of his own.

Turning the Storm Troopers into an effective street-fighting force without firearms while simultaneously keeping them under the control of the party—and following Hitler's chosen "legal path" to power—was a challenging assignment. Hitler told Pfeffer that the Storm Troopers should not see themselves as a separate military organization but rather as an arm of the party and an instrument of intimidation and propaganda.[3] To prevent the Storm Troopers from taking on the character of a clandestine operation, Hitler wanted its members to "march under a bright sky to destroy all myths that it is a 'secret organization,'" as he wrote to Pfeffer. The leader was more interested in men of the fist than men of the brain. "We do not need a hundred or two hundred dedicated conspirators but hundreds of thousands of fanatical fighters for our worldview.... We must show the Marxists that the future boss of the streets is National Socialism, just as one day National Socialism will be boss of the state."[4]

Hitler's third decision involved his newest and most ardent disciple, Goebbels. The little doctor clearly had the sharpest mind, the sharpest words, and the most passion for the cause and for Hitler personally. The Nazi leader had brought the wooing of the intense young talent from the Rhineland to its climax on August 1, when he accompanied Goebbels on a speaking engagement in Augsburg, northwest of Munich. A Saturday crowd of three thousand turned out to hear the small man with the big voice. "It rains flowers on Hitler and me," noted Goebbels afterward. Hitler accompanied Goebbels to the Augsburg train station and, as a parting gesture, presented him with a large bunch of "red, red roses." Goebbels was ecstatic. "Farewell to him. My heart is in pain," he wrote.[5]

The bond complete, Hitler now only had to deploy Goebbels where he needed him—in Berlin.

The Nazi Party's Berlin operation had long been a vexation to Hitler. A giant metropolis of four million, with eight times the land area of Paris, Germany's capital city had a diverse and vibrant culture, swirling immigrant crosscurrents, and, above all, a massive population of industrial laborers. Working-class families often lived in wretched conditions in slum districts such as Neukölln and Wedding, with tenement buildings arrayed four deep from the street, one dismal inner courtyard behind another.* Large, impoverished families dwelled in one or two rooms. Though Chancellor Otto von Bismarck in the late nineteenth century had introduced a form of social insurance to alleviate some of the misery of the poor—and to stem the tide of socialism in the labor movement—the working population of Berlin (estimated at 40 percent of the residents) overwhelmingly supported the "Marxist" parties—the Social Democrats and the Communists. The political coloration gave the city its nickname, Red Berlin.

Hitler's goal was to darken the bright red toward Nazi brown. But the Berlin chapter of the party was small and quarrelsome. On the huge and teeming Berlin scene, it made hardly a ripple. Hitler knew he would never succeed nationally if his crusade remained a regional effort with a

* The name Wedding stems from a twelfth-century noble family, not from a marriage ceremony.

Bavarian base. Only with a conspicuous presence in the German capital could the Nazis gain the necessary notice in the national press. Gregor Strasser suggested that Hitler send Goebbels to solve the Berlin mess and stir the political pot.

A man of the spoken and written word, and probably the brainiest of the Nazi paladins, Goebbels was itching for recognition and approval in the Nazi firmament. Since he lacked the prized Nazi credential of *Frontkämpfer*—a frontline soldier in the First World War—Goebbels needed to prove his mettle in other ways. Though he had hoped to be summoned to Munich to work at Hitler's side, he realized that an assignment to Berlin could be the stepping-stone to power inside the party. While he had proved himself to be a fighter on the lecture podium, for final initiation into the Nazi brotherhood, the little doctor needed to carry his fight into the streets.

Like Hitler, Goebbels despised Berlin. He called it a "stone desert" and a "cesspool of sin." He regarded the city as a screeching concrete jungle and a cultural abomination. With its dance-hall brothels, openly gay sex clubs, and depraved drug culture—all mixed with avant-garde art, music, and steamy nightlife—Berlin was a puritan's nightmare. With its teeming mélange of immigrants—Russian exiles, Eastern Jews, Czech Germans (including Franz Kafka for a time), and black American entertainers—Berlin was anything but pure Aryan. Count Harry Kessler—gay, rich, and cultured—loved Berlin for its "unfathomably deep, chaotic, and titanic quality," just the qualities that Hitler and Goebbels loved to hate.[6] Though Goebbels privately pursued a busy bachelor's love life, he operated generally within bourgeois norms.

Swallowing his distaste for the city and focusing on Berlin's political possibilities, Goebbels arrived at the capital's Anhalter train station on November 9, 1926—the third anniversary of Hitler's failed coup d'état, a holy day of martyrdom in the Nazi calendar. As Hitler's new gauleiter in Berlin, he began work on the very same day.[7]

15

CONQUERING BERLIN

Banned but not dead.

—*Joseph Goebbels's slogan, 1927*

"My first goal when I came to Berlin was to make the city aware of us," said Goebbels. "They could love us or hate us, as long as they knew who we were. We have reached that goal. We are hated and loved."[1]

Goebbels's path into love and hatred began on his first evening in Berlin. He delivered a three-hour stem-winder at a ceremony commemorating those who died during the abortive 1923 putsch. "The *Berliner Tageblatt* is already complaining," noted Goebbels gleefully. To him, a put-down by the Jewish-owned newspaper counted as "my first success."[2]

Goebbels knew that to be taken seriously as a national party, the Nazis had to look like a national party. He moved the run-down Berlin headquarters out of a "dirty, vaulted cellar" on Potsdamer Strasse to smart new quarters on fashionable Lützowstrasse. He drove off the gaggle of political hacks and hangers-on who frequented the party offices. To make his comings and goings look more serious, Goebbels acquired a six-seat Benz automobile. Gregor Strasser complained. Goebbels retorted: "The people must see that this outfit can make a good showing."[3] Goebbels even created a fifty-piece marching band, a demonstrated propaganda tool and recruiting magnet.

Within weeks, as hoped, young Goebbels had become the bête noire of the capital's politics. His fiery, confrontational style drew outsize attention to an undersize movement. He galvanized Berlin's small band of Nazi true believers: their noisy street behavior drew newspaper stories, attracted new members, flushed out enemies, and courted trouble. The Berlin Storm Troopers, under Goebbels's command, baited the combative

Communists into clashes by marching through "Red" working-class strongholds such as Kreuzberg, Neukölln, and Wedding. The political hothouse of Berlin stimulated Goebbels's instinct for endless agitation. "Berlin needs sensation the way a fish needs water," he noted. "This city lives on it, and any political propaganda that doesn't recognize that is doomed to fail."[4]

Along with sensations, he added, his movement needed martyrs. And "where we don't have any, we will create some."[5]

Goebbels got his martyrs soon enough. Five days after his arrival, he launched a uniformed Nazi parade through Neukölln, taunting the Communists. The Reds took the bait and came out in force. Wielding blackjacks, slingshots, and even pistols, both sides beat each other bloody. The Nazis sustained eighteen casualties, including four seriously injured.[6] But to the gauleiter's chagrin, the Neukölln melee went unnoticed in the city's leading newspapers.

In the cacophonous metropolis, more than sixty newspapers printed *three million* copies every day.[7] It took more than a few cracked skulls in a street fight to get media attention—especially since the Nazis had thus far gone unnoticed within the capital's stormy political and cultural life. The Golden Twenties were, after all, in full swing.*

By early 1927 Goebbels made sure his incitements would be noticed when he ventured into Wedding. He plastered Berlin with blood-red Communist-style posters announcing a speech in Pharus Hall, a traditional Communist Party meeting place. On the evening of his speech, fighting broke out between Nazis and Communists wielding fists, brass knuckles, and iron rods.[8] The Nazis outnumbered the Communists and drove them from the hall; the luckless Reds needed a police escort to get them out of harm's way. According to Goebbels, seven Nazis were wounded as well as eighty-three Communists.[9] Best of all, from Goebbels's point of view, the mainstream newspapers wrote about the uproar.

In March, Goebbels created an even larger splash. On a Saturday

---

* Contrary to Hitler's dark picture, all the joys of America's Roaring Twenties—the Jazz Age, the Charleston, flapper wardrobes, women's liberation—were experiencing a parallel renaissance in Germany that became known as *die goldenen Zwanziger* (the Golden Twenties).

night, he led seven hundred Nazi Storm Troopers in a cultish torchlight ritual on a hilltop twenty miles south of Berlin. The following morning, he steered his men onto the main square in the tiny town of Trebbin, where he delivered a rabid speech on "Jewish Marxism." Blood was "the best glue that will hold us together in the struggle to come," he shouted to his listeners. Rowdy Storm Troopers took Goebbels's lurid imagery at face value: on the train ride back to Berlin, they confronted a Communist Reichstag deputy and members of a small Communist reed-instrument band who were boarding the same train.[10] On sight, the bitterly opposed groups waved fists at each other.

According to a Nazi after-action report, several Communists pulled pistols from their bags and pointed them at the Nazis—a cardinal insult to the Nazis.[11] As they jumped onto the moving train, the Nazis vowed revenge. They exacted it the old-fashioned way: by throwing rocks. Whenever the train stopped along the route, the Nazis bombarded the Communist compartments with stones, smashing all their windows. One Storm Trooper climbed atop the train and plunged a flagpole through the roof, injuring several Communists.

When the train reached the Lichterfelde-Ost station, on Berlin's southern fringe, the Nazis pulled all the emergency brake levers; the train could not move. As the Nazis poured onto the platform, a gunshot was fired from the Communist car, hitting a Storm Trooper. The Nazis replied with a renewed hail of stones but faced a fusillade of gunshots—between sixty and one hundred rounds, claimed the after-action report. A Nazi was shot in the head but survived. Train passengers ran screaming from the station and across the tracks, causing an incoming train to screech to a halt.

Suddenly all was quiet. A scene of devastation filled the station. Almost every Communist had been hit by a rock. All the windows were broken, and the band's instruments were destroyed ("a value of 2,500 marks"). After stomping the remaining musical instruments with their feet, the Nazis rushed their injured men to the Lichterfelde Vincent Hospital.

Goebbels had arrived by car in front of the station; he was lifted onto the shoulders of two Storm Troopers and spoke briefly to his men. The troopers began marching into the center of the capital, attacking

Jews—or pedestrians they perceived to be Jewish—as they went.[12] At Wittenbergplatz, adjacent to the stylish Kaufhaus des Westens department store, a hoarse Goebbels spoke again, this time to a crowd of ten thousand, he claimed.[13]

To Goebbels, the weekend turmoil was a near-perfect set piece of agitational propaganda. By storming around in their uniforms, singing, shouting, and intimidating, the Storm Troopers had created a highly visible uproar that generated press coverage and triggered four hundred new enrollments in the Nazi Party, pushing local membership to nearly three thousand. There was one downside: the police and political authorities were beginning to pay much closer attention to the upstart agitator in their midst. A packed Nazi rally a few days later was surrounded by a "giant police presence." One hundred of Berlin's finest entered the hall and announced a weapons search, effectively ending the rally. "It takes strong nerves to do this [job]," Goebbels grumbled.[14] But he loved it: "Interrogations, arrests, trouble, fighting, work—live dangerously!"[15]

Goebbels felt that he was living in the middle of a war. Yet he was pleased that "we few men have been able to tease this city into jumping up and taking notice.... Even the B.T. [*Berliner Tageblatt*] and *8Uhr-Abendblatt* have done me the honor of saying that I've brought things to life here."[16]

Hitler was pleased with Goebbels's inroads and wanted to share in the success. Confident that the Nazi boss could draw a crowd and media attention, Goebbels booked Hitler to speak on May 1—the traditional Communist holiday—in the capacious Clou nightclub. Since Hitler was still banned from public speaking in Prussia, which included Berlin, Goebbels branded the event a "closed" rally by selling admission tickets.

Several thousand enthusiastic listeners showed up. On the podium, Hitler dove into his "living space" theories. Yet he spoke in what the *Berliner Tageblatt*—a sworn enemy of the Nazi Party—described as "a measured tone for a change."[17] The moderately nationalistic *Deutsche Allgemeine Zeitung* even claimed that Hitler had obviously "learned something" from his failed 1923 putsch: he had become practically "democratic"—a hated word in the Nazi lexicon. The paper committed an even worse offense by calling Hitler's speaking talent "decidedly parliamentarian" in style and tone—a strictly taboo term for Nazis. Paradoxically, the newspaper went on to argue that the speaking ban on Hitler should be lifted. "Hitler is really no longer a danger to the state, and one should go ahead and let him make speeches."[18] The Social Democratic Party newspaper, *Vorwärts,* snarky as ever toward the Nazis, declared Hitler's speech a total snooze: "It's all over for Hitler."[19]

Goebbels was outraged. He had expected—and no doubt promised Hitler—a bigger, more belligerent reaction in the Berlin press. He felt the Führer had instead been insulted with trivializing short mentions (the *Vossische Zeitung* even noted that Hitler's chauffeured car had been ticketed for pulling up on the wrong side of the street).[20] Embarrassed and feeling Hitler's simmering discontent, Goebbels decided to retaliate the best way he knew how: with a rant.

Three days later, in the Veterans Association Hall—another hoary political venue in Berlin—Goebbels lashed out at the "Jewish swine" of the Berlin press who had not given Hitler the exposure he deserved. Goebbels even suggested that his listeners locate a certain Berlin journalist who wrote under a pseudonym; they should "pay him a visit and show their gratitude in deeds, not words."[21] Goebbels's undisguised race baiting and incitement provoked a dissenter in the audience to shout, "You're such a perfect Germanic youth yourself!" This brash reference to Goebbels's decidedly un-Teutonic physical appearance—short, dark, partially disabled—brought a hush to the audience.

"You must want to be thrown out of this hall," replied Goebbels.

Whereupon the gauleiter's followers did just that, giving the heckler either a "boxing about the ears" or a thrashing that nearly killed him, depending on who told the story.

Either way, Goebbels's response to the dissenter was a tactical error. The luckless fellow happened to be an elderly Lutheran pastor, described in sympathetic newspapers the next day as "white-haired and respectable."* The clergyman's rough treatment, an otherwise commonplace event, suddenly became a big story in Berlin. With the violence at the Pharus Hall and the Lichterfelde-Ost train station in recent memory, the mainstream

* Some later reports claimed he was also an alcoholic and drunk at the time—and that he was soon defrocked.

newspapers came down hard on the bloody excesses of the Nazis.[22] The Berlin police now had the proximate cause and the public support they needed to lower the boom on the blustery Goebbels and his violent followers. The city government banned the Nazi Party in Berlin from further public activities, including marches and rallies. The ban also muzzled Goebbels, prohibiting him from speaking in public. Only six months into his new job as Hitler's chief agitator in the capital, Goebbels had achieved the worst—or the best—possible outcome: he was robbed of his voice. The prohibition could be a serious impediment or a badge of honor.

To most Nazis, the ban was a mark of success. "Dissolved. It shows we're on the proper path," noted Goebbels.[23] The agile Nazi coined a rhyming catchphrase: *Trotz Verbot nicht tot*—"Banned but not dead." Goebbels would soon find ways to make himself and the Nazis seem very much alive.

16

IMPENDING CATASTROPHE

[Hitler] gestures with hands and arms, jumps excitedly around, and constantly attempts to fascinate the large crowd hanging on his words.

—Report by a police spy, 1927

Hitler had been unbanned. In the winter of 1927, after keeping him on the leash for two years, Bavarian authorities decided to unshackle the raw-voiced Nazi. As long as Hitler espoused no illegal goals, and as long as his Storm Troopers avoided "military activities" and quit arrogating "police powers" to themselves, said the authorities, Hitler could go back on the Bavarian campaign trail. He could speak to the masses.*

Making his Munich debut on March 9, 1927, at the Circus Krone, the city's largest indoor arena, Hitler arrived with martial music, flag waving, and the customary late entrance. The Nazi Party leader's appearance was like a *second* "second coming"; he was greeted with the cheers of more than seven thousand followers. "Women were especially numerous and still enthusiastic," noted a police spy. As Hitler reached the podium, the brass band played a drumroll and cymbal clash, "just like in the theater"—then total silence.[1]

As he had done so often before, Hitler gave his admirers the combative thrill they came for. In the face of what he termed looming national disaster, Jewish perfidy, and disastrous political fragmentation, he offered his usual panacea: a Nazi-created "people's community." He was in full tent-revival mode, according to the police-spy report. "He gestures with hands

* Hitler had already been unbanned in Saxony, but the speaking prohibition remained in place in Prussia and other states—for as long as two more years in some cases.

and arms, jumps excitedly around, and constantly attempts to fascinate the large crowd hanging on his words."

Despite the crowd's apparent enthusiasm, the police observer thought Hitler's performance was "nothing outstanding" but rather a rehash of his "tired phrases" and well-known ideas. "The audience was applauding the man, not the concepts." Hitler uttered his favorite incendiary buzzword, *Kampf* (fight), no more than ten times, well below the Nazi leader's usual count.* Afterward, one listener complained that the speech was "too philosophical." Youngsters leaving the arena talked only about which café they wanted to go to.

The police spy was on to something. At Hitler's next event, three weeks later, also in the Circus Krone, the capacious hall was only half filled. Hitler appeared again three days after that: there was no pushing and shoving at the entrance, and nobody was buying the party's little swastika flags (ten pfennigs apiece). The lame turnout was only partially attributable to rainy weather. Had Hitler peaked?

For all the heady moments at his 1926 Weimar party convention, for all his adroit personnel moves and the publication of the second volume of *Mein Kampf*—in spite of all that, Hitler was by mid-1927 in a funk. Despite steady membership growth, the Nazi Party's finances were in desperate shape, surviving fitfully on annual dues, admissions fees to Hitler's rallies, and thin profits from party publications. These sources hardly brought in enough to run a party with national ambitions. The Führer's attempts, with speeches in June of 1926 and April of 1927, to reach into the deep pockets of the Hamburg elite and the Ruhr region industrialists had yielded plenty of applause but precious little cash.[2] Angry creditors hammered the Nazi Party for payment; no amount of political declaiming could put them off. Some creditors even threatened to drive the Nazi Party into bankruptcy.

Hitler fell into despondency. He later told a group of intimates that he would "sooner have put a bullet in my head" than accept bankruptcy.[3]

* *Kampf* can mean "fight," "struggle," "combat," "conflict," or "battle."

Though Hitler's alleged suicidal utterance was reported only many years later by Goebbels, the threat had a credible ring. The Nazi chief was an all-or-nothing obsessive who had mentioned suicide twice during the 1923 putsch fiasco and had almost done the deed as he was being arrested. "Führer tells me how he wanted to shoot himself [in 1927], because he was over his head in promissory notes, but Kirdorff [*sic*] helped with 100,000 marks," noted Goebbels.[4]

Goebbels was referring to Emil Kirdorf, who became another of Hitler's wealthy benefactors at a critical moment. Like Helene Bechstein and another admirer, Elsa Bruckmann, who often came to Hitler's aid just when his kitty was running dry, Kirdorf reportedly rescued Hitler just as he was facing financial oblivion. White-bearded and bespectacled, Kirdorf was the recently retired king of the German coal barons. Eighty years old, he had for half a century been one of Germany's leading industrialists, a believer in cartels, monarchy, and industrial paternalism.[5] The old pan-German nationalist was a reactionary authoritarian who sternly opposed the labor movement, the Weimar Republic, and democracy—which he considered "the rule of the rabble." Kirdorf was just Adolf Hitler's kind of man.

It was Elsa Bruckmann who first brought the two men together. A well-known Munich salon hostess and political socialite, Frau Bruckmann was the wife of conservative publisher Hugo Bruckmann. Elsa was generous with her husband's money in causes they both supported—including Nazism. She considered it her mission to boost Hitler's mood and fortunes. Well connected in Germany's conservative and nationalist circles, she wrote Kirdorf while he was taking the waters at Bad Gastein, in Austria. "[She] informed me that, as a passionate supporter of the Führer, she had made it her life's work to bring him together with leading men of heavy industry to prepare the ground in our sector for National Socialism," recalled Kirdorf.[6]

The meeting in the Bruckmann mansion lasted four and a half hours. Kirdorf was sold: "The implacable logic and clear structure of [Hitler's] thinking enthused me to the point that I declared myself in agreement with all that he had said." The aging tycoon, according to Goebbels's account, became Hitler's first major donor from the industrial class with his whopping 100,000-mark gift (the equivalent of $350,000 in 2020).[7] He implored Hitler to write down the arguments he had made during their conversation so that Kirdorf might share them with his rich friends in the industrial class around the Ruhr region.

The only thing better than hearing his own voice, for Hitler, was seeing his own words in print. He quickly composed a long essay ("Der Weg zum Wiederaufstieg," or The Path to Resurgence) that hit all the usual notes—Germany's coming calamity, his own intense nationalism, and the need to acquire land commensurate with Germany's agricultural needs (without ever mentioning Russia).[8]

But Hitler was swimming against a new political current. Germany seemed to be regaining its status in the international community and enjoying an economic upswing. Since his movement was predicated on impending catastrophe, Hitler had to refute the prevailing narrative. In his essay, he called any signs of "betterment or resurgence, as people like to say," nothing more than self-deception, or a conscious lie. He repeated his belief in racial purity, the importance of "personality" (strongman dictatorship), and the necessity of eternal struggle for survival. Hitler hinted at the decisive "power of the sword" in international relations yet never stated outright his eagerness for war.

In deference to Kirdorf and his friends, Hitler omitted his customary blasts at the corruptions of middle-class society. But he did not temper his anti-Semitism. He painted "the international Jew" as the busiest promoter of the three sins of internationalism, democracy, and pacifism. He linked Jews to Marxism, the scourge of the business class.

Kirdorf liked the essay. He published it privately, distributing it to his friends in the Ruhr region oligarchy. The old industrialist also took the symbolically important step of joining the Nazi Party. Hoping to grease the money skids, Kirdorf arranged several meetings between Hitler and other industrial moguls in his own villa in the coal country near Duisburg. Yet Hitler's woolly declamations on a classless "national community"—along with the overtones of socialism that clung to Hitler's National *Socialist* German Workers' Party—were anathema to the men of the

Ruhr. Some were also put off by Hitler's plebian manner and his party's reputation for rough behavior. The businessmen listened but held tightly to their wallets. While Hitler was pulling out the stops and carefully navigating the shoals as he saw them, he waited in vain for more financial support.

17

THE ATTACK

The German people is an enslaved people... it is lower than the worst Negro colony in the Congo.

—*Joseph Goebbels,* Der Angriff, *1927*

There was trouble in Berlin. Goebbels had succeeded in making the Nazis noisy and noticed while getting himself and the party banned from public agitation. But he failed at drawing all the top Berlin Nazis in line behind him. A smoldering rivalry would soon cause Hitler headaches and result in stormy confrontations involving threats, sweeteners, and counterthreats—once with a drawn gun.

The clashes pitted Goebbels against his onetime mentor and promoter, Gregor Strasser, and Gregor's younger brother, Otto. The brother with the brains (as Gregor liked to put it), Otto was the more intellectual, dreamy, and radically leftist of the two men. With thinning hair and an oval face like his brother's, Otto was also more somber, lacking Gregor's bluff bonhomie. A confirmed Socialist with a doctorate in law,[1] Otto had supplied some of the extreme ideas Gregor promoted in the Northwestern Working Group—including creating a barter economy and abolishing a party-driven parliament. Upon their initiative's failure, the brothers had set up a separate outlet for their ideas, a publishing operation called Combat Press. It was a National Socialist enterprise yet independent of Hitler and the Nazi Party apparatus. Otto was its editor.

Their little newspaper operation gave the Bavarian brothers unique standing in Berlin. Gregor was a Nazi member of parliament with an office in the Reichstag: he also held the post of Hitler's national propaganda director, making him one of the most influential men in the Nazi Party. Otto's power base was the Combat Press's flagship newspaper, the *Berliner Arbeiterzeitung* (Berlin Workers' Newspaper). It was an ideological mouthpiece aimed at the same working-class readers courted by the Communists, but it had such limited success that Goebbels made fun of it, scorning the plodding style of the newspaper and the Strassers themselves.

"Fat, old Gregor... He's no new man," wrote Goebbels.[2] The young gauleiter had plans of his own: he wanted to publish a Berlin newspaper called *Der Angriff* (The Attack). The Strassers objected.

As the feuding unfolded, Hitler played his minions off against each other. Despite repeated trips to Munich, neither Goebbels nor Gregor Strasser could get Hitler to decide in favor of one or the other. Finally, Goebbels concluded that he had become a mere pawn in a larger power play. "The conflict is not Strasser/Goebbels, it is Hitler/Strasser. I am simply the miserable wretch who has to do the donkey work."[3]

In the end, Goebbels got his way. On July 4, 1927, Goebbels's new newspaper, *Der Angriff*, appeared on the streets of Berlin. Though he was still prohibited from giving public speeches, he could now make his views known in print. He could compete directly with the Strasser brothers. His newspaper would be shriller and more eye-catching, and, eventually, it would make a bigger splash—setting the stage for a long-running conflict between him and the other two alpha Nazis in Berlin.

Der Angriff was a classic Goebbels product. With screaming headlines, a declamatory tone, and plentiful exclamation points in a tabloid format, the newspaper used an edgy typeface on its masthead and an aggressive style in its writing. To introduce it, Goebbels launched a flamboyant publicity campaign a week before publication. He plastered Berlin with large placards, spacing them several days apart. The first poster contained only two words and a question mark: THE ATTACK? The second read, THE ATTACK BEGINS ON JULY 4. The third announced that the newspaper would be weekly, appearing on Mondays.[4] The placard's subtitle, in good agitprop style, read: FOR THE OPPRESSED! AGAINST THE EXPLOITERS!

The paper gave full vent to Goebbels's vituperative wrath and his propagandistic skills. He penned editorials, satires, imagined conversations, and hortatory letters.[5] One early essay, entitled "We Demand...," captured the tone: "The German people is an enslaved people. Under international law, it is lower than the worst Negro colony in the Congo. All its sovereign rights have been removed."[6]

Goebbels constantly attacked the *jüdische Lügenpresse* (lying Jewish press). He and Hitler used as their convenient foils the leading liberal-minded newspapers in Germany, which were owned, founded, or edited by Jews. These included the Jewish-founded *Frankfurter Zeitung;* the Jewish-owned Mosse publishing house, with its distinguished *Berliner Tageblatt,* edited by the renowned Jewish journalist Theodor Wolff; the huge Jewish-owned Ullstein publishing house, which published the *Vossische Zeitung;* and the country's leading wire service, Wolff's Telegraphisches Bureau, founded in 1849 by Jewish businessman Bernhard Wolff (no kin to Theodor). "The Berlin yellow press falls like sharks onto every little bit [of falsehood] and writes its Jewish commentaries," growled Hitler one day about Wolff's.[7]

Goebbels's favorite target in *Der Angriff* was Dr. Bernhard Weiss, the deputy chief of Berlin's fifteen-thousand-man police force—and a Jew. Though a commissioned army reserve officer and a respected law-enforcement professional who held a doctorate in law, Weiss was viciously demonized. The newspaper constantly highlighted the top cop's Jewishness by calling him Isidor, a presumptively Jewish first name that Goebbels imperiously attached to the police official. With constant repetition and relentless pounding, *Der Angriff* was able to make *Isidor* nearly a household word in Berlin. Even Berliners unsympathetic to the Nazis or to anti-Semitism began to believe that Weiss's first name was in fact Isidor.[8] *Der Angriff*'s cartoons brutishly caricatured Weiss as particularly Semitic looking, depicting him variously as a hook-nosed monkey, a jackass, and a snake.[9] Goebbels went so far as to label Weiss's boss, the Berlin chief of police, "a token goy at Berlin police headquarters."

With his malicious little newspaper, Goebbels had his voice back. The diminutive gauleiter was proving—just as he had sloganized—that the Nazi cause might be banned in Berlin, but it certainly was not dead. Goebbels was also showing Gregor and Otto Strasser that he would fight hard for dominance in the capital and for the favor of the one man who really counted: Hitler.

18

ALTERING THE UNALTERABLE

The precondition of freedom is power.

—Adolf Hitler, 1927

In a nation still stung by its battlefield humiliation of 1918, Hitler understood the tonic power of mass assemblies, martial music, stirring rhetoric, uniforms, and flags. Marching around under bright banners in paramilitary garb was a confidence builder. A parade-ground spectacle could mask the financial strains, internal feuds, and political impotence of a movement that was treading water. With his recent infusion of cash from Emil Kirdorf, in August of 1927, the Nazi chief convened his forces for a party convention in Nuremberg.

By abandoning little Weimar for bigger Nuremberg, Hitler was moving the Nazi pageantry—so photogenic for future propaganda—to Bavaria's second-largest city, after Munich. Nuremberg boasted a rich Germanic history: the imperial diet of the Holy Roman Empire of the German Nation had met there during the Middle Ages. The ancient city was especially well suited for big, ritualistic displays. Its central square, broad and long, angled down a cobbled incline toward the meandering Pegnitz River, which was spanned by arched bridges. Rows of half-timbered houses turned the square into a Teutonic proscenium that echoed and amplified the drumbeats and fife trills of the Nazi marching units. Jubilant supporters bombarded Hitler's open car with flowers as he passed through the center of town. The scene doubtless reminded Hitler of one of his favorite Wagnerian operas, *Die Meistersinger von Nürnberg* (The Master Singers of Nuremberg). The Nazis eventually labeled Nuremberg "the most German of German cities."

Even more appealing than the city's main square was its sprawling

Luitpoldhain. A vast open park on the southeast side of town, the Luitpoldhain was a set designer's dream for grandiose events. Here the Nazi masses could pass in broad formations with flaming torches, giant flags, and upraised swastika standards. Military-style review built fighting morale. Men whose lives were a long slog on the periphery of prosperity and self-respect could, with a fresh uniform and membership in a larger unit, find moments of self-assurance and hope.

An estimated twenty thousand Nazis showed up in Nuremberg, including seven thousand Storm Troopers. Among the special guests was Kirdorf. By the end of the party convention, Hitler was certain of one thing: he wanted to return to Nuremberg for all his party rallies.

Despite the successful convention, Hitler was in a sour mood by November. Even after constant sanguinary street battles with Communists in urban centers—and Hitler's many clamorous rants against Marxism—the Nazis were not winning the workers. Though the Nazi Party by then claimed a membership of seventy-two thousand, it was not making serious dents in the membership of the German Communist Party.[1] The Nazi leader was not building a movement around the masses, or at least around his definition of the masses—the poor, the unlettered, and the downtrodden.

Something had to change. Hitler convened his party leaders for a grim meeting in Weimar on a cold Sunday afternoon in November of 1927. In a long lecture to his regional princelings and lieutenants, the Nazi chief said that propaganda efforts had to be diversified and not tailored solely to the urban proletariat. He declared a shift of emphasis from the working class to the middle class and from the urban areas to the rural electorate. Nazi activists were making surprising inroads among farmers, whose economic woes were driving some of them into Nazi meetings and even into party membership. Hitler told the assembled gauleiters that he was personally taking over the job of national propaganda director; he already had plans to make Gregor Strasser the party's national organization leader, or CEO. Hitler remained, always and forever, its chairman.

Hitler's timing was fortuitous. Within two weeks, a wave of discontent arose among northwestern German farmers over the Berlin government's pay raises for civil servants. The farmers were already fuming over depressed agricultural prices. Hitler capitalized on the rural rage with a speech at a protest meeting of farmers from Schleswig-Holstein, Germany's northernmost state, known for its cattle farms. "Everybody knows that if things [for farmers] continue for a few more years as they are now, then it's all over," said Hitler to the cheers of the men from the rural outback.[2]

In a blatant play for the farmers' votes, the Nazi leader made a brazen break with past dogma. He altered the unalterable by reinterpreting one of the supposedly untouchable Twenty-Five Points. The party program included all sorts of grand and very socialist demands, such as point 13, the nationalization of all trusts; point 14, the communal takeover of large department stores, which were mostly owned by Jews and threatened the livelihood of small shopkeepers; and point 16, mandatory profit sharing at all "large firms." Then came a point that would trigger stiff resistance among farmers if left unaddressed: point 17, which demanded "uncompensated expropriation of land for the common good" and a "prohibition on land speculation."[3]

Point 17 was toxic. Written carelessly in 1920 by Hitler and the other political neophytes in his party, the threat of land grabbing by a future Nazi state was anathema to any farmer. To men of the soil, land was life. Many of the small farmers tilled fields that had been in their families for generations, even centuries. Point 17 had to be fixed.

With a national election looming in May of 1928, Hitler declared that point 17's demand for "uncompensated expropriation" applied "only to land that has been acquired illegally or is not managed for the good of our people.... Accordingly, this refers principally to Jewish land speculation companies." So it was all about the Jews again! What a convenient way to neutralize a tone-deaf misstep! Hitler's preferred scapegoat once more served its purpose.

The Nazi boss's breezy revision of unshakable doctrine was as dramatic as it was abrupt. Rarely in his rise to power was there a more crystalline example of the driving principle behind his quest: ideology did not matter as much as raw power. "The precondition of freedom is power," he said.[4]

19

ROCK BOTTOM

We are not coming as friends.... We are coming as enemies! We are coming like wolves into a flock of sheep.

—*Joseph Goebbels, 1928*

After three years of party building, book writing, and subduing internal insurrection, Hitler had consolidated his grip over the Nazi movement and its far-right competitors. Other than the cacophonous gatherings, noisy propaganda, and outbursts of violence, however, the political strength of Hitler's message was uncertain. Its first test would come in May of 1928 in a national parliamentary election.

The election would be a moment of reckoning for Hitler's strategy of pursuing a legal path to power, not a revolutionary one. The springtime balloting would also serve as a referendum on German democracy, reflecting public opinion of foreign minister Gustav Stresemann's politics of détente and the fulfillment of Germany's reparations obligations. Stresemann's policies had led to the peacemaking Locarno Treaties and Germany's acceptance into the League of Nations, accelerating the country's rehabilitation as an equal among the major European powers. The vote would also be a pocketbook election, measuring Germans' satisfaction with the economy, which was on a gradual upswing. In the first quarter of 1928, the number of people without jobs dropped more than 50 percent, falling from 1,371,103 to 642,180. The unemployment rate was shrinking to 5.3 percent—the best since the end of the First World War.[1] A strong showing by the establishment parties identified with the Weimar Republic would be a vote of confidence in the young democracy and a repudiation of its detractors, including the Nazis.

While Nazi Party candidates would be standing for parliament in districts all over Germany, Hitler himself could not run. Having renounced his Austrian nationality in April of 1925, Hitler was stateless. He had still not been naturalized as a German. But that did not stop him, as the famous face and firebrand of the Nazi Party, from campaigning madly all over the country. In any case, voters cast ballots for their district candidates and party lists under the German system, not for a single person running for chancellor. The chancellor would emerge from parliamentary negotiations after the election.

Thirty-two parties entered the 1928 race—a glaring example of political fragmentation during the Weimar Republic. The Nazis mounted a widespread and highly visible operation, especially at the local level. With Heinrich Himmler functioning as Hitler's deputy director of propaganda, a constant stream of guidance flowed from the Munich headquarters into the *gau* offices and local chapters across Germany. Drafted as if they were military orders, directives from the pedantic Himmler lent an aggressive, polemical tone to the Nazi campaign. The local activists threw themselves into the election process with a vengeance, competing to attract the best speakers to their areas.[2]

The Nazis introduced a new ground game to German politics. In seven weeks of electioneering, they boasted of ten thousand meetings, rallies, and "beer evenings." A Munich police report called the Nazis' number "inexact" but acknowledged that "no other political movement has mounted such intensive and nearly uninterrupted agitation throughout the Reich."[3] The agitation sometimes spilled into violence; five Storm Troopers were killed in the course of the campaign.[4]

Crisscrossing the nation from Munich to Hamburg, from Karlsruhe to Chemnitz, Hitler brought a different kind of electioneering to Germany. German elections were generally fought at the district level through posters and press organs; top national party leaders typically made only one or two big speeches during an entire campaign. Election battles were not waged with constant star turns by a national leader. Hitler, a self-nominated charismatic savior and obsessed road warrior, was the exception.

On the campaign trail, Hitler hammered his usual themes, all of them plainly laid out in *Mein Kampf:* Germany's coming downfall; the virtues of "struggle"; the necessity of dictatorial rule by a great "leadership personality"; the need for "living space" for Germans in eastern Europe; the perfidy of Jews. He avoided everyday political jousting and refused even to talk about domestic economic issues. Concerned with bigger things, he claimed histrionically, Hitler focused on the "life and the survival of a whole people."[5]

One evening in Zwickau, Hitler told 3,500 listeners that democracy was a disastrous form of government that, like pacificism and Marxism, thrived "only in times of decay and destroy[ed] the survival instinct of a people."[6] Constantly fanning racial prejudices and twisting logic, Hitler alleged that decadent American phenomena such as New Orleans jazz and the Charleston were proof of democracy's inherent weakness. "When a people dances negro dances and listens only to jazz music, then we need not to be surprised if its souls perish and seek out parliamentary monstrosities," he declared.[7]

Almost against his will, Hitler also waded into a then burning controversy regarding the small Alpine province of South Tyrol. Ceded to Italy after the First World War, South Tyrol was home to more than two hundred thousand German speakers who had for centuries been part of Austria. Suddenly South Tyroleans were forced to speak only Italian in schools, in government offices, and when conducting official business. Liberating South Tyrol from Italian tyranny had become a nationalistic cause in German politics—except with Hitler. Enamored of his own grand scheme of a future alliance with Benito Mussolini's fascist Italy, Hitler simply wrote off the South Tyroleans—to the consternation of the nationalist movement. The decision would cost him votes.

The spring of 1928 was a tough time to sell doom and gloom. In his efforts to convince Germans of their imminent demise, Hitler was swimming against a tide of contentment and fascination with new cultural freedoms. With the postwar scourges of hyperinflation and numerous putsch attempts now behind them, German voters were enjoying relative stability and satisfaction. Even with the pain of reparations payments and postwar suffering in some areas, there was a sense of a brighter future in the nation's capital. *Things Are Already Looking Up!* (*Es geht schon besser*) was the title of a popular variety show that started in Berlin in 1926. The hit of 1928 was a light musical about the joys of department store shopping called *There's Something in the Air* (*Es liegt in der Luft*).[8]

Innovations such as movies, radios, cars, and airplanes transformed popular culture. Mass transportation such as Berlin's noisy elevated S-Bahn trains energized daily life. "Berlin stimulates like arsenic," noted British diplomat and writer Harold Nicolson.

The belated German industrial revolution, beginning in the late nineteenth century, brought production to levels of dizzying growth. In 1928 alone, industrial wages rose 10 percent.[9] The Germans, late to the industrial game but longtime lovers of science and certainty, wholeheartedly embraced modernity. Their universities soared to world leadership in theoretical and applied science, their professors winning numerous Nobel Prizes and turning Berlin's Friedrich Wilhelm University into one of the world's leading educational institutions (eleven of Germany's twenty-nine Nobel Prizes in science or economics before 1933 were won by Jewish Germans). Industrialists matched the scientists: in Hamburg and Bremerhaven, the steamship companies built dazzling luxury liners for the booming United States–bound trade. The *Bremen*, owned by North German Lloyd, captured the transatlantic crossing record with an average speed of 27.8 knots per hour. In Friedrichshafen, on Lake Constance, in southern Germany, a visionary named Count Ferdinand von Zeppelin had developed gigantic dirigibles in the 1890s. His successor, Hugo Eckener, had by 1928 launched the world's largest rigid airship, named for the count himself, the *Graf Zeppelin*. The 776-foot-long blimp was about to undertake its first long-range voyage, to Lakehurst, New Jersey—a great source of joy and pride among Germans.

Postwar freedoms also unleashed a flowering in the fields of architecture, theater, film, music, writing, and painting. All exploded in bursts of creativity that rebelled against traditional German norms of art and culture. The younger generation experimented, sometimes wildly, with new approaches. Their improvisational spirit lustily filled the vacuum left by the crash of Germany's Wilhelmine monarchy, with its staid standards of morality and expression.

The new inventiveness led to the stark Bauhaus design and art school, led by Walter Gropius; the rise of nonsensical Dada; the provocative plays of Bertolt Brecht and Kurt Weill, including *The Threepenny Opera;* the rich theater direction of Max Reinhardt; the "new objective" painting of Otto Dix and Georg Grosz, with its coruscating caricatures of society and politics; the wrenching antiwar woodcuts of Socialist Käthe Kollwitz; the harrowing expressionist films of Fritz Lang and Robert Wiene; the subtle acting of Peter Lorre and unsubtle performances of Marlene Dietrich; and even the writing of expatriates drawn to the flame of Berlin, such as the Englishmen Christopher Isherwood and W. H. Auden. Germany's cultural deluge was "the greatest [artistic] Renaissance of the century," commented Sol Hurok, the New York impresario who set up shop every summer in Berlin's Eden Hotel to book talents such as Artur Schnabel and Rudolf Serkin for American stages.[10]

With the artistic release came sexual and behavioral liberation as well. Dancing clubs, liberal drinking, smoking, and frequent drug use—especially cocaine—became part of a nightlife that, in the sleepless capital of Berlin, often did not begin until midnight. Sexual mores loosened as well; women began wearing short skirts and bobbed hair and going unescorted to dance clubs. Prostitution flourished, as did sexually transmitted diseases. Homosexuality, though still illegal, was flaunted. Both Isherwood and Auden had come to Berlin for its openly gay scene: they frequented a "boy bar" that Isherwood called the Cosy Corner, where "the boys stripped off their sweaters or leather jackets and sat around with their shirts unbuttoned to the navel and their sleeves rolled up to the armpits."[11] In 1922, Berlin police estimated the number of male prostitutes at twenty-five thousand.[12] The erotically charged city teemed with more than one hundred gay, lesbian, and transvestite clubs and hangouts, some of them catering to straight audiences. Pornography thrived.

Former First World War officers, broke and out of work, sometimes became gigolos, escorting well-heeled matrons to respectable dance cafés. A performance artist named Anita Berber, often clad only in a sable wrap and sporting a small pet monkey hanging around her neck, became famous for her nude appearances in casinos and hotel lobbies; she also wore a silver brooch packed with cocaine.[13] Dr. Magnus Hirschfeld ran a museum he called the Institute of Sexual Science, where he conducted pioneering research on sexual identity. Cross-dressing and transgender club performances were popular.

The hottest act in Berlin for a time was the celebrated "banana dance" of the nearly nude African-American performer Josephine Baker, who starred in revues in America and France as well. Count Harry Kessler, who was gay but always ran in Berlin's leading social and artistic circles, recalled a 1926 encounter with Baker that captures the spontaneous, fecund energy of the decade. His own dinner guests having departed at 1:00 a.m., Kessler received a phone call from Max Reinhardt, the renowned theater director, who was at the home of a playwright friend on the tony Pariser Platz. "They wanted me to come over because Josephine Baker was there, and the fun was starting." When Kessler arrived, he found Reinhardt and others "surrounded by half a dozen naked girls. Miss Baker was also naked except for a pink muslin apron.... [She] was dancing a solo with brilliant artistic mimicry and purity of style, like an ancient Egyptian... performing an intricate series of movements without ever losing the basic pattern. This is how... dancers must have danced for Solomon and Tutankhamen." Before the night was over, Kessler and Reinhardt had conceived a new play called *Song of Solomon,* which Kessler would write for Baker and Reinhardt would direct. "Reinhardt was enchanted with the idea," noted Kessler.

While Berlin celebrated its wickedness—and the police vice squads scrambled to keep up with the sometimes grisly crimes surrounding the club scene—the Nazis labeled Berlin a den of iniquity. Despite rumored homosexuality in the highest ranks of the Storm Troopers, Berlin's gaudy decadence served as a political foil for Hitler and Goebbels, who denounced the merry sinfulness as a corruption of the German national spirit. They also dismissed the new artistic experimentation as "cultural Bolshevism," thus pairing the Golden Twenties with the hated politics of "Jewish Marxism."

There was, of course, a vast middle class that held on to bourgeois conventions and looked with skepticism on the licentious excesses of 1920s popular culture. But they took their pleasures in other areas of distraction, such as a sports craze focused on boxing, tennis, track and field, boating, and race cars. Summer afternoons saw Berlin's sprawling bodies of water—the Wannsee, the Müggelsee, and the broad expanse of the Havel River—dotted with sails and oarsmen. Their shores were lined with sunbathers and finely dressed patrons at waterside cafés with attached "dance gardens," where couples displayed their skills to the tunes of a small dance band. Many Berliners embraced the "free body culture" (*Freikörperkultur*) of outdoor nudism that accompanied a wave of health consciousness. Entire families turned up—and dressed down—for the weekly "naked day" at the outdoor swimming pool in the vast Luna Park amusement center.[14] Count Kessler once drove his friend the French sculptor Aristide Maillol to a sports facility that overlooked a swimming pool and sunbathers. "Maillol was in raptures about the unabashed nudity," he noted.[15]

With their inventive breakthroughs and displays of joie de vivre, the 1920s were for some Germans a joyfully experienced moment with no hint of a coming storm. Young Berliner Raimund Pretzel played sports with his friends, taught tennis near Berlin's Kurfürstendamm, and courted young ladies in the city's countless outdoor cafés. He remembered the 1920s as the best period of his youth: "Life was set in a major and not a minor key."[16] (In the 1930s, Pretzel would flee Nazi Germany for England, becoming an anti-Hitler journalist under the pseudonym Sebastian Haffner.)

On election day, May 20, 1928, Hitler was in Munich, probably at Nazi Party headquarters on Schellingstrasse. The party's dreary rooms, up a back stairwell in the rear courtyard of an old five-story building, matched Hitler's mood of impending disaster. Voter turnout under heavy rain had been only 75.6 percent—low by German standards.[17] The weak voter participation was not just the product of inclement weather. It also sent a political signal: people were relatively satisfied with the status quo.

The election results rolled over Hitler like a tidal wave. The Social Democrats and the Communists—blood enemies of the Nazis—scored a stunning victory, winning more than 40 percent of the vote between them (Social Democrats, 29.8 percent; Communists, 10.6 percent). The outcome was a robust endorsement of the budding republican democracy. It also gave a strong boost to Foreign Minister Stresemann's dogged work at rapprochement between France and Germany. "Sunday's vote was without doubt a victory for reconciliation," noted *Le Petit Parisien,* a Paris newspaper with a circulation of more than two million.[18]

The Nazis were crushed, winning only 2.6 percent of the national balloting, coming in ninth—ahead of such slivers as the Christian-National Peasants' and Farmers' Party (1.9 percent) and the German House and Property Owners' Party (0.1 percent). While Hitler's archenemy, the Communist Party, won 2.7 million votes, the Nazi Party received only 810,000. More than 97 percent of the voters had shunned the Nazis. Hitler had run against the status quo, and the status quo had won. Despite Hitler's transparent attempt to woo farmers by "correcting" his "unalterable" point 17 regarding land expropriation, most Nazi campaigners had not grasped the shift from an urban to a rural strategy. Many focused too heavily on working-class districts in industrial cities and preached a "true German socialism."

In Berlin, Goebbels's stronghold, matters were even worse. Despite his electoral gyrations, the Nazi Party captured only 1.57 percent of the vote. Goebbels and his little Nazi band were considered so harmless that they had been unbanned. Goebbels had run hard, not just for the Nazi Party but also for himself. To obtain parliamentary immunity as a firewall against prosecution for his defamatory propaganda—and to obtain the first-class rail pass that came with a parliamentary seat—Goebbels had stood for the Reichstag. On election night, he sat up until 4:00 a.m. at the Victoria Garden restaurant, listening to returns. Despite the party's dismal showing, Goebbels won his seat; his fellow Nazis carried him around on their shoulders. But the citywide tally left him glum. "The left made fabulous gains," he admitted. "Depression in me. . . . I need rest and quiet."[19]

For all their disappointment, Hitler and Goebbels saw a shimmer of hope. Because of Germany's system of proportional representation, their 2.6 percent of the vote actually gave them twelve of the 491 seats in the new Reichstag.* The Nazi leaders knew their tiny beachhead inside the main

* The total number of seats in the German parliament varied from election to election, depending on a complex set of calculations (which is still used in modern Germany). In 1924, the Reichstag had 493 seats; in 1928 it had 491 seats; in 1930 it would have 577 seats; in 1932 it would have 608 seats. In 2019, the parliament had 709 seats.

house of German politics would give them a platform for mischief. "We will enter the Reichstag to obtain for ourselves the weapons of democracy," wrote Goebbels. "We will become Reichstag deputies to cripple the Weimar mentality.... We are not coming as friends... We are coming as enemies! We are coming like wolves into a flock of sheep."[20]

Among the Nazis who would be taking Reichstag seats with Goebbels were Gregor Strasser, Gottfried Feder, Wilhelm Frick—and Hermann Göring. A recent returnee to the Nazi fold, Göring was a First World War flying ace who had joined the Nazi Party in 1922. Hitler had been especially pleased to recruit a war hero who held Germany's highest medal. "Splendid: a war ace with the *Pour le Mérite*—imagine it!" Hitler told a supporter. "Excellent propaganda! Moreover, he has money and doesn't cost me a cent."[21]

Born in 1893 in Bavaria, Göring was the son of a former governor-general of German South West Africa (now Namibia). When he entered Hitler's movement, the Nazi leader gave him command of the ragtag Storm Troopers, which he turned into a tightly run paramilitary unit. But during the 1923 putsch attempt, Göring was badly wounded in the groin. His life was saved by a Munich doctor whose office happened to be nearby; the doctor was Jewish. Göring fled Germany ahead of the law and spent months in hospitals, becoming addicted to morphine. Once released, the former fighter pilot and his glamorous Swedish wife moved to Scandinavia, where he found work as a commercial flier. But life outside Germany was dull. When the German government in 1927 declared amnesty for political crimes, the handsome former officer with the growing girth repatriated to Germany. Göring was drawn again, as he had been in 1922, to Adolf Hitler's hot political flame. He relished the chance to be a big player in the relatively small world of the Nazi Party. Hitler gladly welcomed the charming pilot, who had useful social connections, back into the party.

Despite the devastating 1928 election results, Hitler conceded nothing. Around midnight in Munich's Bürgerbräukeller, he consoled his supporters by making not being totally dead the equivalent of success. Three days later, he exploded in a tirade of finger-pointing from the same Bürgerbräukeller podium, blaming the Jews, the Social Democrats, and a "grandiose system of lying" for his party's drubbing. Hitler took special aim at Erhard Auer, the non-Jewish but outspoken Bavarian SPD leader and editor at the *Münchener Post*. One true believer shouted, "Hang him!"

Though they vented and blustered, Hitler and Goebbels knew the Nazi Party had become a nearly insignificant blip in German politics. In the first test of Hitler's scheme to take power through politics rather than through revolution, they had failed. "We considered Hitler finished," commented SPD politician Wilhelm Hoegner.[22] The leading newspapers didn't even bother to declare the Nazi movement kaput, as they had in the past. They simply ignored the Nazis, not mentioning them at all—the worst fate that could befall a political movement, as Hitler had said himself.[23] Hitler had hit rock bottom.

Hitler did what he always did when he was at an impasse: he withdrew to the high country. Packing his bags for Berchtesgaden, he ran from the real world of unsettled politics in Munich to the idyllic sanctuary of his magic mountain in the Alps. There, he could talk himself into trying again.

Part Two

RESET

(1928–1929)

A time of utter misery now set in for the family. I had to leave school. Once again, we came to know hunger, for it was next to impossible to provide for a family of five on our meager dole.... An abysmal hatred flared up in me against the regime that could not provide employment for a family man who had done his duty in the war.

—*A young Nazi Party member*[1]

When a worker has no work, he starts having bad ideas. He hangs around on the streets. Sometimes he just falls completely apart. If he has no money, he starts stealing. As soon as he does that, it's all over for him.

—*A fourteen-year-old apprentice in Berlin*[2]

20

HITLER'S SECOND BOOK

To me those were the best times of my life.

—*Adolf Hitler, on being in Berchtesgaden in 1928*

The vaulting Alpine landscape was a tonic for Hitler. After driving the 110 miles from Munich, motoring up through the mountain villages of Bad Reichenhall and Bischofswiesen, turning into the steep streets of Berchtesgaden—it was like striding through a looking glass. On the slopes of the nearby Obersalzberg, Hitler was no longer the beleaguered politician and harried party boss. He shed the mantle of hectoring agitator and became the reflective highland philosopher he imagined himself to be. Cut off from big-city bustle, he could spiritually connect with the man who had brought him to Berchtesgaden and to many of his beliefs, the man to whom he had dedicated *Mein Kampf:* Dietrich Eckart. The muse lay buried only a short walk from Hitler's hotel.

Best of all, Hitler could write.

Writing was Hitler's way of finding out what he thought; writing was the echo chamber of his inner voice. Since his time in prison, he had relied on the written word to right himself and refresh his own self-belief. For a person with limited formal education whose early ambition was to become a man of images—a painter—Hitler had become, almost totally, a man of words. While his writing was rarely graceful, natural, or measured, it was nonetheless clear, forceful, and unfiltered. Even when wooden, as it sometimes was, his prose was persuasive to those looking for political inspiration.

The Nazi leader lived by words, thousands and thousands of them—poured out in his multihour speeches; poured out in lengthy essays for the *Völkischer Beobachter* and the *Illustrierter Beobachter;* poured out in two wordy books; poured out in endless monologues in cafés and restaurants to his spellbound, and sometimes fatigued, companions. ("He's in form tonight, and it will be a long session," Ernst Röhm once warned his colleagues as Hitler left a café late in the evening and invited everyone to his apartment for still more conversation.)[1] Some thought Hitler's rants were compensation for his social uneasiness, for never overcoming the class anxiety of his humble origins. While declaiming, he was on stage and felt himself on secure ground.[2] His inexhaustible declamations—larded with seeming sophistication and expertise—had the additional benefit of feeding his growing personality cult.

By the summer of 1928, Hitler felt the need to explain things again. He would tell the world why it was all wrong about him, about his movement, about his strategy for future German alliances. He would justify his politically risky rejection of South Tyrolean nationalism in the name of a coming German-Italian alliance—Hitler's grand plan for shifting Europe's big-power constellation.

Though on his back politically, Hitler set about rearranging the world. He would write another book. On this summertime journey to his writing retreat in the mountains, his willing stenographer was Max Amann, his former wartime sergeant and now head of the Nazi publishing house, Franz Eher Nachfolger—the publisher that had issued both volumes of *Mein Kampf*. Amann reportedly paid Hitler the stunning sum of one hundred thousand marks (around $350,000 in 2020 dollars) as an advance for the book that Hitler now proposed to write.[3]

Three weeks after the humiliating 1928 election, Hitler and Amann took up quarters in Berchtesgaden's Hotel Deutsches Haus, on busy Maximilianstrasse. At first Hitler had a room in the front of the hotel but soon moved to a quieter spot in the rear, which he preferred. "I was really spoiled there," he said later. "To me those were the best times of my life."[4]

After a long morning walk up the Obersalzberg, Hitler would sit down with Amann for a long afternoon of dictation. Hitler jabbered on about future German alliances not only with Italy but possibly also with England. He vented viciously about the "maggots of the international Jewish community," linking his preoccupation with blood and race to his demand for "living space" in the east. The chief goal of foreign policy was conquering land to feed one's own people, he said.[5] Conquest had to be achieved "by the sword" rather than by diplomacy or negotiation—an unmistakable threat of war. Subjugated and colonized peoples whom Hitler considered racially inferior would never be absorbed into the German ethnic community, he emphasized. They would simply be pushed out of the way. "There is no question of Germanization," he told Amann.[6]

Much of what Hitler wrote in his new book was well known and repetitive. But there was one surprising element: an almost obsessive fixation on the United States of America. Mentioning "the American union" more than fifty times, he expressed both admiration and envy of America's industrial might, bold inventiveness, and worldwide trading potential. Though Hitler had occasionally denigrated America as a "mongrel" nation with a degenerate popular culture, the Nazi author now praised its inhabitants as "a young, racially select people" who did the right thing by passing the Immigration Act of 1924. The severely restrictive new American law limited US immigration by "undesirable" ethnicities such as Asians and Jews and gave large immigration quotas to Germans and other "Nordic" Europeans.[7] Hitler praised strict US health controls on arriving immigrants to ensure a physically stronger population.

Until shortly after the First World War, Germany, too, had relatively open borders. Its liberal immigration policy allowed German farmers to employ low-wage Polish seasonal workers on their vast eastern estates but also left the door ajar for Eastern Jews fleeing Russian pogroms. The steady influx of unassimilated Jews gave rise to ethnic Jewish enclaves such as Berlin's Scheunenviertel (Hay Barn Quarter), whose street life resembled, in some ways, shtetl culture in Poland. By 1920, German officials began tightening the borders, partly in response to a heavy influx of ethnic Germans driven out of the regions of Silesia and West Prussia, which had been lost in the First World War. In a country struggling with a postwar housing shortage and unemployment, new immigrants of any ethnicity were suddenly unwelcome. Hitler's focus, however, was on the non-German newcomers. If his country did not pay as much attention as America did to its racial composition, he groused in his new book, the nation would "deteriorate into degenerate, brutish gluttons who will not even remember past greatness."[8]

Hitler's coarse anti-Semitism and racism were deeply influenced by the teachings of eugenics. He had absorbed the writings of pseudoscientists such as Englishman Francis Galton and Americans Charles B. Davenport and Madison Grant. They argued that "scientific racism" and controlled reproduction through sterilization could weed out the feeble while promoting the strong. In his book *The Passing of the Great Race; or, The Racial Basis of European History,* Grant wrote that woolly-headed humanitarians had thwarted both science and nature by perpetuating the lives of "the weaker elements" that filled the jails, insane asylums, and poorhouses.[9] Before such misguided interventions, when man lived in "the savage state of society," the less capable members were "allowed to perish and the race [was] carried on by the vigorous and not by the weaklings."[10]

Though not a scientist—he was a lawyer and conservationist—Grant asserted that genetic heredity was socially determinative. He embraced the notion of superior races—Nordic Europeans—and inferior races, generally from the south and east of Europe. The inferior races, he argued, always produced more criminals, more asocial behavior, more people with disabilities. The mixing of the races would always have a deleterious effect on the superior race. Grant believed that only Germans and Swedes possessed "true race consciousness"—precisely the quality that Hitler was trying to promote.[11]

Without crediting Grant, Hitler frequently invoked the "iron laws of nature" in his writings and speeches—a clear echo of Madison's claim that "nature cares not for the individual.... She is concerned only with the perpetuation of the species."[12] *The Passing of the Great Race* was published in German in 1925 by Hitler's supporter Julius F. Lehmann; Hitler almost certainly read it. In a laudatory letter to Grant, Hitler is reported to have called the American's book his "Bible."[13]

In his new book, Hitler's focus on America went well beyond racial issues to a startling claim of a coming conflict with the United States. Grandiosely, he forecast war with the burgeoning transatlantic power, which he labeled a hegemonic threat.[14] With America's rise, he noted, "a new power factor has emerged on such a scale that it threatens to nullify all previous state power relationships."[15] Germany and Europe had to prepare themselves for an existential fight with the American giant, Hitler wrote—a megalomaniacal leap in his vision of world conquest. Beyond western Europe and Russia, Hitler had now added the world's fastest-growing economic force to his list of potential enemies.

At around two hundred pages, Hitler's new book was, effectively, the third volume of *Mein Kampf.* Considerably shorter than the first two volumes, it was more concerned with foreign policy than either of its predecessors was. In fact, the book may have given away a bit too much of Hitler's future plans for a world that he intended to vanquish. The manuscript nakedly revealed his radical and nearly unalterable plans to wage war and shape world history. Probably for that reason—and out of concern that a new book would crush sales of the slow-moving second volume of *Mein Kampf*—Hitler and Amann decided to put the new book on ice for the time being. The manuscript was locked up in a safe at Nazi Party headquarters, its existence unknown to all but Hitler's tightest circle. And there in the Nazi Party repository the manuscript would stay for more than two decades, never to be published in Hitler's lifetime. Yet the very drafting of such a book in a moment of abject political defeat showed that Hitler in 1928 remained certain of his destiny as a world changer—and was unafraid to write it down, at least while cogitating in his mountain aerie.

21

TAKING STOCK

I am now thirty-nine years old, which gives me at best just twenty years.

—*Adolf Hitler, 1928*

Refreshed by his weeks in the mountains, Hitler prepared in the late summer of 1928 to lead the Nazi Party out of the wilderness.

Hitler felt he was short of time. His martyr complex convinced him that he would not live to be an old man. Troubling health issues, such as recurring stomach problems, made him hypochondriacal. "I am now thirty-nine years old, which gives me at best just twenty years," he wrote to a fellow Nazi.[1] Certain of his messianic calling, the Nazi leader still believed he was among the chosen few on earth "who will someday make history," he wrote. Despite the 1928 election disaster, the fanatical politician (who had no other professional prospects) intended to press on, whatever the odds, and the odds were hardly favorable. The Nazi Party's coffers had been drained by the failed election effort. Hitler could not even afford an annual convention in Nuremberg. Instead, he summoned the gauleiters to Munich for a kind of group therapy session in August of 1928. In two combative and sarcastic speeches, the Nazi boss told his lieutenants that "a movement based on a fundamentally sound idea with determined supporters cannot be destroyed by setbacks."[2] Rejecting the narrative of a moribund party, Hitler worked himself into a revivalist rant over the course of several hours. The old fire-breathing rabble-rouser brought his regional leaders cheering to their feet.

Gregor Strasser, the Nazi Party CEO, also reenergized the assembled gauleiters with a new party organization plan. It was designed to rationalize, centralize, and resuscitate the movement. As with almost everything the burly Strasser undertook, his initiative met with enthusiasm from Nazi Party activists. Liked by the rank and file, Strasser was a practical man who could put meat on the bones of Hitler's high-flown promises.[3] Following the election debacle, Strasser had pounced on the gauleiters for not sufficiently heeding Hitler's call for a shift from an urban political strategy to a rural and middle-class focus.[4] "A deep look at the [1928] election results shows two things," Strasser wrote in a detailed analysis. "First, Marxism is the real winner.... Second, our National Socialist voters were drawn mainly from basic middle-class and agricultural strata of society—the first because of anti-Semitism, the second because of nationalism. The proletarian percentage recruited by our socialism represents by far the smaller portion [of our vote]."[5] In other words, forget the proletariat; win the farmers and the petit bourgeoisie.

Making the rural strategy work meant reaching voters in the sparsely populated countryside. That task fell to Heinrich Himmler, the deputy director of propaganda, who wrote a striking memorandum. It unveiled a flood-the-zone style of campaigning that would reshape Nazi electoral methods and eventually play a key role in bringing Hitler to power.[6] Himmler outlined an inundation strategy that called for saturation propaganda—a blizzard of leaflets, posters, newspaper articles, and the heavy presence of uniformed agitators for a short time in a single area. Rather than spread propaganda efforts thinly over a large region, he instructed local organizers to create a jammed schedule of *seventy to two hundred* meetings and rallies in a single *gau* in the space of *seven to ten days*.[7] The events were to be announced from cars and trucks bearing giant posters. The local party was to stage special "recruitment evenings" for the Storm Troopers and Hitler Youth in venues that were "not too large," so they would be filled to bursting.

Before each meeting, a Storm Trooper band should march through a town playing music that was locally popular. The recruitment evenings should include wrestling or jujitsu performances, theatrical sketches, singing, plus a film from a Nazi Party convention with massive scenes of proud Storm Troopers parading past Hitler. "It is taken for granted that every speaker in each *gau* will appear at every scheduled evening to the limits of his ability," wrote Himmler.

The bundling of so much activity in such a short time would force the "enemy press" to drop its "usual tactic" of ignoring the Nazis but instead write about the party and "make propaganda" for the Nazis, asserted Himmler. Even if the aggressive Nazi style led to a backlash, any event that generated publicity, negative or otherwise, would be considered a success. Hitler had laid out the primacy of propaganda in *Mein Kampf*: "It makes no difference whether they laugh at us or revile us... the main thing is that they mention us, that they concern themselves with us again and again, and that we gradually... appear to be the only power that anyone reckons with at the moment." Under Himmler's strict guidelines—which included party-controlled graphics styles and Munich-directed messaging—the Nazi Party was following Hitler's plan precisely and increasingly speaking with one voice.[8]

No longer banned from speaking, Goebbels in the autumn of 1928 again became a busy stump orator and crowd agitator. He drew ten thousand followers to Berlin's Sports Palace—a huge arena built for ice hockey, speed skating, and bicycle races but often used for political events. Goebbels gave a vitriolic speech. "Blood is the best adhesive," he yelled, inciting Berlin Storm Troopers and party members who were bloodying the streets outside the arena even as he spoke.[9] As Goebbels noted in his diaries:

> In the Sports Palace... endless enthusiasm. Outside combat with the Communists. Twenty-three wounded, three badly. Hopefully the worst injured will survive. In the hall enormous excitement.... Outdoors the streets are filled with people—screaming, heaving, bellowing, cheering. Fighting! My heart jumps for joy.... I visit one of the injured men. Gruesome. But I can justify it. Getting out—rocks flying! Boos and whistles. Hate and love. Finally, I sit peacefully for an hour among friends. How tired I am![10]

Goebbels's incendiary labors merited a congratulatory letter from Hitler: "Berlin—that is your work."[11] Goebbels responded by arranging a grand moment for the Führer—a speaking date in the Sports Palace on

November 16 (Prussia had lifted the speaking ban on the apparently harmless Hitler). Sixteen thousand eager listeners showed up—the largest crowd Hitler had ever faced. For the first time, his bombast was amplified throughout a cavernous hall by "electro-acoustical magnification"—loudspeakers.[12] Welcomed like a conquering hero, he delivered his usual extremist rhetoric, thrumming his audience's prejudices with salacious references to "racial defilement" and "Negro music"—what he called the "bastardization" of culture and morals.[13] Hitler contrasted the cultural contribution of Beethoven with such shabby imports as the Charleston and the shimmy, all the rage in Berlin.[14]

"The boss is very happy," Goebbels noted after staying up late chatting with Hitler, Hess, and several others. "He laughs with me a lot, and we congratulate each other." Hitler's appearance was even treated respectfully in the Berlin newspapers. Goebbels wrote, "Even the Jewish press is surprisingly objective . . . But careful! If a Jew offers praise . . ."[15]

The Sports Palace turnout told Hitler that his movement could recover from the election disappointment of six months earlier. Confident of someday ruling Germany, the Nazi leader was already redesigning the German capital in his mind's eye. "He has in his head the transformation of Berlin into a great metropolis of the coming Germany," Hess wrote.[16] "He has already sketched some of it beautifully on paper . . . We've often laughed (but with an earnest undertone) when we stroll with him around Berlin and, with a flick of his hand, he demolishes unsightly old housing complexes to give existing and especially future buildings extra space for a more imposing appearance."

In the private sphere, Hitler led the life of a rising potentate. He had discovered a charming mountainside home on the Obersalzberg called Haus Wachenfeld. The two-and-a-half-story Alpine house commanded sweeping views of the Untersberg and the Watzmann. Best of all, it was for rent for only one hundred marks per month. Hitler grabbed it in October of 1928 and never let it loose.

By the end of 1928, though badly outnumbered by the Social Democrats and the Communists, Nazi Party membership had grown to around one hundred thousand. Hitler was playing the long game, burrowing on like a hedgehog in the hope that he could someday capitalize on unforeseen opportunities that political or economic events might offer—events such as a worldwide depression.

The notion of an economic collapse was not as far-fetched as it might have seemed in late 1928. Despite the surface appearance of success and growth, Germany's rising prosperity rested on the wobbly foundation of short-term capital in the form of mostly American loans. "We've been living for the last few years on borrowed money in Germany," said the foreign minister, Gustav Stresemann. "Should a crisis occur here and [the Americans] call in their short-term credits, then we are bankrupt.... We are not only militarily disarmed, we are also financially disarmed. We have no money left."[17]

Stresemann's warning went largely unheeded.

22

1929

If men wish to live, then they are forced to kill others.

—*Adolf Hitler, 1929*

Nineteen twenty-nine began unremarkably. In Berlin, people gathered for their morning coffee and *Brötchen* (rolls) at the famous Café Kranzler, on the Unter den Linden boulevard. Ladies in broad-brimmed flowered hats showed up for the afternoon tea dances at the elegant Hotel Esplanade. Even around Berchtesgaden, the Alpine mountain trails and lifts were open for those with the funds and leisure to enjoy them. American money from investors eager to cash in on the German recovery flowed into the Ruhr region industrial machine at a steady pace.

Hitler was operating under the radar. Ignored by 97 percent of the voters in 1928, the Munich fanatics—the Nazis—seemed to be a world apart: a sect of brown-shirted evangelists who passed out leaflets on street corners and held their apocalyptic revival meetings in beer halls and in small pubs around the country. To most Germans, the Nazis might as well have been speaking in tongues.

The inattention suited Hitler. He used the uncertainty of the times to build his mass movement and exploit propagandistic opportunities. Unrestrained by the spotlight of press attention, Hitler's speeches in the first months of 1929 bristled with radicalism and portents of violence that left no doubt about the Nazi boss's bellicose intentions. "He who does not fight with deadly weapons and does not possess the strength to plunge them into the heart of the opponent will never be able to lead a people in the mighty battle of destiny," Hitler thundered at one meeting.[1] "If men wish to live, then they are forced to kill others," he said at another.[2]

In what would be a fateful decision, Hitler promoted Heinrich

Himmler from deputy propaganda director to head of the Schutzstaffel—the SS. With the same dogged attention to detail that he brought to his previous assignment, the bespectacled bureaucrat began turning the black-shirted paramilitary force into an embodiment of Teutonic fealty and knightly honor—a virtual cult of death. By year's end Himmler would boost SS membership to three thousand men. At the same time, Gregor Strasser was still building local Nazi chapters, no matter how small, all over Germany. Traveling tirelessly, he created a base of loyalty among local leaders and gauleiters who appreciated the attention from the down-to-earth national organization leader. His efforts yielded a precious political resource: an index card system of more than one hundred thousand names of members and potential members.

In a move to increase propagandistic impact, centralize ideological control, and help fill the party coffers, Strasser and Hitler demanded that local chapters subscribe to the *Völkischer Beobachter* and the *Illustrierter Beobachter*—the heavily illustrated monthly that specialized in panoramic shots of Hitler speaking before tens of thousands. The monthly publication also carried virulently anti-Semitic stories such as "The Jew and the German Woman," which included a photo captioned: "Brutal murder of a Christian girl by the Jew 'Schwarz' Gerolzhafen."[3] To boost *Völkischer Beobachter* sales, party headquarters announced a subscription campaign that offered rewards to the chapters that recruited the most new subscribers. Prizes ranged from a replica of the Blood Flag of 1923 to a new Opel sports car. The energetic Saxony *gau* won the car.[4]

Busy Nazi leaders were also implementing Hitler's rural strategy. Like union organizers looking for disgruntled coal miners in Appalachia, Nazi Party agitators and recruiters were drawn to Schleswig-Holstein, north of Hamburg, where dissatisfied farmers had turned themselves into a violence-prone protest group. Farmers in northern Germany had been whipsawed since 1926 by downward fluctuations in hog prices, followed later by crashing cattle and crop prices worldwide. The national government's economic policies boosted urban consumption but downplayed agricultural interests, leading to farm foreclosures and bankruptcies.[5] The farmers bitterly protested, marching under a black flag emblazoned with a plough and a sword, naming themselves *Landvolk* (country people) after a medieval peasant movement of the same name. The aroused rural folk were not above acts of terrorism, hurling bombs at government offices and even placing one at the Reichstag.[6] They found allies in the Nazis, who, in turn, recruited the protesters into their party.

The rural turbulence could sometimes turn lethal. In March of 1929, a rural demonstration exploded when Communists attacked Storm Troopers marching in support of farmers in a windswept North Sea village called Wöhrden. According to a report from Nazi participants, the Communists unexpectedly jumped the Storm Troopers, killing two of them with lances fashioned from sharply honed cabbage-harvesting blades. Seven Nazis were severely wounded, and twenty-three were lightly injured.[7]

Outraged, Hitler traveled all night by train from Munich to attend the deceased Storm Troopers' funerals—and to enhance the party's self-mythification by declaring his fallen men martyrs in the holy cause. Reaching Hamburg, he motored northward in a jammed little Adler automobile, only to arrive late at the first service because fuel ran low. On the following day, he attended the second funeral and visited a severely wounded Storm Trooper at his bedside. Hitler lionized the murdered Nazis with long articles in the *Völkischer Beobachter*, lending iconographic standing to the "bloody night of Wöhrden" (*Blutnacht von Wöhrden*)—a memorable phrase already used in mainstream press reports on the violence.

In Berlin, Goebbels—undaunted by the 1928 election losses—insisted on maintaining the Nazis' street presence to demonstrate their "indomitable" fighting spirit and to attract news coverage. On May Day, the traditional Communist and Socialist holiday, the Nazis and the Reds turned Berlin into a tableau of bloodshed. Goebbels noted "barricade battles in Wedding and Neukölln, nine killed, one hundred badly injured, one thousand arrests—street fighting and open civil warfare."[8]

Not everyone, however, was preoccupied with the savage politics on the fringes. In another part of Berlin, near Nollendorf Square, in the fashionable Western shopping district, a cultural counterpoint was unfolding as Christopher Isherwood, a young gay British author, wrote about the libertine life of a man named Arthur Norris and a woman he called Sally Bowles. Isherwood's novellas *Goodbye to Berlin* and *Mr. Norris Changes Trains* later gained international fame and became the basis for the play and the film *Cabaret.* To Isherwood, the Nazi-Communist "civil war" was just background music to all else that was fascinating and germinating in Berlin. The city's creative energy was driven, he felt, by an "indestructible something... that is immensely exhilarating."[9] Isherwood recognized that Berlin led a double life: the zany excesses of the privileged community in western Berlin surrounded by misery and want in its working-class slums: "The bright part of Berlin was terribly bright, but the dark side was very dark indeed, a kind of sinister jungle."[10]

The underbelly of Berlin was not the only dark spot in the country. In a portent of worse economic times to come, Germany's hardscrabble Silesian coal fields and weavers' warrens in such impoverished towns as Waldenburg had been hit with falling prices and unemployment, driving some weavers into the coal pits and some miners onto the dole. That Germany might soon feel more waves of misery was powerfully augured in a semidocumentary silent movie, *Hunger in Waldenburg,* which opened to large audiences in Berlin in early 1929. "Only six hours from Berlin, a hell of infant mortality, rickets, tuberculosis, and unemployment," read the film's first subtitle.[11] Few could imagine that similar conditions could, in less than a year, begin to grip the rest of the country.

23

ALFRED HUGENBERG

How can the National Socialists join Hugenberg?... How can Hugenberg join Hitler?

—*Adolf Hitler, 1929*

Hitler had hitched his wagon to Alfred Hugenberg. Or vice versa. Hugenberg would never quite be sure who was in control.

A thickset man with startled-looking hair and an impressive mustache, Alfred Hugenberg was a unique figure in German politics. A onetime Prussian civil servant who had become a captain of industry as chairman of steelmaker Friedrich Krupp AG, Germany's largest corporation, Hugenberg had reinvented himself as a political force by acquiring a media empire. His nationwide newspaper chain was Germany's largest; his Berlin publishing house, August Scherl, produced three newspapers with a combined circulation of 350,000 copies per day; his movie company, Ufa (Universum-Film Aktiengesellschaft), dominated the market. In 1928, Hugenberg had gotten himself elected chair of the conservative German National People's Party, an amalgam of eastern landowners, wealthy industrialists, monarchists, and lower-middle-class Protestants who were both anti-Catholic and anti-Semitic.

Hugenberg's politics, like Hitler's, were racist, hypernationalist, antidemocratic, and expansionist. The sixty-four-year-old newspaper baron had been advocating social Darwinism and "racial hygiene" since he cofounded the Pan-German League in 1894, when Hitler was just five years old. Like Hitler, he was a strong believer in military expansion eastward to ease Germany's perceived population squeeze. Hugenberg unabashedly promoted the conquest of Poland to create a land rush for small German farmer-businessmen, with their allegedly superior racial traits and modern agricultural skills.[1] In many ways, Hugenberg was just another Hitler—or a pre-Hitler. Given their overlapping extremist politics, the two men were bound to intersect.

Despite a busy economy and a deluge of American business loans made possible by the 1924 Dawes Plan, Germany still labored—and chafed—under the reparations obligations imposed by the Treaty of Versailles. Again, American bankers took an interest in keeping Germany afloat by easing the repayments burden. In 1929 a committee led by General Electric chairman Owen D. Young proposed lowering Germany's indebtedness by nearly 20 percent and stretching the remaining payments over a full fifty-nine years, until 1988. A clear improvement over the terms of the Dawes Plan, the Young Plan also included a French promise to evacuate the Rhineland immediately—five years ahead of the treaty schedule.

But stretching Germany's reparations obligations over nearly six decades insulted Hitler's and Hugenberg's sense of honor. Along with other passionate nationalists, they vehemently opposed the Young Plan. Starting in July of 1929, Hugenberg led a major campaign to block the scheme, even though Foreign Minister Stresemann had already signed it and would soon submit it to the Reichstag for ratification. Hugenberg's radical alternative was the maximal position: complete cancellation of German reparations and a repudiation of Germany's 1919 acceptance of sole responsibility for the First World War. By obtaining enough petition signatures, Hugenberg was able to force a national referendum on the issue; it was scheduled for December of 1929. The German National People's Party chief was supported by hypernationalist leaders Franz Seldte and Theodor Duesterberg, of the 250,000-strong Steel Helmet veterans' association; Heinrich Class, of the racist Pan-German League; and prominent industrialist Fritz Thyssen. After some hesitation, Hitler decided to join Hugenberg's effort, too.

It was not an easy collaboration. Hitler and Hugenberg were the odd couple of German politics: Hitler, forty, the razor-voiced tribune of the people, in his jackboots and quasimilitary regalia; Hugenberg, sixty-four, the black-suited magnate with the odd haircut and gold watch chain conspicuously looped across his ample girth. Stocky and comical looking, the mulish Hugenberg had what Hitler needed—a sprawling newspaper chain, control of Germany's leading movie studio, and bourgeois respectability with a heavy dose of antirepublicanism.

Hitler also had what Hugenberg coveted: emotional appeal to the voters. Though skeptical of Hitler's sometimes radical antics, Hugenberg knew Hitler had a useful populist base. Playing on the same field of right-wing politics, the two men had to embrace. It was a marriage of convenience; they were not to make a felicitous pair. Yet joining Hugenberg's campaign was a shrewd short-term political move for Hitler. The Nazi leader's name and visage were catapulted from the narrow world of his party press into mainstream newspapers all over Germany. One prominent photo showed a stern-looking Hitler in a Storm Trooper uniform standing beside Hugenberg and Admiral Alfred von Tirpitz, one of Germany's most celebrated (and controversial) commanders during the First World War. Printed all over the country, the picture became Hugenberg's stamp of approval for the Nazi.[2] Throughout their shared campaign against the Young Plan, however, Hitler insisted on calling his own shots, making his own speeches, even criticizing Hugenberg when it suited him. On the campaign's final day, Hitler and Hugenberg appeared together in Munich's Circus Krone, Hitler's home turf. Their roles were entirely reversed: Hitler, with his biting rhetoric, was the star; Hugenberg, the dull speaker, played second fiddle.[3]

For all their efforts, the referendum to block the Young Plan failed. It was supported by only 13.8 percent of the electorate; 51 percent was required to pass. The referendum's failure signaled the end, for the moment, of attempts to create a united nationalist bloc in German politics. The differences among the right-wing groups were considerable and sometimes personal. The rivalries between alpha leaders such as Hitler and Hugenberg were nearly insurmountable.

Though the anti–Young Plan crusade was dead, Adolf Hitler was very much alive and now seen as part of the respectable right wing—one more mosaic stone in the Nazi leader's calculated and cumulative image building.[4] It would not be the last time Hitler's zigzag path to power would collide with Hugenberg's.

24

CONQUERING NUREMBERG

Something has to happen — we're on a razor's edge!

— *Storm Trooper in Nuremberg, 1929*

Hitler was solvent enough to do what he liked best: put on a show. In August of 1929, he staged a four-day Nazi Party convention in Nuremberg—now his preference for party gatherings. Nuremberg had the space, the history, and the politics he liked. He called the city "a wondrous trove of German art and German culture."[1] Nuremberg also had the fiery orator Julius Streicher and a friendly police chief, Heinrich Gareis, who made life considerably easier for a group that wanted, effectively, to occupy the city for four days.[2]

Nearly forty thousand Nazi Party members and Storm Troopers streamed into the historic old city—twice as many as had attended the last convention, in 1927. Most arrived on thirty-five special trains, with exuberant young Nazis leaning out the railroad cars. Greeted by marching bands, many were led by a fife-and-drum corps to their quarters. Some camped in open warehouses with straw-covered floors. Teenagers in Hitler Youth bivouacked in large white tents pitched in a nearby poplar woods. The men and boys ate from steaming soup kitchens set up by Storm Troopers; they washed and shaved at long outdoor water troughs, where they cut up and splashed one another like lads on a great summer outing.[3] Hitler paid a visit to the campers among the poplar trees, who hopped up from eating out of their mess kits to give the Nazi salute.[4]

To enhance his movement's aura of gravitas, Hitler invited guests of honor to the convention, including Emil Kirdorf, his new best friend in the coal-and-steel world. From the royal house of Hohenzollern came Prince August Wilhelm, a pro-Nazi son of the abdicated kaiser. Widely known in Germany by the nickname Auwi, the prince was regarded by some, including Goebbels, as senile—though he was only forty-two years old. One British correspondent uncharitably described him as "chinless and knock-kneed."[5] Others took note of his rumored homosexuality.[6] No matter: he was the progeny of the kaiser. Also among the special guests was Winifred Wagner, Hitler's admirer from Bayreuth and the bearer of one of Germany's most celebrated names. In addition, there was a younger woman—Hitler's half niece—named Geli Raubal.[7]

There was plenty of backroom intrigue, too. Goebbels brought his innate suspiciousness to conversations held all over town and well into the night. "Had a conversation last night with [Bernhard] Rust. He has uncovered a conspiracy.... Now I see all the connections. Now is the time for me to hold firm. I'll stay where I am. Beside Hitler. We will chop off the snake's head."[8]

Despite real or imagined plots, Hitler's men put on a good spectacle. A Nazi Party convention was, in Hitler's view, not a place for talking but a place for showing. Ridiculing the "fruitless discussions" that other parties had at their annual conventions, he effectively shut down any possible challenges to his leadership or policies by declaring the Nazi convention a debate-free zone—even though numerous petitions, motions, and questions had been submitted to party headquarters before the gathering. The party conclave was to be a "clear and understandable demonstration of the will and the youthful strength" of the National Socialist movement, Hitler decreed.[9] It was, in short, a piece of propaganda with Hitler as the main attraction.

Nuremberg was overrun with Nazis, and the Nurembergers seemed, at first, delighted. Merchants in the city center welcomed the run of Nazi parades and mass events—marches, marches, and more marches. There were two impressive torchlight processions, one culminating in a great fireworks show on the spacious Luitpoldhain meadow. Twenty thousand Storm Troopers saluted a gigantic fiery swastika as it whirled in the night, sending sparks flying off its spinning rims.

There were, of course, speeches, working groups, and much happy milling about. But the youngish assemblage took its greatest pleasure—judging by the ninety-minute film produced afterward by the Nazis—in ceremonies such as the cultish "consecration of the colors."[10] In this ritual, Hitler held in his hand the tip of the hallowed, never-washed Blood Flag from the 1923 putsch. As each Nazi delegation from each region of Germany marched past, he touched the Blood Flag to a corner of the local group's banner. The blood of the martyrs now figuratively flowed in every Nazi unit in the nation, just waiting to be avenged.

The convention was not all ceremony and discipline. Youthful energy mixed with radical beliefs; young guys in uniforms were emboldened to act like masters of the universe. Roving bands of Storm Troopers picked fights with political opponents, trashed pubs, and demolished a streetcar. "Brown shirts dominant everywhere," noted Goebbels.[11] One group attacked the local trade union headquarters, a stronghold of Marxism. Wherever they crossed paths, the Nazis went after members of the Social Democrats' Reichsbanner militia, in one case attacking a man on a bicycle just to rip away his black-red-and-gold banner—a fray that ended with one Socialist killed and the accidental death of one Nazi's wife.[12] Police responded with attack squads and officers on horseback. One newspaper called the scene a WILD-WEST IN NÜRNBERG.[13]

Hitler became alarmed. Following his final speech on Sunday afternoon, he returned to the podium to implore his troops to remain calm in the face of provocation. "We already have many wounded, some of them stabbed, some shot!" Hitler shouted.

A Storm Trooper retorted: "Something has to happen—we're on a razor's edge!"

"Be reasonable, now, be cool; think about the success of our movement," replied Hitler. "In good time we will see to it that these [enemies] will be destroyed root and branch!" That satisfied the restive men at the rally, who burst into peals of "Heil!"[14]

Yet reports of fatalities circulated. Hitler and Goebbels toured the city by car for hours, ordering Nazis off the streets. Clearly, Hitler did not want his four-day show marred by reports of violence. But it was too late. What little reporting the national newspapers did on the Nazi Party convention was all about fisticuffs and fatalities. The Nazis' reputation for thuggish overreach grew.[15]

Hitler did not get the national news coverage he craved. Even the Nazi violence was relegated to the inside pages. The party was competing for coverage with grand and inspiring events Hitler could not control. The great German airship *Graf Zeppelin,* the pride of the nation, had just completed the initial stage of its journey, the first-ever circumnavigation of the globe by a dirigible. It had docked in Lakehurst, New Jersey, just as Hitler was finishing his Sunday afternoon speech in Nuremberg. The big blimp merited far more prominent play in Monday's German newspapers than did the Nazis' rowdy convention. People were more interested in reading about Susie, the mascot gorilla on the airship, than about Adolf Hitler, the rabid rabble-rouser. After all, Susie had just recovered from a bout of airsickness and "looked forward to her journey across America."[16]

Despite its rocky ending, the Nazi Party convention's size, dynamism, and sheer noise lent Hitler's movement the appearance of revived purpose and permanence. After the 1928 election debacle, the Nuremberg gathering marked another turning point. The Nazis were back from the nearly forgotten, and they were not going away. Even so, in the early autumn of 1929, no one in the movement could see a clear path to power—absent some cataclysmic change.

25

CATACLYSM

> [Stresemann] looked like a Prussian barkeeper, overweight, bald, with undistinguished features, a harsh voice.
>
> —*Edgar Ansel Mowrer, American journalist*

The cataclysm came in October—in two parts.

Foreign Minister Gustav Stresemann—the man who led Germany back to international respectability, the man who made Germans seem normal and civilized to the outside world, the man who symbolized pragmatic moderation in a turbulent time, the only man who had served in every German government since 1923—fell ill and died.

A politician with a fine feel for massaging the press, Stresemann maintained his habit of a Friday afternoon schmooze with the foreign correspondents corps in Berlin to the very end. At his last such coffee klatch, at the foreign ministry's Leopold Palace, on September 28, 1929, he seemed to Associated Press correspondent Louis Lochner "deathly pale and flushed." Five days later, at the age of fifty-one, he was dead of a stroke.[1]

Stresemann had been the glue that held the German body politic together for the previous six years. With his skillful mix of nationalism and accommodation, he had navigated the crosscurrents of international politics to bring Germany into respectability while cutting the best available deals for his countrymen. Stresemann's chief accomplishment, along with key treaty negotiations, was putting Germany on friendly footing with its historic archenemy, France. The German foreign minister pulled off this masterstroke over ample quantities of good food, good wine, and excellent cigars with French foreign minister Aristide Briand, a passionate believer in the reconciliation of former adversaries. The two men became fast friends.[2] For their efforts, Stresemann and Briand (along with

British foreign secretary Austen Chamberlain) had been awarded the Nobel Peace Prize.

Just as significant as Stresemann's diplomatic finesse was his domestic political touch. With his dull looks and plainspoken style, Stresemann was the born moderate, loved by few but hated by almost no one in the center of German politics. One American journalist who covered his years as foreign minister described him bluntly: "He looked like a Prussian barkeeper, overweight, bald, with undistinguished features, a harsh voice."[3] Yet Stresemann was full of personality, charming foreign statesmen, international journalists, and even some of his opponents in the German political swirl.[4] The embodiment of stolidity and caution, he nonetheless had a taste for the occasional bold stroke. As the only politician who had lasted through nine governments, the thick-necked foreign minister was a one-man bastion of continuity in a changing government tableau. In government upheaval after upheaval, Stresemann was always asked to remain as Germany's foreign minister. He had been the last man standing. Now he was gone.

Few realized how deeply Stresemann's unexpected death would affect Germany's future. Within two weeks of his demise, government and economic leaders were preoccupied with the second part of the October cataclysm: the stock market crash. On October 24 and 29, 1929, and in the days that followed, the New York Stock Exchange lost more than half its value. Few in Germany had any inkling that America's stock market crash would unleash the Great Depression and trigger their own country's spiral toward totalitarianism. For the moment, they were too busy celebrating one of Stresemann's last triumphs: the hauling down of the French tricolor over the German city of Koblenz, on the Rhine River, on November 30, three years earlier than was mandated by the Treaty of Versailles. Thanks to Stresemann, French troops were now gone from German soil.

Part Three

TURNING POINT

(1930–1931)

The breakdown threatened to bring all economic life to a standstill. Thousands of factories closed their doors. Hunger was the daily companion of the German workingman . . . many an honest workingman had to resort to theft to obtain food. A case in point is the extensive pilfering of potatoes all through harvest time. . . . Early in 1930, I joined the National Socialist Party.

—*Unskilled laborer*[1]

People lacked the very essentials of living, and suicides were daily occurrences in the large cities.

—*White-collar worker*[2]

26

FONDNESS FOR FIGHTING

> The mass of the working classes wants nothing but *panem et circenses* [bread and circuses]! They will never understand the meaning of an ideal.
>
> —*Adolf Hitler, 1930*

"I've almost never prophesied the moment of our movement's success," Hitler wrote in an unusually frank letter on February 2, 1930. "Yet today I can make a prediction with almost oracular certainty."

The Nazi Party boss seldom wrote letters, notes, or anything personal; his preferred medium was a massive speech to a massive audience. Beyond making constant vague claims of an impending National Socialist millennium, Hitler avoided timeline promises and deadline prognostications. But in this rare missive to a German supporter living abroad, he broke his customary reserve, writing with astonishing political accuracy:

> If destiny keeps me in good health and no unforeseen catastrophe occurs, the German people will have passed the deepest point of their humiliation in two and a half to three years. I believe our victory will occur within this time period, and... our people's resurgence will begin.[1]

The Wall Street crash, in October of 1929, hit Germany especially hard. In the months thereafter, undercurrents of instability were breaking to the surface as thousands of manufacturing plants closed, small businesses shuttered their doors, and jobless men crowded the sidewalks in search of nonexistent work. Children of the unemployed were often forced to eat at public soup kitchens. In January of 1930, German labor officials reported a 14 percent unemployment rate—3.2 million persons out of work. Counting those forced into part-time work, the jobless figure reached 20 percent, or 4.5 million persons.[2] Germans were already remembering the horrors of 1923, when hyperinflation wiped out many middle-class families' life savings and left some citizens begging on the sidewalks or rioting in the streets.[3]

But Hitler was on the upswing. The Nazis' unprecedented 11 percent showing in a Thuringian state election held in December of 1929 had given the party leader a jolt of confidence. In Weimar, Thuringia's state capital and Hitler's home away from home, the Nazis had done even better, winning 23 percent of the vote. The breakthrough to double digits had made the Nazis the swing factor in a prospective coalition with Thuringia's middle-class and nationalist parties, whose chief aim was to exclude the Social Democrats and the Communists from the state's governing cabinet.[4] To form a majority that would span the center and right wing, these parties needed the Nazis.

Hitler was thrilled. On the verge of cracking the club of respectability with a share of power, the Nazi Party chief gloated in his letter to the overseas German: "It is downright astonishing how the arrogant, conceited, and stupid rejection of the [Nazi Party] of a few years ago has turned itself into an expectant ray of hope. A great shift in public opinion has occurred.... No wonder the former coalition partners in Thuringia are turning to us for the first time to request our membership in the government."

In negotiations over joining the Thuringian government in early 1930, Hitler used a tactic that would later serve his needs at the national level. He demanded two key portfolios: the interior ministry and the education ministry. The first would give the Nazis dominion over the police and the civil service; the second included oversight of schools, universities, and cultural policy. "Whoever holds these two ministries and ruthlessly exploits their power can achieve extraordinary things," wrote Hitler.[5]

The Nazi Party's potential coalition partners in Thuringia were appalled when Hitler proposed one man for both ministerial jobs: Wilhelm Frick. A committed Nazi who, like Hitler, had been convicted of treason following the 1923 putsch, Frick was a hard-liner who favored draconian law enforcement. Despite objections to Frick, Hitler outmaneuvered the other parties; they were forced to accept his choice. Once Frick assumed the two posts, he set about driving Social Democrats, Communists, and their perceived fellow travelers out of the Thuringian civil service, the police, and the schools.[6] Reaching directly into the state's most respected cultural institution, the University of Jena, Frick created something new: a professorial chair for racial studies as a branch of social anthropology. It was Hitler's first chance to put his radical racial beliefs on a pedestal of academic respectability.

Racial studies served as cover for pseudoscientific ways to discredit non-Aryans, especially Jews. And no one was better suited for the new professorship than Hans F. K. Günther, Germany's best-known eugenicist and exponent of racial stereotyping. A linguist and writer, Günther was called the pope of racist analysis; his nickname was Racial Günther (*Rasse-Günther*). Like Hitler, the pseudoscientist had drawn much of his "scientific racism" from eugenicists Madison Grant and Sir Francis Galton. Günther also embraced the "racial demography" of French aristocrat Arthur de Gobineau. The German's best-known books were *Racial Elements of European History* and *Racial Characteristics of the Jewish People.* Creating typologies of racial variance, Günther used phrenological drawings and photographs to support theories of inferior and superior races. Judging by skin tone, eye color, perceived emotional characteristics, and even religious background, the busy Günther even subdivided Germans according to their regional appearance. He distinguished the (superior) Nordic-looking individual from the (inferior) Mediterranean types, the Swabians from the Balts, the Alpine Germans from the lowlanders. By this scale of differences, Günther determined the "racial soul" of each group, a concept that had a considerable following in an era when stereotyping was commonplace.

Günther got his university chair, and Jena got its place in Nazi history. But Wilhelm Frick did little more damage than that. His plan to purge the Thuringian police was stymied by the long arm of the national government—the Reich interior ministry. Within a little more than a year, Frick was undone and out. His aggressive style helped trigger a vote of no confidence in the Thuringian coalition, which fell, taking the Nazis with it.

Meanwhile, Goebbels was continuing his flash-bang propaganda campaign in the German capital. Ever alert for human drama that fit the Nazi narrative, Goebbels in early 1930 seized on the shooting and eventual death of a Storm Trooper named Horst Wessel to create a celebrated martyr. In a clash with Communists, the young Nazi—who had been accused of pimping for a prostitute—had been shot in the face. As Wessel lay for weeks in a hospital, Goebbels published a series of fawning articles about the fallen hero in his newspaper, *Der Angriff*. When the luckless Storm Trooper finally succumbed, on February 23, Goebbels turned his funeral into a Nazi cult event. Five hundred Storm Troopers marched with flaming torches past Communist Party headquarters on Bülowplatz: the Communists responded by belting out their anthem, "The Internationale." Nearly twenty thousand people lined the streets of the cortege, claimed Goebbels. On a cemetery wall, Communists had painted, in large white letters, A FINAL "HEIL HITLER" FOR WESSEL THE PIMP! Rocks were thrown, and a near riot ensued. At the interment's end, a poem written by the young Wessel was sung to the tune of a traditional soldiers' chorus for the first time in public. The "Horst Wessel Song" ("Raise high the flag—the ranks tightly closed!") was a stirring march that became the Storm Troopers' new anthem and a hallowed song in the Nazi movement, sung frequently at party gatherings and outings. Goebbels's martyr was made.

The Nazis' fondness for street altercations carried over into their own ranks. Goebbels still feuded with the Strasser brothers over Otto's insistence on Socialist doctrines in the Combat Press newspapers. Sidewalk vendors of Goebbels's *Der Angriff* faced fistfights with sellers of the Strassers' *Der Nationalsozialist* and the *Berliner Arbeiterzeitung*. Even Hitler was furious with the Strassers for revealing privileged party discussions in their publications.[7] In April of 1930, the Nazi chief summoned his top leaders to Munich. During a two-hour disquisition on party discipline and the heresy of Marxism, he unloaded his displeasure. Hitler reminded his paladins that the Nazi Party wasn't a party in the conventional sense; it was the "organized German will," whose realization depended not on "fruitless intellectual discussions" but on toeing the party line.[8]

Goebbels was delighted. Hitler had finally struck at the "salon Bolshevists." Better still, he shocked everyone by announcing that Goebbels would become national propaganda director, making the Berlin gauleiter the third most important man in the Nazi Party after Hitler and Gregor Strasser.

"[Gregor] Strasser goes white as chalk," gloated Goebbels in his diary. "Strasser and his little circle are shattered."

The Goebbels-Strasser feud was an ongoing irritant to Hitler. Once in 1928 he had showed up at Otto's office in Berlin to complain.[9] "I was at work in my enormous study," recalled Otto, "when Hitler burst in unannounced." Hitler made a bald-faced threat: "What will you do when ten of Herr Goebbels's Storm Troopers attack you in your office?"

Otto calmly pulled a big revolver from a drawer and placed it on his desk. "I have eight shots, Herr Hitler. That will be eight Storm Troopers less. . . . I shall shoot anyone who attacks me. . . . Brown shirts can't frighten me." (It was not unusual for men to keep loaded firearms handy in those days; Hitler always did.)

Hitler changed his tune. He seized both of Otto's hands, staging the syrupy reconciliation scene that Hitler so loved. "The tearful eyes, the trembling voice, the whole studied performance was wasted on me," wrote Otto. The truculent editor spurned an offer by Hitler to buy out Combat Press.

By 1930, Hitler had concluded that Otto's ideological apostasy and contrariness could no longer be tolerated. The Nazi chief wanted at all costs to avoid a nasty party schism. With Saxony state elections scheduled for June 22, he hoped for a compromise that would keep Otto quiescently under the Nazi tent.

One day Hitler summoned Otto to his room at Berlin's Hotel Sanssouci for an "urgent conversation." The meeting turned into a marathon showdown of seven hours spread over two days. During their hotel-room confrontation, the party boss once again tried to buy Combat Press, reportedly offering Otto and Gregor a jaw-dropping eighty thousand marks ($280,000 in 2019 dollars) apiece if they would sell. He offered to make Otto his national press spokesman—if he would relinquish the publishing operation.

"Herr Hitler, I am not for sale," sniffed Otto.[10]

Hitler ripped into Otto, calling his writings "nothing but Marxism—in fact, Bolshevism!" Continuing his rant, Hitler said that the National Socialist movement would select leaders from a new master class of men "who will not allow themselves to be guided, like you, by the morality of pity." In one of the most telling lines he ever uttered, Hitler shouted his disdain for the very people he longed to lead: "The mass of the working classes wants nothing but *panem et circenses*!* They will never understand the meaning of an ideal."

The ideological haranguing continued the following day. Finally, the turbulent meeting was over, and so was Otto Strasser's role in the Nazi movement. Hitler denounced Otto to Goebbels as "an intellectual white Jew" and a "Marxist of the first water."[11] After the Saxony election in June gave the Nazis 14 percent of the vote, making them the second-largest party in the state, Hitler authorized Goebbels to undertake a "relentless cleansing" of the party in Berlin. The gauleiter was to pay particular attention to the "rootless debate-club literati" like Otto. Only too happy to comply and baring his teeth, Goebbels promptly clothed himself in Hitlerian authority by printing the leader's edict in *Der Angriff*.

But Otto got a beat on Hitler and Goebbels; he quit the Nazi Party before he could be thrown out. He formed his own splinter group, later dubbed the Black Front. Goebbels feared that Otto might lead a significant number of Nazis into his new competing movement, but the Black Front peaked at around five thousand members. Goebbels need not have worried. Whatever remnants of socialism that had lingered in the Nazi Party were now almost certainly gone. So was Otto. All Goebbels had left to worry about was Gregor.

* Bread and circuses.

27

A BLACK DAY

Are we Germans a single nation or are we just a heap of special interests?

—*Hermann Dietrich, German finance minister, 1930*

On an overcast Thursday afternoon in March of 1930, Germany's fragile democracy began its decline into extinction.[1]

Since the 1928 election, Germany had been governed by a five-party "grand coalition" cabinet led by Social Democratic chancellor Hermann Müller. The coalition stretched from Müller's Social Democrats and the left-liberal German Democratic Party, on the left, across the middle to the (Catholic) Centre Party and (Catholic) Bavarian People's Party, then kept going to the conservative German People's Party, on the right. Combining the working-class Socialists, who had won nearly 30 percent of the vote in 1928, with the middle-class parties was a brave attempt to span the core of German politics. Its goal was to marginalize the extremes—the revolutionary Communists on the far left and Hitler's racist Nazis and Hugenberg's hypernationalist, authoritarian German National People's Party on the far right.

But the center would not hold.

The members of Müller's overstretched coalition constantly put their own party interests ahead of the broader national interest. The coalition frequently stalemated. In the spring of 1930, they were deadlocked over the Depression-driven question of how to salvage the strained unemployment insurance program in the face of dramatically rising layoffs. At issue was whether to increase the employers' mandatory contribution from 3.5 percent to 4 percent. Small though the increase would be—one-half of 1 percent—it became the stumbling block that broke the government. The ill and exhausted Chancellor Müller could not assemble a majority of his coalition members behind any workable solution. His last resort was a request to President Hindenburg to rule by decree under article 48 of the German constitution so he could force the issue. This was a solution to stalemate that had worked several times in years past—notably, when Chancellor Gustav Stresemann in 1923 sought to break a deadlock and end hyperinflation. But Hindenburg, who was eager to stymie Social Democratic influence in any German government, said no. Gridlock met obstinacy; political compromise succumbed.

After twenty-one months in office, Hermann Müller threw in the towel. On March 27, 1930, he and his government resigned. The Social Democratic chancellor's departure marked the sixteenth time in the eleven-year life of the Weimar Republic that a government cabinet had relinquished the reins of office. But this time it was different. With the end of Müller's five-party government went the last, best attempt at centrist coalition politics based on parliamentary strength. With it went the fundamental democratic idea of the Weimar Republic.

The *Frankfurter Zeitung* branded March 27 "a black day."[2]

With Hermann Müller gone, the mantle of leadership fell to Heinrich Brüning, a bespectacled economics expert and leader of the Centre Party. A forty-four-year-old workaholic bachelor who lived in a modest Catholic retreat in Berlin, Brüning was a conservative nationalist with monarchist leanings.[3] The devout academician was best known for his financial expertise, not his political skills. Goebbels called him a "bloodless Jesuit." Brüning's solid wartime credentials as a frontline officer who had earned an Iron Cross made him palatable to the former field marshal President Hindenburg—a distinct plus, since Brüning would be ruling without majority support in the parliament but with the full support of the president.[4]

On March 30, Brüning became the Weimar Republic's ninth chancellor in eleven years, forming its seventeenth cabinet.[5]

Chancellor Brüning's first months in office were not auspicious. Like a strict accountant, he believed that only budgetary austerity could shield Germany from collapse under the weight of its outstanding loan obligations. The new chancellor was bent on proving to the international financial markets that Germany could get its house in order, even at the expense of its economically suffering populace. Brüning pushed through—with Hindenburg's support—a series of measures that would cut government salaries, reduce welfare programs, and raise taxes. The bespectacled Jesuit was bitterly labeled the Hunger Chancellor.

Hitler in the spring of 1930 was busy tending his own patch of politics in Munich. Convinced that his fortunes would soon turn, he and publisher Max Amann issued a new edition of *Mein Kampf* that combined both volumes into a single book. The new "People's Edition" ran to nearly eight hundred pages but was offered at the everyman price of eight marks.[6] Hitler's and Amann's instincts were right: the book started selling as soon as it hit the streets, in May of 1930, and would become a big earner in the coming years.[7]

Trends seemed to be running in Hitler's favor; he decided on a daring real estate investment. It was time to move the shabby Nazi Party headquarters on Schellingstrasse into imposing new accommodations near Munich's stately Königsplatz, with its grand monuments and museums. Securing a rumored large loan from a benefactor while announcing a fund-raising campaign among party members, Hitler purchased an elegant but neglected villa called Palais Barlow for more than 800,000 marks (the equivalent of $2.9 million in 2019). The edifice stood on fashionable Briennerstrasse only half a block from the four-story mansion of Hitler's wealthy friends Hugo and Elsa Bruckmann, where Hitler often attended Friday evening salon gatherings. To remodel his new villa into a party headquarters, Hitler engaged Paul Ludwig Troost, an architect known for the sumptuous interior design of luxury ocean liners. Unafraid to adopt the trappings of the haute bourgeoisie even as he built a mass movement that included the working classes, Hitler wanted to give his insurgent party the look of a government-in-waiting.

After a little more than three months in office, Chancellor Heinrich Brüning's government stalemated. The chancellor had created a cabinet not based on party power in the parliament but rather on expertise: he filled it with men possessing proficiency in finance, economics, defense, and other fields—a "cabinet of experts," as the newspapers called it. These experts supported Brüning's deflationary policies, which put even more desperate and hungry people on the streets. Using Hindenburg's offer of "presidential" powers under article 48 of the constitution, Brüning forced civil servants and salaried employees to make "emergency contributions" to the federal budget.[8]

But Brüning went too far. When the parliament was asked on July 18, 1930, to ratify the chancellor's austerity budget, the motion backfired. That triggered a vote of no confidence by the Reichstag, which still had the constitutional right to vote a government out of office and force new elections. The Nazis instantly endorsed the no-confidence motion, throwing their clamorous support behind it. The final vote on the motion would be close; the Nazis needed all their twelve parliamentarians on hand for the balloting. They were missing one man: Joseph Goebbels.

The peripatetic Nazi propaganda chief was out of town. Always caught up in one fevered love affair or another, the bachelor Goebbels was off visiting his latest girlfriend at her parents' home, a forester's lodge forty-eight miles north of Berlin. When Hermann Göring telephoned with the summons that he urgently needed to return to the capital, Goebbels's first thought was not about the windfall prospect of bringing down the Brüning government—and dissolving the parliament—but about the threat to his own freedom. A parliamentary dissolution meant losing his parliamentary immunity. Goebbels had reason to be worried: he faced an array of charges for incitement to violence and other crimes from which he was shielded as a sitting member of the Reichstag.

"If the Reichstag is dissolved, they will arrest me right away," noted Goebbels. "But I don't give a shit!"[9]

The Nazi propaganda boss made a mad dash on narrow roads for Berlin, his driver sometimes reaching the hair-raising speed of sixty-two miles per hour. Arriving at the Reichstag at noon, Goebbels noticed a newspaper headline that read: IT COMES DOWN TO JUST ONE VOTE. Goebbels's heart was pounding as one Fräulein Bettge, a Nazi secretary at the Reichstag building, yelled to him, "Get inside, quickly!" He made it with just five minutes to spare.

Chaos reigned inside the Reichstag chamber. Brüning's finance minister, Hermann Dietrich, made a last-minute plea for unity, imploring parliament to close ranks behind the government and its proposed budget. "We have to stop playing special-interest politics!" he said on the Reichstag floor. "The present question is: are we Germans a single nation or are we just a heap of special interests?"

With his bitingly accurate but politically volatile phrase—"a heap of special interests"—the luckless Dietrich had just handed Adolf Hitler a new rhetorical cudgel.

Brüning's budget was voted down, 236 to 221 (with 10 abstentions). The Reichstag was dissolved, and the chamber erupted. The Communists burst into a lusty rendition of "The Internationale"—they liked their chances. Others shouted, some cheered, and Count Reventlow, the reluctant Nazi, went "white as a sheet," noted Goebbels.

A new election was called for September 14. All the political cards were now in the air, waiting to drop in some new configuration. German history had once again come to a halt.

Goebbels was on the run. A national election was exactly what the Nazis wanted, but Goebbels still had to stay out of jail. "Sneaked out of the parliament building undiscovered. Went to Göring's. Tonight I'll travel with Göring to Hitler. Hopefully I won't be arrested beforehand."[10]

Even as the workers suffered, the economy cratered, and the politicians flailed, life in Golden Twenties Berlin continued in the jaunty style to which it had become accustomed. On the night of the parliament's dramatic dissolution, on flashy Kurfürstendamm just a few minutes' drive from the Reichstag, a scene of a different kind unfolded at the Gloria-Palast movie theater. It was the premiere of *Der Blaue Engel* (The Blue Angel), the movie that would launch the sultry Marlene Dietrich to international fame. All the notables of the entertainment and culture scene turned out. The tragicomic film, about a respectable professor who descends into madness, was one of the high points of a rich moviemaking era for its Austrian-American director, Josef von Sternberg, and its German star, Emil Jannings. For Marlene Dietrich, a formerly unknown performer in unremarkable shows, it was the launchpad of a lifetime. To the Nazis, however, the heavy-breathing movie, with its cabaret seduction scenes, was yet another descent into decadence and depravity. If Hitler and Goebbels needed more proof that democracy was a failure and autocratic control was needed, *Der Blaue Engel* provided it.

After taking her bows at the Gloria-Palast, Dietrich quickly put herself beyond the clutches of the Nazis and their future crackdowns. She departed Berlin the same night to board a transatlantic liner that would carry her to America and Hollywood. For the rest of her life, she returned home only twice for brief visits. The film star was among the first of the hordes of creative and intellectual talent to flee Germany as the Nazis squashed the thriving culture. With Dietrich's hasty nighttime exodus, two eras—the glory of Germany's artistic flowering and the coming horror of Nazi repression—passed in the night.[11]

28

TWO MONTHS THAT CHANGED THE WORLD

The brown shirt is a garment of honor. The wearer must above all represent the National Socialist worldview and conduct himself appropriately.

— *"Ten Commandments of the Storm Troopers," 1928*[1]

Sneaking past "white mice"—roving police patrols—Goebbels and Göring made it onto the overnight train to Munich. They arrived the next morning in what Hitler loved to call "the capital city of the movement" just in time for an impromptu meeting of Nazi Party leaders and other gauleiters who had streamed in from around the country. Everyone knew the unexpected September parliamentary election could be their chance to make a comeback from the disastrous 1928 election.

Hitler viewed the election as both a windfall and an existential challenge. He had to cross into the realm of credible contenders for the leadership of Germany or see his movement fade to the margins. The Nazi Party could not withstand another resounding defeat. The election would test the party's enhanced ground game; it would plumb voters' receptivity to the Nazi message for the first time since the 1929 Wall Street stock market crash and its brutal economic impact on Germany. Histrionic as always, Hitler cast the upcoming vote as a "turning point in Germany's destiny." He was upbeat: "Unless all the signs are wrong, Germany's fate is slowly beginning to turn. We are approaching a period of major internal shifts and upheavals."[2]

Hitler was either bloviating or brilliant. In either case, his instincts were right.

Thanks to Gregor Strasser and a battalion of busy bureaucrats in Munich, the Nazi Party had turned into a tightly run and growing organization. Led by Hitler's monomania, the party had been shaped into a small army of fanatical followers. When Brüning's cabinet fell, Hitler and Strasser were ready to try out their new political machine. Germany was again in chaos, and they meant to leverage that chaos.

It took Hitler only half a day to start. Seven hours after the Berlin government resigned, the Nazi leader commandeered the stage at the Circus Krone, elbowing aside scheduled speeches by Strasser and Wilhelm Frick. Seizing the moment and the microphone, Hitler got a jump on all the other political parties. Eight thousand supporters showed up, lustily cheering their leader. In an unusually poignant speech, Hitler nimbly adopted the just-resigned German finance minister's lament, in his Reichstag swan song, that Germany was "a heap of special interests." Painting a vision of his vaunted "national community," which would bury differences and embrace all Germans from all classes, professions, and both major Christian denominations, Hitler said:

> In our ranks we don't have the middle class or the working class, not the businessmen or the white-collar workers, not farmers or city folks, not Catholics or Protestants, not monarchists or republicans. *We have only Germans among us*![3]

Hitler delivered his lines with a cadence and a pace designed to sweep up his audience in a mass embrace, putting nationality above all other values in a time of peril. With his rousing final words—*"We have only Germans among us!"*—Hitler cleverly channeled Kaiser Wilhelm II at the start of the First World War: "I no longer know any political parties: *I know only Germans!*" That patriotic line had unified an often-divided Germany in the massive war effort. While Hitler's definition of Germans naturally did not include Jews, his reference to "only Germans" in this speech was not a statement of ethnic exclusion but of broad inclusion of the fractious elements of the German body politic: it didn't matter if you were Protestant or Catholic, bourgeois or proletarian, field hand or factory worker; all that mattered was that you were German.*

This was a bold leap. Politically tribalist, Germans were locked into a form of identity politics, almost religiously attached to their political persuasions: Socialist, Catholic, or Protestant-bourgeois.[4] The tribes were subdivided into at least eight main political parties, with many more small parties thrown into the mix. In this alphabet soup—the Weimar Republic was one of the most complicated political periods in history—Hitler was exhorting voters to rise above the narrow concerns of party division and join his mass movement as a single German community, almost as though the Nazi Party were not a party at all.

In actual practice, Hitler knew the toughest tribes to crack were the Socialists—both Social Democrats and Communists—and the Catholics, who had a historic attachment to the Centre Party (and its Bavarian sister, the Bavarian People's Party). This affiliation grew out of Catholics' minority status in German society (roughly 35 percent Catholic versus 65 percent Protestant) and from the nineteenth-century disputes between the German government and the Catholic Church known as the "cultural struggle," or *Kulturkampf.* In the coming elections, Hitler would draw the majority of his support from the Protestants.

To his rapt listeners in the Circus Krone, Hitler promised that on election day in September of 1930, the young Nazi movement would "beat loudly on the doors of the German government" and shout, "Open up! The special interests must get out! The German people are moving in!"[5]

A sense of desperation that the coming election was Germany's last chance for a new start seized some editorial writers. "The Reichstag has fallen—long live the Reichstag!" wrote the *Vossische Zeitung,* imploring German voters to "get it right this time." Practically screaming for the political world to quit its petty squabbling and overcome its partisan

* Heretical though it may sound, Hitler's words in German have a salving cadence that inescapably reminds the reader of Illinois senator Barack Obama's stirring call at the 2004 Democratic National Convention—not for a red America or a blue America but for a "*United States* of America." Hitler's ability to cast such an inclusive and persuasive verbal embrace helps explain his appeal to voters.

differences, the editors beseeched Germans to seek common ground in order to prevent the country from descending into "a war of all against all."[6]

Yet "all against all" captured the state of German politics. More than thirty very disparate parties were soon slugging it out on the German campaign trail. Each party, no matter how tiny, was convinced of the rightness of its cause, unable to sacrifice its singular interests for the broader national interest. Each wanted its slice of the political pie, no matter how small. The election unfolded as a playground brawl. And none brawled more eagerly than the Nazis. By August, the brown shirts seemed to be everywhere: intense, dedicated, always active. "We were at it day and night," recalled a Nazi campaign worker, "doing sometimes rather dangerous propaganda service before every election... putting up stickers, hanging banners, building scaffolding."[7]

That Nazism was far more than a one-man movement became starkly clear during the 1930 campaign. Tens of thousands of Nazi activists flooded the hustings in towns and villages across the country. Continuous agitation countered the party's image as a marginal fringe movement. "There was a feeling of restless energy about the Nazis," reported a housewife in the little Lower Saxony town of Northeim. "You constantly saw the swastika painted on the sidewalks or found them on pamphlets put out by the Nazis. I was drawn by the feeling of strength about the party, even though there was much in it which was highly questionable."[8]

Nazi campaign rallies became a form of mass entertainment, with music, banners, uniforms, rituals, and a passionate political message. Goebbels's propaganda department adopted modern advertising techniques, employing simple slogans, bright colors, and frequent repetition to generate what one historian called "an assault on the collective subconscious."[9] Sporting events and so-called German evenings—beer and rhetoric—were popular attractions that also generated revenue for the Nazis' coffers.[10] Augmenting the activism was the Nazi publishing machine: besides the daily *Völkischer Beobachter* and weekly *Illustrierter Beobachter,* there were several dozen smaller Nazi newspapers around the country. The non-Nazi media paid attention, too, carrying Hitler's name and party identification to readers throughout Germany.[11]

The Nazis had a new secret weapon: a speakers' school. Hitler endorsed the efforts of a Nazi gauleiter to promote a correspondence course to train Nazi orators.[12] The gauleiter, Fritz Reinhardt (no kin to Max Reinhardt), devised a step-by-step method to inculcate in would-be Nazi public speakers the minutiae of National Socialist doctrine and policies. "This course is not intended to teach you how you should move your mouth and body while speaking," Reinhardt wrote. "You should not become an actor, but rather a National Socialist advocate and then a National Socialist speaker.... You must possess the idealism you propose to instill in the hearts of our fellow countrymen, and you must, with your heart, understand the concepts of Volk and Fatherland."[13]

By the 1930 election, Reinhardt had trained several thousand speakers to carry a uniform message into the small towns and villages that Hitler could never reach with his mass rallies in major cities. "Speakers to the barricades!" exhorted the *Illustrierter Beobachter*, echoing Hitler's faith in the impact of the spoken word.[14] Tailoring their remarks to specific audiences, such as civil servants, farmers, and small shop owners, the speakers connected the dots of fanatical commitment, German rebirth, and the racial roots of Hitler's ideology as well as programmatic points on the economy, the military, and foreign policy. Reinhardt's training even included the dark arts of negative campaigning—heckling, disruption, and argumentation. Without the battalions of trained orators to round out the hoopla of Storm Trooper marches and lively party rallies, the Nazis' exertions might not have generated long-term political gains and votes on election day.[15]

In the seven-week election battle, the Nazi speakers would give an estimated six thousand speeches and talks. Even that impressive number was just a fraction of the thirty-four thousand rallies, assemblies, meetings, and marches that the Nazis announced for the final month of campaigning. The staggering number of Nazi political gatherings had a two-way benefit: besides reaching voters, the voters' concerns also reached the Nazis. "That is why we get closer to the people than do those [other parties] who sit in Berlin," Hitler bragged to a British journalist.[16]

The campaign unfolded in the age of print. Television was nonexistent, and state-controlled radio was not available to the political parties.

Placards and handbills were powerful political tools. "We will work the electorate systematically—everywhere in Germany, the same placards will be posted, the same leaflets distributed, and the same stickers will appear," announced Goebbels to the district leaders.[17] The party's chief slogans, Goebbels decided, would be "Freedom and bread!" and "Down with the Young Plan!"

The sloganeering of the era was often a primal scream. One muscular Social Democratic poster depicted a shirtless workingman slamming a Nazi in the head with one elbow and coldcocking a Communist under the chin with the other. Another fierce SPD placard showed a man painfully chained to a gigantic swastika: "The worker in the Reich of the swastika!" it proclaimed.[18] A Communist poster portrayed a peaked-cap worker about to bring his fist down on a boardroom of top-hatted capitalists who were labeled "The System." In their competition for workers' votes, the Socialists and the Communists devoted much of their energy to attacking each other rather than the Nazis.

The Nazis produced a grisly placard that showed their party driving a dagger into the head of a menacing serpent. The snake bore a Jewish Star of David and was festooned with the usual Nazi bugaboos: Marxism, Bolshevism, the Dawes Plan, the Young Plan, the Locarno Treaties, war guilt, inflation, corruption, and "girl trafficking."[19] On another poster boldly addressed to "Marxists!" the Nazis tried to peel off SPD voters by pointing out that many of their candidates and leaders were "JEWS."

In this election campaign, the Nazis embraced new technologies such as slide shows and films. If the primary purpose of propaganda lay in "attracting the attention of the crowd," as Hitler wrote in *Mein Kampf*, few things drew the curious and the undecided as well as moving pictures or even still photos with captions and spoken commentary did.[20] In a pre-television age, a public slide show or a film screening was a novelty and a form of entertainment.[21] The Nazis had both.

The innovative Nazi slide shows were the brainchild of a fervent anti-Semite named Bruno Czarnowski. A First World War veteran and a Storm Trooper in Upper Silesia, Czarnowski was a born polemicist who often spoke to local Nazi groups. Seeking to intensify his anti-Semitic message, he lifted cartoons by Hans Schweitzer (a.k.a. Mjölnir), the house caricaturist at Goebbels's combative newspaper, *Der Angriff.* Czarnowski used Schweitzer's drawings to create garish slide shows with titles such as "The Blood-Drunk Bolsheviks." That show was a gory depiction of the Russian Revolution, blaming Jews, the progenitors of communism, for mass murder and other atrocities. The best-known show in Czarnowski's lineup was called, simply, "Isidor." This cartoon-based narrative drew from Goebbels's frequent smears of Berlin's Jewish deputy police chief, Dr. Bernhard Weiss.

Czarnowski's slide shows, made available to Nazi campaigners across Germany, were a hit. Czarnowski also offered projector rentals for 10 marks. "With the slide apparatus the smallest village can put on a great show," announced the *Völkischer Beobachter.* "Slide performances easily pay for themselves if you charge admission."[22]

In addition to slides, the Nazis had begun moving into film production. As early as 1929, Goebbels had created something new—a sound film with staged scenes and high production values. The Berlin gauleiter's first movie was called *Battle in Berlin,* a tableau of anti-Semitic imagery paired with filmed street fights between Nazis and Communists. The combat scenes were probably staged or openly instigated for the cameras. Still, the bloody pictures conveyed the Nazis' commitment and willingness to use violence for their cause.[23] Even if street violence bruised the Nazis' public image, it had the political upside of keeping them in the news. In Goebbels's Berlin film, the roughneck imagery was augmented by documentary footage of long-bearded Eastern Jews on Berlin's fashionable Kurfürstendamm—pictures that underlined the Nazi message. Goebbels's *Battle in Berlin* was screened in 1929 at sixty *gau* gatherings in front of a total of thirty thousand people. By the 1930 election, eight films had been produced for distribution to party meetings.

As the campaign unfolded, the flood of Nazi propaganda and loudspeaker-driven events sometimes offended small-town taste and propriety. Yet the overall impact was positive. A can-do image was fostered by orderly Storm Trooper marches through market squares and solemn commemoration ceremonies at local war memorials.[24] Concerts staged in local parks by smartly uniformed Storm Trooper marching bands lent the Nazis more visibility than the other parties, making their movement look larger than it actually was. Such actions convinced some voters that the brown shirts could be depended on not just to talk but also to act.[25]

The Nazis became known as the party of youth.[26] Hitler's rebranding a decade earlier—changing the name of his party from simply the German Workers' Party to the *National Socialist* German Workers' Party—was proving to be an inspired choice for attracting young voters. Nationalism, with its aura of patriotism, evoked a macho fighting spirit that appealed to angry young men, including university students. Socialism, with its implied promise of an egalitarian future, appealed to the disenfranchised, the idealists, and the young voters, especially women. Many of the young men and First World War veterans swinging their blackjacks at Communists and Socialists were convinced that they were on the right side of history, fighting for a providential cause. "We firmly believed that our combat would someday achieve unity in the German people," recalled one Nazi.[27]

Cunningly, the Nazis also portrayed themselves as just what Germany needed to impose order on street mayhem, though they were themselves the instigators of most of it. Despite their reputation for rowdiness in urban areas, the Storm Troopers could also project respectability and decorum. A list of the "Ten Commandments of the Storm Troopers" had been handed out in Stuttgart and contained the following edicts:

> The brown shirt is a garment of honor. The wearer must above all represent the National Socialist worldview and conduct himself appropriately. When the Storm Trooper assembles for a march, it is especially important that he not have his hands in his pockets or a cigarette in his mouth.... Cultivate the company and companionship of your fellow members, but let such meetings be orderly. Do not let them degenerate into drunken brawls.... Be diligent in your private life, for you work for the great ideas of Adolf Hitler.[28]

By the time of the election, the Depression had begun sweeping through Germany like a scythe, leaving broad segments of workers on the streets, without hope or prospects. Jobless homeless men, some wearing suits, often had nowhere to sleep. They would pay pennies for the chance to doze while sitting in a jam-packed shelter—with their heads awkwardly leaning across a rope for support. Even those with jobs, such as female textile-mill workers, led brutal lives. "The workday begins at 4:45," said one Bavarian woman who also had a husband, a home, and children to care for. "I do my [factory] work standing, nine and a half hours a day.... After twelve hours, [it's] back home....In Bavaria, the poor women live like slaves."[29]

To men stuck in chronic unemployment or straitened circumstances in backwater towns, entering the Nazi Party, and especially joining the Storm Troopers, could be an act of upward mobility. Attending meetings and gaining membership in something greater than one's own small circle was a step above stagnation. Suddenly a man was no longer standing on street corners, his destitution on full display, but rather going to organized events, talking about the future, distributing leaflets. To former frontline soldiers, the remembered camaraderie of the trenches was sometimes experienced in the tight discipline of party activities and Storm Trooper formations. "Common suffering and common peril had welded us together and hardened us," remembered one veteran fighter after joining the Nazi Party.[30] Weekly discussion evenings on the topics of politics and National Socialism, usually held in a local restaurant or pub, were obligatory. On Sundays the new Nazis took part in "propaganda parades." Recruitment was direct and personal: a newly converted Nazi would invite a friend to come to the next meeting with him, much as a religious evangelist might spread his message. The entire experience drove a growing sense of egalitarianism inside the party.

At the grassroots level, so carefully cultivated by Gregor Strasser, the rank-and-file Nazis were already practicing their own version of a classless national community, treating one another as equals. They greeted each other not as "Mister" (*Herr*), the expected form of German address, but rather as "party comrade" (*Parteigenosse*). This appellation marked a dramatic break with traditional German formality; it unashamedly borrowed the techniques of the Nazis' archenemies, the Communists and the Socialists.

This egalitarianism thrilled a new Berlin party member named Gustav Heinsch. A family servant and chauffeur, Heinsch was surprised to find himself raised to the post of cell leader in Berlin. "Class arrogance had been completely eliminated among us in the party," he recalled.[31]

The Nazis copied the Communists in other ways. One was in the creation of a dense web of small neighborhood cells that followed the Communist structure of grassroots party building. Devised by Reinhold Muchow, an organizational whiz in Goebbels's Berlin office, the street cell organization transformed the German capital into hundreds of small political villages with familiar neighborhood leaders. These leaders operated just as a ward politician in Chicago or New York might. Joining a neighborhood club with friends who met frequently at the corner pub was far easier than affiliating with a big national organization that met in huge halls. By 1930, Muchow's Berlin network included nine hundred street cells organized into forty sections with 280 cell leaders. Many cells produced little newspapers intended for single city blocks.[32] They could speedily plaster their neighborhoods with posters and leaflets, generating on just two days' notice a packed house for a Nazi rally in the 18,000-seat Sports Palace, Berlin's largest indoor arena. Muchow's model was soon followed in other cities.

Throughout the 1930 campaign, Hitler continued to denounce "special interests." Yet Gregor Strasser was savvy enough to know that certain narrow interests had to be served if the Nazis' big-tent strategy was to attract key groups such as lawyers and doctors. Strasser created a meshwork of organizations designed to link affiliation groups—especially those in the middle class—to the Nazi movement. These included the National Socialist German Lawyers' League, the National Socialist German Doctors' League, and the National Socialist School Pupils' League, aimed at youngsters in Germany's college-prep high schools, the *Gymnasia*. These students were typically the children of the educated bourgeoisie, a notch above the proletarians in the Hitler Youth. The school pupils' league complemented the established National Socialist German Students' League, founded in 1926, focused on university students. Women were organized into the National Socialist Women's League.[33]

The Nazi Party also created a special department to attract farmers and reached out to Germans focused on outdoor activities, fitness training, and other hobbies. Embracing the popular enthusiasm for cars newly available for general purchase, the Nazis founded the National Socialist Automobile Club. At meetings of the Berlin chapter, the primary topics were mechanical issues, car racing, and motorcycle racing.[34] But the members were ready to assist the Nazis by ferrying Storm Troopers to rallies—sometimes in several towns on the same day. Darting around the countryside in cars and open vehicles fed the image of the Nazis as a dynamic, omnipresent political force. The automobile club effectively mechanized Nazi propaganda at no cost to the party.[35]

By mid-August of 1930, all the political parties were running at full tilt. Truckloads of Communists coursed through city streets waving large red flags, tossing out thousands of leaflets, and sporting large placards on the sides of their vehicles. The SPD sent out long wagons bearing immense billboards. Boys in short pants made the rounds with stacks of flyers; well-dressed men in fedoras tossed leaflets into the air. Mothers pushing baby carriages had information sheets pressed into their hands.[36]

A political frenzy was loose in the land.

29

HITLER ON THE HUSTINGS

Everything's cool.

—*Joseph Goebbels, 1930*

To mount his fervent wall-to-wall 1930 campaign, Hitler had to ricochet from corner to corner in a country considerably larger than the Germany that later generations would know. The nation stretched nearly one thousand miles from its southwestern fringe, on the Franco-Swiss border, to its northeastern extremity, on East Prussia's Baltic Sea coast. The Nazi Party leader traveled from Kiel, on the northern coast, to Breslau, in the southeastern depths of Silesia; from Cologne, in the Rhineland, to the cavernous arena of Berlin's Sports Palace; from Essen, in the heart of the Ruhr region, to Königsberg, in distant East Prussia (getting to East Prussia required crossing the hated Polish Corridor, mandated by the Treaty of Versailles; the corridor extended Poland's boundaries northward to the Baltic Sea, separating Danzig, an ethnically German city, from the rest of Germany).* While the Nazi foot soldiers recruited supporters one by one, Hitler swooped across the land, staging rallies for the multitudes and offering himself as the redemptive leader on whom they might pin their hopes.

Hitler was the Nazis' traveling prophet, thundering doomsayer, and self-styled savior. After the first three weeks of the seven-week campaign, he became hoarse. But he benefited from a new technology: loudspeakers. He quickly learned to stand three or four feet back from the microphones so that his declamatory rants, often rising to an angry shout, would not

* Today's Germany is 25 percent smaller. Defeat in the Second World War cost Germany East Prussia, Silesia, and most of Pomerania. Königsberg was lost to Russia; it is today's Kaliningrad. The greatest distance in Germany today, corner to corner, is 670 miles.

distort his words as they echoed across huge halls and great open spaces. "The loudspeaker was invented just at the right time for Hitler," noted Rudolf Hess.[1]

Hitler's campaign began to catch fire, drawing larger crowds than those of any other party's candidates: 10,000 in Hamburg, 12,000 in Essen, 15,000 in Cologne, 17,000 in Frankfurt-am-Main, 18,000 in Berlin, and an astonishing 25,000 in Breslau's Centennial Hall—with another 6,000 outdoors listening to loudspeakers.[2] At the Frankfurt-am-Main rally, Hitler preached the menace of decay and attacked "the system," a term for everything that ailed the Weimar Republic.[3] The "system" included those who supported the republican government as well as boogeymen such as Jewish businessmen. The "system" was broad, menacing, and completely vague: a useful demagogic device.[4]

The Frankfurters loved Hitler's performance, according to news reports. But one dismissive journalist from the elite Berlin-based Ullstein press service ridiculed the event as "nothing but a circus parade." He dismissed the attendees as people who "were satisfied with Hitler's politics of destruction."[5] Missing the power of the message, the newsman blamed Hitler's seemingly deplorable voters for liking it.

Even in a democratic election, Hitler was comfortable advocating dictatorship. Just twelve years earlier Germany had lived under a monarchy; the impulse for republican government had come from political leaders at the top rather than through revolution from the bottom. The new form of government—democracy—had never been fully accepted by many elements of German society, including parts of the military, the landed elite, the leadership class of the Wilhelmine bureaucracy, and fervent nationalists at all economic levels. To many in German society, authoritarian rule was not a preposterous idea; it seemed the right solution for an unstable situation. "In moments of greatest hardship, nations have always reached for dictatorship, not democracy," Hitler shouted to hearty applause in Munich. In Würzburg, a charming baroque town in Franconia, the Nazi leader flatly proposed the replacement ("by legal means") of the Weimar Republic with a strong-willed dictator.

Hitler rolled out elements of his worldview at various times and in various places. In Cologne, the heart of the Catholic Rhineland, Hitler rumbled in apocalyptic terms that Germany's downfall was at hand.[6] In the port city of Kiel, Hitler laid out the raw reasoning for his claim to "living space" in eastern Europe: "Land has been in a constant state of redistribution for millennia," he said. "It would be insane to suggest that this game is suddenly over—and that the current state of distribution is set forever." Existing borders were suddenly meaningless.

As usual, Hitler was notably imprecise on policies and programs. The Nazi platform was whatever swam in people's heads. "Here is our program in one sentence," said Goebbels. "Under National Socialism everything will be different."[7]

Sometimes Hitler waxed positive. He evoked a glowing picture of a thriving, ingenious Germany as proof that the country should be released from the servitude of postwar reparations and second-class status. "Wherever one looks in the world, our people stand at the pinnacle of the really useful achievements on earth," he told a packed house in Munich.[8] Conveniently, Hitler failed to mention that many of Germany's signal accomplishments had come from Jewish minds, including those of Nobel Prize winners Albert Einstein, Otto Fritz Meyerhof, and Gustav Hertz.

As the September election neared, Germany witnessed a peripatetic campaign the likes of which it had never seen. Hitler gave twenty-one speeches in seven weeks, greeted by one jubilant crowd after another. His listeners were chortling and cheering, getting their money's worth in political theater, riding the crest of shared schadenfreude and the frisson of protest politics. In industrial Essen, a steelworkers' and coal miners' town, Hitler fanned the anger of a roughshod audience that was spoiling for corporeal vengeance against the authors of all ills: Communists, Jews, big business. The crowd roared when Hitler issued a blunt endorsement of thuggish tactics. If five hundred Communists stormed the hall—filled with eight thousand Nazi supporters—Hitler said he would simply tell the police, "Leave this to us!"[9] Everyone in Hitler's audience knew what he meant, especially the young men no doubt rubbing brass knuckles in their pockets.

Though the Storm Troopers and other militias were officially unarmed, they always had blackjacks and other weapons at the ready. To forestall the threat of violence, President Hindenburg issued a ban on "the public carrying of weapons for hitting, stabbing, or beating." The state of Hesse, including Frankfurt-am-Main, Darmstadt, and Wiesbaden, prohibited marches, motorcades, and even bicycle parades by both Nazis and Communists.[10] Several states banned the Nazis from wearing their signature brown shirts. "Even if they take the shirts off our backs, they can't take out our hearts," shouted Hitler to his followers.

The Storm Troopers began sporting white shirts instead of brown shirts, sometimes with swastika armbands. The government could hardly outlaw the wearing of the most common color of men's shirts. The Storm Troopers' white-shirted brigades stood out even more than the brown shirts had before. The bleached shirts were quickly recognized as the new Storm Trooper uniform, a gesture of defiance.

Yet bloody clashes continued all around the country, especially between the Nazis and the Communists.

For all the Nazis' sound and fury, Germany's governing elites were far from silent. Though doubts about democracy were rampant, the men of the center-left fought back. On August 11, 1930, the eleventh anniversary of the 1919 adoption of the Weimar constitution, the voices of republicanism were raised in ceremonies throughout the country. Constitution Day was the closest thing Weimar Germany had to a national holiday. Berlin's Sports Palace was filled for a prodemocracy celebration that included the "Hallelujah" chorus from Handel's *Messiah* and the final choral movement from Beethoven's Ninth Symphony.[11] Afterward, a crowd estimated at several hundred thousand, stretching from the Berlin Cathedral to the Reichstag, held a prorepublic torchlight parade. Led by uniformed members of the Social Democratic Reichsbanner militia, the marchers formed a flickering human river for one and a half miles. The display took on near-religious fervor when, at 10:00 p.m., one hundred flag bearers emerged from the Reichstag's high-pillared main portal, passing beneath the famous inscription on the pediment, DEM DEUTSCHEN VOLKE (to the German people). The procession was followed by Reichstag president Paul Löbe, a Social Democrat. As if to tell the Nazis that they did not exclusively own the symbols of patriotism, the crowd launched into a mass singing of Germany's national anthem, with its opening line, "Deutschland, Deutschland, über alles." The crowd then raised a lusty "Heil!" to the German republic itself.

Hitler's spirited campaign—Nazis everywhere, speakers on every stump, literature flying through the air—hit a bump. Hitler and Goebbels were blindsided by an internal party revolt that threatened to cripple their campaign and derail their march to power. A key group of Storm Troopers in and around Berlin staged a mutiny. In late August of 1930, with the election campaign in full swing, they seized and trashed Goebbels's offices while he was out of town, overwhelming loyal SS troops who tried to defend the suite, leaving the SS men's blood on the gauleiter's furniture and carpets.

The rebellion had been led by a decorated former First World War officer named Walter Stennes. The uprising sprang from both petty grievances and political differences. The Storm Troopers were angry over their low pay in the face of profligate spending by the party bosses in Munich on luxuries such as the new party headquarters in a stately mansion. Stennes was furious that no Storm Troopers had been included on the Nazis' candidate list for the election. Like many Storm Trooper commanders, Stennes was tired of being relegated to strong-arm assignments and propaganda marches: he demanded political sway as well. He let Goebbels know he wanted three slots on the Nazi candidate list for his men.[12] "They want to give us an ultimatum—[parliamentary seats] or an attack on us," wrote Goebbels. "Right in the middle of the [election] battle. I can't believe it."

Hitler rushed to Berlin. Plunging into a round of hands-on peacemaking, the Nazi boss and Goebbels spent an evening running around the city to Nazi "storm pubs" and other Storm Trooper hangouts. Hitler was enthusiastically received everywhere, but the underlying mood was gloomy. "Everything is on a razor's edge," thought Goebbels. "On some points, the Storm Troopers are not totally wrong. Their financial demands are justified."

Stennes was summoned to Goebbels's apartment, where he and Hitler parleyed until 6:00 a.m. On the street outside, rebel Storm Trooper units chanted protest slogans. Sick at the prospect of losing the party's unprecedented campaign momentum, Goebbels counseled Hitler to meet the rebels' demands for the present but to deal with them more harshly after the election.

The next day Hitler announced increased funding for the Storm Troopers but also fired Franz Pfeffer von Salomon as head of the paramilitary group. In a bold stroke, the Nazi chief made himself the organization's supreme commander.[13] The Storm Troopers could no longer lament their status as the neglected stepchild; they had the attention of the party Führer himself. That evening Hitler made an emotional speech to two thousand of the uniformed men jammed into Berlin's Veterans Association Hall, a favorite political gathering place. Stennes read out the news of increased funding for their ranks.[14] Rising nearly to hysterics, Hitler announced that he, personally, was now their leader, triggering great jubilation, according to a police report.[15] In his practiced manner, Hitler called on his men to swear an oath of loyalty to him and his cause: "We shall at this moment declare that nothing can separate us, so help us God against all devils! May God bless our struggle!"

The men rose in a roar. Hitler invited an eighty-year-old war hero, General Karl Litzmann, a newly minted Nazi, onto the stage for the usual hand clasp and deep-in-the-eyes look.[16] Hitler's magic was still working.

Goebbels could finally exhale. "The end of the Stennes putsch... The rebellion has been suppressed," he wrote that night in his journal. "Everything's cool [*Alles ist Butter*]."[17]

30

TURNING POINT

National Socialism, with its promise of a community of blood, barring all class struggle, attracted me profoundly.

— *Railroad worker*

[Germans] are ready to try anything else for a change, even giving their support to [the Nazi Party], whose leaders and promises are irresponsible.

—*American diplomat*

What a disgrace! How close we are, really, to civil war!

— *Victor Klemperer, diarist*

For once, there is truth to the phrase: it's one minute to midnight.

— *Ernst Toller, political dramatist*

By election day—Sunday, September 14, 1930—Hitler's triumphal march through the provinces convinced him that he'd touched a political nerve; his movement felt revived. Four days before the ballots would be cast, he made a previctory speech in Berlin's Sports Palace. The big arena was filled to the rafters—Goebbels claimed that one hundred thousand supporters had tried to get tickets for the eighteen-thousand-seat hall. Swept up in the adoration of the crowds and now convinced that "the German people are awakening," Hitler waxed lyrical on his familiar theme of uniting Germans in a single political and social force:

> We are but small leaves on a great tree. The key is that our trunks must remain healthy and our nation must be as strong as it has been

> for millennia. If one takes the long view, all the petty class differences disappear. Then one sees people of the same blood in a single community and understands that this great mass must be vigorous for the whole nation to remain healthy and have a future life. There is only one way to overcome social differences—by giving people a great ideal that is higher than egoism.[1]

Hitler's idealized vision brought his followers to their feet. "The people went crazy," claimed Goebbels. "Victory is already in our pocket!"[2]

Germany had never seen an election of such intensity or violence. In street clashes with Communists, the Nazis claimed that forty-two of their men had been killed; the Communists claimed forty-four of their own had succumbed.[3] On the campaign's final day, a final spasm of violence by Nazis in front of the Communist headquarters in Berlin left two persons dead.[4] The police arrested 170 people.[5]

The stormy 1930 election campaign was all over but the voting.

On the morning of the election, Berlin's *Vossische Zeitung* printed a large black-bordered front-page box exhorting its readers to "Vote republican!" The newspaper was desperately promoting the survival of Germany's democracy: "Vote for progress, not overthrow! Vote for reason, not fanaticism! Vote for leaders (*Führer*) not seducers (*Verführer*)!" The play on words was clearly aimed at the Führer of the Nazi Party, though the newspaper just as vehemently opposed the antidemocratic Communists.

Aside from Hitler's and Goebbels's demagogic and hyperbolic prophecies, few analysts forecast a political earthquake. British ambassador Sir Horace Rumbold notified London to expect a Nazi take of perhaps fifty or sixty seats in the 577-seat Reichstag—a significant but not overwhelming increase from their twelve seats in the last parliament. Even Goebbels privately predicted that the Nazis would win only forty or fifty seats—a satisfying leap from 2.6 percent to 8 or 9 percent of the vote. Even that, he insisted, would be a great victory: "Our reward for years of work and worry."[6]

Observers in the German political establishment confidently anticipated a centrist election outcome that would thwart the extremes of left and right—the Communists and the Nazis. "Despite the customary exchange of acerbities which has marked the campaign rhetoric of the past two weeks," noted the *New York Times,* "negotiations for the consummation of a 'Socialist-Bourgeois' government are already under way."[7]

Commentators from the liberal-left publications had no feel for the popular impact of the Nazis' frenzied campaigning. The Nazis were a "noisy presence with absolutely no future," wrote Carl von Ossietzky, editor of the leftist weekly *Die Weltbühne.*[8] The *Berliner Tageblatt*'s respected chief editor, Theodor Wolff, dismissed Hitler's movement as a "society of incompetents." Even if the Nazis did well in this election, argued Wolff, they would experience only transitory success: "The crown worn by the kings of the rabble-rousers will slip, and Herr Hitler will fade into the sunset."[9]

Election turnout was enormous. At 82 percent, voter participation was the highest since 1919; more than thirty-five million Germans voted. Polling places were swamped, and so were the cafés, restaurants, pubs, and beer gardens that always filled up after people cast their ballots in Germany (always on a Sunday). In Berlin, from morning to night, the political electricity crackled. "At every moment of the day, in the neighborhoods of the city center, the north and the east, the propagandistic activity never relented," wrote a French reporter. Men wearing sandwich boards with party slogans crowded the sidewalks. Nazi trucks carrying long party banners cruised the city, filled with young Nazis bellowing, "Deutschland erwache!" (Germany, awaken!). In working-class districts, the Communists rode around shouting, "Red Front!"[10] A striking number of women were voting, noted an observer.

In the capital's newspaper quarter, around Kochstrasse, people craned their necks to watch election results projected on a high screen. "It was no time for joking," wrote the French journalist. "A group of children dressed all in red passed by, accompanied by a dog holding a poster between its teeth that read, 'Vote for the Communists'—but nobody laughed."[11]

Hitler stayed in Munich. On election day, he calmed his nerves by going to a play during the early part of the evening. But then his *Völkischer*

Beobachter printer, Adolf Müller, showed up with early returns suggesting that the Nazis might win sixty or seventy seats. "If the German people have any sense, they must give me more than sixty," said a superconfident Hitler—or so he recalled many years later (possibly embellishing his recollection). He added, "I was thinking to myself: suppose we win one hundred seats! One hundred seats at a stroke! Müller sprang for a round of drinks at that idea."[12]

By midevening, it became clear that Hitler's wild notion would become reality. Germans watched with mounting surprise as news tickers and telephone reports tacked up astonishing gains for the Nazis and the Communists—and losses for nearly everyone else. By late evening, it was obvious that Germany had been hit by a political tsunami. The biggest winners were the Nazis.

Shockingly, the Nazi Party's share of the national vote had surged from 2.6 percent in 1928 to 18.3 percent in 1930. The Nazis had made a quantum leap forward, winning 6.4 million votes in 1930 compared to only 810,000 votes in 1928. That translated into 107 of the 577 seats in the new parliament—twice as many seats as Hitler and Goebbels had forecast in their giddiest moments before the election.[13] These results made the Nazis the second-largest political party in Germany after the Social Democrats (who garnered 24.5 percent of the vote and 143 seats). The Munich firebrand had now passed through the looking glass of plausibility; he was contending seriously for the leadership of Germany.

To modern ears, 18 percent of the vote may not sound like a lot—until one considers that nearly forty parties had run in the election and fifteen had made it into the new Reichstag.[14] With their nearly 25 percent, the Social Democrats were still number one, but their vote share had dropped five points from 1928. Hitler would need only two million more votes to overtake the SPD. In third place were the Communists, with 13.1 percent (77 seats), up by nearly three points from the last election.

Hitler's Nazi Party had swamped Hugenberg's German National People's Party (DNVP), which lost two million votes, falling from 14 percent to only 7 percent of the vote (41 seats). That gave Hitler a clear hold over the far-right antidemocratic nationalists. All others—especially the middle-class parties in the moderate center of German politics—had lost votes, in some cases dramatically so. Most stunning was the collapse of the late Gustav Stresemann's German People's Party (DVP), which sacrificed nearly half of its following and failed to crack 5 percent. The Nazis had drawn voters from all these parties, including one-third of habitual DNVP voters (Hugenberg's people) and, astonishingly, 10 percent of SPD voters.[15]

To some Germans, Hitler's appeal lay in his assurance of a magical solution to the Depression misery, including vague promises of full employment. "Most of those who joined the Nazis did so because they wanted a radical answer to the economic problem," said Lower Saxony resident Erhardt Knorpel. "Then, too, people wanted a hard, sharp, clear leadership—they were disgusted with the eternal political strife of parliamentary party politics."[16] Despite Hitler's railings against Social Democrats, some voters were drawn to the "socialist" part of the Nazi Party's name. "We believed the common people should have a better life and that socialism was essential," said one impassioned woman. "We were idealists."[17]

Among Germans committed to the struggling parliamentary system, the most depressing number was 37—the percentage of voters who had cast ballots for three parties that opposed democracy altogether. The Nazis, the Communists, and Hugenberg's nationalists all favored authoritarian government; together they captured more than thirteen million votes. That meant that well over one-third of German voters had given up on the republican enterprise; they associated democracy with disorder and economic failure. Some folks who resisted the extremes of Hitler's ideology were simply overwhelmed by events. "It was the depression and business was bad," remembered Kurt Zeisser, whose father owned a small-town print shop. "The Nazis used to ask my father for contributions, and he refused. As a consequence, he lost business. So he joined the Nazi party. But this lost him other customers, so he was discouraged by the whole situation. He probably wouldn't have joined of his own choice."[18]

With the traditional Prussian class structures still intact, giving the military and the aristocratic landholders outsize influence in public life and politics, nationalism was on the rise. The Weimar Republic was becoming a democracy without democrats, a nation slouching toward a dramatic shift. The body politic was radicalizing—in both directions, right and left, leaving the center without strength and energy. "[Germans] are ready to try anything else for a change, even giving their support to [the Nazi Party], whose leaders and promises are irresponsible," wrote one American diplomat.[19] A British military attaché pessimistically noted that Hitler had successfully tapped into the dynamism of the German Youth Movement, with its nature-based idealism and romantic nationalism. "It can't be stopped," he wrote.[20]

At a stroke, Hitler had leaped from the fringe of German politics to the center of the national discussion. Set back on their heels, the other parties—and especially the government of Chancellor Brüning—knew they would somehow have to deal with the fierce new political presence in their midst with its rising radical star, Hitler. The left-liberal political establishment was apoplectic. "A black day for Germany," wrote Count Harry Kessler, calling the election "a delirium of the German lower middle class [that can] bring ruin on Germany and Europe for decades to come."[21] Others were simply perplexed. The *Frankfurter Zeitung* described Hitler's upset victory as a "bitterness election"—a howl of discontent from a disaffected people who had been goaded into a mood of angry protest.[22] Some fell into the trap of name-calling. Kurt Tucholsky, a star writer for *Die Weltbühne*, dismissed Hitler as "an upstart Mongolian" and a mere "house painter." Editor Carl von Ossietzky labeled Hitler a "nowhere fool" and a "half-insane rascal."[23]

But some recognized the Nazi upsurge as a serious menace. "One hundred seven National Socialists [in parliament]—what a disgrace!" wrote Victor Klemperer, a Jewish-born professor at the Technical University of Dresden. "How close we are, really, to civil war!"[24] Dramatist Ernst Toller, a far-left activist who in 1919 had led Bavaria's short-lived Socialist republic and then spent five years in prison, saw clearly: "Chancellor Hitler is waiting just outside the gates of Berlin. For once, there is truth to the phrase: it's one minute to midnight."[25]

Who were Hitler's voters? How did he septuple his vote in just two years? Where did his supporters come from?

These questions have concerned researchers for decades. For at least a generation of post–Second World War historians, the prevailing theory was that Hitler's support came predominantly from the middle and lower-middle classes. Small shop owners, small farmers, and small businessmen were considered most receptive to the Nazi leader's message. But subsequent research showed that, in fact, Hitler's supporters stemmed from all segments of society.[26] They ranged from blue-collar workers to a smattering of educated professionals—the mark of a catchall party of protest.[27] The Nazis' greatest gains came in the Protestant and agrarian regions of the northern and far eastern provinces, not in the Catholic south or Rhineland west. The cattle farmers and potato growers of Schleswig-Holstein, the northernmost state, gave Hitler 27 percent of their vote, up from a mere 4 percent in 1928.

The 1930 election's high turnout also benefited the Nazis. Four million more Germans voted than in 1928. Frenzied campaigning by Hitler and his far-flung troops helped drive the excitement, especially among first-time voters. Crisscrossing the land like an avenging hero, Hitler morphed into a matinee idol to many young women and men.

Exit polling did not exist in 1930, but a 1934 survey of Nazi Party members by Columbia University sociologist Theodore Abel suggested certain trends that help explain Hitler's surprise election successes.[28] Abel's research consisted of an essay contest approved by Goebbels. Abel asked willing Nazi participants to write about themselves and why they joined the Nazi Party. First prize was a whopping 125 marks; fifth prize was 10 marks. More than six hundred Nazis responded with personal essays, ranging from one page to eighty pages in length—some handwritten, some typed. The research model is obviously flawed by modern standards. It is not randomized; the participants were self-selected and may have wanted to please the Nazi leadership. Nonetheless, the essayists' comments, along with subsequent analysis by scholars such as political scientist Peter H. Merkl, shed light on the parts of Hitler's message that appealed to voters.

Hitler's aspirational rhetoric about a "national community" that included all elements of German society, excluded all non-Germans, and subordinated private gain to the public good apparently had significant impact.

The notion of a classless society clearly appealed to those disadvantaged by class. "Why was there such a thing as higher classes with so many privileges?" asked Gustav Heinsch, the Berlin house servant who became a Nazi convert precisely because he discovered in Hitler's rhetoric a "true people's community."[29] A former Communist, an electrician, declared that after reading Hitler's speeches and reconsidering his views, "I was politically reborn."[30]

Hitler's attacks on "the system" appealed to some. Two-thirds of the respondents in Abel's 1934 sample cited Hitler's strong anti-Marxism as an important reason they had been attracted to the party in 1930 and in subsequent elections. "The slogan 'Workers of the world, unite!' made no sense to me," remembered one Nazi. "National Socialism, with its promise of a community of blood, barring all class struggle, attracted me profoundly."[31]

For some Nazi converts, the sense of comradeship in hard postwar times was the draw. "While I was an apprentice, I met young people who practiced marches and sang martial songs on Saturday afternoons and Sundays," wrote Hermann Jung, a carpenter from Kaiserslautern. "My enthusiasm for the comradeship that I experienced as a seventeen-year-old among these groups knew no bounds.... During campouts or bivouacs, we would be taught the basics of the Führer's thinking by older comrades."[32]

Critically, the Nazis who participated in the 1934 study cited "the content of the speeches" as the key factor that brought them into the Nazi Party. While some had been "swept off [their] feet" by the marching music and the hoopla of the Nazi mass meetings, most new party members claimed to have been persuaded primarily by what they heard and learned. Frustrated upward mobility was a common socioeconomic factor—especially among those forced by depressed circumstances to move from the countryside to a city.[33]

Hitler's 1930 election turnaround landed in the outside world like a bombshell. FASCISTS MAKE BIG GAINS IN GERMANY was the alarmed lead headline in the *New York Times* on September 15. Germany's bourgeoisie had been defeated by "the cry for a dictator" who would lead the country out of the slough of parliamentary despond, wrote Berlin correspondent Guido Enderis. The rise of the Nazis, he noted, constituted "one of the most upsetting developments" of German postwar politics.[34] The Associated Press reported that the landslide of "Fascist and Communist votes shook the foundations of parliamentary government in Germany." In Paris, *Le Figaro* wrote: "The success of M. Hitler's party confounded all predictions."[35] Blindsided by Hitler's somersault to a top political spot in Europe's largest and most troublesome country, financial markets reacted with a dramatic sell-off by international investors, especially on the German stock market.[36]

Diplomats at a League of Nations conference in Geneva talked of nothing but the German election. Coincidentally, the German dirigible *Graf Zeppelin* landed on election day at the Swiss city's airport, where its crew enjoyed a Champagne reception and cheers from tens of thousands of Swiss spectators.[37] Longer than two American football fields, the massive blimp was a striking example of technological superiority and a source of growing worldwide admiration for Germany.[38] But by evening, as the German election returns rolled in, a sour mood seized the international delegations. French foreign minister Aristide Briand, a self-declared friend of the late Gustav Stresemann, pronounced himself "personally hurt" by the results. Briand abruptly cut off scheduled talks with Germany over economic issues, sending his delegation back to Paris. German foreign minister Julius Curtius reported to Berlin that the improved Franco-German relations of recent years had just gone into a deep freeze. The conference ended with Briand's final commentary on the turbulent, violence-laced German election: "Ah! Quels cris de haine! Quels cris de mort!" (What cries of hatred! What shouts of murder!)[39]

But not all the world viewed Hitler's political breakthrough as an unmitigated disaster. Some quarters in British public life that had promoted reconciliation with Germany now embraced the upstart force that seemed to be reshaping the country's politics. The most astonishing reaction came from Lord Rothermere, a conservative monarchist who owned the populist *Daily Mail*, with more than one million readers. The press baron, born Harold Harmsworth in 1868 and later given the title 1st

Viscount Rothermere, frothed: "A new Germany is rising before our eyes.... [Hitler] is erecting a strengthened bulwark against Bolshevism." The apparently smitten British press lord loved the idea of another Mussolini on the European continent who would preserve "Western civilization" from an onslaught from the East.[40]

Hitler could not get enough of Rothermere's bear hug. He reprinted the British magnate's full essay in the *Völkischer Beobachter.* He invited the *Daily Mail*'s Rothay Reynolds for an interview. "Hitler spoke with great simplicity and with great earnestness," reported Reynolds, echoing his boss's embrace of the Nazi leader. "He is conscious that he possesses the rare quality of leadership." Hitler, in turn, laid on thick praise of Rothermere and used the convenient platform to issue a warning to Europe:

> What Lord Rothermere has made English people understand is that Germany must have the same rights as other countries after being 12 years in the penitentiary of Versailles. If Europe decides to make Germany serve a life sentence [by paying fifty-eight years of reparations under the Young Plan], then she must face the danger of having an embittered nation, desperate to the verge of crime, in her midst. A child can figure out what that would mean—Bolshevism.... To have a strong party in Germany which will form a bulwark against Bolshevism is in the interests not only of England but of all nations.[41]

The brash Rothermere had put himself at odds with most British newspapers and the political establishment. He rushed into print again, denouncing his critics as "pompous pundits who pontificate" for publications "whose sales and influence alike sink steadily month by month towards [the] vanishing point." Rothermere made one concession to his detractors: the Nazis should follow Mussolini's example and get anti-Semitism out of their program. "Jew-baiting is a stupid survival of medieval practice," he wrote.[42]

The *Daily Mail* was not the only British publication interested in hearing from Hitler. The *Sunday Express,* another high-circulation British newspaper, took the extraordinary step of giving Hitler more than a page of space for a long essay.[43] "My Terms to the World" was the article's assertive headline. Hitler waved the flag of coming disaster, claiming Europe faced a choice of him or the deluge. "Germany will either have to become a free nation again or, by losing faith in any other future, be driven into the beckoning arms of Bolshevism," he wrote. The Nazi leader also brandished the specter of the German beast unleashed, claiming that his country was in a state of "high fever." The world should beware "the coming revolt of the German soul," he wrote. "The shock and surprise of the election is nothing [compared] to the shock and the surprise that is coming."

Germany's Jews were naturally horrified by the sudden turn of events. "Our first feeling as cultured people is one of deep shame," wrote the Jewish weekly *Jüdisch-liberale Zeitung.* "Is it comprehensible that six and a half million German voters let themselves be led into madness by one party's 'rat catcher' melodies?"* Published by reform Jews and written from a culturally German point of view, the newspaper challenged Hitler's claim to be building a "national community." Though religiously Jewish, the editorialists considered themselves thoroughly German: "After this election, it's every German Jew's duty to make a greater effort than before to cultivate relationships with non-Jews," they wrote.[44]

If the Jewish community was in shock, Jews as individuals were confused by the unexpected rise of the radicals. "Most people from a Jewish background are fully disoriented," noted Thea Sternheim, a non-Jewish author, in her diary.[45] Even Bella Fromm, a society and diplomatic writer for the *Vossische Zeitung* whose hand would soon be kissed by Hitler, was flummoxed.[46] As a fully assimilated Jew, she'd never considered forsaking Germany, but now the question was upon her: "Should one leave Germany and wait outside to see what will happen?"[47] A "suitcase-packing mood" arose in the Jewish-owned companies Ullstein and Mosse, publishers of the *Vossische Zeitung* as well as the *Berliner Tageblatt,* the *Berliner Zeitung,* the *B.Z. am Mittag,* and others.[48]

* "Rat catcher"—*Rattenfänger*—is usually translated into English as "Pied Piper." In this context, a literal translation better captures the idiom.

One Jew took an oddly naive view of Hitler's sudden success. Cogitating from his prestigious perch at the Prussian Academy of Sciences, Nobel Prize–winning physicist Albert Einstein, Germany's most famous scientist and best-known Jew, reasoned that there was no cause for despair. "The Hitler vote is only a symptom, not necessarily of anti-Jewish hatred but of momentary resentment caused by economic misery and unemployment within the ranks of misguided German youth. . . . I hope that as soon as the situation improves the German people will also find their road to clarity."[49]

Within three years Einstein would flee his German fatherland for America.

31

HEARTS AND MINDS

All of a sudden we are "respectable."

—Rudolf Hess in a letter to his parents, 1930

Hitler had become a credible competitor for power. Germany's future governing structure—democracy or authoritarianism—was still undecided, and Hitler was the wild card. At the Circus Krone two days after the 1930 election, the Nazi leader took a giddy victory lap. Touting his "great win," the party chief mocked those who had thought they could halt the Nazi movement with the silent treatment.[1] Surprisingly, Hitler opened a rare window on his own feelings. As an Austrian high school dropout, he had keenly sensed the condescension of the German social and governing elite. By birth, by class, and by manners, he had been excluded from their ranks. Now his political breakthrough had ended a period of self-doubt. The time of being ignored—"the bitterest period in the life of any individual"—was over, said Hitler. He had crashed the party and done it with the tools of democracy, assisted by demagoguery and bursts of violence.

In the German capital, all was uncertain. Chancellor Heinrich Brüning was still running a caretaker government with a "presidential" cabinet—he derived his governing powers not from parliament but from President Hindenburg's willingness to sign emergency decrees drafted by the cabinet. Operating without parliamentary legitimacy but also without significant pushback from the Reichstag, Brüning intended to hold on to his office and keep Hitler out. The best Hitler could hope for were ministerial seats in the Brüning administration. But the chancellor adamantly refused to consider bringing the Nazis into his government as a way of taming the party's threat. "No; never; under no circumstances!" he said, dismissing the Nazi upsurge as "a temporary fever."[2]

In fact, the Nazis were more like a rambunctious elephant. Tantalized by the notion that he might soon be part of the government, Hitler played the respectability card. He called on pillars of the establishment such as Wilhelm Cuno, a former chancellor who was now head of the booming Hamburg-America Line. Cuno harbored hopes of succeeding the aging and ailing Hindenburg as Germany's president. Hitler, in turn, hoped Cuno could boost the Nazi Party into a place in the new cabinet. Visiting the shipping magnate in Hamburg, Hitler assured him that Nazi economic policies would represent no threat to free enterprise. He also insisted that there would be no violent persecution of Jews in a coming Third Reich, only efforts to reduce the "Jewish predominance in the state."[3] Cuno couldn't help Hitler into a coalition cabinet, but he gave the Nazi leader his seal of approval by arranging for him to speak again to Hamburg's National Club of 1919, the closed circle of the city's conservative elite.

The bumptious election campaign was over, but German democracy was effectively paralyzed. Mainstream politicians were torn between embracing and shunning the Nazis. Some conservative nationalists argued for easing the Nazis into positions of responsibility to aid "national regeneration." Trying to ignore and exclude the Nazis would backfire, they feared. They recalled Chancellor Otto von Bismarck's attempt in the late nineteenth century to strangle the Social Democratic movement by exclusion and banning under a set of "Socialist laws." The Iron Chancellor's strategy had failed abysmally; the SPD had grown to become Germany's largest political party.

The dramatically altered postelection atmosphere was captured in a letter by Rudolf Hess to his parents, who lived in Egypt:

> You can't imagine how the situation in our movement and especially with Hitler himself has shifted literally overnight. All of a sudden we are "respectable." People who used to keep considerable distance from Hitler now "must" have a meeting with him. The domestic and

> foreign press is beating down our doors; we get telegrams from America offering money for a one-hundred-word reply; phone calls from London. They all moan terribly when Hitler instructs us to tell them that he is not available. Leaders of industry are secretly asking for meetings. Not to mention all those who write or somehow let us know that they "*always* really personally supported our movement."[4]

Hitler's dream seemed to be coming true. He had survived so many brushes with political death: the failed 1923 putsch; his 1924 conviction for treason and year in prison; the 1926 renegade challenge of the Northwestern Working Group; the 1928 election disaster; Otto Strasser's 1930 apostasy and departure from the party with several thousand followers; the 1930 Storm Troopers' revolt, led by Walter Stennes. Any of these challenges could have ended Hitler's march to power. He had overcome each setback, however, and lived to fight his way to a surprise victory.

All the world was now listening to Hitler's every utterance. People wanted to know how he would play his hand as leader of Germany's second-largest party. Hitler reveled in proving to the world—and to doubters in his own party—that he could come to power through the ballot box, "by legal means," as he constantly put it. A few days after the election, the Nazi Führer had a chance to make his point again and to do it on a unique platform. His venue would be not Berlin or Munich but Leipzig, the home of Germany's Supreme Court.

On the morning of September 25, 1930, thousands of exuberant citizens jammed the streets in front of Leipzig's cupola-domed Reichsgericht, the German high court.[5] The raucous scene resembled a political rally more than a courthouse appearance: it suited Hitler's belief in politics as a permanent campaign, a never-ending struggle. Arriving at 9:00 a.m.—he had just traveled the 120 miles south from Berlin—the Nazi leader was hailed as a conquering hero. On the Supreme Court steps, he gave the crowd his raised-arm salute, triggering a roar that could be heard deep into the massive building.

The peripatetic Hitler had come not to make a speech but to give testimony. He had been called as a defense witness in the trial of three Reichswehr officers accused of conspiracy to commit treason by overthrowing the state. In the course of their plotting, the officers—all described as hotheads by their own attorney—had visited Nazi Party headquarters in Munich in an amateurish effort to recruit fellow putschists.[6] Hitler was called to the stand to show that the accused officers could hardly have conspired with a nonrevolutionary party to start a revolution. The Nazi leader's motives for testifying were, of course, political, not legal. He welcomed yet another national stage where he could proclaim his purity. Calling Hitler to the stand had been the idea of Hans Frank, the lawyer for the three officers, who was also Hitler's personal attorney and sometime confidant. The courtroom setting, with its dark wood paneling and black-robed judge, was dignified—a perfect podium for a political statement. The national and international press were in attendance.

Knowing Hitler's reputation for political peroration and courtroom grandstanding, the chief judge, Alexander Baumgarten, warned the Nazi leader not to make "a multihour propaganda speech for your party."

Yet within minutes of taking the witness stand, Hitler launched into a tutorial on the Nazi philosophy. He began with his usual lament about Germans denying "our own inner racial strength." Though twice admonished by the judge, Hitler managed to turn the courtroom into a political soapbox, just as he had done at his own 1924 treason trial. "In three years we will be the strongest party," Hitler continued, predicting a Nazi leap from 107 to 250 parliamentary seats.[7] In his long-winded presentation, he was trying to make points with the German military establishment—an institution so powerful it was often labeled "a state within the state." Calling the Reichswehr "the most important instrument in reestablishing the German state and the German people," the Nazi leader dismissed the idea of a Nazi-sponsored putsch. Joining with the three defendants to displace the German army would be "madness" and "the greatest imaginable crime," he said.

Hitler's rhetoric worked.[8] He endeared himself to skeptics such as forty-year-old Major Alfred Jodl. A Reichswehr officer who would later become deputy commander of Germany's armed forces during the Second World War, Jodl said that his original strong opposition to Hitler was reversed by the Nazi leader's passionate Leipzig testimony.

Despite Hitler's disclaimers, Judge Baumgarten wanted to know about the Nazi chief's questionable past statements. How could he purport to be pursuing politics strictly by "legal means" when he had also threatened "revolutionary" revenge? The jurist cited Hitler's predictions that, during the struggle for power in Germany, heads would "roll in the sand, either ours or those of others."

The judge's challenge triggered not contrition or dissembling but a flash of Hitlerian fire. If his movement succeeded, said Hitler, the Nazis would convene a people's tribunal that would exact retribution from the "November criminals of 1918" who had staged the German revolution and brought the country to its current miserable state.

He repeated the words: "Heads will roll in the sand."[9]

A shudder must have rippled through the courtroom. Hitler's lurid language conjured guillotines and beheadings in a new Nazi-run state. The Nazi chief's true believers loved it. "Bravo!" they shouted, only to be admonished by the judge.

Hitler was having it both ways. His show of respect for the army and claim of adherence to electoral "legality" sent mollifying messages to the military and to polite society. But his pitiless threat of beheadings on public squares fed red meat to his belligerent base. As Hitler left the Supreme Court, an enthusiastic follower pressed a posy of flowers into his hands.[10]

The Leipzig performance put Hitler all over the front pages again. *Die Weltbühne*'s Carl von Ossietzky faulted the high court for not interrupting Hitler's "guillotine fantasies." The liberal editor exhorted supporters of the Weimar Republic to "cease sticking their heads into the very sand where their heads will soon roll, according to Hitler's pronunciamiento."[11] London's *Daily Herald* called Hitler's courtroom antics "the boasting of an unbalanced man."[12] Two Paris dailies put Hitler's intemperate remarks and photos from Leipzig on their front pages. The *New York Times*'s page 1 story recounted Hitler's grisly description of German political leaders' heads being lopped off by "a guillotine functioning after approved historic precedent"—evoking tumbrels, drums, and blood in the sand.[13]

The second-strongest party in Germany had again seized the world's attention. The German stock market sagged anew. The Leipzig sideshow had given curious observers a vivid glimpse of a Nazi future. "That's just fine!" wrote Goebbels that night in his diary. "Our day of fulfillment is that much closer."[14]

Though now inside the political system, Hitler had still not gained access to the levers of power. He sent word to Chancellor Brüning's camp that he would be willing to join a governing "coalition with three members"—but without specifying which third party he had in mind.[15] When he heard nothing back, Hitler put out feelers to other parties, but none was interested in forming a cabinet with the Nazis. Chancellor Brüning had negotiated a cease-fire with the Social Democrats; the SPD agreed to "tolerate" his minority government without actually joining it. Brüning would enjoy at least a show of support for most of his policies and have a firewall against a parliamentary vote of no confidence.

But given Hitler's ostentatious embrace of legality over revolution during the Leipzig trial, Brüning felt obliged to meet with him in secret on October 5.[16] Arriving sub rosa after dark at the home of politician Gottfried Treviranus, Hitler, accompanied by Gregor Strasser and Wilhelm Frick, sat down to tea with Brüning. The chancellor's goal was not to offer a coalition deal to Hitler but to obtain his support for a domestic austerity program. Holding the purse strings tight, argued Brüning, was essential to securing a $125 million international loan, desperately needed to keep Germany solvent. Hitler should act as the loyal opposition, said the chancellor, and throttle his constant harangues about fully canceling Germany's reparations debts.

Instead of winning Hitler to their version of political and fiscal reality, though, Brüning and Treviranus got an hourlong lecture in the Nazi's signature style. It was "as if he were addressing a mass rally," remembered Brüning. "After a quarter of an hour... his voice was getting louder and louder." Brüning was struck by the violence in Hitler's monologue, especially the frequent use of the word "annihilate" (*vernichten*). The targets of his annihilation included the Communists, the Socialists, France, and Russia. By now, Brüning had got it: with Hitler, it was always "first power, then politics."[17]

To the outside world, the chief question was what Hitler would do in the realm of foreign policy if he came to power. Not that Hitler had ever disguised his aggressive intentions toward Russia: he had been speaking of "land and soil" in the East since the early 1920s, of "living space" on Russian territory since 1924, and of Germany's need to find space in the East for "twenty million too many people" throughout the 1930 election campaign. Only now were observers outside Germany beginning to take his blathering seriously.

To address rampant curiosity about the rising Nazi, the *New York Times* ran a detailed Associated Press analysis based on *Mein Kampf*—whose sales had recently picked up. The *Times*'s headline read: CONQUEST OF RUSSIA ONE AIM OF HITLER. No one knew how Hitler planned to realize that aim.[18] What exactly would happen if Hitler became Germany's chancellor?

The German parliament convened for its first session following the seismic 1930 election on October 13. Among the 577 deputies were, for the first time, more than one hundred Nazis. With shouts and catcalls, they turned the Reichstag's opening ceremony into a mockery of parliamentary decorum. For starters, they violated standing rules by wearing their brown-shirted uniforms into the chamber, looking like an overgrown troop of Boy Scouts and provoking laughter from the other deputies.[19] With Goebbels egging them on, they bellowed "Heil Hitler!" throughout the roll call. Most of the Nazis were first-timers in a legislative body. Bringing their street manners into the parliament, they provoked the Communist deputies into a shouting contest that came within inches of a brawl. Speaking from the podium, Gregor Strasser said: "Right now we support the constitution [and] we support the Weimar democracy... as long as it suits us." The burly Nazi added: "And on democratic grounds we will demand all positions of power—and then keep them as long as we wish."[20]

"Second-rate theatrics," groused the *Vossische Zeitung*. "Dr. Goebbels should have known that tricks and gestures that work in the Sports Palace fall flat or look ridiculous in the Reichstag."[21]

Outside, the drama was worse. Emboldened by their new political standing, hundreds of Hitler's roughneck followers went on a rampage. They attacked Jewish stores and a café; they forced the nearby Jewish-owned newspapers *Berliner Tageblatt* and *Vossische Zeitung* to lower their window shutters for protection. Swinging at anything in their path, the rioters smashed all street-level display windows at the elegant Jewish-owned Tietz department store. "A little foretaste of the Third Reich," said one of the Nazi rowdies.[22]

For their excesses, the Nazis earned an international black eye. A large photo of the parliamentary uproar appeared on the front page of Paris's *Le Matin,* which called the session a "grotesque comedy."[23] The *New York Times* described the four hours of smash-and-dash on Berlin's streets as a "virtual reign of terror."[24] Around midnight, Count Harry Kessler wandered to the scene of the rioting and was disgusted: "Such pig-headed stupidity and meanness makes me want to vomit."[25]

The man behind it all stayed out of sight. As a stateless person—no longer an Austrian but still not naturalized as a German—Hitler was unable to run for office or enter the Reichstag chamber. Holed up at the Hotel Sanssouci, just a few blocks from the tumult, Hitler followed events closely. After the rioting, he sent word that he condemned the vandalism.[26] He told a journalist that the street actions "had nothing to do with our movement"—though police records showed that nearly all the one hundred persons arrested were Nazis or Nazi sympathizers. Hitler was again portraying himself as a man of reason who denounced violent excesses while letting his supporters send a forceful message to his base: here's what we have in mind for Jews and big capitalists.

Hitler continued to use the Anglo-American press to invoke the Marxist menace and portray his motives as pure. In interviews, he claimed that Germany was "like a powder keg that could be ignited by a single spark." The Nazi leader only wanted for Germany what Americans wanted for America—"a German Monroe Doctrine," he said. "We want Germany for the Germans, just as Americans want America for Americans."[27]

Three days after the turbulent Reichstag opening, Thomas Mann, Germany's leading writer and cultural icon, delivered a scathing denunciation of Hitler and his party. In a speech at Berlin's gilded Beethoven Hall, Mann—the author of *The Magic Mountain, Buddenbrooks,* and other works that had won him the 1929 Nobel Prize in Literature—denounced Hitler as a "grotesque" politician who favored "Salvation Army–style affectations" such as fairground-stall bell ringing and "mass fits" until everyone was "frothing at the mouth."[28] That Mann, a pillar of bourgeois respectability, would find Hitler offensive was unsurprising. More shocking was the renowned author's suggested remedy: desert the faltering middle-class parties and support the Social Democrats. A natural conservative, Mann typified the wealth and inherited privilege that was antithetical to Socialist history and doctrine. But he was telling his Beethoven Hall audience—like him, members of the haute bourgeoisie—to drop their antipathy for a working-class movement and join the Weimar Republic in forming a bulwark against the greater evil, the Nazis. Noting that the Social Democrats had consistently backed the "great" Gustav Stresemann's efforts to achieve German equality in the world, Mann argued that this party of the workers represented German interests in the broadest sense. Mann put himself in the company of the country's "rational republicans" (*Vernunftrepublikaner*), who embraced the republic not out of love of democracy or moral conviction but out of recognition that no reasonable alternatives existed.

Goebbels tried to derail Mann's message. He arranged to salt the Beethoven Hall audience with Nazi hecklers. The police were summoned, and the hecklers were ejected, drawing even more attention to the famous author's speech. Goebbels was furious. "Our people spat on Thomas Mann's head," he wrote in his diary. "[He called us] barbarians!"[29] The *Völkischer Beobachter* denounced Mann's oration as "an advertisement for the Marxists."[30]

Coasting on his new political celebrity, Hitler delivered speeches all over Germany. He kept the Nazis on the front pages and helped achieve electoral successes in local and regional elections. A rush of new Nazi Party membership applications forced the Munich headquarters to add a late shift—6:00 p.m. to 11:00 p.m.—to handle all the paperwork.[31] Nazi Party enrollment expanded to 389,000 members by year's end.[32]

Still, the Nazis' political future remained unsettled. The Storm Troopers were spoiling for trouble. They held frequent events to ridicule Chancellor Brüning's ban on their brown uniforms. Trim and spiffy in white shirts with ties, the Storm Troopers marched in military-style formations under a mocking banner that read: THE SHEEP ARE BAAING AND COWS ARE LAUGHING BECAUSE OUR BROWN SHIRTS THREATEN THE STATE. (In German, the lines rhyme in an amusing doggerel: "Es blökt das Schaf/ Es lacht das Rind/ Weil Hemden staatsgefährlich sind.")[33]

In December of 1930 Goebbels smelled an event ripe for exploitation—the opening in Berlin of the American movie *All Quiet on the Western Front.* Based on German writer Erich Maria Remarque's wildly successful but controversial novel, the antiwar film offered a withering portrayal of trench warfare during the First World War. Pitilessly realistic, the movie included bayonets to the belly and soldiers descending into shell shock. Remarque's narrative subverted the myth of frontline heroism and comradeship, a central tenet of Nazi lore and of Hitler's self-styled soldierly persona. Though the movie won the Academy Award for Best Picture in 1930, Hitler, Goebbels, and many other German nationalists bitterly denounced it and tried to block its showing in Germany.

When *All Quiet* nonetheless opened in Berlin to a full house on a Thursday night, it was received with quiet and sober reflection. "No movie has ever had such a direct impact on an audience," wrote a reviewer.[34] Goebbels had something else in mind for the following night. The Berlin gauleiter arranged for Nazis—including many Storm Troopers—to buy up large blocks of tickets. Goebbels took a seat in the balcony's first row as the film began. During a scene in which bedraggled German soldiers received only starvation rations, the Nazis began shouting: "German soldiers were brave!... It's a disgrace that such an infamous movie was made in America."[35]

Goebbels sprang from his seat in the balcony and began making a speech, claiming the film would destroy Germany's reputation in the world. Stink bombs were thrown among the viewers. Several cartons of white mice surreptitiously brought in by the Nazis were released. Climbing onto seats, some people swung walking sticks or their fists at one another. "Down with the Jews!" shouted one Nazi. "Hitler is at the gates!" shouted another. Leni Riefenstahl, Hitler's future documentary film director, was there: "The theater was ringing with screams so that at first I thought a fire had started. Girls and women were on their seats shrieking."[36]

Goebbels staged street marches and demonstrations against *All Quiet on the Western Front*. The Nazi propagandist spun a self-fulfilling prophecy, convincing the public that the film was too explosive to be shown in Germany because it triggered a violent response—even as the Nazis were supplying the violence. "We are once again the steel point of the hard wedge," Goebbels chortled into his diary.[37] Within days, the German film review board canceled further showings of the film. Though the movie had in fact been denounced by many other nationalists and German patriots, it was Goebbels and the Nazis who made the most noise and claimed victory.

32

WAITING FOR HITLER

Without a doubt a certain part of our educated classes looks down on our young movement—they consider us "proles" and "arrivistes."

—*Adolf Hitler, 1931*

It makes me want to throw up!

—*Joseph Goebbels, 1931*

In or out of office, in the Reichstag or in the streets, the Nazis had made themselves the free radicals of German politics. By early 1931, Hitler could smell, taste, and almost feel power within his grasp. "[He] wants to achieve power at any price and wants it right away," noted Goebbels.[1]

To counter his image as an extremist carnival barker, Hitler sought connections with esteemed names. One of those was Hjalmar Schacht. Born to parents with a fondness for America—his full name was Hjalmar Horace Greeley Schacht—the conservative economist had served in several of Germany's highest economic posts, including as head of its central bank. In May of 1930, Schacht surprised his friends by resigning from the bank in a disagreement over the government's reparations policies; he then embarked on a self-organized lecture tour of the United States. Upon his return to Germany, the apostate financial expert—and former cofounder of the German Democratic Party—was looking for new political alliances. He and Hitler fell into each other's arms.

Schacht was first wooed by Hitler at a January 5, 1931, dinner in Hermann Göring's well-appointed apartment in Berlin's Bayerisches Viertel neighborhood. This upscale part of town was also favored by prosperous Jews such as Albert Einstein. The man who brokered the dinner was Fritz

Thyssen, scion of the great coal and steel family, one of Hitler's first and friendliest supporters from the Ruhr region's plutocrat class. In the coziness of Göring's flat, Hitler was able to reel in the willing Schacht with his intensity and rhetoric. Struck by Hitler's poise, confidence, and the "absolute conviction of the rightness of his outlook and his determination to translate this outlook into practical action," Schacht concluded that Hitler was the man of the future.[2] Afterward, the former banker tried to convince his friend Chancellor Brüning to include Hitler in a new government, if only to curb the Nazis' excesses.[3] The chancellor rejected Schacht's appeal.

Hitler's consorting with the captains of industry and high finance met with consternation from more extreme Nazis such as the impatient Storm Trooper leader Walter Stennes. But Hitler had a keen political sense: he was unbound by ideological purity, and he understood that no transformative political insurgency could come to power in Germany without the tacit consent of the military and top business leaders. All his talk of a popular "uprising" (*eine nationale Erhebung*) was metaphorical spin to drive an electoral bandwagon. While kindling a rebellious spirit among the masses, Hitler was working a negotiated takeover among the elites. In the drawing rooms of the better neighborhoods, Hitler sought the sympathies of the salon, not the street.

In the Reichstag, Hitler encouraged his 107 unruly deputies to fulfill their pledge of political obstructionism. They gladly complied, but the parliamentary moderates fought back. Wilhelm Hoegner, a Social Democratic deputy from Bavaria and a longtime Hitler enemy, tried to alert other parliamentarians to the sinister portents of Nazi rule. Hoegner had led an investigation into Hitler's 1923 Beer Hall Putsch; he understood the murky underbelly of the coup attempt and forecast a reign of terror if Hitler came to power.

On the floor of the Reichstag, Hoegner cited a draft constitution found in the pocket of one of the Nazis killed in the putsch. A radical and bloodthirsty document, the draft was intended to replace the Bavarian and German constitutions if Hitler's putsch had succeeded. The new constitution would have suspended parliament, outlawed strikes and unions, eliminated Jews from public employment, seized Jewish property and money, and required anyone deemed "unproductive" or a security risk to be interned in "collection camps"—a forerunner to concentration camps. More chilling, the draft mandated an immediate death penalty for a host of offenses such as refusal to work, participating in illegal meetings, and helping a Jew hide any parts of his estate from confiscation. Even refusal to turn over funds "earned from the suffering of the German people during the war"—a dig at alleged Jewish profiteers—would get capital punishment.

In all, said Hoegner, the draconian constitution named forty grounds for summary execution. "The death penalty shall be carried out by hanging or shooting," read the document.[4]

Hoegner's words had little or no impact. The Reichstag was preoccupied with finding a way to do business as the nation struggled economically. Meanwhile, the Nazis were focused on hastening the demise of democracy. In their parliamentary disruptions, they often received strange-bedfellow support from their archenemies—now frenemies—the Communists. Their joint tactics culminated in a stormy session of the Reichstag on February 9, 1931. "It was as though the National Socialists had lost all inhibitions—with jeering, clamoring, and insulting that surpassed any parliamentary debate in memory," wrote a journalist.[5]

The Reichstag went into extended chaos. The trigger was a bill that would change the rules of debate to curtail exactly the kind of tactics the Nazis were now employing. The Nazis walked out of the parliamentary chamber, followed by the Communists, in order to kill a quorum. Then the two radical parties walked back in, only to depart again, over and over. The farce continued until three o'clock in the morning of Tuesday, February 10, when the bill was finally passed three hundred to zero without the Nazis or the Communists in the chamber.

The following day, the Nazis declared a complete boycott of the parliament. Exiting the chamber on Göring's orders, the 107 Nazi deputies announced that they were gone for the duration. Most departed Berlin for their hometowns.[6] Keen to maintain the appearance of a "nationalist front" with the Nazis, the bullheaded Alfred Hugenberg decided his DNVP delegation should follow the Nazis in boycotting the Reichstag.

Crippled and disempowered, the German parliament temporarily put itself out of business, adjourning on March 26 for six months. The adjournment was euphemistically called the "Easter Break." The long absence of the legislative branch was designed to give the Brüning cabinet a chance to get its program together. Yet with no ruling majority, Brüning was running a minority cabinet that derived all its power from one man: President Hindenburg. The Reichstag could revoke those powers by majority vote—but it chose not to. For all practical purposes, parliamentary governance had ground to a halt in Germany.

The forces of the center again tried to assert control. Government action was triggered by a crime that drew national attention—the brutal murder by three Nazis of a Communist in Hamburg.[7] At Chancellor Brüning's request, President Hindenburg signed a sweeping emergency decree "for the suppression of political excesses." Issued on March 28, the decree gave the government the power to suspend most civil rights, including freedom of speech, freedom of the press, freedom of assembly, and freedom from search and seizure. The Nazi press howled at the new restrictions; so did the Communist newspapers as well as Hugenberg's publications. But the establishment press welcomed the measures as necessary to curb the extremists. The president's decree was "no coup d'état," insisted the *Vossische Zeitung:* "The Nazis and the Communists have often enough sneeringly proclaimed that they intended to supply the republic with the rope to hang itself."[8]

The emergency edict was clearly aimed at the Nazis. It banned the wearing of political uniforms and insignia, a prohibition resented bitterly by the Nazis and the Storm Troopers, whose quasimilitary look was central to their identity and recruitment appeal. A ban on using open trucks to transport political activists undercut one of the Nazis' most effective rallying techniques.[9]

Hitler was worried. In the 1920s, he had for nearly two years been under a public speaking ban. The prohibition had blunted the Nazi Party's impact. To avoid a renewed party ban, Hitler ordered all Nazis—including the Storm Troopers—to obey President Hindenburg's new decree in letter and in spirit. The rules required all political flyers and posters to obtain police clearance in advance—pure political censorship.

Goebbels had been slapped with a speaking ban by the Berlin police and feared that his newspaper could be shut down.[10] "I'm trembling every day over *Der Angriff*," he wrote.[11] Yet Goebbels felt the Nazis ought to be making more mischief, not less. "We should have stuck with our posture as looming troublemakers and enigmatic sphinx," he wrote. Goebbels especially faulted the smarmy Göring, his onetime pal, for cozying up to conservative power brokers such as Schacht. "It makes me want to throw up!" wrote Goebbels.

Goebbels had other worries. During a trip to East Prussia—where he was knocked unconscious during a police attack—he had picked up rumors that Storm Trooper commander Walter Stennes was still fomenting unrest. "Something stinks in the Storm Troopers," noted Goebbels. "Stennes is behind it all. He's very focused on his goal. The indolence in the Brown House gives him plenty to work with."[12]

The Brown House, Hitler's splendid new party headquarters in Munich, was an indulgence that the party leader thought he deserved. Expensive remodeling by architect Paul Ludwig Troost had turned the old Palais Barlow, built in 1828, into a grand home for the once bedraggled Nazi Party. The converted mansion now had a Hall of Banners, a Hall of Standards, and a lavish Hall of Senators. For Hitler, moving from dingy rooms on innocuous Schellingstrasse into a stately edifice on monumental Briennerstrasse was like crashing the barriers of class inferiority. From his new perch, Hitler could finally get back at the condescending *Bildungsbürgertum*—the cultured upper middle class. These were the snobs and sophisticates who had long dismissed him as a rube from the Austrian outback. "Without a doubt a certain part of our educated classes looks down on our young movement," Hitler wrote. "They consider us 'proles' and 'arrivistes.' Now we want to show these folks *that we possess more culture than do our critics*. They should compare our headquarters with those of the other parties, with all their millions of marks—and then make their judgment."[13]

The Nazi leader also had to prove to skeptical Nazis that his costly purchase of a fancy building was a political necessity. The Brown House was a key piece of propaganda, he argued—and propaganda was the lifeblood of politics. To contend for national power, the Nazi movement needed to look the part of a serious national party. Even as Hitler was defending his cushy headquarters, it did not go unnoticed among the Nazi rank and file that, in the middle of the Depression, their party chief lived in a nine-room apartment in an upper-bourgeois neighborhood of Munich; that he leased a mountain home in Berchtesgaden; that he traveled everywhere in one of his several large Mercedes automobiles. While Hitler believed his elevated lifestyle was only fitting for a man destined to lead the nation, it was a point of bitter consternation among men like Walter Stennes.

The Storm Troopers had kept the pot boiling. With a strong appeal to young men out of work, they adroitly used soup kitchens and even the offer of temporary lodging as lures to membership. Spirits were boosted by the fact that Hitler had recalled Captain Ernst Röhm, the respected First World War veteran, out of exile in Bolivia to take command of the paramilitary. With his war-wounded face and implacable discipline, Röhm was a man ready for the fight.

An atmosphere of near civil war prevailed in Berlin. Storm Troopers used their usual "storm pubs" as staging spots for street activism and violence.[14] Hitler had to deny rampant rumors of a planned putsch. Flipping reality on its head, he claimed that "the Reichsbanner and Moscow are inciting civil war in Germany with their outrageous lie that the Nazi Party intends a coup d'état."[15] Yet Hitler also admonished the Storm Troopers to stay away from banned weapons and remember that the Nazi Party planned to conquer Germany by legal methods alone. This was a shot aimed straight at Stennes, whose command stretched from Berlin to the far northeastern corner of Germany. Stennes and other radical Storm Troopers still harbored dreams of an armed march on Berlin in the style of Benito Mussolini's putative 1922 March on Rome, which led to a takeover of the Italian government. The Storm Troopers' grumbling became a whisper campaign floating the idea that Hitler had become too timorous to mount a takeover by force. This was too much for the Nazi leader. He summoned several Storm Trooper leaders into Munich headquarters for a showdown. He was "most certainly *not* too cowardly" to lead an armed revolt, averred Hitler. "But I *am* too cowardly to throw Storm Troopers in front of the machine guns [of the police and the army]," he said. "We need the Storm Troopers to perform far more important tasks—namely, the creation of the Third Reich."[16] In a gauzy web of togetherness, Hitler exhorted every Storm Trooper, once again, to swear allegiance by raising his right fist and shouting, "The new Germany will arise through the fist."[17] Once again, they complied.

Hitler hoped his Munich sermon would be heard in Berlin. But if the restless Stennes was listening, he drew the opposite lesson from the one Hitler intended.

33

OPEN REVOLT

Hitler puts on a good face, but he is broken.

—*Joseph Goebbels, 1931*

Storm Trooper commander Walter Stennes rebelled again. On April Fools' Day in 1931, he led a mutiny against Goebbels's headquarters and his newspaper, *Der Angriff*. Stennes's rebels issued a public denunciation of Hitler's "un-Germanic and uninhibited despotism within the party and [his] irresponsible demagoguery."[1] The assault was nothing less than an attempted palace coup. Goebbels called the new mutiny an existential threat—"the greatest but perhaps final crisis of the party.... We have to fight our way through it."[2]

From its earliest days, the Nazi movement had borne within it the seeds of rivalry and strife. The first insurrectionist was Hitler himself. Within months of joining the party, in late 1919, the young firebrand had deposed the group's original founder, Karl Harrer. Within another eighteen months, he had pushed out Harrer's cofounder, Anton Drexler.[3] In the coming two years, Hitler faced rebellious tendencies among Storm Troopers who wanted to convert the party militia into a separate and sometimes truculent force. During Hitler's year behind bars, the Nazi Party's sundry rivals splintered into feuding factions. Ernst Röhm even created a new version of the Storm Troopers that he called the Frontbann, an apostasy that led to a break with Hitler and to Röhm's overseas banishment for several years. Even after Hitler's refounding of the party, in 1925, the Nazi chief faced several upstart challenges to his sole leadership.

Now he faced another rebellion—the most serious one so far. The

Stennes revolt laid bare the internal stresses of a party "held together only by a program of having no program," cackled a commentator in the left-liberal press. With the Nazi Party's deep fissures splashed across front pages, the essayist asked what else could be expected from a movement in which one man, Adolf Hitler, "is both pope and Caesar."[4]

News of the Storm Trooper insurrection reached Hitler and Goebbels in Weimar, where they were meeting with Röhm and other Nazi leaders. With the telephones ringing constantly, Goebbels learned that *Der Angriff*'s trusted business manager, Ludwig Weissauer, had joined forces with Stennes. The renegade Storm Trooper commander accused Hitler and Goebbels of betrayal. He faulted the "Munich clique" for its extravagant spending on the Brown House while Storm Troopers did not even have "the pennies necessary to repair their worn-out marching boots."[5]

Worse, Stennes upbraided Hitler for pursuing "special-interest politics," the very thing the Nazi leader had campaigned against in 1930. Hitler was described as a relic of a failed past. Stennes announced that he had deposed Goebbels as gauleiter and declared himself the commander of "the independent Sturmabteilung." The new formation would continue down the path for which they once fought alongside "the old Adolf Hitler," he claimed.[6] The messy squabble played out in full view of the national and international press. The *New York Times* noted the "common failing of all German political parties, division into right and left wings and sub-right and sub-left winglets."[7]

From Weimar, Röhm was dispatched back to Berlin to reassert control over the Storm Troopers. Hitler and Goebbels took an overnight train to Munich, sharing a sleeping compartment. The Nazi Führer looked thin and pale, wrote Goebbels. "I feel sorry for Hitler. . . . We talk a lot, but the mood isn't there. Hitler puts on a good face, but he is broken."[8]

By morning, Hitler's fighting spirit rebounded. Working the phones, he and Goebbels called in loyalty chits from Nazi leaders all over Germany. With forceful persuasion—and proof that they were undaunted by the Stennes revolt—the two men squeezed declarations of faithfulness from gauleiters everywhere. Even while regaining control, Hitler and

Goebbels lived for several days in a "continuous state of nervous tension." Goebbels learned that Göring had played along with Stennes, trying to grab for himself Goebbels's proxy to speak for Hitler in the capital. "I'll never forget that!" groused Goebbels in his diary. "It gives one doubts about people. It's all a pile of frozen shit."[9]

The insurrection was soon suppressed. Hitler once again authorized Goebbels to carry out a draconian purge of the Nazi Party and Storm Troopers in and around Berlin.[10] But he also felt the need to justify himself in the eyes of his doubters; he composed a long, impassioned essay. A fast writer with great confidence and coherence under pressure, Hitler piled one argument on top of another; his article ran over two full pages in the *Völkischer Beobachter*.[11] He seemed to be refounding his movement yet again. Reminding his followers of his modest origins and his time in "the hardest school of life" (in Vienna), Hitler evoked his years of "misery and need" along with his service as a "simple musketeer" in the First World War. (Hitler was exaggerating: he carried a rifle but rarely fired it; he was a courier, not a rifleman.) The Nazi chief once again trotted out his thirteen months in prison as proof of his dedication to the Nazi cause. He came down especially hard on those who thought they could deviate from the "legal path" to power. Taking up revolution against the armed might of the state, he wrote, would be the act of "a fool, a criminal, or an agent provocateur."

Hitler triumphed. With Stennes now expelled from the Nazi Party, Hitler met on April 12 in Weimar's German National Theater with all the gauleiters. He adroitly turned the Storm Trooper crisis into an affirmation of Nazi solidarity and loyalty to him. Twelve thousand Storm Troopers marched past Hitler afterward, saluting the party chief in front of the Hotel Elephant, on Market Square. "A breath of salvation," Hitler called the event the following day in a letter to conservative publisher Julius Lehmann.[12]

One more potentially fatal bullet had been dodged. But even in triumph Hitler and Goebbels had been sowing the seeds of future trouble with the Storm Troopers by elevating Ernst Röhm's role and control. Röhm had clearly been the right man to reorganize the Storm Troopers, bringing the brown shirts from an estimated 88,000 members at the beginning of 1931 to 260,000 by the end of the year. But Röhm, too, had ambitions and an agenda that would soon be out of sync with Hitler's.[13] For now, those differences were papered over.

In the summer of 1931, Germany was in a state of suspended political animation. As the country slid further into the Great Depression—Germany was hit harder economically than any other European country—a sense of anomie prevailed. The psychological dislocations and fears of a crumbling order were captured in Fritz Lang's landmark film about a serial child killer in Berlin. Called *M—A City Searches for a Murderer*, the movie starred Peter Lorre and explored the compulsions of a homicidal maniac roaming Berlin's seamy underside. The viewer was left with a disconsolate sense of social and mental breakdown for which there was no solution.

While the left-liberal media often celebrated the limitless artistic creativity of this permissive period, the Nazis dwelt on the dark aspects of a capital city with loose controls over public morality and widespread public corruption. The Nazi version played well in the provinces. Germans' faith in their political system dwindled. Desperate times called for desperate measures, but democracy did not seem up to the task. Germany's efforts to ease its economic pressures were not working. An attempt to stimulate the economy through a customs-free trading zone with Austria was blocked as a violation of the Treaty of Versailles. Austria's most important bank, the Creditanstalt, owned by the Rothschild family, collapsed, accelerating the downturn. Hitler trumpeted the widely felt ramifications of its bankruptcy as proof that Jewish financiers sought world domination.

Chancellor Brüning's insistence on deflationary policies—slashing state spending rather than boosting it—exacerbated the economic slump with soaring unemployment that would soon reach 34 percent.[14] In Düsseldorf, more than 1,400 German industrialists took the desperate step of urging Brüning to move directly to dictatorship (though they later backed off their demand).[15] President Hindenburg, who normally stayed regally aloof from the fray, felt compelled to make a rather abject appeal to US president Herbert Hoover for "relief from abroad."[16] Hindenburg's plea was supported by US ambassador Frederic M. Sackett in Berlin, who conferred frequently with President Hoover by transatlantic telephone, still a novelty. For fear of eavesdroppers, the president and the ambassador tried to disguise their conversation by using American slang most of the time.[17] Hoover was sympathetic to Germany's plight, proposing a one-year moratorium on its reparations obligations and war debts.

The Hoover moratorium was approved in July of 1931 but did little to ease the crisis. Within one week, the Darmstädter und Nationalbank (called Danatbank for short), one of Germany's leading commercial lending institutions, announced that it "had been forced to keep its teller windows closed"—it had collapsed.[18] That Black Monday, as it was called, was followed by the crash of the Dresdner Bank, triggering a general run on banks. The government shut down the banking system altogether for two days: it took two weeks to resume full operations.[19]

Meanwhile, thousands of jobless, homeless men camped out under the green foliage of Berlin's sprawling Grunewald forest, living in tents or tin-roof sheds. In an echo of Depression-era measures in the United States, the German government organized a labor corps that was sent to excavate land and clean up swamps: make-work for a crippled nation.[20] Other regions suffered dramatically, including desolate Silesia. Entire families moved into semiunderground barracks outside towns with windowlike entrances at ground level; they lived hand to mouth, like ferrets seeking shelter from the elements.[21] Even farmers could barely survive. "My mother and my father had to work on the land from early in the morning until late at night," remembered one Nazi Party member. "Although both of them worked very hard, we had just enough for the most necessary things."[22]

The Nazis took full advantage of the growing economic crisis. In May, they had, for the first time, become the largest party in a state legislature, winning 37 percent of the vote in Oldenburg, a tiny city-state on Germany's northwestern flatland. In Hamburg, Germany's great northern port, a city normally tilted hard to the Socialists and Communists, the Nazis rose to 26 percent. Several months later, in a spectacular surge, the Nazis reached 37 percent in elections in Hesse, the state that included the cultural and business metropolis of Frankfurt-am-Main.[23]

There was another state that Hitler coveted even more: Prussia. Germany's biggest and most powerful state, Prussia stretched over more than eight hundred miles, from the Rhine River in the west to Königsberg, on the Baltic Sea. The massive state included 60 percent of Germany's land area and population. By far the most dominant of Germany's seventeen states, Prussia represented to Hitler the biggest political prize short of winning the national government. The capital of Prussia was also the capital of Germany—Berlin. Its state offices and state parliament formed an independent power center, sometimes in competition with the national government. With control of a massive police force, Prussia could directly influence public order and public mood, bringing pressure on the Reich.

Though Prussian politics had long been dominated by the Social Democrats, the Nazis had already made deep inroads. In the 1930 parliamentary election, Prussians—like the rest of the Germans—had given the Nazis 18 percent of their vote. While the Reichstag election had no direct impact on the Prussian legislature—not due for an election for two more years—the surprise outcome scrambled the state's political equation. Hitler was sufficiently emboldened by his party's new standing among Prussia's voters to attempt a kind of legal coup d'état against the Prussian government through a referendum. First introduced by the Steel Helmet veterans' association and several other nationalistic groups, a plebiscite could prematurely force out the Prussian government of Social Democratic governor Otto Braun. His administration would be replaced by one that reflected "the popular will" as expressed in the last election, asserted the initiative's sponsors.[24] In a stark illustration of Germany's shifting constellations, the Communists joined with the Nazis in supporting the referendum; the liberal press denounced it as a distraction from Germany's more pressing problems.[25] Though plainly extraconstitutional, the political ploy came to a vote. The campaign was feverish; on balloting day thirteen people were killed in Berlin during clashes between Communists and the police.[26]

But Hitler's blustery lunge for power through the side door of Prussia was another leap too soon. The August 9 referendum failed, gaining only 37 percent of the vote. Hitler was bitterly disappointed. He still could not break out of the stalemate that had mired his rise to power. Goebbels called it a "heavy defeat" and a "triumph for the Jews."

By now, Goebbels was wondering if the Nazis could ever achieve power by votes alone. "Can we really make it through the legal route?" he asked.[27]

To Hitler, the answer was always yes—given enough time. But many of his followers shared Goebbels's doubts. The Nazi leader felt the pressure for action building from below—the same kind of pressure that had impelled him to his botched putsch in 1923. Now he was trying again to have it both ways. While cautioning his followers against excesses that could bring the wrath of Brüning's emergency decrees down on them, Hitler did not initially object when five hundred Storm Troopers went rogue on an autumn night in Berlin. In a vicious wilding on the evening of September 12, the beginning of the Jewish New Year, Storm Troopers terrorized Jewish shopkeepers and "Jewish-looking" people on fashionable Kurfürstendamm. The hotheaded malefactors were egged on by their Berlin commander, Count Wolf von Helldorf, who patrolled up and down the avenue, directing the action.[28] The "pogrom-like rioting"—in the words of the Central Association of German Citizens of the Jewish Faith—was widely denounced.[29] Thirty-three brown shirts landed in prison. Even Hitler was finally forced to distance himself from the excesses of the Storm Troopers.

But his disavowals were hollow. At a closed meeting in Munich three days later, the Nazi leader showed his hypocrisy. Unaware that his words would wind up in a police-spy report, Hitler told Storm Trooper leaders that the party would publicly denounce violence like the Berlin attacks on Jews. But, he added, he understood the commanders' need to "undertake something to satisfy the revolutionary mood" of their restive troops—

like beating up Jews.[30] Even if denounced or expelled from the Nazi Party in the short run for violating the government's emergency decrees, the Nazi street fighters' "contributions" to the cause would not be forgotten in the future. The young firebrands would be welcomed into the party's full embrace "when the time was ripe," said Hitler.

In the mind of a man convinced of his inevitable success, the time of triumph could not be far away.

34

HITLER AND WOMEN

> [Hitler] was erotic with the women by whom he surrounded himself, but never sexual.
>
> —*Christa Schroeder, Hitler's secretary*

Hitler's seemingly inexorable climb to power was suddenly stalled by a scandal. On September 19, 1931, in his posh Munich apartment on Prinzregentenplatz, in a well-lit bedroom facing the square, a dead body was discovered. The deceased was a fetching twenty-three-year-old Austrian woman named Geli Raubal. She was Hitler's half niece. She may also have been his lover and, as some speculated, his victim. Beside Geli lay Hitler's 6.35mm Walther pistol.

The potentially disastrous impact of Geli's mysterious death on Hitler's political future was immediately apparent to him and those around him. Though a distraught Hitler clearly loved his niece, the politician's first comment to the investigating detective included a lament that "this had to happen *to him*."[1] The ambitious politician saw Geli's demise as a political impediment as much as a personal tragedy. The questions surrounding the puzzling death of the young woman did, in fact, have the potential to end Hitler's career just as he seemed on the cusp of success. To Rudolf Hess and other top Nazis, the first job was to publicly spin Geli's death as suicide, probably committed out of despair over a failed singing career—and to threaten newspapers that suggested otherwise. While the full truth was never ascertained, the still clouded tale of Hitler's relationship with his young niece remains the melodramatic high point in the disputed history of the Nazi leader's odd and uncertain relationships with women.

One of the secrets of Hitler's unlikely success was his appeal to the opposite sex. A generation younger than most party leaders, the unmarried Hitler was a kind of erotic wild card in German political life. He attracted a coterie of motherly matrons—including his wealthy benefactors Elsa Bruckmann and Helene Bechstein—as well as excited young female admirers stirred by his very presence. "Girls in the front row became delirious," reported an American journalist at one of Hitler's Sports Palace speeches.[2] A magnetic speaker full of radical ideas and messianic confidence, the Nazi leader's pheromone quotient could be felt not only at massive rallies with throbbing music but also at small Munich pub gatherings. "Only a few yards away [from me] was a young woman, her eyes fastened on [Hitler]," recalled Ernst Hanfstaengl about his first visit to a Hitler speech. "Transfixed as though in some devotional ecstasy, she had ceased to be herself and was completely under the spell of Hitler's despotic faith in Germany's future greatness."[3]

The frenzy shown by Hitler's female admirers may have been reciprocal: "For Hitler, [sexual] gratification came from the ecstasy of the masses," said his longtime secretary Christa Schroeder.[4] She believed that Hitler never had actual sex with any woman, including Eva Braun, the shopgirl who was to become Hitler's mistress and, in the Third Reich's final days, his wife. Said Schroeder: "[Hitler] was erotic with the women by whom he surrounded himself, but never sexual." As in any good soap opera, Schroeder's source was Eva Braun's hairdresser.[5] Others have asserted that Hitler had intimate relations with at least seven women.[6]

Hitler knew that female adulation gave him a political advantage. "I need to stay single so I can get the women's vote," he told a friend. The party leader denied himself the joys of family life for the greater good of the nation—or so he claimed. Just as he had told the young Maria Reiter in Berchtesgaden in 1926, Hitler later said to a Nazi supporter: "I have another bride: Germany! I *am* married to the German *Volk,* to its destiny!"[7] Behind Hitler's airy claims of mystical matrimony to the German people lay a shrewd political calculus: Germany had lost nearly two million young men in the First World War; prospective husbands were in short supply, and female voters were in large supply.

Almost every aspect of the improbable Hitler saga invites exaggeration, but none more than the issue of his sex life and his anatomy. The Nazi leader's odd behavior around women fed conjecture for decades that he had physical malformities or venereal diseases—most of it based on innuendo, half-truths, or outright lying. A growth industry flourished in unsubstantiated legends about Hitler's possible incest, homosexuality, or impotence. Such theories seem driven by the search for personal aberration to explain Hitler's political and military deviancy; proof of private perversions would support the belief that appalling public acts could not have come from a normal person. Seizing upon an illustrative flaw, especially a sexual one, is irresistibly appealing to the popular imagination.

Yet one assertion about Hitler's sexuality has in fact been documented: he had an undescended testicle. Called cryptorchidism, the condition was long ridiculed in a British marching ditty (sung to the tune of the "Colonel Bogey March") claiming, "Hitler / Has only got one ball!" But that was only a song. Russian forensic examiners claimed after the Second World War that Hitler's burned corpse was missing its left testicle. But Russian deceit and secretiveness led Western historians to doubt the reports. In 2015, however, German historian and archivist Peter Fleischmann uncovered, for the first time, a credible doctor's notation that confirmed Hitler's condition. In the 1923 admissions ledger to Landsberg Prison, where Hitler spent 1924, the year after his putsch, Fleischmann deciphered the medical notation: *rechtsseitiger Kryptorchismus* (right-side cryptorchidism)—the condition of an undescended testicle. The doctor had originally written "left-sided," but crossed out "left" and substituted "right." So while a bit of mystery remains—was it right or left?—Fleischmann's discovery erased any doubts that Hitler had only one properly descended testicle. The long-lost 1923 prison admissions book made its way through a flea market, an auction-house offering, and finally, in 2010, into the possession of the Munich State Archive. But no historian before Fleischmann had decoded the wobbly handwriting of the elderly prison doctor, who penned his scrawl in the now-defunct Sütterlin script of that era.[8]

An undescended testicle is usually surgically corrected in infancy. Adult cryptorchidism, as in Hitler's case, means that a man has a low sperm count and his chances of fathering a child are reduced. Whether Hitler was aware of this, and whether he felt embarrassment about his condition, remains unknown. Did his unusual anatomical feature make him wary of experiencing intimacy with a woman? Could his "one-ballism" have induced impotence? Could fear of being considered something less than a full man have warped his sexual preferences? While an undropped testicle into the scrotum sac is a shaky foundation upon which to base a theory of war and mayhem, knowing that Hitler had cryptorchidism may contribute to our cloudy understanding of his stilted relations with women and some of the drama surrounding those entanglements. Such as his relationship with Geli Raubal.

35

GELI

Geli was an enchantress.... [Hitler] always followed her like a faithful lamb.

—Heinrich Hoffmann, Hitler's photographer

Up until her shocking and bewildering death, Geli had been, by most accounts, the love of Hitler's life. She flashed through his world like a comet, distracting him as no other woman ever had. The story of their relationship is a full bodice ripper, involving deep attachment, bitter jealousy, possible incest, high suspense, and, ultimately, murder or suicide—depending on which ending seems more plausible.

Born in 1908 in Linz, Austria, Geli was the daughter of Hitler's half sister, Angela, and her husband, Leo Raubal, who died when Geli was two (Geli is short for Angela; mother and daughter had the same name). After moving to Munich in 1927 to begin medical studies, Geli soon switched to music and took singing lessons. A skeptical Uncle Alf, as Geli called Hitler, paid for the instruction—even though Geli's teacher called the lively young Austrian "the laziest pupil I ever had."[1]

Geli (and sometimes her mother) increasingly became part of Hitler's roving political show. They traveled together to Nuremberg, to the Bayreuth Festival, even on vacation (with several others) to the North Sea islands of Heligoland. In a photograph, a happy Geli stands next to Hitler on a windswept pier, her thick brown hair tossed into a Medusa-like tangle of dark tresses.

Then nineteen, Geli soon fell in love with Hitler's chauffeur, the tall, darkly handsome Emil Maurice. At Christmastime in 1927, Maurice approached Hitler to ask for Geli's hand. The Nazi chief flew into a violent rage and reportedly raised his dog whip, chasing Maurice out a window.[2] "I seriously think he would have liked to shoot me dead at that moment," recalled Maurice, who was soon fired.[3]

The Hitler-Geli saga—and the heat of the rumor mill—intensified when Hitler invited Geli to live in his spacious apartment on tony Prinzregentenplatz. She moved in during October of 1929 and had her own sunny room overlooking the busy square. On its face, Hitler was trying to give shape and purpose to Geli's young life as well as provide supervision and free rent. What was really going on between the two was a matter of racy speculation in the Nazi world. Nonetheless, the wives of the leading Nazis, including Ilse Pröhl Hess, twenty-nine, took the young woman under their wings. Hitler, Hess, Ilse, Geli, and a revolving roster of Hitler's closest associates lunched almost daily at the Osteria Bavaria, on Schellingstrasse. They also often traveled with the Führer, even on his sudden overnight drives from Munich to Berlin. "The girls were in the back and we had the job of singing, so the driver didn't go to sleep," remembered Ilse.[4]

Openly squiring Geli around Munich, the Nazi chief took his niece to afternoon gatherings at his beloved Café Heck and to evenings of theater and music. Attending concerts and other events together, the two—though nineteen years apart in age—seemed almost like a married couple. She was the only person who dared interrupt the Nazi Führer's self-centered monologues. "When Geli was at the table, everything revolved around her," recalled photographer Heinrich Hoffmann. "Geli was an enchantress."[5]

Al fresco outings on the Bavarian lakesides were among Hitler's favorite diversions. Photographs of one such picnic show the men in suits and ties, the women in dresses, all sprawled on blankets beside a copse of trees.[6] Geli was no great beauty; she had the broad features and sturdy build of her square-faced mother. But she was cheerful and often bursting with laughter. She had become close friends with Henriette Hoffmann, the photographer's bright-faced daughter. "To us the world was a garden," remembered Henrietta. "We considered life a party that was just beginning." During one picnic, the two young women disappeared behind a stand of bushes to go skinny-dipping in the lake. "We swam naked and let ourselves be dried by the sun. . . . A swarm of butterflies descended on the naked Geli."[7]

Munich's odd couple—Hitler and Geli—was the object of feverish gossip. "[Hitler] hovered at her elbow with a moon-calf look in his eyes in a very plausible imitation of adolescent infatuation," claimed Hanfstaengl.[8] Hitler even accompanied Geli on shopping trips for clothing, standing around, it was reported, "like a faithful lamb" and paying the bills, sometimes for very expensive fashions.[9] Party leaders grumbled that Hitler was not only playing with fire by escorting his young niece around in public, he was also squandering hard-gathered party funds on her Champagne tastes.[10] Hitler retorted: "Nobody can tell me what to do if I want to drive somewhere... with my niece. It is no business of the movement! I get no salary from the party."[11]

Rumors flew that while Geli was Hitler's one true love, she seemed frustrated by the restrictions placed on her by her perpetually watchful and possibly jealous uncle. A flash point occurred during the annual devil-may-care Carnival period in Catholic Bavaria, which culminated on Fat Tuesday, or Mardi Gras. The season was noted for late-night carousing in risqué costumes whose wearers wore masks to conceal their identities. Young Geli was keen to join in the reveling. When she sketched the Carnival costume she wanted to wear to the Munich parties, Hitler flew into a rage over the dress's deep décolletage. "You might as well go naked!" he fumed.[12] Hitler, who saw himself as Geli's guardian, allowed his niece to attend the Carnival balls only in the company of a chaperone such as Heinrich Hoffmann.[13]

On the afternoon of September 18, 1931, Hitler prepared to embark on a political journey to Nuremberg and points north. According to at least one account, he and Geli had a heated argument before he left. "Really! Nothing ties me to my uncle anymore!" Geli reportedly said to Frau Winter, Hitler's housekeeper.[14] Shortly after Hitler's departure, the housekeeper noticed Geli enter Hitler's room (where he kept his pistol) in a flustered state, then return quickly to her own room. A thud emanated from Geli's room, as if a bottle of perfume might have been knocked over.[15]

The next morning, Geli did not show up for her usual breakfast.

Knocking on Geli's bedroom door, Frau Winter got no response. Since Geli was the reigning princess of the household, the housekeeper did not persist. At 10:00 a.m., her husband, Georg, decided to force the double door with a screwdriver.[16] What he found inside was gruesome.

Lying facedown in a smear of her own blood was a dead Geli.[17] The bullet from Hitler's small pistol had penetrated her lung.[18] Nowhere was there a suicide note or an explanation for her death. Only a barely started letter to a friend in Vienna, mentioning an upcoming trip to the city, was found.

The alarmed servants immediately notified Rudolf Hess, who reached Hitler at his Nuremberg hotel. Hitler screamed: "Hess, answer me—yes or no—is she still alive?...Hess, on your word of honor as an officer—tell me the truth—is she alive or dead?"[19]

Hitler—along with his photographer, Hoffmann, and chauffeur, Julius Schreck—raced down the ninety-mile highway toward Munich. They were stopped for driving too fast, and Schreck was issued a speeding ticket that would later serve as a handy alibi for Hitler, proving that he had been out of Munich when Geli died.[20] Back at his apartment—Geli's body had already been removed—Hitler fell into a funk. Within hours, he was close to a nervous breakdown and was considering leaving politics, according to Hess.[21] With Schreck and Hoffmann close at his side, Hitler fled Munich for the quiet country house of his friend and printer, Adolf Müller. There, on the shores of the Tegernsee, the Nazi leader holed up with his demons for several days. He stayed alone in a darkened room, pacing up and down, recalled Hoffmann. Schreck secretly hid the pistol that Hitler always carried with him.[22]

As Hitler brooded alone, the Nazi Party hierarchy flew into damage-control mode. A killing in the Führer's own apartment, whether by suicide or murder, could cripple him politically. Geli's demise had been an accident of improper gun handling, they said. Then they began labeling her death a suicide—Geli was upset, they claimed, about her unsuccessful singing career. Yet within a day, the Munich press was stirring speculation. HITLER'S LOVER COMMITS SUICIDE headlined one newspaper, with a sketch showing a whip-holding Hitler standing over a dead woman's body. The anti-Nazi *Münchener Post* was only slightly more subtle, calling

Geli's demise "a mysterious affair." Suggesting that a violent clash with Hitler left his niece with a broken nose, the newspaper claimed that Geli had wanted to go to Vienna to become engaged, over Hitler's outraged objections. The newspaper cited Geli's unfinished letter to her friend in Vienna, fanning doubts that the young woman's death could have been a suicide.[23]

Hitler fired off a broadside denial, but that did not stop the rumor mill. A Communist newspaper denounced the Nazis as a party led "by bachelors and homosexuals." Wilder theories were floated: Geli was engaged to a violin teacher in Linz, and he was Jewish; better still, she was pregnant by him. Or she was pregnant by Hitler himself. Hitler's lawyer, Hans Frank, threatened the newspapers with legal action if they sought to keep the rumors alive. His admonitions seem to have worked: to the Nazi Party's great relief, the sex-and-murder saga quickly faded from public view.[24]

Meanwhile, Geli's remains were transported back to Austria and buried, without an inquest, in Vienna's central cemetery. Only a week later did Hitler visit her grave for a final farewell. Geli's death was ruled a suicide, and no amount of conjecture in the following decades would present convincing evidence to the contrary. All that remained uncertain was the reason she apparently took her own life.

For years, Hitler clung to the memory of his high-spirited niece. He ordered that Geli's room in his apartment be left unchanged and kept as a kind of shrine with fresh flowers frequently deposited in it. Uncle Adolf had a small bust of Geli sculpted and kept it with him, her familiar visage often facing him from the mantelpiece of his Berlin hotel room.

Yet however severe his grief, Hitler quickly found his way back to the only thing he really understood—pursuing political power. Less than a week after Geli's passing, he spoke to more than ten thousand cheering supporters in Hamburg. It was as though he had returned from a purgatory, reborn to the world he was trying to conquer. With Geli gone, Hitler seemed liberated. "Now I'm internally and externally free," he told a fellow Nazi. He repeated his assertion that he was not committed to any woman but rather to the German people.[25]

Hitler's love affair with the German nation did not shield him entirely from the lures of feminine attraction. He was soon fixated on a dashing divorcée and socialite named Magda Quandt, who had become a Nazi activist. Smitten when he first met Magda over tea with a group of Nazis in the lobby of Berlin's Kaiserhof Hotel, Hitler was crushed to learn only an hour later that she was already the paramour of his propaganda chief, Goebbels.[26] Though Magda was committed to Goebbels, the stylishly flirtatious woman had in her first meeting with Hitler silently reciprocated his apparent interest with penetrating looks and suggestive comments. The young woman's infatuation with the Nazi chief probably remained unconsummated, yet a charged bond grew between Goebbels's future wife and Hitler. When Goebbels and Magda were married, in December of 1931, Hitler served as best man and hosted the wedding breakfast. Even though Magda was married to Goebbels—they would eventually have six children together—she was also spiritually wed to Hitler. This odd love triangle would last for fourteen years, until their deaths.[27]

For more earthly pleasures, Hitler had already begun seeing a young shop assistant he had met at Heinrich Hoffmann's photo studio: Eva Braun.

36

HINDENBURG, HUGENBERG, AND HARZBURG

He can lick me from behind.

—President Paul von Hindenburg, 1931

Adolf Hitler and President Paul von Hindenburg had never met. By the autumn of 1931, the Great War's field marshal and the western front's trench courier had become the antipodes of German politics—each with great certainty about his mission, each with a constituency and a unique kind of power. Hitler commanded a popular following that had shifted politics on its axis. Hindenburg controlled the ultimate lever, the power to appoint the chancellor. Between those two poles lay the entirety of the political establishment: the government, the parliament, all the other parties. Hitler was trying to leapfrog them all. Hindenburg was standing at the other end, his door closed.

With Germany plunging deeper into economic depression and with joblessness soaring, the Nazis were garnering an average of 29 percent of the vote in state and local elections. The party's electioneering was a "work of genius," reported the *New York Times*.[1] Yet Hitler was still not in the chancellor's chair or even in the cabinet. Nor had he laid eyes on the man who stood in his way: President Hindenburg.

On Saturday, October 10, Chancellor Brüning called Hitler in for a conference. Brüning had now shifted his position: he was trying to lure the Nazi leader into a coalition as a junior partner—if Hitler would agree to a dubious scheme to keep President Hindenburg in office for another seven-year term. With the president's current term slated to end in the spring of 1932, Brüning wanted at all costs to avoid a bitter presidential election just when he was trying to right the German economy in the eyes of international investors. The chancellor proposed a constitutional amendment to allow Hindenburg to be installed as president for life without the divisive thrashings of a popular balloting. Though of highly questionable legality, this initiative, Brüning felt, could be passed with a two-thirds majority of the Reichstag. For that, he needed Hitler's Nazis.

Hitler refused Brüning's proposal as extralegal. Without telling Brüning, the Nazi leader also had an ulterior motive: he was already mulling the prospect of running for the presidency himself—as a side door to political power. Yet Brüning did not give up. He asked Hitler, Why don't you sit down for a conversation with President Hindenburg? Having traveled so far, having butted his head against the wall of exclusion, Hitler would not refuse. Brüning made the arrangements for that same afternoon.

The chance to meet with the most revered living hero in Germany was a political triumph for Hitler. Dismissed not so long ago as a carnival huckster, he was now ushered into the presidential palace, on Wilhelmstrasse—the sanctum sanctorum of German political life—for an audience with the hero of the First World War, Germany's highest constitutional officeholder. The six-foot-five-inch aristocrat and the five-foot-nine-inch stateless commoner finally shook hands.

The meeting was not a success. Though the conversation in Hindenburg's chambers started well enough, with Hitler showing appropriate humility, the Nazi's demagogic instincts soon took over. Straining to prove himself a man of worldly knowledge and leadership qualities, Hitler subjected the eighty-four-year-old president to his usual endless ramble on politics, foreign policy, and history. Hindenburg, a man of strategic silences, listened stone-faced. The meeting ended without decision or warmth. Reports on Hindenburg's reaction to Hitler are mixed. The most common account—and the one that fits with later events—has Hindenburg coarsely noting to an aide that while Hitler might be a good speaker, he clearly was best suited for the office of postmaster—"so that he can lick me from behind, on my stamps" (an odd variation on the usual barnyard epithet).[2]

Just across the street, in the Kaiserhof Hotel, Hitler—unaware of Hindenburg's scathing put-down—gave a glowing account to his paladins. In

Hitler's recollection, Hindenburg had listened carefully, and the president's influential chief of staff, state secretary Otto Meissner, had even supported some of Hitler's points. "End result: we are now socially acceptable," gloated Goebbels.[3]

It had been a dramatic day—yet nothing had happened. Hindenburg had seen Hitler, the noisome political comer, and developed a distaste for him. Hitler had clearly profited: being received by the German president conferred on the Nazi leader the status of a serious political figure. Though indecisive, the encounter was only the first of a series of meetings that would eventually change history.

At 7:00 p.m., Hitler and his chief lieutenants left the Kaiserhof for a nighttime drive to the Harz Mountains, in western Germany. They were scheduled to take part the following day in a great show of unity of the "nationalist opposition." Hitler was a reluctant participant. When his caravan arrived at two o'clock on Sunday morning in the small spa town of Bad Harzburg, he was in a rage about the whole undertaking. He was furious at being forced to participate in someone else's game. That someone was Alfred Hugenberg.

Hugenberg and Hitler had been playing footsie since their failed joint attempt in 1929 to derail the Young Plan through a referendum. After the 1930 parliamentary election, with the Nazis in primacy on the right, Hugenberg's German National People's Party (DNVP) began taking some of its cues from Hitler's party. The Hugenberg followers liked to call their coalition of convenience with the Nazis a "nationalist front." But the alliance was a loose one. Both party leaders wanted authoritarian rule, but each man wanted to be the ruler. On paper, Hugenberg should have had the advantage: he owned a massive share of the German press; he was an insider in top business circles; he looked the part of the traditional German politician, even with his loopy mustache.

But Hugenberg did not have Hitler's youth, energy, or visceral connection to the masses. The old man in the bulging suits and wing-collar shirts did not look like a new beginning, which people were demanding. Hugenberg had none of Hitler's special appeal to that burgeoning bloc of voters, women. Nonetheless, Hugenberg considered himself the main man of the nationalist right.[4] To the media baron and former head of the Krupp steel company, Adolf Hitler was still only a political "drummer" who could give rousing speeches but not run anything.

Bad Harzburg was crawling with politicians, businessmen, noblemen, phalanxes of military men, and paramilitary forces. All the uncompromising opponents of the republic were there, except, of course, the Communists. Even the former kaiser himself—living in exile in the Netherlands—was unofficially represented by two of his sons, Princes August Wilhelm (Auwi) and Eitel Friedrich. A wide assortment of business leaders (though no truly big names) had heeded Hugenberg's call for a united front. Even Hjalmar Schacht, the renegade former head of the Reichsbank, Germany's national bank, showed up and astonished everyone with an unscheduled speech. In it, Schacht bad-mouthed the German economy and trumpeted the perils of its deep indebtedness to American lenders—triggering outrage the next day among German financial leaders trying to stave off a crash. The *Berliner Tageblatt* bemoaned "Schacht's criminal speech in Bad Harzburg." Taken together, the quiltwork of political characters and forces gathered in the mountains became known as the Harzburg Front.

But the front cracked immediately. Hitler, still out of sorts, showed up at Sunday morning's ceremonies only long enough to take in the march-past of two thousand Storm Troopers, then showily departed the reviewing stand as an even larger contingent of Steel Helmets passed in review. The insult was quickly protested by Steel Helmet leaders Franz Seldte and Theodor Duesterberg. Hitler also snubbed Hugenberg by skipping the luncheon for the leaders, disingenuously claiming that he could hardly enjoy a sumptuous meal when his Storm Troopers were sometimes going hungry. When he finally made his scheduled afternoon speech, he did not even mention the unified nationalistic front. The Nazi leader again had it both ways—benefiting from the publicity of a big splash organized by Hugenberg while still maintaining full independence from his rival. Hitler was, as always, a force unto himself.

The Harzburg meeting was a bust. The nationalistic right, like the rest of German politics, was too splintered to achieve its sole purpose: pushing

Brüning out of office. Even if most elements had coalesced, without the Nazis they could swing no weight. And Hitler had made it clear that the right wing's only path to power would be with him in the lead.

To prove that the Nazi Party did not need Hugenberg as much as Hugenberg needed Hitler, the Nazi leader one week later mounted a massive show of strength in Braunschweig, a Nazi stronghold not far from Bad Harzburg. One hundred thousand Storm Troopers arrived for parades and processions in more than thirty-eight special trains and several thousand trucks.[5] Hitler consecrated the colors of twenty-eight new Storm Trooper units, and a torchlight parade sparkled through the surrounding roads in the evening. While Alfred Hugenberg might be able to arrange a glittery gathering of well-heeled leaders in a spa town, Adolf Hitler could stir the hearts of the common people in a working-class city. Hitler had the foot soldiers and the votes.

37

BOXHEIM AND THE AMERICAN MEDIA

> Every order from the Storm Troopers, the state militia, and others, no matter their rank, must be followed immediately. Resistance will be punished by death.
>
> Anyone caught with a firearm after this deadline will be treated as an enemy of the . . . German people and shot on the spot.
>
> —*Boxheim Document, November 1931*

A secret document had exploded in the German press. It was an outline for a brutal Nazi regime in Hesse, a small state along the Rhine River. The document's disclosure, in November of 1931, ignited a firestorm, tarnishing Hitler's reputation and threatening, once again, to forestall his juggernaut.

Called the Boxheim Document because of its origins in a Rhine River winery of the same name, the draft had been composed by overeager local Nazis. Reacting to rumors of a coming putsch attempt in Hesse by the Communists, the Nazis outlined a preemptive coup d'état that would introduce draconian martial law. Their draft orders mandated drumhead courts, firing squads, and summary executions for a host of sins, such as not obeying a Storm Trooper or simply not showing up for work. The document warned of the confiscation of private property that would be carried out at the whim of the new Nazi regime. Selling or even bartering food would be banned.[1]

The Boxheim Document sparked national outrage. Incensed commentators called the text eerily similar to the constitutional draft found on the body of a dead Nazi in Munich after the 1923 putsch attempt. Federal prosecutors opened an investigation of treason charges against the Nazis in Hesse.[2] Some saw the Boxheim revelations as proof that Hitler and his party, despite their veneer of legality, were a radically violent band. A "reign of terror" like that described in the Boxheim Document could be expected from the Nazis should they come to power nationally, wrote *Vossische Zeitung* editor Carl Misch.[3] To the Nazis, "the joy of power is the joy of murder," opined the Social Democratic Party newspaper. Even in conservative Bavaria, the newspapers called for charges of treason against the Boxheim Document's principal author (Werner Best, the Nazi who drafted the original text, was indeed charged but never convicted). The French national daily *Le Temps* labeled Hitler's rise "the most dangerous adventure for world peace that could be imagined."[4]

Hitler claimed he was blindsided. He had known nothing, he insisted, about the Boxheim confab, a meeting of only six local Nazi leaders where the grim document had been discussed and adopted three months earlier. But his denials rang hollow, since only nine months earlier he had written in the *Völkischer Beobachter*: "Nothing happens in the National Socialist movement without my knowledge and approval, no matter how far away I may be."[5] Those words were thrown in his face by editorialists around the country. Given Hitler's aggressive speeches and imprecations that "heads will roll in the sand," the Boxheim bombshell seemed an accurate reflection of the Nazi spirit—even if unauthorized by Hitler.

In an effort at damage control, Hitler managed to convince Chancellor Brüning and other leaders that he was ignorant of the doings of his underlings in Hesse. He dispatched Hermann Göring, his go-to man for dealing with the high establishment, to offer soothing words to President Hindenburg. To his party members, Hitler sent a typically ambiguous message: he banned freelance "legal preparations" like the scheming of the Hesse group at the Boxheim vineyard. Yet he assured his followers that the Nazi Party, once in power, would "act ruthlessly against all those vermin who damage our people or fatherland."[6] The "vermin" were unspecified, but Hitler's supporters knew he meant the usual suspects: Jews, profiteers, racial polluters, and the "November criminals" who had in 1918 overthrown Germany's monarchy and established the hated Weimar Republic.

Because Chancellor Brüning was still trying to win Hitler's support for keeping President Hindenburg in office for another term, he accepted

Hitler's claims of ignorance. With winter approaching, he was also grappling with an emergency scheme to distribute ten million marks' worth of coal and foodstuffs—potatoes, bread, and perhaps even meat—at discounted prices to the growing masses of jobless Germans.[7] Brüning did not need the Boxheim distraction.

Yet the clamor over the Nazis' flirtation with dictatorship put the chancellor in a quandary. In a bitter exchange of statements with Hitler, he showed that he saw through Hitler's hollow claims of legality. "If one declares that, having come to power legally, one will then break the bounds of the law, that is not legality," wrote Brüning.[8] The government quickly enacted a broad ban on political activism—but only for the coming holiday season. In a forty-six-page decree, Brüning prohibited all political meetings or outdoor demonstrations until January, with the threat of three months in prison for defamation of any public official. The decree outlawed the sale of blackjacks and other blunt instruments and, once again, forbade the wearing of "political uniforms"—a swipe at the Nazi Storm Troopers.[9] The brown shirts simply donned their white shirts without calling the starchy look a uniform.

Caught once again dancing on the political edge, the Nazi chief needed to turn ignominy into a political plus. With more than six million voters in his pocket from the 1930 Reichstag election—and reason to expect considerably more in the next balloting—Hitler could operate with chutzpah. He launched an aggressive media strategy that soon left the grisly details of the Boxheim scheme nearly forgotten.

Hitler's charm offensive began at the Kaiserhof Hotel, his preferred Berlin residence, located kitty-corner from Chancellor Brüning's office on Wilhelmstrasse. The Kaiserhof was nearly as palatial as the chancellery itself. Hitler's full staff often took up an entire floor of the hotel (usually the top one). His Kaiserhof perch give him and his entourage the air of a government-in-waiting, pounding at the gates of power just across the street. It was the perfect location, Hitler thought, for a big press conference to deny his complicity in the Boxheim affair and get his name and rhetoric into the newspapers.

Ernst Hanfstaengl, now Hitler's international press secretary, knew that if the party called a regular news conference, the leading German newspapers would simply boycott the event, making Hitler look foolish. Hanfstaengl proposed to invite only the foreign press. If prominent overseas newspapers wrote about Hitler, the German press would be forced to write about the foreign press writing about the leader of Germany's second-largest party. Hitler loved the idea.

The Kaiserhof bar had already become a regular stop on the elbow-bending and news-gathering circuit of the foreign correspondents in Berlin. Like newsmen everywhere, they knew a good story could often be found over good drinks, whether with primary sources or with their underlings. Clearly, Hitler was the coming story, the man who was stirring the German political pot. Dismissed and even despised by many foreign reporters, he nonetheless had to be heard. "Each morning foreign correspondents in Berlin expected the Brüning Government to fall and Fascist Adolf Hitler... to seize the Government," wrote *Time* magazine.[10]

Warmed up by Hanfstaengl's clever provision of glasses of sherry and a light buffet at the Kaiserhof, the foreign reporters were ready at 4:00 p.m. on December 4, 1931, to take a fresh look at the Nazi leader.[11] Arriving late, Hitler proceeded to predict his certain victory in the next parliamentary election, whenever it might come. Denying responsibility for the Boxheim affair, he admitted that "my will is law" in the Nazi Party but said that he could not prevent some of his several hundred thousand party members from "having ideas of their own."[12] Hitler ranged widely over economic and foreign policy topics, stroking the newsmen's need for words of conciliation among former enemies. He claimed to have worked for twelve years to eliminate the old German phrase "God punish England!"[13] France, of course, remained an implacable enemy (French journalists had reportedly not been invited to the news conference). For his American audience, Hitler insisted that he and his party were Germany's only bulwark against Marxism—a sure winner with the anti-Communist US media.

The Kaiserhof schmooze was the beginning of a chain of media stories that lasted until year's end. Paying particular attention to the American and British press, Hitler gave interviews to the Associated Press, the *New*

York Times, the *Detroit News*, the *Christian Science Monitor*, and the *Sunday Graphic and Sunday News*. Articles ran in the *New York Herald Tribune*, the *Chicago Tribune*, the *Daily Express*, the *Daily Mail*, and again in the *New York Times*. Hitler wrote a lengthy essay for the hugely influential North American Newspaper Alliance, syndicated all over the United States.[14] For good measure, he also sat for interviews with Italy's *Gazzetta del Popolo* and Japan's *Nichi Nichi Shimbun*.

In his interviews, the indefatigable Nazi leader pounded consistent themes, painting himself as a reasonable man with no desire for a Boxheim-style revolution and, again, as the West's best defense against Bolshevism. He invoked existential threats (Communism), professed his own purity ("What we want is equality"), and set up boogeymen (the Treaty of Versailles; France). He also blithely asserted that the Nazis were already the strongest party in Germany, with fifteen million voters behind them. The fall of the Brüning government (and Hitler's presumptive ascension to the helm) was "only a question of weeks or months," he claimed in the *New York Times*.[15] Assuring nervous American capitalists that the Nazis respected private property, Hitler claimed he would honor private and commercial debts. The Nazi leader singled out for praise the isolationist US senator William Borah, an Idaho Republican who chaired the Senate Foreign Relations Committee. Borah—who had denounced the Treaty of Versailles as too harsh toward Germany—was an example of "genuine Americanism asserting itself in plain everyday language," said Hitler.

When Hitler scheduled a second international press conference for December 11, he hit a stumbling block. The Prussian interior minister, Carl Severing, brandished the Damoclean sword of possible deportation of the stateless Nazi leader. To Severing, the Boxheim Document's portents of violent overthrow and repression met the minimum requirement for pushing the Austrian-born Hitler out. Severing could only deport Hitler from Prussia, not from the whole of Germany. Still, Prussia comprised more than half of German territory, including Berlin. The minister could at least force Hitler into the political ghetto of Bavaria. Severing's scheme was a sly move; it would have humiliated and partially neutralized Hitler. But Hitler canceled his news conference before Severing could pounce.

Since the Brüning government denied Hitler access to German radio, he decided to take to American radio instead. He prepared an address to deliver to Americans via a telephone hookup to the Columbia Broadcasting System—CBS—with an English translation to follow.[16] A nationwide speech to the American people was the Nazi chief's boldest attempt yet to sway German voters through the back door of the international media. But since the government controlled both the airwaves and the telephone lines, it denied Hitler the necessary hookup to London, where the address would have to be retransmitted to New York. Hitler's speech would never be heard.

The agile Hanfstaengl released the radio text to the American press. The powerful anti-Communist Hearst newspaper chain printed Hitler's address throughout the United States.[17] In it, Hitler offered soothing words. "I know what war is like," he wrote. Repeating his new favorite mantra, he added: "We want nothing but a Monroe Doctrine.... America for the Americans and Germany for the Germans"—Hitler's pious way of justifying ethnic exclusion.

Hitler's words made their way right back into the German media. The *Vossische Zeitung* ran a front-page story the very next day. While reporting on Hitler's address, the newspaper was also at pains to downplay it. "Anyone who knows how avidly the American press chases 'news' also understands how quickly their interest fades," sniffed the paper.

Hitler's peace-loving claims clashed with reports of his party's dirty doings. A meeting of the National Socialist Pharmacists and Physicians was prominently covered on December 8 on the front page of the *New York Times*.[18] The Nazi druggists and doctors touted "racial purification" as one of the prime goals of the Nazi Party, all in support of the Nordic race—"the finest flower on the tree of humanity," as one speaker put it. Echoing eugenics doctrine in America, the Nazi doctors called for racial classifications to segregate undesirables so they could be sterilized and eliminated. Loudest among the orators was the pharmacist turned politician Gregor Strasser, Hitler's number two. Once in power, said Strasser, the Nazis would restore Germany's "primitive vigor," return women from the factories to the kitchen, execute Marxists by hanging, and abolish such "Jewish abstractions" as "stock companies" and trade unions.

Yet in the same issue of the *New York Times,* on page 6, a three-column-length article ran under the byline "By Adolf Hitler." It was the North American Newspaper Alliance essay, and it was mostly sweetness and light.[19] Hitler claimed to stand only for the forgotten virtues of "frugality, inner discipline and honesty." Germany, Hitler pleaded, was on its sick-bed economically and needed "an entirely different treatment from that prescribed by the Versailles quack doctors in 1919." In a single issue, the *Times* had showcased Hitler's habitual tactic of having it both ways.

In mid-December Hitler's media caravan culminated in a cover story in *Time,* the world's leading newsmagazine.[20] While archly describing Hitler as a "small, sparse" man with "the little mustache and the great, rasping voice," *Time* granted that Hitler's goal of taking power was in sight. The magazine ridiculed the "Brüning dictatorship" for "trying to out-Hitler Hitler" with its harsh austerity policies. Meanwhile, "Adolf Hitler sat in Berlin giving press interviews as though he were already Chief of State."

Hanfstaengl had converted the foreign press into a primary source for the German press. "No one can be completely informed about what is happening here without consulting the foreign correspondents," groused Bella Fromm, a *Vossische Zeitung* writer.[21]

Glaringly absent from Hitler's wordy interviews had been any reference to the Great Depression, to racial purity, to his burning desire to conquer Russian territory, or to his rabid nationalism. Strikingly, he made no mention at all of Jews—until his last American interview of the year. On December 28, 1931, he was visited at the Brown House in Munich for a five-minute conversation with Annetta Antona, a longtime columnist for the *Detroit News.* After touching on the usual topics, the interviewer posed a simple question:

"Why are you anti-Semitic?"

Hitler's reply was swift: "Somebody has to be blamed for our troubles. Judaism means the rule of gold. We Germans are land-minded, not money-minded."

Antona asked why a large oil painting of Henry Ford, the famed carmaker and notorious anti-Semite, hung behind Hitler's desk.

"I regard Henry Ford as my inspiration," replied Hitler.[22]

The international media parade was not over. The most influential—and most mistaken—of Hitler's American interlocutors was a renowned and rising journalist named Dorothy Thompson. A respected correspondent for the *New York Evening Post,* Thompson had in December of 1931 snagged an audience with Hitler for an article in a 1932 issue of *Cosmopolitan,* a prestigious American magazine. When Thompson walked into Hitler's Kaiserhof hotel suite, she was expecting to be impressed. Instead, she was taken aback:

> I was convinced that I was meeting the future dictator of Germany. In something less than fifty seconds I was quite sure that I was not.
>
> It took just about that time to measure the startling insignificance of this man who has set the world agog.
>
> He is formless, almost faceless, a man whose countenance is a caricature, a man whose framework seems cartilaginous, without bones. He is inconsequent and voluble, ill-poised, insecure. He is the very prototype of the Little Man....
>
> His movements are awkward, almost undignified and most un-martial. There is in his face no trace of any inner conflict or self-discipline.[23]

Thompson's withering first impression did not prevent her from judging that the Nazis had become in all probability the strongest political movement in the Reich: "They are ripe for power."[24] The writer even granted that Hitler might in the next election get the fifteen million votes he was predicting. *"But fifteen million Germans CAN be wrong,"* Thompson insisted, in italics. She condescendingly asserted that the Nazi Party was "a peasant movement" whose supporters were only "little people."[25]

Thompson's article, "I Saw Hitler!," appeared in *Cosmopolitan*'s March 1932 issue and was immediately published as a small book that became a bestseller. The writer's belittling view of the Führer and his movement added to the conviction among educated elites that Hitler was a clown and a charlatan who could be dismissed.[26]

Adolf Hitler and heavily bemedaled Hermann Göring saluting Storm Troopers in Nuremberg. [*Alamy*]

Hitler loved speaking at Munich's upscale Bürger-bräukeller beer hall, where his 1923 putsch failed and his 1925 comeback began. [*Bundesarchiv*]

Alamy

In the spring of 1925, Hitler finished the first volume of his political manifesto, *Mein Kampf*. He worked in a small cabin on the Obersalzberg, a mountain near Berchtesgaden. He called his retreat a *Kampfhäusl*, or combat cottage. [*akpool*]

[*Bayerische Staatsbibliothek*]

[*National Archives*]

The alleged love of Hitler's life was his half niece Geli Raubal (*left*). Picnicking with Geli and his entourage around Bavaria's lakes was one of Hitler's favorite diversions. In 1931, using Hitler's pistol, Geli committed suicide in his Munich apartment. [*National Archives*]

The Nazis made their "restless energy" felt with constant marching, singing, and politicking. [*National Archives*]

Joseph Goebbels (*left*) boosted Nazi operations in Berlin with fiery speeches and Storm Trooper violence. [*Alamy*]

Gregor Strasser (*right*) was the organizational brains behind Hitler's electoral success. Hitler later had him murdered. [*National Archives*]

A vicious 1930 Nazi campaign placard depicted Jews as a snake infested with Hitler's bugaboos—Marxism, war guilt, inflation, corruption, and "girl trafficking." [*Bundesarchiv*]

In the early 1930s, jobless coal miners in Silesia moved their families into primitive semi-underground barracks. [*Alamy*]

Leaning on a rope, out-of-work German men paid pennies to sleep for an hour in a warming shelter. [*Alamy*]

In 1932, Hitler reinvented electoral campaigning with an airborne whistle-stop tour. He also covered thousands of kilometers in an open-top car—his preferred mode of travel. [*National Archives*]

[*National Archives*]

Politics in the 1930s became a bloody business. Hitler continually lionized and honored the wounded and dead among his violence-prone followers. [*National Archives*]

In 1932, Hitler ran for president against the incumbent, Field Marshal Paul von Hindenburg (*left*)—and lost. But in January of 1933, the president's son, Colonel Oskar von Hindenburg (*in uniform below*), urged his father to make Hitler chancellor. Other members of the influential camarilla around the president included Franz von Papen, Kurt von Schleicher, Otto Meissner, and Joachim von Ribbentrop, a Champagne dealer whose villa was used for secret negotiations with Hitler. Alfred Hugenberg nearly stopped Hitler's ascent, but he gave in at the last minute.

Hindenburg [*Alamy*]

Papen [*Alamy*]

Schleicher [*Alamy*]

Meissner [*Alamy*]

Ribbentrop [*Alamy*]

Hugenberg [*Bundesarchiv*]

Meissner often rode with Papen in Berlin's sprawling Tiergarten park. [*Alamy*]

On January 30, 1933, Hitler's unfathomable ascent succeeded. Waving from a chancellery window, Germany's new chancellor soaked up the cheers of more than thirty-five thousand Storm Troopers, members of the Steel Helmet veterans' association, and civilians celebrating his takeover with a torchlight parade. [*Alamy*]

[*Alamy*]

Yet another close observer underestimated Hitler. US ambassador Frederic Sackett had been trying for months to warn Washington that Hitler was as dangerous as the Communists, but the State Department did not appreciate the gravity of his cautions. A Harvard-educated lawyer, successful businessman, and former US senator from Kentucky, Sackett decided he should get a closer look at the man who was commanding so much attention from the media. Since meeting openly with Hitler might offend the government to which he was accredited, Sackett arranged a secret Saturday afternoon social gathering at the home of Emil Georg von Stauss, a director of the Deutsche Diskonto Bank. As cover, wives were included in the invitation to Sackett and to his fellow US diplomat Alfred Klieforth, who acted as translator. On the Nazi side, Göring, Hanfstaengl, and Rudolf Hess showed up. Hitler, the main object of the little tête-à-tête, was invited under his hoary but thin cover name, Herr Wolf.

The afternoon tea soon lapsed into the familiar farce of Hitler orating—"as if he were addressing a large audience"—and everyone else listening. The Nazi leader never looked the American ambassador in the eye. Sackett was surprised that such a quirky character could be leading a powerful political movement that might someday rule Germany. The ambassador ratcheted down his assessment of Hitler, describing the Nazi leader as a "fanatical crusader" possessed of "forcefulness and intensity" who would nonetheless be found unacceptable by educated people—and thus unelectable. Hitler's speaking ability gave him appeal only to "those classes that do not weigh his outpourings," Sackett wrote to the secretary of state, Henry L. Stimson. Trapped in his elitist bubble, the American envoy ignored Hitler's rousing emotional appeal to the six million voters he had won a year earlier. Sackett informed the secretary of state that Hitler was certainly "not the type from which statesmen evolve."

Part Four

GRASPING FOR POWER

(1932)

People lacked the very essentials of living, and suicides were daily occurrences in the large cities.

—A white-collar worker

My wife underwent untold hardships throughout these years. To enable me to pay my party dues, and spend an occasional penny, she worked hard at sewing.... Frequently, if I returned home at night from a meeting or a propaganda trip, I still found her bent over her work, happy to see me come home unharmed.

—Unemployed Nazi Party member[1]

Morning after morning, all over the immense, damp, dreary town and the packing-case colonies of huts in the suburb allotments, young men were waking up to another workless empty day to be spent as they could best contrive; selling boot-laces, begging, playing draughts in the hall of the Labour Exchange, hanging about urinals, opening the doors of cars, helping with crates in the markets, gossiping, lounging, stealing, overhearing racing tips, sharing stumps of cigarette-ends picked up in the gutter.

—Christopher Isherwood, 1932

38

A FLOATING POLITICAL GAME

Now I've got them in my pocket! They have recognized me as a partner in their negotiations.

—*Adolf Hitler, 1932*

I have to stiffen Hitler's spine.

—*Joseph Goebbels, 1932*

Hitler had lost momentum. Despite a string of recent successes in local and state elections, the self-proclaimed savior was no closer to high office at the beginning of 1932 than he had been a year earlier. His rise to the control of Germany was not quite as predestined as he had just boastfully claimed in his New Year's message to the party. All the Nazis had to show for their 107 seats in the Reichstag was noisy obstructionism and political stunts. Too many volatile forces, competitors, and unpredictables were in play for Hitler or anyone else to have a lock on Germany's future.

But the economy was in free fall. By early January, wages were sinking, and joblessness had risen to nearly six million—an unemployment rate of 30 percent, twelve points worse than in the United States.[1] Tightly yoked as it was to plunging US fortunes, Germany's production machine was battered externally as well as internally. The country's industrial output dropped to barely half of its 1928 levels. Chancellor Brüning's rule by decrees from President Hindenburg—endorsed by the defense and interior minister, Wilhelm Groener—was not working well.[2]

On New Year's Eve, President Hindenburg had dolefully addressed the German people by radio. The best he could offer in the trough of the Depression was a chin-up appeal that Germans beset by disaster should simply "see it through," just as he had done in the 1914 Battle of Tannenberg, when he vanquished Russia's seemingly superior First and Second Armies. But the lameness of the presidential message was highlighted by an unexpected interruption of the broadcast: In midspeech, his oration was broken by a voice shouting, "The shadow of the Red Front is over Germany! Let all proletarians unite in opposition to the emergency decrees and the dictatorship!" Communist dirty tricksters had found a way to tap the radio transmission lines and disrupt Hindenburg's attempt to rally the nation.[3]

Germany's economic crisis was on fullest display in Berlin, the outsize city with outsize problems. Slum districts teemed with out-of-work men and hungry people. Wandering into a tenement quarter, an American journalist reported:

> An iron screen guarded the buffet and behind the bars lay a fly-specked platter of fried horse meat and a pair of horse meat sausages. The guests were hungry. They sat at their tables and gazed through the bars at the horse meat. It was dinner time, but they ordered nothing. . . . A tall young man, his skinny neck sticking out of a tattered overcoat that flapped about his ankles, wandered through the room holding out a once-white dress shirt. He was willing to trade the shirt for the price of a horse meat sausage. He found no takers. His own chest was shirtless.[4]

The Nazis were worried. "The new year must be decisive," Goebbels confided to his diary on New Year's Day.[5] He openly admitted to Storm Troopers in the Sports Palace that seizing power had become an existential matter for their movement. "The decision will come in the next four to five months. If the Nazi Party does not come to power by then, Germany's downfall and breakup is unavoidable."[6]

Goebbels was as usual full of apocalyptic hot air, but his bluster could sometimes drive events. His histrionic wailings were in fact a sly attempt to build a fire under Hitler. The propaganda chief wanted Hitler to reenergize his political bandwagon by shifting his focus from the chancellorship to the unlikeliest office of all for a stateless man from Austria: the presidency of Germany. Goebbels wanted Hitler to shoulder his way into the halls of power through the portal of the presidential palace.

Running for president was a bold idea, but Hitler was undecided. Keeping every option open, the Nazi leader was playing dodgeball in a floating political game. He was the uncertain factor that everyone both feared and wanted. Brüning and the coterie of advisers around President Hindenburg still sought a way to make Hitler adhere to a larger political force that would give him standing while limiting his power. Smothering Hitler with a political embrace was their goal. Hitler knew the game and was avoiding the hug. He was also temporizing over Goebbels's insistence that he raise the stakes, and his profile, by taking on Germany's greatest living icon, Hindenburg.

In fact, the eighty-four-year-old field marshal did not want to be president anymore. Tired, frustrated, and longing to retire to his East Prussia estate, Hindenburg was especially disinclined to mount a political campaign to hold on to the job. But Brüning and his advisers saw no alternative. Desperate to project an image of political stability and calm to the outside world, Brüning needed Hindenburg's reassuring presence in office to forestall a complete drain of US money from the German economy. Still hoping for Hitler's backing of a second Hindenburg term through a dodgy constitutional amendment, the bespectacled chancellor turned for help to his defense and interior minister, Wilhelm Groener, who agreed, along with Hindenburg's chief of staff, Otto Meissner, to make a renewed approach to Hitler. They telegraphed the Nazi leader in Munich, inviting him to Berlin to discuss the matter.

This was the moment Hitler had longed for. After seven years of dogged campaigning, he was being summoned to the inner sanctum of the power brokers. Reading the telegram in the *Völkischer Beobachter* offices, Hitler held the paper up for Alfred Rosenberg and others to see. "Now I've got them in my pocket!" he exulted. "They have recognized me as a partner in their negotiations."[7]

The Nazi chief traveled to Berlin, but the meeting was a failure. By some accounts, Groener and Meissner indirectly offered Hitler the

German chancellorship if he would agree to propose Hindenburg's prolongation as president. Whether that was true or not, Hitler did not take the bait. Instead, he demanded new elections; he was rebuffed. Everybody was turned off and unhappy. The Nazi leader clearly had no one in his pocket. Groener's conclusion was that Hitler should be kept away from political power "at all costs."[8]

Goebbels continued to press Hitler to declare his intention to run for president. Hitler procrastinated. And then he made a speech.

Hitler's address on January 26, 1932, to the exclusive Industry Club in the stylish Rhine River city of Düsseldorf became the most noted political event of the new year. A high temple of German capitalism, the club boasted an elite membership of magnates and would-be magnates who gathered there for meals and schmoozing. Once per month, the club invited a notable dinner speaker. On the night of the Nazi leader's appearance, the scene around Düsseldorf's Park Hotel, where the club was housed, resembled a military siege. The hotel's first-floor windows were shuttered, its main entrance heavily guarded. Police cordons held back angry Socialist and Communist demonstrators who surged against the security lines, shouting taunts and epithets at the buttoned-up gentlemen in dark suits headed for the club banquet. "Down with Hitler, slave of the capitalists!" was a favorite gibe. Hitler was headed for a "pig-out" at the "banquet table of the steel kings," announced the Communist newspaper.[9] Nervous about the crowds in front of the hotel, Hitler's driver pulled into an inner courtyard, where the Nazi chief could slip in through a side door.[10]

All six hundred tickets to the Industry Club's closed-door banquet were sold out.[11] As usual, it had been the Nazi-friendly steel baron Fritz Thyssen who brokered Hitler's invitation to the club (Thyssen had originally wanted Gregor Strasser, seen among businessmen as the reasonable Nazi, but Hitler grabbed the invitation for himself). The press was barred from the event—but details of Hitler's speech quickly leaked out. Right from the beginning of the two-hour oration, club members got what they came for: a dazzling display of the renowned firebrand's rhetorical gift. Though the Nazi leader stuck to his usual script—Germany's downfall, the National Socialist promise of redemption through a national community—most of the men of the Industry Club had never heard it before, certainly not from Hitler's lips. He spun out his complex views on history and politics with references to Bismarck, Frederick the Great, and General Carl von Clausewitz (1780–1831), the Prussian military theorist. Stroking his audience, the Nazi political philosopher lauded elite leadership as preferable to a democracy that was only "the rule of stupidity, mediocrity, half measures, cowardice, weakness, and incompetence." His address was less about Germany's plight in the pit of the Depression than about the condition of mankind and the decay that had beset the German people since the 1918 revolution—good applause lines for nationalists and industrialists. Hitler knew he was among sophisticated people, not a beer-hall audience; he avoided attacking Jews or even mentioning his lust for land in Russia.

Hitler ended his marathon discourse in his usual exhausted state. Thyssen quickly shut down Albert Vögler, one of the Ruhr region's top industrialists, who tried to initiate a discussion. Hitler did not stay for dinner, leaving the gustatory pleasures to the increasingly Falstaffian Hermann Göring, who had accompanied Hitler to the event. Göring's social skills made him good company among the elites; he never saw a banquet he did not like.

The assembled captains of industry gave Hitler "long, stormy applause" after his speech, but attempts to turn praise into monetary support fell flat. Nazi efforts to gather donations or even pledges at the banquet were largely spurned.[12] More significant was the negative reaction that Hitler's appearance provoked outside the Industry Club. In Depression-racked Germany, the Nazi chief was denounced in the liberal press for his elbow rubbing with the business class and "fraternization over Champagne." The Communist newspaper published cartoons of Hitler scarfing down a seven-course feast, though he had skipped the meal. Even Hitler's own camp was nonplussed by their leader's bald-faced foray into the belly of the capitalist beast; Nazi newspapers were uncharacteristically quiet.

Hitler's and Goebbels's iron maxim that any publicity is better than no publicity had backfired. The Düsseldorf event was a misstep, more costly in political terms than profitable in economic terms. Burned, the Nazis turned down an invitation for Hitler to speak again to businessmen in Hannover. The Nazi leader lapsed into a bohemian reverie and retreated for a rest in the mountains.

Goebbels was frustrated. "I have to stiffen Hitler's spine," he told himself.[13] The propaganda meister's efforts to push his boss into the presidential race had not gone unnoticed by the Nazis' opponents. Albert Grzesinski, the plainspoken chief of Berlin's huge police force and a passionate Social Democrat, tried to derail a Hitler candidacy before it started. In a much-noticed speech to twenty thousand listeners in Leipzig, Grzesinski played the citizenship card, proposing that "the foreigner Adolf Hitler" be chased out of Germany "with a dog whip."[14] Grzesinski's colorful language came as a gift to Goebbels, who loved such taunts—useful fodder for arousing the masses.

The question of presidential succession overshadowed all political discussions. After a special committee of notables was formed and three million signatures were gathered on a petition begging President Hindenburg to run again, the Old Gentleman relented. In a historic switch, the Social Democrats threw their support behind him, though in 1925 they had bitterly opposed the field marshal in his first election. Hindenburg, the old Junker, stood for almost all that the Socialists opposed—the military class, the monarchy, big capital, and big landowners. But the Socialists were horrified at the prospect of a Hitler presidency; they chose Hindenburg as the lesser evil.

As soon as Hitler learned that the "Marxists" were backing Hindenburg, he decided to run. With the president now politically tied to the left wing (he also had the support of the center), Hitler thought he could corner the conservative nationalist vote. He allowed Goebbels to break the news of his candidacy on February 22 in front of twenty thousand Storm Troopers in the Sports Palace. The audience acted as though Hitler had just walked on water. "People laugh, people cry, many are beside themselves," scribbled the Berlin gauleiter.[15] Hitler wanted to hear all the details of the Sports Palace event; he invited himself over to Goebbels's apartment at midnight. Goebbels and his new wife, Magda, gladly climbed out of bed to welcome the boss.

To Goebbels and Magda, sudden late-night visits by Hitler were becoming routine. In marrying Goebbels, Magda had known that she would enter a life of nonstop politics. Thrilled to be at the epicenter of Germany's most energetic and controversial political movement, she had even begun hosting weekly late-afternoon teas for prominent Nazis and influential journalists—"my five o'clocks," she called the gatherings. She had turned the Goebbelses' spacious apartment in Berlin's prestigious West End into a sought-after Nazi salon.[16] Hitler had begun using their flat as a refuge and retreat. Probably in love with Hitler as much as she was with Goebbels, Magda welcomed the party chief's visits, even after midnight. When Hitler arrived, the propaganda meister described a scene of "frenzy upon frenzy [at the Sports Palace] until the roof threatened to cave in." Hitler left the Goebbelses' apartment in the wee hours with tears in his eyes. He could already envision himself as president of Germany.[17]

Hitler's candidacy did not please Alfred Hugenberg. The bumptious publisher-politician was still bitter over Hitler's dismissive behavior five months earlier at Bad Harzburg. Staunchly opposed to a Nazi dictatorship,[18] Hugenberg threw his diminishing political weight behind another presidential candidate: Theodore Duesterberg, deputy chief of the Steel Helmet veterans' association. Hard-core nationalist voters would now be drawn in three directions—to Hindenburg, to Hitler, and to Duesterberg. The split practically guaranteed that there would be no outright winner in the election's first round. A runoff would no doubt be necessary.

Hitler faced one last hitch: he was still not a German citizen. Through some fast-paced maneuverings by the Nazi-friendly government of the city-state of Braunschweig, Hitler was sworn in on February 26 as a *Regierungsrat*—a government counselor. Hitler's new title came with no particular duties but conferred German citizenship. In Braunschweig's legation building in Berlin (all seventeen states had legations in the capital), officials were treated to the unlikely sight of the famed and fiery orator taking the oath of a petty bureaucrat—and vowing to "be loyal to the Reich and state constitutions, to obey the law, and to faithfully fulfill the duties" of a government counselor. Hitler was sworn to protect the very constitution he hated, a technicality he would cast aside at the first opportunity.

Forty-two years after his birth as an Austrian, Hitler had become officially what he always claimed to be emotionally—a German.

39

RUNNING FOR PRESIDENT

Venerable old man—you can no longer provide cover for those whom we intend to destroy! Step aside! Clear the way!

—*Adolf Hitler, campaigning against President Hindenburg, 1932*

He who can explain this remarkable phenomenon can throw light upon the singular wave of mass emotion that is sweeping over Germany and will roll up millions of votes... for the National Socialists in the Presidential election.

—*Harold Callender,* New York Times, *1932*

Hitler was four hours late. Still, the Breslau mob—fifty thousand excited Silesians—waited expectantly, listening to marching bands, noshing on their victuals, watching the crowd grow. A local newspaper reported on the unprecedented turnout:

> Trucks brought National Socialists from Silesian villages—their roofs were covered with people. Likewise, on public buses, private autos of every kind, including some ancient heaps... people hung on in the most uncomfortable positions or atop the buses, not scared off.... The stream never stopped: horse-drawn wagons, bicycles, and motorcycles.... They brought their own lunches and an evening snack. Vendors peddled fruit and refreshments through the crowd. Volunteer first aid personnel were on hand, SS officers directed the crowds—all in all, a colorful, lively scenario.[1]

Hitler's presidential campaign had quickly turned into a replay of the 1930 road show—only bigger and more spectacular. Giving twelve major speeches in eleven days, he stumped Germany like an itinerant preacher. The campaign lasted only two weeks, from March 1 to March 13, 1932. At age forty-two—exactly half Hindenburg's age—Hitler was a political whirlwind, dashing from Stettin to Stuttgart, from Nuremberg to Cologne, from Hamburg to Frankfurt. His crowds were enormous—20,000 in Frankfurt, 35,000 in Cologne. Meanwhile, the Old Gentleman sat stone-faced and unmoving in his Berlin palace.

Hindenburg appeared in public only once, standing in review of the Berlin Guards Regiment, saying nothing but occasionally raising his baton in salute.[2] In his full field marshal's regalia, a head taller than almost anyone in the crowd, the president looked like a born king; his political handlers made sure that the scene was included in the newsreels shown in movie theaters all over Germany. Hindenburg's Social Democratic supporters, spooked by Hitler's recent successes in regional elections, came up with a simple negative campaign slogan: "Beat Hitler—elect Hindenburg!"

Besides Hitler and Hindenburg, the other two serious candidates for president were Steel Helmet leader Duesterberg and Ernst Thälmann, the fiery leader of the Communists, with a base that usually won 10 percent in national elections. But the election was really all about Hitler and Hindenburg. Hitler ran around casting himself as a self-styled bearer of German salvation. He sermonized to the jammed crowds as a messiah come to lift them from their despair. The Nazi leader appealed not to his listeners' economic concerns but to their emotional core—to visceral issues of identity and national pride. Germany's problem, he said, was not "a broken economy but a broken people." Hitler blithely leaped over facts, figures, and economic details. Rather than a jobs program or policies for overcoming the Depression, Hitler proposed rebirth. His vision was utopia. By joining the National Socialist movement, the *Volk* would be whole again, baptized into the single creed of Germanness.

In his Breslau speech, Hitler had reminded Germans of the humiliating Treaty of Versailles, the Rhineland military occupations, the horrifying hyperinflation, and, now, the crashing economy. Grandiose, histrionic, often historically inaccurate, Hitler's hypnotic preachments seemed to lift his admirers into a collective ecstasy.[3] In Frankfurt, *New York Times* correspondent Harold Callender was astonished by the fervent patience of a crowd of 20,000 that noshed on sandwiches, drank beer, and squirmed in their seats until Hitler arrived at 10:30 in the evening; his car had broken down on the route from Weimar. After waiting nearly seven hours, the assembled masses heard a hoarse Hitler deliver thirty-five minutes of "vehement generalities," noted Callender. Yet even a tired Hitler could put on a rhetorical display. Shaping words with his busy hands, wagging a finger downward like a thunderbolt-hurling demigod, gathering the longings and frustrations of his listeners into splayed fingers cupped toward himself like an enveloping embrace, Hitler massaged his audience with both speech and gesture. In his screeching style, he once again attacked the evils of *das System*. "The system" was the perfect target: it sounded mean and wicked; it sounded overwhelming; it sounded secretive—a projection surface for people's fears. Was it the government? The scheming party politicians? The lying press? The industrialists? The Jews?

It was any and all of those. Hitler was issuing a blanket indictment of Germany's system of governance. He was proposing not just a regime change but also a system overthrow—through the ballot box.

People came to Frankfurt and other cities to experience a Hitlerian laying on of hands—the promise of rescue in a world of misery.[4] "He who can explain this remarkable phenomenon," Callender wrote, "can throw light upon the singular wave of mass emotion that is sweeping over Germany and will roll up millions of votes—more millions than in 1930—for the National Socialists in the Presidential election."[5]

Sometimes the campaign strain got to Hitler. After a late-night speech in Hamburg, he fell the next morning into a state of near helplessness, giving observers a rare glimpse of his weaknesses. "M'zoup! M'zoup!" he whimpered to his staff, complaining that his breakfast soup had not yet arrived in his plush room at the Hotel Atlantic. By the time Hamburg gauleiter Albert Krebs arrived with the morning newspapers, Hitler appeared to be a bent and burdened man slurping vegetable soup alone.

Hitler quizzed Krebs on vegetarian diets, turning the conversation into a classic Hitlerian monologue. Krebs watched the spellbinding speaker of the previous night fall into feeble hypochondria. Hitler said he suffered from sweating, trembling, extreme nervousness, and stomach cramps. He feared that he might not have long to live. "I have no time to wait!" he told Krebs. "If I had time, I would never have run for the presidency at all. The old man [Hindenburg] won't last much longer anyway. But I can't lose a single year more. I *must* come to power soon to be able to finish the gigantic tasks in the time left to me. I must! I must!"[6]

Refusing to campaign, President Hindenburg gave only one speech; it was on the radio, not in front of a political rally. Nonetheless, radio was a powerful medium for reaching a national rather than a local audience. Even with his stilted speaking style, the president's address drew a huge listenership.*

Angry as hell, Hindenburg was at pains to justify his candidacy as something far more than a concession to appeals by the Social Democrats and by Brüning's Catholics. He was running, said the president, as a nonpartisan candidate of "unity" to prevent "a radical candidate of the right or of the left" from seizing Germany's highest office. He meant Hitler. Steaming mad at "untruths being spread about me," the normally emotionless Hindenburg spat out the word *untruths* and banged his fist on his desk so vigorously that the nationwide radio audience could easily hear it.[7] The gesture was a rare and endearing show of feeling by the stolid Prussian officer, who otherwise spoke in the stiff tones of a trained soldier, not a politician.

To counter Hitler's repeated boast that he, as a former army private, represented Germany's heroic frontline generation, the old field marshal invoked the "spirit of 1914," reminding listeners of his First World War triumphs. Hindenburg was running on his name and reputation alone. "I

---

* Germany by now had 4.2 million registered radios with an estimated regular listening audience of 11 million people—probably more for a presidential address.

don't consider it necessary to hold a programmatic speech. My life and my life's work say more about my aspirations and my intentions than words ever could."

Chancellor Heinrich Brüning, meanwhile, was a man afire. Keeping Hindenburg in the presidential chair—and Hitler out of it—was critical to his own program and his political survival. Rushing around the country in support of Hindenburg's candidacy, the Jesuitical ascetic morphed into an avenging angel. His rallies, like Hitler's, drew tens of thousands. The normally restrained economics professor became the Old Gentleman's alter ego, casting brimstone where Hindenburg only cast disapproving glances. Brüning predicted the apocalypse if Hitler became president. "Hindenburg must be victorious because Germany must survive," he said.[8]

The Social Democrats, old hands at red-meat agitprop, insisted that a "reactionary" Hitler presidency would mean "the destruction of all civil liberties as well as the destruction of the press, cultural organizations, and labor unions."[9] They echoed the Hindenburg campaign slogan: "Beat Hitler—elect Hindenburg!" The SPD formed an antifascist, prorepublican alliance called the Iron Front.[10] By embracing one of Germany's iconic symbols—iron—the leftists in the Iron Front cloaked themselves in the mantle of patriotism and steadfastness, reminding voters of Bismarck's 1862 description of "blood and iron" as the essentials of German might. Though Hitler often invoked Bismarck's words, it was the Socialists who, during this election, made the Iron Front a brand of their own, linking the steely Hindenburg with the revered Iron Chancellor, Bismarck.

After his first meeting with Hindenburg, in 1931, Hitler told his intimates that the field marshal had become "a doddering old geezer who can't even pee anymore."[11] Now Hitler was struggling to walk a fine line between respect and dismissal by portraying Hindenburg as a man who had done great service to the nation but whose time had passed. In Nuremberg, however, the Nazi leader's words went over the edge: "Today I see before me an eighty-five-year-old [*sic*] geriatric and I must call out to him: 'Old man, you no longer carry the future of Germany on your shoulders. Now we must have our turn. You can no longer assume our responsibilities. We, the war generation, will do it ourselves. Venerable old man—you can no longer provide cover for those whom we intend to destroy! Step aside! Clear the way!'"[12]

40

CERTAIN OF VICTORY

Had a phone call with Hitler. He is shocked beyond measure.

—*Joseph Goebbels, 1932*

[Hitler's] gone crazy.... Hess, you need to call a doctor. That's not normal—impossible!

—*Gerdy Troost, 1932*

As the presidential election day neared, fears of a coup d'état or even a civil war rose dramatically. One newspaper darkly reported that units of Nazi Storm Troopers with field rations and bandages were on the march toward Berlin from Silesia in the east and the Rhineland in the west.[1] A Nazi putsch attempt was suspected if Hitler should *lose* the election; another more insistent rumor predicted a coup if Hitler *won* the presidency and decided to replace the Brüning administration with a Nazi-dominated cabinet without holding a parliamentary election.

Interior Minister Groener believed that an intra-Nazi conspiracy of Goebbels, Strasser, and Wilhelm Frick would oust Hitler from the Nazi leadership if he failed in his "one last chance" to achieve power on "the legal path."[2] Groener authorized the temporary closing of various Nazi newspapers as well as raids on Goebbels's offices in search of weapons and incriminating material. All political demonstrations were banned on election weekend. Even "standing around by pedestrians" would attract police attention. All vacation time and leave for Berlin police officers and the Prussian state forces were canceled for four days.

Hitler liked his odds. The federal election board had calculated that the eligible electorate for 1932 was forty-four million voters—three million more than in 1930. Most of the newly eligible voters were young Germans, a cohort that had strongly supported the Nazi leader in the last election.[3] Hitler told H. R. Knickerbocker of the *New York Evening Post* that he expected to best Hindenburg in the first round: the president would receive "no more than 12,000,000 votes," while he, Hitler, "cannot get less than 12,000,000."[4]

Hitler estimated that neither man would win an absolute majority in a multicandidate first round. But in the second round, in April—when the winner could be decided by a plurality—Hitler believed there was "no question of the outcome."

Goebbels, too, anticipated victory. "Fantastic numbers estimated for Hitler," he wrote.[5] Campaign money, a concern only a few weeks earlier, had suddenly begun flowing. "Just got 200,000 marks—that aces it for the final week," Goebbels noted.

On Sunday, March 13, 1932—election day—Hitler made the four-hundred-mile drive from Berlin to Munich. He was thrilled to see long lines at polling places all along the route. The election was drawing a historic turnout: of 43.9 million eligible voters, 37.6 million went to the polls—a participation rate of 85.6 percent, the highest in the life of the Weimar Republic.

A delighted Hitler stopped in Nuremberg to call Goebbels; the Nazi chief told the Berlin gauleiter that he was "certain of victory."[6]

In Munich, Hitler spent the first part of the evening at the Brown House. Gathering up his usual entourage, he then decamped to his table in the right rear corner of Café Heck to listen to election returns on a radio. They came in slowly at first, then in a rush. The glow of expected victory rapidly faded. Blow by blow, it became clear that Hitler was not winning. "The news was getting worse and worse," recalled Gerdy Troost, sitting at Hitler's table with her husband, architect Paul Troost. Hindenburg was running far ahead of Hitler. The Hindenburg forces must have "turned out every last little grandpa and grandma" to vote for the president, said Gerdy. "The German people had said no" to Hitler.[7] And they had given a huge yes to Hindenburg.

With 18.6 million votes, President Hindenburg had won 49.6 percent of the vote—startlingly close to outright victory. Hitler's total lay far behind: 11.3 million votes, or 30.1 percent. The field marshal had thrashed the private by nearly twenty points.* It was a strong endorsement of the existing order and a rebuke to Hitler.

After midnight, Hitler's inner circle was ready to give up and go home. With President Hindenburg so close to victory, there was no rational reason for Hitler to challenge him in a runoff. Hindenburg would need only 150,000 more votes for an outright majority; Hitler would need seven million new votes to overtake him. The Nazi could graciously concede and quit the field. But Hitler's raw survival instincts clicked in. As he had done after his failed putsch, as he had done after the disastrous election of 1928, as he had done in other moments of despair, Hitler summoned the stubborn tenacity that kept him going.

"Let's go back to the Brown House," he said to Rudolf Hess. "I'll dictate a statement that the struggle goes on!"

Gerdy Troost was taken aback. "He's gone crazy. This is nuts!" she whispered to her husband. Turning to Hess, she said: "Listen, Hess, you need to call a doctor. That's not normal—impossible!"

By then, Paul Troost was trying to silence his wife. "Stop! Shut up!" said Troost. "He knows what he is doing."[8]

Paul Troost was right. Hitler knew no other way to deal with defeat than to go on the offensive. At the Brown House, he put out statements to rally the troops. Brazenly spinning the election outcome as a success, he noted that his vote total was 78 percent higher than in 1930—11.3 million votes over 6.3 million votes. "We are now without question the strongest political movement in Germany," crowed Hitler, though the Social Democrats and the Centre Party had not even fielded candidates, preferring instead to back Hindenburg.

Hitler was the unbending scrapper of old: "The first election campaign is over, but the second one begins today—and I will personally lead it."[9]

In Berlin, Goebbels had fallen into a funk. Expecting victory, he and Magda had invited political friends to their capacious apartment on

* Thälmann, the Communist, received 4,983,197 votes, or 13.2 percent. Duesterberg, the hapless nationalist candidate supported by Hugenberg, received only 2,558,000 votes, or 6.8 percent.

Reichskanzlerplatz. "Everybody was there," he wrote. "And then the radio. Reports trickle in. It doesn't look good. By 10:00 p.m. it is obvious: we've been beaten. Terrible prospects! . . . Had a phone call with Hitler. He is shocked beyond measure by the outcome."

But Hitler's surprise plans to challenge Hindenburg in a runoff revived the Berlin gauleiter. "Now [Hitler] is big. Giving all of us new courage. I'm flying to Munich immediately to confer with him."[10]

To Brüning and the prodemocracy camp, Hindenburg's near victory and Hitler's defeat were cause for celebration. The Nazi leader's decision to enter a runoff was heartily mocked. HITLER WILL NOT GIVE UP HIS HOPELESS CAMPAIGN, headlined one newspaper.[11] US ambassador Sackett reported a "malicious joy" in government circles, since Hitler would now be subjected to "the chagrin of suffering the same defeat a second time."

41

HITLER OVER GERMANY

I shall attack, attack and attack again.

—Adolf Hitler to a British journalist, 1932

Is Hitler racially pure?

—Bavarian newspaper, 1932

Following the March 13 presidential vote, Chancellor Brüning and Interior Minister Groener proclaimed a three-week "Easter break" during which no political campaigning would be allowed. While the hiatus was ostensibly called to give exhausted German police forces a respite from the political street clashes that had generated countless injuries and many deaths, the pause also put the brakes on Hitler's feverish nationwide campaigning. The runoff would be squeezed down to a single week, with voting on April 10. Yet even with the forced political cease-fire, an atmosphere of foreboding was felt.

"I hear some very strange reports which leave no doubt but that both sides, left and right, are making comprehensive preparations for civil war," wrote diarist Harry Kessler.[1]

Politically, the runoff looked like a shoo-in for President Hindenburg. Theodor Duesterberg, the Steel Helmet leader, had thrown in the towel, but Communist leader Ernst Thälmann, who had won 13.2 percent in the first round, was still in the race. The main question, however, was Hitler. What would he or could he do to stymie Hindenburg's certain victory?

Hindenburg's political machine was taking no chances. With a war chest of 7.5 million marks (one million more than Goebbels had), the Old Gentleman's handlers flooded cities, towns, and villages with one hundred thousand picture posters and more than ten million leaflets, most of them air-dropped from a fleet of thirty airplanes.[2] In Berlin alone, 130 banners spanned streets and intersections, including one on the iconic Brandenburg Gate—VOTE FOR HINDENBURG! Hindenburg's campaign took advantage of a new technology called miracle letters, which projected the field marshal's name onto the night sky when clouds were thick. While most images of Hindenburg simply showed his famous rocklike visage, one lusty poster dared to place the president's formidable head atop a muscleman body clad only in a loincloth.

To counter Nazi portrayals of Hindenburg as ancient and incompetent, the president's campaign created ready-to-use illustrated newspaper supplements depicting him at work on high stacks of mail, greeting foreign diplomats on New Year's Day, and out for his morning walk, sometimes with his grandchildren. Not to be outdogged, so to speak, by Hitler's well-known affection for German shepherds, Hindenburg even appeared in one supplement that emphasized the president's love for his deceased shepherd Rolf. The supplements were carried by more than one thousand of Germany's four thousand newspapers.

Hitler's prospects of beating Hindenburg seemed slim to nonexistent. But Hitler and Goebbels saw the runoff as another chance to put their political crusade on national display. Besides, Hitler now had his eye not so much on the presidency as on the brass ring of the chancellorship. Recovered from the shock of defeat in the first round, he aimed in the second to maximize his vote share, setting a new benchmark for the next Reichstag election, whenever it might come. A good showing at the ballot box would also maintain the Nazis' momentum going into a cluster of crucial state legislative elections scheduled for late April, right after the presidential runoff. Prussia and several other significant states would be voting; 80 percent of the German electorate would go to the polls again.[3] The state votes were practically another national election, the year's third major cycle.

Hitler had a bandwagon, and he wanted to keep it rolling.

With only one week to woo voters, Hitler faced the quandary of how to magnify his campaign reach. Still barred by Brüning's government from speaking on German radio, he and Goebbels came up with something new. Their innovation was ideally suited to a modern political crusade that was built not on programs and policies but on optics, drama, propagandistic impact, mass appeal, and the charisma of a political star.

They rented an airplane.

Campaigning by chartered plane had never been tried before—not in Germany, not in Europe, not in America. Hitler had already transformed German electioneering with his appearances at mass rallies all around the country—a very uncommon practice. Now he would magnify the tactic by using an airplane to appear in more than one city per day—sometimes in three or four per day. It was a brand-new style of campaigning: the airborne whistle-stop tour.* Having directly reached between two hundred thousand and three hundred thousand voters in the election's first round, Hitler hoped to speak directly to one million in the second.

Hitler's airborne electioneering began on April 3. As his pilot, Hitler had chosen Hans Baur, a First World War flying ace now with the fledgling Lufthansa airline. When he interviewed Baur, he confessed that he had a fear of flying—he hated being airborne and feared airsickness. Nine years earlier, during the first flight of his life, from Munich to Berlin, he had experienced both fright and vomiting as his small plane hit bad weather and made an emergency landing. Pilot Baur assured the politician that airplanes had come a long way since 1923, when rickety, low-powered First World War aircraft were still in use. The new trimotor Junkers was bigger, more comfortable, faster, and safer. With a boxy fuselage and overhead wings that screened the sun's rays while giving good views from the passenger windows, the Junkers D-1720 would give Hitler a cocoon-like feel. It would become his flying home for a week.

With Baur at the controls, Hitler took off from Munich on a dazzling Sunday morning for the first leg of his electoral blitz. Hitler's entourage

---

* It was not until later in 1932 that Democratic presidential candidate Franklin D. Roosevelt mounted the first of his famous railroad whistle-stop campaign tours. By then Hitler was flying circles around Germany with his airborne campaign, years before the practice became common in America.

called the sunny day "Hitler weather," aping the old Wilhelmine expression "kaiser weather." By the time Baur set down in Dresden, the classical city on the Elbe River, all doubts were erased that Hitler could recover his momentum. A crowd of sixty thousand greeted the Nazi Führer in a jammed bicycle-racing stadium. They gave him the loudest greeting he had ever heard.

Hitler told the expectant crowd that, since the radio waves were denied him, his goal in the one-week campaign was to "speak personally in just a few days to the millions of people that the [other candidates] can more easily reach with their media." Hitler's followers loved hearing and sharing his umbrage at being scorned by the political establishment. Yet despite the obvious support of the adoring crowd, Hitler's speech was remarkably defensive. He felt compelled to refute post-Boxheim charges that a Nazi-led government would trigger chaos and civil war.[4]

And so it went for the rest of the day—and the week. At a stroke, the airplane turned Hitler into a candidate who seemed to descend from heaven. After Dresden, Baur flew the short hop to Leipzig. Forty-five minutes later, he and Hitler were airborne again for Chemnitz, where another horde of forty-five thousand greeted the candidate.[5] By evening the Junkers airplane was headed to Plauen, where Baur landed it in the dark. Four cities in one day: Hitler was so pleased that he presented his new pilot with a large bouquet of flowers. "Baur, you've done your job well. I'm enthusiastic about air travel now."[6]

Goebbels had scheduled the largest event of the week for the next day on Berlin's Lustgarten square. All Monday afternoon Berliners streamed into the vast quadrangle surrounded by the Berlin Cathedral, the City Palace, the Old Museum, and the Spree River. Hours before Hitler's 5:00 p.m. speech, Storm Troopers from around the city marched into position, bands playing, flags flying—a "pseudomilitary spectacle," noted one journalist.[7] Hitler and Goebbels knew that there was nothing like sharp uniforms and military music to lift spirits.[8] The method and the moment worked: an estimated 150,000 people assembled on the sprawling square, one of the largest political rallies in German history.

Hitler's loudspeaker-assisted declamations bounced off the high-columned museum, the hulking church, and the pompous palace. He promised that a coming Third Reich would make it easier for all "German maidens" to find homes and husbands to support them, a prospect lustily cheered by women in the crowd.[9] Yet Hitler was just as defensive in Berlin as he had been in Dresden, raising and rebutting allegations of bedlam and civil strife should he come to power. The normally aggressive Hitler was now "electioneering in sheep's clothing," wrote a reporter. The Nazi leader's effort to distance himself from his previous threats of "heads rolling in the sand" was nothing more than a desperate attempt to shed the "boogeyman odor" that clung to the Nazi Party because of "ghosts of Boxheim," wrote the journalist.[10]

The most remarkable moment of Hitler's Berlin rally came not from Hitler but from Albert Grzesinski, the Social Democratic Berlin police chief. Loved on the left, the police boss was hated on the right, especially by the Nazis. Grzesinski emerged onto a balcony of the City Palace to view the massive turnout. The very sight of Berlin's top cop—with his bullet head and dark brows, Grzesinski was easily recognizable—stirred the crowd to an "earsplitting whistle concert" (whistling was the equivalent of booing).[11] "Down with him!" shouted the crowd, driving the chief back into the palace.

Campaigning by chartered aircraft was a gamble, both politically and physically. It had to work on a schedule that could be thwarted by unforeseen impediments—or by a failure of nerve. On the campaign's fourth day, Hitler was scheduled to fly from Fürth, near Nuremberg, to Frankfurt-am-Main, near the Rhine River. But the route crossed the two-thousand-foot-high Spessart Mountains, and Baur told Hitler that hailstorms were forecast. Hitler insisted on flying anyway; he had a speech to make. Over the mountains, the hail hit, and Baur was flying blind. The boxy Junkers airplane was "lashed by rain and hail against a dark background of threatening clouds," he recalled.[12] Flying low, the pilot managed to avoid disaster and bring the aircraft down safely. On the ground, Hitler told Baur the experience had felt like a scene in Wagner's *Die Walküre* (The Valkyrie).

Cynics dismissed Hitler's innovative use of an airplane as a campaign stunt. But Goebbels knew it sent a highly visible message: the Nazi Party is energetic and modern, embracing the latest technology in a changing age. The sight of Hitler's Junkers D-1720 high above the clouds or descending into distant towns was rich material for photographers. Nazi newspapers daily published large photo spreads depicting Hitler's historic air tour as a conquest. Hitler was a kind of godsend coming from on high to rescue Germany—or rising into the clouds as a conquering hero.

Heinrich Hoffmann, Hitler's photographer, joined the Führer in the Junkers aircraft. He captured Hitler pensively gazing out a window at the broad German landscape; speaking to massive crowds in panoramic photos; driving past adoring mobs on the streets; smiling and shaking hands in front of the trimotor aircraft while signing autographs on the plane's wing. Goebbels chartered a second plane—a Junkers F 13 flown by a colleague of Baur's—to ferry journalists and Hitler's bodyguard, SS man Sepp Dietrich, ahead of Hitler's plane. Goebbels also hired a film crew to document the new flying campaign.

To brilliant effect, Goebbels dubbed the airborne road show "Hitler over Germany" (*Hitler über Deutschland*). Within weeks, the film crew's documentary was out, and so was Hoffmann's one-hundred-photograph book, both entitled *Hitler über Deutschland.* Hoffmann's book, available for two marks from the Nazi publishing house, bore on its cover a striking artist's sketch of Hitler's airplane high over a map of Germany, its wings spanning the breadth of the nation.[13] Inside, the book showed Hitler accepting a bouquet of flowers in East Prussia, autographing a newspaper for a delighted schoolboy on one of his plane's rear stabilizers, and speaking to a panoramic scene of more than one hundred thousand supporters in Berlin. Hitler did seem to be all over Germany.

Sefton Delmer, the British *Daily Express* correspondent in Germany, was the sole foreign reporter invited to fly with Hitler on his historic airborne campaign. Delmer had been born to Australian parents living in Berlin and spoke only German growing up before being sent off to England for further education (his father lectured at Berlin's leading university).[14] Returned later to Germany, Delmer—known as Tom to his friends—

HITLER OVER GERMANY

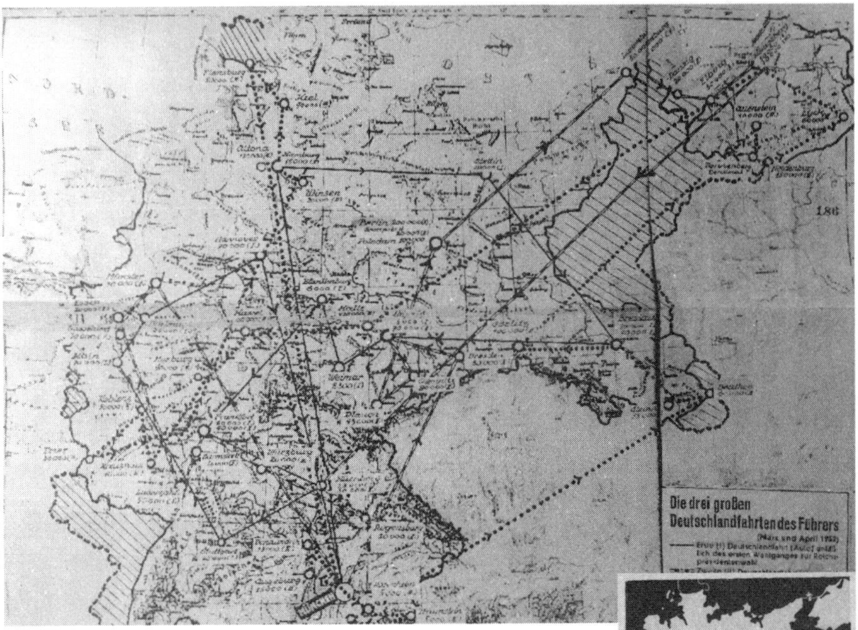

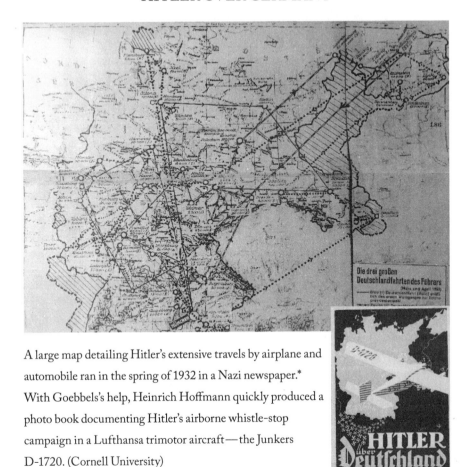

A large map detailing Hitler's extensive travels by airplane and automobile ran in the spring of 1932 in a Nazi newspaper.* With Goebbels's help, Heinrich Hoffmann quickly produced a photo book documenting Hitler's airborne whistle-stop campaign in a Lufthansa trimotor aircraft—the Junkers D-1720. (Cornell University)

* "Die drei grossen Deutschlandfahrten des Führers (März und April 1932)," *Der Nationalsozialist,* undated, in Materialsammlung-RSA, Institut für Zeitgeschichte, Munich.

became a renowned figure in the foreign press corps. His German fluency ingratiated him with the Nazi elite; so did the Bechstein piano he rented so that Ernst Hanfstaengl could drop by his flat for a drink and a spell at the piano, banging out Nazi marches and Harvard fight songs. Delmer's tactics paid off when he was invited to fly exclusively with Hitler on the morning of April 6.

"Hitler was prepared to have me around because I spoke German like a German and... because he thought I sympathized with him in his fight," wrote Delmer. "And up to a point, I did. I loathed the hypocrisy with which Chancellor Brüning posed as a great champion of parliamentary democracy, while in fact he governed without parliament.... He banned the pro-Hitler newspapers on the most spurious pretexts. He denied the Nazis and their Nationalist partners the right to speak over the radio.... All this made me feel a certain sympathy for Hitler."

When Delmer arrived at Berlin's Tempelhof Airport, where Hitler's plane stood ready, he saw Goebbels pull up in a brand-new beige-and-brown Mercedes convertible. Everyone swarmed around the shiny open car, which contained not just the propaganda meister but also his striking wife, Magda. In a comically awkward scene, the persuasive Magda dragged Hitler over to inspect the new car, forcing him to sit down next to her in the driver's seat, as he smiled "nervously because of the closeness of Frau Goebbels' Chanel No. 5," noted Delmer.

Pilot Baur took off for distant East Prussia. In the passenger compartment, sitting a few seats behind Hitler, the British newsman was surprised to see Hitler sink into what appeared to be a morose apathy. "He just sat there, staring gloomily out the window... [with] wads of cotton wool in his ears," noticed Delmer. This glum figure, not standing before a cheering crowd, provided "an entirely new picture of Hitler for me... a complete contrast to the glad-hand extrovert who had said goodbye to Magda Goebbels and the others at Tempelhof. Never again have I seen such a contrast between the public and the private figure as [I did] in Hitler."

Once the plane landed and the door was flung open, "the other Hitler took over," recalled Delmer. Hitler resumed his practiced Führer pose, raised his arm in the Nazi salute, and projected what the British reporter called a *leutseliges Leuchten*—a beatific gleam in his eyes that struck so many as Hitler's source of hypnotic power. The gaze, the posture, the quasimilitary trench coat—it all gave Hitler the look of "Siegfried the Light-God," wrote the irreverent Brit.

The day's furious pace imparted a taste of modern political electioneering long before it became the norm. Struggling to stay as close as he could to the fast-moving candidate, Delmer found himself being stroked by admirers who were trying to touch Hitler. Suddenly part of the candidate's entourage, Delmer was caught in a bubble that he could not escape. Seated right behind the Nazi leader on a stage, the reporter squirmed miserably for two hours because he needed a smoke. At the next meeting, the stout Delmer had to hustle to keep up. "Hurry! Run!" shouted Hanfstaengl as Hitler disappeared into a meeting with supporters. When Delmer caught up, he was cheered as an adjunct hero "because of my closeness to the Messiah." In fact, "one poor woman who missed with an attempt to kiss Hitler's hand promptly made a dive for me."

Sitting again behind Hitler, Delmer had a good view of the audience. It was not what Hitler said that impressed people, Delmer concluded, but "the magnetism of his physical presence." By denying Hitler the use of the radio waves, Chancellor Brüning had driven Hitler into a frenzy of face-to-face meetings, where he was especially effective. No matter what happened in the presidential race, thought Delmer, Hitler's new barnstorming method would heighten his appeal to the masses to a degree "which Brüning would certainly be made to regret."

After his few days with Hitler, Delmer's ears were still ringing with "the wild cheering and enthusiastic singing of the overwhelming crowds which have been deafening us all the time we have spent on the ground. Nearly 200,000 German men and women have today seen, heard and cheered Herr Hitler," he wrote.[15]

It had been an exhausting week. In seven days, Hitler had made twenty-three speeches. Bouncing around in Baur's chartered airplane, Hitler may have spoken to a million people, though Goebbels, with typical exaggeration, claimed it was two million. Whatever the number, it was far greater than any candidate had ever addressed before in one week's electioneering. Hitler had redefined political campaigning.

Short though it was, the one-week campaign was not without its upheavals and surprises. At the beginning of the week, Goebbels had to fight off scandalous eruptions in the press. The left-leaning *Welt am Montag* published material showing Storm Trooper commander Ernst Röhm to be homosexual. While the former First World War officer was widely believed in Nazi circles to be gay, his outing in the national press—based on an exchange of Röhm's letters with a friend—posed a problem for Hitler, especially since the story alleged not only a salacious lifestyle but pederasty as well. Hitler was devastated, but lawyer Hans Frank assured him that the allegation of boy trafficking was untrue. Hitler defended Röhm and kept him as Storm Trooper chief.

Later in the week, the same newspaper revealed what it called the Nazis' penchant for expensive luxury while posing as a party of the common people. THIS IS HOW HITLER LIVES, announced a headline on a story claiming that the bill for Hitler and his entourage at the Kaiserhof Hotel for ten days in March of 1932 was 4,008 marks—a princely sum. In fact, subsequent research showed the claim to be exaggerated, but the newspapers' many readers—and even Goebbels—did not know that at the time.[16] Three days before the runoff vote, Hitler declared the bill to be a fake, but with little effect. The report was seized upon by other newspapers to attack Hitler's Everyman pose.

Hitler's claim to a heroic war record and frontline experience "in the trenches" was also called into question in two newspaper articles obviously written by men who had served with him during the First World War, though their names were withheld.[17] One piece, in the *Volksfreund* of Braunschweig, noted that Hitler had "worked out for himself how to get out of the line of fire" by snagging a messenger's assignment. While most foot soldiers spent seven to ten days at a time lying in wet trenches or standing in mud up to their stomachs, Hitler lay on a safe cot in a reinforced old house at regimental headquarters, six miles behind the battle lines. "Thousands of fathers with families at home could have filled the little post behind the lines," noted the writer, but the unmarried Hitler felt no inclination to swap assignments with doughboys at the front, "as he is trying to tell blinded German youth today." Yet another newspaper noted that Hitler was born and grew up in a province of Austria along the Czech border and was probably not fully Germanic but rather "an Aryan mongrel." The newspaper's headline asked, IS HITLER RACIALLY PURE?—a major insult in the Hitlerian world of ethnic spotlessness.[18]

After the fierce seven-day campaign, Germans trekked to the polls on Sunday, April 10. As expected, Hindenburg won, but with only 53 percent of the vote—not as comfortable a margin as his backers had hoped. While the president had gained 708,000 new votes over the first round, Hitler had won two million new votes, rising from 30.1 percent to 36.8 percent of the total. In losing, he had won. "An overwhelming victory for us," crowed Goebbels. "Hitler is very happy. Now we have a springboard into the Prussian elections."[19]

Hitler, too, gloated and girded for future fights. "Adolf Hitler tonight is as happy as a sandboy," wrote journalist Delmer after sitting down with the party Führer at the Brown House in Munich for a final interview. "He is smiling all over his face. His political chiefs, who are with him, are congratulating him and slapping him on the shoulders."[20] In Delmer's telling, Hitler took an unabashed victory lap:

> In one week's campaigning [said Hitler], I have succeeded in accomplishing the impossible. I have increased my votes by more than two million. That is a feat which has never been equaled and I have done this despite the unconstitutional ban placed on my broadcasting election appeals. All my newspapers were muzzled, and I had only my own voice with which to refute the lies and slanders spread about me.... I ascribe my triumph entirely to the fact that I did not capitulate [after] my apparent reverse at the first ballot. I will confess it. My election troops after the first battle were momentarily disheartened. The political Eastertide truce intervened and prevented me from inspiring them with new courage. But all that has been swept away by my week's whirlwind campaign.... It gave a new confidence.... I shall continue as I have begun, I shall attack, attack and attack again.[21]

And attack he would. Hitler had gone from trying to win the presidency outright to simply conquering Germany through steady party building and vote-getting in a series of elections. The next balloting was only two weeks away, in late April of 1932. From Hitler's point of view, it was a good thing that he had failed to win the presidency: he was not burdened with official responsibilities; he could continue the perpetual campaign. His constant electioneering and speechifying would suck waves of new supporters into his wake.

Sooner or later, Hitler felt, he would overwhelm everybody and everything. In a year and a half, he had doubled his share of the votes. While Hindenburg had won the election with a broad but vaguely defined coalition, Hitler had won his votes as exactly what he was, a Nazi. He could now honestly claim that the Nazis were Germany's largest political party.

42

GROUNDSWELL

Something has to happen. We have to have power. Otherwise we'll just win ourselves to death.

—*Joseph Goebbels, 1932*

The economic depression overshadowed everything. Long lines of men sought food and jobs in every city, just as they did in the United States. Yet Hitler still refused to give specifics of a Nazi Party economic program. When pressed, he simply heaped blame on the ruling parties and coalitions of the previous thirteen years. The Nazi Party, he implied, was the only logical remaining choice. "Today the question is not what *we* will do but what *they* have done!" he said.[1]

Lack of jobs was boosting recruitment by the Storm Troopers. Asked how many of his purported four hundred thousand brown shirts were out of work, Hitler claimed that three hundred thousand were—and that the number would swell to six hundred thousand all-volunteer members once prohibitions were lifted, such as the ban on wearing brown shirts.[2] Hitler's admission to the presence of a high percentage of jobless men in his ranks was telling.[3] Unemployment was his friend, sending large numbers of idle men into his movement, where they could find camaraderie and a sense of purpose.

During the state election campaign, culminating on April 24, Goebbels promised to deliver a "propaganda masterpiece," and he did. Among his innovations was a rented bus plastered with oversize posters bearing the Nazi slogan "Work, freedom, and bread!" Wherever the bus stopped, a bugler would step out like a carnival barker to blow a fanfare and attract potential voters.

With hardly a break, Hitler rushed back onto the hustings. He spoke to twenty-six rallies in eight days. A broad swath of states was voting for legislatures and governments. Prussia was the main prize. Hitler's goal was to rack up significant vote shares in the legislative tallies—maybe even outright victories. The Nazi leader could fairly feel the ground swelling underneath his feet.

When the returns came in, half a dozen states had awarded the Nazis the single largest partisan share of the vote. Most important was their triumph in Prussia, where they took 36.6 percent of the ballots—almost exactly the same as Hitler's national share in the presidential runoff. In winning nearly 37 percent, the Nazi Party had easily bested the Social Democrats, who had ruled Prussia throughout the life of the Weimar Republic. The once mighty Socialists now finished second, with a lame 21 percent. The victory carried the Nazis from six seats to 162 seats in the Prussian legislature, the second-most-important lawmaking body in Germany after the Reichstag.[4]

Even in Bavaria, where Hitler courted less sympathetic Catholic voters, the Nazis effectively tied the Catholic-based Bavarian People's Party with 32.5 percent. In Anhalt, a small state southwest of Berlin, the Nazis soared to 40 percent; they could claim the governor's chair. The Nazis had showed that Hitler's surge to nearly 37 percent in the presidential election two weeks earlier was no fluke. The party had now repeated the feat in the state elections.

Goebbels called the state election results a "phenomenal victory." Yet within that success lay a niggling doubt: Had Hitler peaked? Despite their best efforts—and the expenditure of nearly all their resources—the Nazis had not been able to push their bandwagon any further along. They had once again won just over one-third of the German electorate, but no more. Hitler's base was stuck at 37 percent.

"What now?" wondered Goebbels. "Something has to happen. We have to have power. Otherwise we'll just win ourselves to death."[5]

43

INTRIGUE AND BETRAYAL

The bomb went off. The system has fallen.

—*Joseph Goebbels, May 31, 1932*

In the spring of 1932, the political establishment was tying itself in knots, trying to figure out how to acknowledge Hitler's political popularity while limiting his real power. Paul von Hindenburg was still Germany's president, and Heinrich Brüning was still its chancellor, but Adolf Hitler had become the *x* factor in German politics. He felt confident he needed only a new Reichstag election to make his final leap. But the next parliamentary balloting was not constitutionally due until 1934.

Rumors again swirled that the Nazis, driven by their impatient and rowdy Storm Troopers, might make a lunge for power by force, unleashing the uprising that many brown shirts still dreamed of.[1] The Prussian police had uncovered documents containing the purported code words that would signal the start of a coup d'état: *Oma tot!* (Grandma dead).[2] Though former Storm Trooper commander Walter Stennes had been banished to the sidelines of the Nazi movement, he had not shed his ambitions, and he still had a following. He was agitating for a putsch, at least according to Goebbels's information. "A wild nervousness and restiveness everywhere—putsch, putsch, putsch!" Goebbels wrote. The Berlin gauleiter had special security set up outside his apartment.[3]

The Storm Troopers were organized, young, committed—and exasperated.[4] Though unarmed, they could easily find their way to weapons in a country riddled with secret arms caches, some of them under the control of the Reichswehr, which was supposed to be limited in its size and firepower by the Treaty of Versailles. Defense and Interior Minister Groener wanted to "break out the poison teeth"—the Storm Troopers—to deprive Hitler's movement of its belligerence in the streets. Once shed of its violent wing, argued Groener, the Nazi Party would be respectable enough to become a coalition partner.[5]

"Of course, the Nazis mustn't be allowed to govern alone anywhere, especially not in the national government," wrote Groener. "But in a few state governments an attempt will have to be made to bind the Nazis into a coalition and bring them down from their utopian visions with honest government work."[6]

Such was the desperate thinking among government leaders in the face of Hitler's meteoric rise. They imagined that Hitler could be tamed with governing responsibilities and the hard labor that comes with them. The establishment had no idea what an untamable animal Hitler really was—or what opposition they might face within their own ranks, especially in the military leadership. A key to that opposition was General Kurt von Schleicher.

Kurt von Schleicher was a unique figure who would play an outsize role in the turbulent coming months. Born in 1882 in Brandenburg, just west of Berlin, Schleicher was the son of a Prussian officer and entered the military as a teenager. He spent most of the First World War on the General Staff of the German Supreme Army Command, far from any battlefield. Yet his staff position enabled him to move rapidly up the ranks, leapfrogging other officers of his age. By war's end, in 1918, he was on the staff of General Groener, who assumed command of the armed forces when Germany capitulated.

In 1930, the rapidly promoted General von Schleicher was already in a position to influence President Hindenburg's choice of Heinrich Brüning as chancellor. The president's gatekeeper role in deciding who could form a government gave the head of state exceptional political influence. A small cabal around the president, including Schleicher, sought to use this unique presidential power to shift German politics toward conservative, nationalistic, militaristic, and authoritarian administrations. They wanted to shut out the German left—especially the Social Democratic Party—from any future governments. Other members of the secretive camarilla around Hindenburg included Colonel Oskar von Hindenburg, the president's son and chief adjutant, and the state secretary, Otto Meissner, the head of the president's office, who lived with his family in the presidential palace. Bull-necked, bespectacled, and scar-faced, Meissner was the Old Gentleman's chief aide and ear-whisperer, making him one of the most influential men in Germany.

By 1932, Schleicher was again serving as special adviser to Groener, who had become Germany's defense minister. With his pale skin and shaved head, Schleicher was known for his suave charm; he had become exceptionally well connected in political circles. Naming Schleicher to head his office of political-military affairs—the military's chief lobbyist to the political community—Groener viewed Schleicher as "my Cardinal in politics."[7] Essentially a political animal in an army uniform, Schleicher often quipped, "You can't rule with bayonets."[8] From his perch at Groener's right hand, Schleicher had become the defense minister's prying eyes and ears in the political world while staying well wired with the military brass. At the same time, he was turning the supposedly neutral military into a force in German politics.[9]

Schleicher was more than just the connective tissue among power centers. He had his own agenda and ideas for solving Germany's sticky political dilemma—especially for dealing with Hitler and his paramilitary might. Like most of his friends among the generals, Schleicher saw the Storm Troopers not as a violent horde but rather as a rich source of new recruits for the enlarged German army they hoped to create. Merging the Storm Troopers, along with the Steel Helmet association and the Reichsbanner, into a still-to-be-created German national militia might dodge the Treaty of Versailles restrictions, which limited Germany to only one hundred thousand men in uniform.[10] To the scheming Schleicher, this plot had political benefits, too. Absorbing the brown shirts into the army would take the Storm Troopers out of play as a Hitlerian cudgel, putting four hundred thousand men beyond the reach of the Nazi leader's casual whims. A consolidation into the military would convert the Storm Troopers from a reckless terror band into a training and feeder organization for the German army.[11] A strengthened German armed force could in turn create a kind of military dictatorship with a civilian head, or so went

Schleicher's logic. He and the generals thought such a scheme might finally make Hitler manageable.

But Defense Minister Groener disagreed. The former army commander, now cabinet minister, wanted no part of legitimizing Hitler's rough paramilitary. Rather, he wanted the opposite: he felt the brown shirts should be repressed. Groener had received a tip from an inside source claiming that Storm Trooper units in Silesia were preparing to arm themselves and had, "with great diligence, figured out where Reichswehr weapons were stored."[12] With fears of civil war in the air, Groener and Chancellor Brüning convinced Hindenburg that the psychological moment had come to sign an emergency order banning the Storm Troopers and asserting the state's monopoly on organized force.[13] The ban was issued on April 13.

Schleicher was apoplectic.[14] So was the Storm Trooper chief, Ernst Röhm. When state police began occupying Storm Trooper offices and motor pools, Röhm wanted to resist with force, even without firearms: after all, the Storm Troopers outnumbered the Reichswehr and most state police forces. But Hitler knew only chaos and death would ensue and his seven-year climb toward power would be over. Though he hated the ban, Hitler threw all his authority into keeping a lid on Storm Trooper ambitions, commanding Röhm and his men to obey the emergency order. "Comrades, I understand your feelings," Hitler wrote in a *Völkischer Beobachter* essay. "You have for years followed the legal path to the conquest of political power. During this time you have been persecuted and tortured in horrific ways." With the stroke of a pen, the Nazi chief also converted all Storm Troopers into regular members of the Nazi Party. As Storm Troopers they were banned: as plain party members they could continue agitation and propaganda—minus the militaristic marches, the brown shirts, and the street fighting.

The ban on the Storm Troopers dampened public violence and, for a while, had a paralyzing effect on the Nazi movement. The move may have been the government's finest moment in trying to oppose the Nazi menace and keep German politics on a democratic path. But it backfired. The banning of the Nazis marked the beginning of the end of Groener's influence—and Brüning's, too. By taking on Hitler directly, Groener had fallen into a trap. His most aggressive move to save Germany from a train wreck would prove his undoing and, finally, bring down the men who engineered the Storm Trooper ban.

Groener's downfall came not directly from Hitler but from Schleicher. Even though Groener once said he viewed Schleicher nearly as his own son, the protégé was now turning on the patron. On April 28, 1932, Schleicher met secretly with Hitler, informing the Nazi chief of his and the generals' strenuous opposition to Groener's ban on the Storm Troopers and the SS. Overreaching his brief, Schleicher discussed with Hitler the possibility of the Nazis joining a governing coalition.[15] Nine days later, on May 7, Schleicher secretly met again with Hitler—to instigate a palace coup. Schleicher brought with him two of the most powerful men in Germany, though neither man held political office: Oskar von Hindenburg and Otto Meissner. Accompanying Hitler were Storm Trooper chief Röhm and the commander of the Berlin Storm Troopers, Count von Helldorf.

Schleicher laid out a plan to bring down Chancellor Brüning and replace his government with a right-wing "presidential cabinet" that would be more palatable to Hitler. In exchange for the Nazi leader's support of his scheme, Schleicher offered the two things Hitler most needed: a lifting of the ban on the Storm Troopers (and SS) and a dissolution of the Reichstag, which would automatically trigger new elections. This spectacular offer suddenly made Kurt von Schleicher the most important political player in Germany: he was effectively speaking for the only man who could make good on the proposed deal, President Hindenburg. Hitler did not hesitate; he accepted the offer. It was a resounding victory.

That evening, he celebrated. "We drank Champagne," reported Goebbels. "The boss is relaxed and funny."

So pleased was the Nazi chief that he and his entourage capped their celebration with a late-night joyride north to Schwerin, near the Baltic coast, arriving at 2:00 a.m. During a drive the next day through the surrounding forests, Hitler and Goebbels made plans for the promised new elections. "We are free to agitate and will deliver a masterpiece," wrote

Goebbels. "A squad of airplanes will jump from one province to another.... It will be a huge hit. The Storm Troopers can march in their brown shirts—woe to our enemies!"[16]

Schleicher wasn't done. Completing his betrayal of his boss and patron, he seized upon a poorly delivered Reichstag speech by Groener (he was sick and bandaged) to inform him that the Reichswehr generals had lost confidence in the defense minister—a situation that Schleicher had done much to create. Groener's resignation came swiftly, undermining the government's ban on the Storm Troopers and further weakening Brüning. "We get message from General Schleicher: the crisis continues according to plan," noted Goebbels.[17]

The plan's next piece was forcing the resignation of the man who in March and April had done so much to ensure President Hindenburg's reelection, Chancellor Heinrich Brüning. Like Hindenburg's closest advisers, Schleicher felt the conscientious Catholic chancellor had allied himself too closely with the Social Democrats. Schleicher and the Hindenburg camarilla wanted a nationalistic, right-leaning cabinet. They convinced Hindenburg that Brüning had to go—though Brüning felt he was "only one hundred meters from my goal" of achieving financial stability and support for Germany in international negotiations.

The ostensible cause of Brüning's dismissal was a disagreement with the president over a proposed plan to repopulate a number of aristocratic estates in the East Elbian flatlands. This was President Hindenburg's homeland, and here lived many of his friends in the Junker class of prosperous landholders. However, many of the huge domains were bankrupt. Under the land-reform plan favored by Brüning, they would be bought at forced auctions, then subdivided into small plots to be cultivated by desperate farmers resettled from Depression-racked parts of Germany.[18] Not surprisingly, the landed agrarian interests—though sometimes penniless—loudly protested the proposal; Hindenburg got an earful while vacationing at his own eastern estate. His Junker friends denounced the resettlement scheme as "agrarian Bolshevism."[19]

Brüning was summoned to a meeting with President Hindenburg on May 30. When he arrived, the chancellor noticed Schleicher's coat and hat hanging in the president's anteroom—a clear enough sign of his own subordinate's role in what would happen next.[20] Brüning was kept waiting for nearly an hour and a half, then given three and a half minutes with Hindenburg. The burly old president brusquely informed the ascetic chancellor—who for two years had thrown himself heart and soul into a losing strategy for saving Germany—that his services were no longer needed.

"The bomb went off," noted Goebbels, who kept steady track of events in his journal. "The system has fallen."[21]

44

HIGH-WATER MARK

Papen enjoyed the peculiarity of being taken seriously by neither his friends nor his enemies.

—André François-Poncet, French ambassador to Germany

President Hindenburg's dismissal of Chancellor Heinrich Brüning in late May of 1932 was but the first step in Kurt von Schleicher's plan to steer the German ship of state in a more authoritarian direction. The plan was happily shared by the presidential camarilla and the president himself. The scheme's second step, conceived and executed largely by Schleicher alone, was the choice of an obscure political nonentity as Brüning's successor. The nonentity's name was Franz von Papen.

A gentleman officer from the landowning Westphalian Catholic elite, Franz von Papen was almost nobody's idea of a political leader. Born in 1879, he was a man of high social standing and low political profile. Well born but intellectually lightweight, Papen had never spoken on the floor of the Prussian legislature, of which he had been a member for years. When he was posted to Washington in 1913 as military attaché to the German embassy (and to the embassy in Mexico), the thirty-four-year-old Papen gained a reputation as a secretive intriguer. He bizarrely conspired to have German Americans disguised as cowboys stage an invasion of Canada—though it never happened. When the First World War broke out, Papen plotted to undermine US support for its Western allies by fomenting strikes in plants that produced arms for the British and French militaries. Declared persona non grata and expelled from the United States in December of 1915, Papen returned to Germany to take command of an infantry unit on the western front. In 1917, however, he was transferred to Turkey, where he helped command Ottoman troops. There he befriended another German officer—Joachim von Ribbentrop.

After the war, Papen renewed his friendship with Kurt von Schleicher, whom he had known when they were young officers. Papen was only three years older than Schleicher. The two men often drank and chatted at Berlin's exclusive Deutscher Herrenklub, a British-style gentlemen's club. Founded as a watering hole for the economic and political establishment, which was bent on saving Germany from Marxism, the club on any given day hosted such members of the Berlin elite as French ambassador André François-Poncet. In this setting, Papen—tall, mustachioed, well tailored—was the quintessential German gentleman.

As General von Schleicher, now the chief political schemer, sought a successor to the deposed Chancellor Brüning, he wanted neither great power nor a great mind. He preferred a placeholder until his own day in the sun might arrive. He considered several candidates before settling on his drinking friend Papen—the man who would be easiest to manipulate. But when Schleicher mentioned the little-known Westphalian cavalryman as a prospective chancellor, his suggestion was "met with incredulity" by the political class. "Papen enjoyed the peculiarity of being taken seriously by neither his friends nor his enemies," noted Ambassador François-Poncet. "He was reputed to be superficial, blundering, untrue, ambitious, vain, crafty, and an intriguer."[1]

When one astonished friend told Schleicher that Papen was not much of a brain, Schleicher replied: "He need not be one—but he'll wear a fine hat!"[2]

With his three-piece suits, bow ties, and blue-blooded demeanor, Papen did indeed look the part. Yet even Papen sensed that he might not be up to the job of chancellor. When President Hindenburg summoned him on June 1, 1932, to offer him the post, he tried to turn it down, but Hindenburg's appeals to Papen's patriotism prevailed. No sooner was the deal struck than Schleicher, who had been listening in a side room, emerged to congratulate Papen. Schleicher brazenly presented the newly anointed chancellor with a list of cabinet members already selected by Schleicher and the camarilla; it included Schleicher as defense minister.

Most of the new ministers were, like Papen, noblemen—a cabinet of barons, it was called. The puppet was in place.

With Papen sworn in as chancellor, Schleicher, the kingmaker, had effectively coopted the German government—or so he thought. He then turned his attention to Hitler. Schleicher was still trying to harness the Nazis' popularity into the larger scheme of marginalizing the German left. He and the camarilla fervently sought to accommodate President Hindenburg's demand for a government without Social Democratic influence. Schleicher was flipping the equation: whereas Chancellor Brüning had tried to govern from the middle with the "toleration" of the Social Democrats—a de facto center-left coalition—Schleicher was shaping a cabinet under Papen that would govern with the "toleration" of the Nazis—a de facto center-right coalition. Hitler, himself a schemer of the highest order, had his own hug-and-hold strategy. Like Schleicher, he saw any new cabinet as merely a holding operation until events placed control in his hands. He agreed to Schleicher's proposal.

But in his own mind, Hitler was already manipulating the man who was trying to manipulate him.

With Brüning barely out the door and Papen freshly installed, President Hindenburg made good on the first part of the pact that Schleicher had struck with Hitler in their secret May 7 meeting: the president dissolved the Reichstag. New parliamentary elections were set for July 31, 1932. Then came the second part: Hindenburg canceled the ban on the Storm Troopers and the SS. The president's volte-face met with an outcry from some political leaders, especially Bavarian governor Heinrich Held. Unleashing the Storm Troopers, said Held, was tantamount to "carte blanche for murder, manslaughter, and the worst sort of terrorizing."

Held's forecast quickly came true. Back in uniform and back on the streets, the Storm Troopers reverted to form. With the July 31 Reichstag election campaign already in high gear—Germany's fourth election in five months—the Storm Troopers staged provocative marches, noisy rallies, and parades through left-wing neighborhoods. Germany fell into the worst wave of violence since the founding days of the Weimar Republic. June and July of 1932 became a long, hot summer, with daily reports of brutal clashes and bloody victims. Sundays were the preferred days for battle between Communists and Nazis—a weekend civil war. By the end of June, seventeen political murders had been recorded. July was worse: eighty-six people were killed and hundreds seriously injured. "Day for day, Sunday for Sunday, this is a continuous Saint Bartholomew's Day massacre," lamented Harry Kessler.*

The worst clash occurred on July 17 in the Hamburg suburb of Altona. Seven thousand Storm Troopers were given a permit to march through a mostly "red" locale. The police lost control. Clashes between Communists and Nazis included massive gunfire. Seventeen were killed, and more than two hundred were injured.[3] The day became known as Altona Bloody Sunday, a low point in German national life.

Political violence lowered the tone of electioneering. One Social Democratic Party poster depicted the Nazis as a grinning skeleton wearing a swastika-emblazoned cap, with the caption: "The Third Reich? No!" The *Arbeiter-Illustrierte-Zeitung* (Workers' Illustrated Newspaper) ran a full-page cartoon by German caricaturist John Heartfield showing Hitler with his arm raised in the Nazi salute—so that a fat cat in the background could lay a wad of money in his hand. "The real meaning of the Hitler salute," read the caption. In Munich, the anti-Hitler editor Fritz Gerlich blatantly took on Hitler's racist politics with a front-page photomontage showing Hitler with a bride on his arm—a black African woman. The banner headline asked: DOES HITLER HAVE MONGOLIAN BLOOD?[4] Playing his own racist card, Gerlich argued that Hitler had Slavic-Asian features.

For all their harsh propaganda, the Social Democrats knew they were on sinking ground. After thirteen years as Germany's strongest party, they were certain to be overtaken by the Nazis in the upcoming July 31

* Kessler's reference was to the massacre that took place in August of 1572, on the eve of the Feast of Bartholomew the Apostle, when French Catholic mobs slaughtered thousands of French Protestant Huguenots.

election. Even in Prussia, they were barely holding on. Governor Otto Braun and Interior Minister Carl Severing, in league with the (Catholic) Centre Party, had managed to cobble together a wobbly caretaker coalition after their weak showing (and Hitler's strong showing) in the April state elections. To politicians like Chancellor Franz von Papen, Prussia looked ripe for the picking. The time had finally come to push aside the last remaining Socialist-dominated bastion of republican thinking.

On July 20, with the outrages of Altona Bloody Sunday as his pretext, Papen struck.

The chancellor of Germany staged a coup—not against his own government but against Germany's largest state. Summoning Braun and Severing to his office, Papen showed them an emergency decree, signed by President Hindenburg, relieving them of all their offices. Because of the state of near civil war in Germany, intoned Papen, article 48 of the German constitution was invoked, and the Free State of Prussia was now under the control of the national government. Prussia would be ruled by a commissioner, said Papen—himself. In their weakened state, Braun and Severing, along with their entire cabinet, had no choice but to acquiesce.[5] Even the traditional best weapon of the Socialists—a general strike—was not an option, given the catastrophically high unemployment rates.

Papen's Prussia coup was a stunning, unconstitutional display of brute power—and an unexpected show of boldness by the supposedly spineless chancellor. The *Preussenschlag*, as it was called in German, was carried out by a government so emboldened by its backing from President Hindenburg that it blithely ignored outcries from across the country. Even though Germany was a federal republic with independent powers in all seventeen states, 60 percent of the country—Prussia—was now under the direct administration of the national government in Berlin.

The July 31 Reichstag election would objectively test Hitler's repetitive refrain that the Nazis were now Germany's strongest party. This time the contest was a national parliamentary race, the one that mattered most. Winning the Reichstag was far more important than doing well in a presidential election or gaining seats in the state legislatures.

Hitler again took to the air in a chartered plane. People scrambled anew to be part of Hitler's drop-from-the-sky spectacle; they sometimes spent whole days to reach his rallies and would picnic on the grounds for hours until the star of the show arrived. After the "flights over Germany" in the spring, a Nazi-friendly newspaper had published a map of Germany overlaid by the spiderweb lines of Hitler's air and ground travels. The two-page spread was an impressive graphic that showed the Nazi campaigner's corner-to-corner embrace of the German electorate.[6] His new tour would outdo the last two flying campaigns in distance and appearances. Over three weeks, Hitler would appear in fifty different cities, often speaking to audiences kept waiting in darkness and rain.

To many of his fervent followers, helping Hitler gain power was an existential matter. "If we won, Germany was saved," remembered one Nazi activist. "If we were defeated, a gate would open up in the east and Moscow's red hordes would swarm in and plunge Europe into night and misery."[7]

On the campaign's first day, pilot Hans Baur flew Hitler seven hours from Munich to Tilsit, on the East Prussian border with Lithuania. "For the first time I heard his voice," recalled a local farmer who soon joined the Nazi Party. "His words went straight to the heart."[8] Hitler hopscotched around the northeast before heading for the Baltic Sea coastal cities, where his air tour underwent one of its most adventurous and frightening moments—and his supporters waited for him until after midnight. Flying into the little port town of Warnemünde, Baur met heavy rain and cloud cover down to 150 feet; he could not land. "I didn't know the place and I should have had to land in the dark at [10:00 p.m.]—and there was no wireless to help me," recalled Baur.

The pilot told Hitler they would have to proceed to the next rally—at Stralsund, fifty miles to the east. But the military banned Baur from landing at Rechlin, the airfield near Stralsund. The pilot was forced to fly 160 miles south to Berlin, where Hitler telephoned Göring and asked him to put pressure on his military friends to allow a landing in Rechlin. The flying troupe departed Berlin at 11:00 p.m., heading for a field that also had bad weather and no lights. On his first approach, Baur missed the landing strip and "was digging up potatoes in an adjoining field."

Long after midnight, Baur set Hitler down in the right location, landed and alive. He was able to make it to the Nazi rally at 2:00 a.m.—where a crowd of twenty thousand had been waiting for nearly seven hours in a cold rain. Most of them were still there. Their reward was to hear Hitler speak for twenty minutes.[9]

Two days later Hitler flew to Göttingen, a storied university town in Lower Saxony that also was a hotbed of Nazism. There, an audience of around fifteen thousand waited in a persistent drizzle. To keep their spirits up, Hitler had Baur fly over the wet and patient mob—a signal from on high that the messiah was coming. Baur then turned to the only usable airfield, thirty-two miles away in Kassel, where Hitler's heavy Mercedes was on hand. Arriving an hour later on the soggy meadow outside Göttingen, Hitler spoke, bareheaded and hoarse, for only fifteen minutes. To the local pro-Nazi newspaper, the *Göttinger Tageblatt,* the moment was worth two full pages, lots of photos, and a claim of thirty thousand listeners.[10] To the more sober *Volksblatt,* Hitler's "giant rally was actually a giant letdown."[11] Half the crowd had departed before the Führer arrived, it claimed. Such were the perils of a high-speed, tightly scheduled airborne campaign.

Still, there were occasional relaxed moments. During a rare day off, Hitler took Baur to visit the charming Belvedere Palace, on the edge of Weimar, with its sprawling grounds and elaborate botanical gardens. When they stopped for refreshments at the palace's outdoor café, Hitler ordered local Nazi leader Fritz Sauckel to round up some young women to join Hitler's traveling party for dinner. "All day long I'm surrounded by men, and I'd like to hear women's voices for a change."

By 5:00 p.m., Sauckel had duly produced more than a dozen lovelies to sit with Hitler's party. But Sauckel's efforts had lit up the local grapevine, so that scores of young women began turning up or driving past, just to look at the famous Führer. Hitler noticed a comely lass in a passing car and turned to his pilot. "Look Baur: there's a lovely little woman for you—as pretty as a picture!" When Baur expressed concern about Hitler's apparent lack of female companionship, the Nazi chief replied: "I'm in the limelight of publicity, and anything of that sort could be very damaging. Now if *you* were to have a passing affair, no one would bother his head about it, but if I did there'd be the devil to pay. And women can never keep their mouths shut."[12]

Hitler's furious campaigning had drawn massive attention.[13] Though Germans had already made three treks to the polls earlier in the year, on July 31 they turned out in record numbers—84.1 percent of all eligible voters cast ballots, the highest ever in a parliamentary election. More than fifty parties were running, yet the Nazis were the massive winners. Hitler proved that his party had become the nation's strongest by polling 13,745,680 votes—37.2 percent of the ballots cast. In his runaway victory, Hitler had more than doubled the Nazi Party's 18.2 percent in the previous parliamentary election, just two years earlier. The Nazi share of seats in the Reichstag soared from 107 to 230.*

The election showed, above all else, that Germans were fleeing the center for the extremes. With the Nazis winning 37 percent of the vote, the Communists polling 14 percent, and Alfred Hugenberg's German National People's Party winning 6 percent, more than half of all Germans—57 percent—had voted for three parties that vehemently rejected republican democracy. They had given up on the Weimar Republic, with its swirling politics and ineffective administrations. They wanted an authoritarian government to solve their intractable problems.

Hitler's success had been a sensational leap forward—yet it also smacked of a Pyrrhic victory. At 37 percent, the Nazi Führer was right where he had been twice before—in the April 10 runoff against Hindenburg and in the April 24 state elections. He achieved only a fractional increase over the 36.8 percent he had won in the April presidential runoff. For all Hitler's airborne exertions, for all Goebbels's saturation

* The Social Democrats, historically Germany's strongest and most prodemocracy party, dropped to an embarrassing 21.5 percent, down from their high of 37.9 percent in 1919. The Centre Party, with its stable Catholic base, held steady at 12 percent. Two old parties of the bourgeois middle, the German Democratic Party and the deceased Gustav Stresemann's German People's Party, had sunk nearly to extinction, winning only 1 percent and 1.2 percent respectively.

propaganda, for all the Storm Troopers' parades and violence, Hitler had won 37 percent three times running. He had hit a ceiling.

Goebbels was glum. "We have won a tiny bit," he lamented. "Now we must come to power... one way or another. Something must happen.... We won't get an absolute majority this way."[14]

45

AT THE GATES OF POWER

I could not see how a man of his type, a plebian Austrian of limited mentality, could ever gain the allegiance of a majority of Germans.

—*Hans von Kaltenborn, CBS radio journalist, 1932*

Can't believe it—at the gates of power.

—*Joseph Goebbels, 1932*

While the establishment parties stewed over how to swaddle Hitler in a confining wad of responsibilities, the Nazi boss secretly set off in another direction. He contacted the man at the vortex of the political swirl, General von Schleicher. The two men met secretly again on August 6, sitting down together in the little town of Fürstenberg, fifty miles north of Berlin. Over the course of several hours, Hitler did to Schleicher what Schleicher had done to Papen—presented him with a finished list of cabinet posts and other assignments in a new government that would be headed by Hitler himself. He was willing to share some power with appointees from other parties, he said, but he wanted key positions for the Nazis. Gregor Strasser would become interior minister; Hermann Göring would run a new air ministry; Hjalmar Schacht would run the national bank; Wilhelm Frick would be a state secretary in the chancellery; Joseph Goebbels would get a new ministry for popular education—propaganda by another name. Even with other parties in the cabinet, Hitler's list corralled enough critical posts for the Nazis to have a stranglehold on power.

Slyly, Hitler said nothing about appointing a defense minister—the job that Schleicher currently held in the Papen government. Schleicher, no Nazi, was nonetheless part of Hitler's plans—at least for as long as it took the Nazi leader to get past Hindenburg. Being in Hitler's cabinet would suit Schleicher just fine and make the rest of the package more palatable to the president, who held the final say. With Schleicher as the minister who oversaw the army and all its weapons, Hindenburg could feel that one of his own team had a degree of control over Hitler's potential excesses. For Schleicher, being inside Hitler's cabinet but with back-channel connections to the president's inner circle—and to the army leadership—was a conspirator's dream.

Following his rather grandiose scheming with Schleicher, Hitler retreated to his highland eyrie in Berchtesgaden to enjoy his victory and make plans. Goebbels, along with the eight-and-a-half-months-pregnant Magda, joined Hitler in the mountains. The two men could already taste power. They sat up until 4:00 a.m. working through the ins and outs of taking over the government. So confident were they of their imminent leap onto the stage of glory that they fell into sentimental reminiscing about the years of struggle and all that had brought them to this historic moment. They shared recollections of their youth, including memories of each man's tyrannical father and loving mother. "Hitler is quite touched.... He and I lived through almost exactly the same upbringing," noted Goebbels.[1]

The men in Berchtesgaden were awaiting the signal from Berlin to form a new government. "Things will burst open within the week," recorded Goebbels. "We will never concede power unless they carry us out in coffins. This is a total solution. It will of course cost bloodshed, but that will be cleansing and clarifying. [Hitler and I] stay up late talking, weaving plans late into the night. Can't believe it—at the gates of power."[2]

But the gates quickly slammed shut. Schleicher had traveled to the president's country estate, Neudeck, in East Prussia. The confident general laid out Hitler's proposed cabinet choices for the Old Gentleman—and got a resounding rejection. Hindenburg was still smarting from Hitler's insults to his advanced age during the spring presidential campaign. The president was also angered that Hitler had broken a vow to "tolerate" the Papen cabinet rather than make a play for Papen's job. The president feared that a Nazi-led cabinet, despite a sprinkling of other parties, would be all Hitler all the time—and might even challenge presidential authority.[3] Hindenburg wanted no part of appointing Adolf Hitler as Germany's chancellor.[4]

Hindenburg also bore animus toward Hitler as a brash, no-name upstart from nowhere. To the old monarchist who had fought for the kaiser in the 1866 Austro-Prussian War and in the 1870–71 Franco-Prussian War, it was too much to expect him to "entrust the empire of Kaiser Wilhelm and Bismarck to a private from Bohemia." Or at least that was the comment attributed to the president in some reports.* True or invented, the comment reflected Hindenburg's feelings toward the Nazi interloper.

Hitler had overplayed his hand. His challenge now was to sell himself to the old president. He sent Röhm on a scouting mission to feel out Schleicher, Papen, and Meissner—now the most important men in German politics besides Hindenburg. Röhm reported back that the three were ready to work with Hitler—Chancellor Papen "very much so." Unfortunately, President Hindenburg was not.

"Only the Old Gentleman has reservations, no doubt whispered into his ear by the German Nationals [Hugenberg]," noted Goebbels. "His objections: the presidential cabinet would be gone; Hitler is too partisan; south Germany would rebel; he [Hindenburg] feels loyalty to Papen; what happened to Hitler's promise to tolerate a Papen cabinet?"[5]

Saturday, August 13, dawned oppressively hot in Berlin. The capital had gone febrile with speculation about a coming change of government. Even the most left-liberal commentators recognized that the Nazis had to be accommodated.

The Nazi leader felt that his providential march to power could still succeed; he decided to press his case. At noon he traveled to the defense ministry to meet with Schleicher, who endorsed Hitler's plan to try to unseat Papen while keeping Schleicher in charge of the military. Hitler

* Hindenburg confused Hitler's hometown of Braunau am Inn, Austria, with another town with a similar name in Bohemia, part of Czechoslovakia.

motored to Papen's chancellery office on Wilhelmstrasse. People were already gathered on the sidewalks and street corners, talking, gesturing, reading the latest editions of the newspapers—and expecting something big.

Would the Nazis come to power? Would this be Germany's historic day? Would there be a dramatic new beginning?

Inside the chancellery, Hitler met an impasse. Rejecting Hitler's cabinet proposal, Papen refused to step down. Instead, he offered Hitler the vice-chancellorship in his own cabinet, a powerless position. Suddenly a man with a political mind of his own, Papen called the bluff of a challenger he still did not take seriously. He had earlier found Hitler "curiously unimpressive" and lacking an "inner quality which might explain his extraordinary hold on the masses." To the upper-crust Papen, known for speaking with an aristocratic Westphalian accent, the Austrian-accented Hitler was still an uncultured rube with a "curious hair style" and a strange mustache that gave him a vague "bohemian quality."[6] Papen could see none of the magnetic force in Hitler that he had heard so much about. He tried to buy Hitler off with a title but no real power.

Deeply offended, Hitler saw straight through the ploy. As leader of the largest party in Germany, he refused to subordinate himself to anyone else as chancellor.[7] After two heated hours of discussion, Hitler left Papen's office in defeat and in a huff. He retreated to the Goebbelses' apartment for succor. The Nazis seemed forever stuck in the role of opposition party.

At 3:00 p.m. Goebbels's phone rang. It was a call from the presidential office. President Hindenburg wanted to see Hitler. Hitler sulkily declined, saying that if a decision had already been made, "it serves no purpose for me to come."[8] But a presidential aide hinted that the door might be open for reconsideration. Hitler decided to go. Arriving shortly after 4:00 p.m. with Röhm and Frick as his entourage, Hitler met with Hindenburg, Papen, and Otto Meissner. The president wanted to "officially" ask the Nazi leader "a simple question: are you prepared to be part of the next government?"[9]

An irritated Hitler replied that he had already explained to Chancellor Papen why he would not join a government that his party was not leading.

"So you're demanding the whole government?" asked Hindenburg.

"That's not necessarily the case," replied Hitler. "We'll have to have negotiations about the makeup of the cabinet, and that can't be done overnight."

Now Hindenburg was irritated. He well remembered Hitler's promise to Schleicher that he would support a new government after Brüning was deposed if, in return, the president dissolved the Reichstag, called new elections, and lifted the ban on the Storm Troopers and their uniforms. With Meissner taking notes, the president gave Hitler a simple civics lesson, telling the Nazi leader that by joining the governing coalition he "would be able to show what he could achieve." If Hitler could produce positive results, said Hindenburg, he would acquire increasing and perhaps even dominating influence in a coalition government.[10] Failing that, said the Old Gentleman, he could not—"in front of God, his conscience, and his country"—justify giving the entire power of government to a single party and "especially not one so hostile toward people of different political persuasions."[11]

Hindenburg's explicit mention of the Nazi Party's brutal hostility toward people "of different persuasions" was influenced by a "white book" that the president had recently received from the most influential Jewish organization in Germany, the Central Association of German Citizens of the Jewish Faith. The white book documented the wave of terror against Jews, Jewish institutions, and Jewish businesses, especially the numerous attacks on storefront windows around the country. Hindenburg had just sent the association a letter denouncing anti-Jewish violence as well as any proposed attempts to limit the Jews' rights in Germany.[12]

At loggerheads with Hitler, Hindenburg brought the meeting to an end with the admonition that the Nazi leader conduct himself "honorably" as an opposition party. Warning against terror and violence, Hindenburg shook Hitler's hand and reminded him that the two men should remain what they were—"old [war] comrades whose paths may cross again in the future."[13]

On this exceptionally hot day "the atmosphere was icy" by the time Hitler took his leave of Hindenburg, recalled Papen.[14] The Nazi chief's walk out of the presidential offices was one of the hardest of his life. He had scurried to the feet of the powerful only to be kicked in the teeth again, he felt. Fuming, Hitler made the trek down the steps of the chancellery before the waiting crowds on Wilhelmstrasse. They could plainly see the abject disappointment and failure on his face, leaving the seat of power empty-handed and spurned.*

Within hours, Hitler's sense of rejection worsened when State Secretary Meissner's notes of the meeting with Hindenburg were converted into a public statement. The presidential press release seemed intended to humiliate the Nazi leader, claiming that Hitler had demanded "the entire power of the state" and that the president's "duty and conscience" prevented him from granting such power to a party "that would use it one-sidedly." Hitler quickly retorted that he had not asked for the full power of the state but only for government leadership. It made no difference. To most outside observers, and even to some Nazi insiders, it seemed that Hitler was an all-or-nothing monomaniac, unsuited for compromise or negotiated politics.

August 13 became a black day on the Nazi calendar. It represented a new low in rejection. Hindenburg's brusque rebuff was a personal defeat for Hitler, a bitter reminder that, in some circles, the rabble-rouser was still not socially acceptable—a supersensitive point in Hitler's psyche.[15] He considered himself a religious prophet who had now been offered a cushy post in the high temple of some other religion—if he would just shut up. He saw through the establishment's gambit to defang him. "I shall never sell my birthright for a mess of pottage," Hitler hotly told a Nazi-friendly newspaper, citing the biblical Esau's folly in renouncing his primogeniture just to get a bowl of warm stew—as described in the book of Genesis.[16]

Goebbels shared Hitler's umbrage. "They talked down to Hitler like [they were] speaking to a sick animal that should be satisfied with a vice-chancellorship," he wrote. "Hitler was lured to Hindenburg as a trap.... Hitler as vice-chancellor under Papen—how grotesque!"[17]

What Goebbels considered grotesque was seen by some other Nazis as a

* President Hindenburg was temporarily working in the chancellery while the presidential palace underwent renovations.

missed opportunity. Outside Hitler's tight Berlin team of Goebbels, Röhm, Frick, and Göring, there was consternation among Nazis. Gregor Strasser and the Storm Trooper leadership believed that accepting half a loaf—the vice-chancellorship—would have finally gotten the long-marching, long-suffering Nazis through the portals of power. Storm Trooper officers complained that they could barely keep their restless men under control.[18]

Hitler departed Berlin to seek solace in the Alps.

To explain his decision to his puzzled followers—and to strike back at the Hindenburg camarilla—Hitler again seized the ready opportunity of interviews with the American media. The first reporter through the door of Haus Wachenfeld, on the Obersalzberg, was Karl von Wiegand of the *New York American.* Hitler disputed the accusation that he had asked President Hindenburg for "everything or nothing." Hitler told Wiegand he had only demanded his appropriate share of leadership of a new cabinet: "Holding only 37 percent of the nation's votes, how could I demand all portfolios? I didn't.... As a matter of fact, I left six portfolios open." Whatever the case, Hitler added, his plan now was to "get 51 percent of the votes, or an even larger percentage."[19*]

Wiegand emerged from the interview frustrated. "That man is hopeless. He gets worse every time I see him.... Ask him a question and he makes a speech," he told the two other waiting correspondents—Louis P. Lochner of the Associated Press and US radio commentator H. V. Kaltenborn. When Lochner and Kaltenborn got their turn, Hitler recited the same political equations he had given to Wiegand. Mindful of a postelection wave of Storm Trooper violence and a bomb attack on a synagogue in Kiel, Lochner asked Hitler if the Nazis might still try to take power by force in an imitation of Benito Mussolini's 1922 March on Rome.[20]

"Why should I march on Berlin? I am already there!" replied Hitler. The Nazi chief told the correspondents that he was still intent on turning Germany into a dictatorship even without a takeover by force. A dictatorship

---

* No party ever won more than 37.9 percent of the parliamentary vote during the Weimar Republic.

was justified in Germany "once the people declare their confidence in one man and ask him to rule," he insisted.[21]

Kaltenborn, not based in Germany, was unafraid to ask Hitler a pointed question. "Why does your anti-Semitism make no distinction between the Jews that flooded into Germany during the postwar period and the many fine Jewish families that have been German for generations?"

Hitler fired back: "All Jews are foreigners. Who are you to ask me how I deal with foreigners? You Americans admit no foreigner unless he has good money, good physique, and good morals. Who are you to talk about who should be allowed in Germany?"[22]

Kaltenborn had struck a nerve. But he was also misled by Hitler's little rant: "After meeting Hitler...I could not see how a man of his type, a plebian Austrian of limited mentality, could ever gain the allegiance of a majority of Germans."[23]

46

FALLING COMET

It is obvious that [Hitler] is now headed downhill.

—Vossische Zeitung, *November 7, 1932*

Revolting, retching... We suffered a heavy setback. Now we face tough fighting ahead.

—*Joseph Goebbels, November 1932*

Hitler's juggernaut was now in limbo. The chastening August 13 rebuff by President Hindenburg had punctured Hitler's claim of inevitability and thrown the Nazi leader into a radical mood. He felt personally affronted the way he had in 1923, when he staged a coup d'état only to find himself betrayed midputsch by the German military. When he was hauled off to prison, Hitler even blamed the German people for not recognizing his valiant efforts to save them. "That bunch of bums!" he shouted to a prison counselor. "You put your life on the line for the greatest cause, and then they betray you!"[1]

In his fevered state, Hitler began lashing out at Jews. Though he had tempered his anti-Semitic outbursts during the 1932 election campaigns to avoid alienating middle-class voters, the Nazi leader was now unconstrained, with Goebbels joining the nastiness. IT IS THE JEWS' FAULT! screamed a front-page headline in *Der Angriff*.

All across Germany, the Storm Troopers and the SS began smashing Jewish-owned shop windows and attacking synagogues. In industrial Krefeld, simultaneous assaults with tear-gas bombs were launched against the Jewish-owned Tietz department store and against Woolworth's, an American chain mistakenly thought to be Jewish-owned. In coastal Kiel, the Karstadt department store and the main synagogue were bombed. In

Berlin's Neukölln neighborhood, all five large display windows of the Leiser shoe store were smashed, and a large crowd formed to protect the attackers from arrest by police.

To the Jewish weekly *Das Jüdische Echo* (The Jewish Echo), the wave of terror in Germany was a "guerrilla war" against Germany's small but highly visible Jewish community. "Daily, even hourly, come reports of new bombings and display-window attacks from different parts of Germany," the newspaper reported.[2] Hamburg Jews desperately reached out to their fellow Germans with an appeal to reason. In a lengthy flyer, they refuted many of Hitler's attacks on Jews, from racial stereotyping to the suggestion that Jews were either Marxist or rich businessmen. Likewise they defended Jewish success in the professions as an act of historical necessity. "Does it really appear so surprising that people would turn more to intellectual vocations who for centuries on end were forcibly kept away from all jobs having to do with manual labor and so were forced to occupy themselves intellectually?" they wrote. "If all vocations but commerce are closed to a person, is it then so surprising that many Jews are engaged in commerce?"[3]

Not all the violence targeted Jews. Storm Troopers in East Prussia and Silesia, bitterly disappointed that Hitler had been unable to seize power after the July election, rampaged at random. They weren't angry only at the establishment but at Hitler and his "legal path" as well. "[The men] are pressing for an attack," reported one unit in the state of Hesse. "To them, an open fight is preferable to this endless electioneering [*Wählerei*]."

Faced with escalating violence, Papen's government issued a new emergency decree elevating political violence to stiffer punishments—including the death penalty.[4] Soon, five Nazi Storm Troopers were put on trial for the exceptionally brutal murder of a Communist in the small Silesian village of Potempa. The Nazis had hauled the man from his bed in the middle of the night and stomped him dead in front of his own mother and brother. On August 23, 1932, the five Potempa killers were sentenced to death.

Hitler was outraged. He very publicly sent the five Storm Troopers a telegram of support. "I feel tied to you with limitless loyalty," he wrote. "[Obtaining] your freedom is from this moment forward a point of honor for us."[5]

Hitler's indignation was fueled in part by a coincidental sentencing, on the very same day, of two members of the Social Democrats' Reichsbanner paramilitary. They had murdered a Nazi Storm Trooper several weeks earlier in a different town. But the Reichsbanner killers received much lighter sentences because their crime had occurred weeks before the government's new capital punishment decree had been promulgated. That distinction was lost on the Storm Troopers, who went into a nationwide fury.*

While Hitler rode the crest of Nazi protest with his telegram of solidarity to the "dear comrades" of Potempa, the incident exposed his hypocritical posture toward Nazi violence while piously pursuing the "legal path." Hitler's telegram—a frothy display of sympathy from the leader of the country's largest political party—made its own headlines, repelling the bourgeoisie but exhilarating Hitler's base. He even sent Röhm to visit the men in prison; Göring provided money for their families. Citing the Potempa incident as a good reason not to accept the vice-chancellorship of a government capable of such injustice, Hitler lashed out at Papen.[6] His tactics worked: Papen and Hindenburg backed down; the murderers' sentences were commuted to life in prison.

With the question of Hitler's role in governing Germany still unsettled, the new parliament that had been elected on July 31, 1932, formally convened on August 30.[7] With the Nazis now the largest delegation, holding 230 seats, Hermann Göring was easily elected president (speaker) of the body. But as he grasped the bell (the equivalent of a gavel), he was already conspiring against the state. In a late-night meeting at his apartment, Göring and other Nazis discussed how to circumvent the blockade posed by President Hindenburg to Hitler's final ascent to power. They

* In all, eighty-six Nazis would die in political violence in 1932, though the Nazis put the number at 198. More than fourteen thousand Nazis made insurance claims for injuries sustained in political confrontations that year.

considered deposing the president through a parliamentary coup d'état—on the grounds that he was no longer competent to hold the office. It would take a two-thirds majority of the Reichstag to introduce a referendum, followed by a majority of the German voters, to remove Hindenburg. In their initial feelers, the Nazis thought they had the concurrence of the Centre Party for their scheme—until former Chancellor Brüning got wind of it and angrily denounced the plot. The conspiracy died.

Chancellor Papen hoped to stay as head of government even without a parliamentary majority behind him. He paid a visit to President Hindenburg at his East Prussian estate, Neudeck. There he outlined his plans for stimulating the still-ruinous German economy to stem unemployment and bankruptcies.[8] He left with the president's blessing. On Monday, September 12, 1932, the Reichstag met for its first regular business session. The first item on the agenda was to be Chancellor Papen's report on the economic crisis. The chancellor had good news to deliver: his finance minister had reached an agreement with the all-powerful National Association of German Industry to reverse the deflationary policies of the Brüning administration.

But before Papen could begin his account, the German parliament took a near-comical but historic turn. A Communist leader, Ernst Torgler, called for a vote of no confidence—a blatant and bold attempt to bring down the Papen cabinet. No one expected such a tactic so early; Torgler's surprise motion threw the Reichstag into an uproar. Chancellor Papen hurriedly sent a messenger back to the chancellery, eight blocks away, to fetch an emergency order already signed by President Hindenburg that allowed the chancellor to dissolve the parliament preemptively at his pleasure, thereby forestalling a no-confidence vote. But by the time the messenger returned with the red box containing the order, Speaker Göring was ready to begin the vote on the unexpected motion. The Nazis had chosen to side with the Communists to bring down Papen.

A wild scene ensued. Trying to exercise his prerogative to speak, Chancellor Papen was blatantly ignored by the imperious Göring, who turned away from the government bench on his right to gaze upon the proceedings to his left. When Papen finally stood right in front of Göring, demanding the floor, the plump Nazi replied only that the voting had already begun. Papen slapped down the red box containing Hindenburg's signed dissolution order and marched out of the chamber—accompanied by his entire cabinet. Well-honed Nazi tactics of disruption and political carnival had reached their apotheosis.

What followed was the greatest humiliation of a sitting government in German history. The no-confidence vote carried, 522 to 42. More than 90 percent of the elected representatives of the German people expressed their dissatisfaction with Papen and his government, voting them out of office. Once again, the German political process was brought to a standstill. Five weeks after a major national election, German politics were scrambled again. The only solution was yet another national election—the fifth of the year. With Papen's cabinet still governing in a caretaker role, the balloting was scheduled for November 6.

Papen's sudden fall was a mixed blessing to the Nazis. It left the chancellor's cobbled-together oligarchy in a shambles, discrediting elitist attempts to run Germany without regard to mass support. Yet it exposed the Nazi juggernaut to the fickle will of the people again. "Election outlook rather pessimistic," wrote Goebbels, who was again worried about money.[9] "The fat cats are with Papen."[10] Goebbels also knew that the Nazi Party membership surge had ebbed. People were dropping out as fast as they dropped in.

Hitler put on his game face, turning again to the English-language press. He talked to Randolph Churchill, the son of the former First Lord of the Admiralty (and future prime minister) and now representing the *Daily Mail.* Hitler insisted that in the coming vote the Papen forces were "bound to collapse like a house of cards. . . . I could go back to the Bavarian highlands, forget politics, and take my ease if I wanted to while Herr von Papen and his colleagues do my propaganda work for me."[11]

But the Nazi boss had no intention of taking his ease. He knew no other mode than frenetic electioneering. The very sight of a podium, the sound of a crowd, the magic of the campaign trail—these were Hitler's drugs of choice. Using a larger airplane, a Junkers JU 52, Hitler again flew all over Germany in three and a half weeks, making fifty speeches and reaching into crannies of the country that had previously been neglected.

Hitler's slogan was "Against Papen and the reactionaries." The Nazi campaign began to ring of class warfare and a reversion to Strasser-style principles of socialism.[12] Goebbels made a surprise decision, approved by Hitler, to join the Communists in supporting a Berlin public transit workers' strike. The move created the impression of a Nazi slide to the hard left. "Hitler is fooling around with Marxism for the moment—Berlin transport strike!" noted the diarist Luise Solmitz, a Hamburg schoolteacher who switched from the Nazi Party to Hugenberg's German National People's Party. "Woe unto Hitler and to Germany that he has missed his moment."[13]

Hitler felt compelled constantly to explain his August 13 decision not to accept the post of vice-chancellor of Germany. He was acutely aware of doubters lurking at the edges of his party. In the small North Sea town of Aurich, he cast the offer as an attempt to shut him up with the perks of office:

> What is the use of being a minister without portfolio?... You have no influence at all.... The gentlemen figured that they [would be] in charge but the National Socialists would have to take responsibility whenever the police were used against the masses. They were convinced that within six months, we would be finished.

In Breslau, Hitler told a huge crowd: "The only thing that tempts me is leadership itself—genuine power and nothing else."[14] In the Nazi press, Hitler's race around Germany was a triumphal march toward victory. But the mainstream media described a campaign that was faltering and no longer filling its venues. In the Festival Hall, at Nuremberg's Luitpoldhain—hallowed ground for the Nazis—only half the seats were taken.[15] Journalist Konrad Heiden later characterized Hitler's slackening path as "a falling comet in the November fog."[16]

On November 6, Germans went to the polls yet again. Voter fatigue showed, with turnout falling to 80.5 percent, four points lower than in

July. Some voters had given up hope. Though Heinrich Brüning, the reviled Hunger Chancellor, was gone, Chancellor von Papen had been unable to relieve the suffering in the land. Nothing drove political disillusionment with the dysfunctional parliamentary system more than economic misery, which often erupted in public places. "Hunger!" shouted a woman over and over in a small-town city hall until the police ran her out. Another citizen on another day started yelling at welfare officials: "I'm hungry! I have hunger and nothing else!" He kept up his mantra all the way to the local jail, where the police locked him up.[17]

Yet in November, fewer voters than in July saw the Nazis as their deliverance. When the November 6 vote was tallied, Hitler and his party had suffered a severe setback. They lost two million votes: their share fell four percentage points—from 37.2 to 33.1. They sacrificed thirty-five seats in the Reichstag. Though still Germany's largest party, the Nazis seemed to have peaked and were on the downslope of their meteoric arc. "The conviction of inevitability and unstoppable forward motion is broken," wrote the *Vossische Zeitung*. "And that means everything for a party without ideological foundations that did not grow and mature gradually and organically.... It is obvious that [Hitler] is now headed downhill."[18]

A big winner was the far left. The Communists jumped to 16.9 percent, their highest share ever. The Communists' newfound strength gave them, for the first time, one hundred seats in the parliament: it was further proof, warned Hitler, of the imminent danger of a Bolshevist takeover of Germany—a scare tactic that resonated with German businessmen and industrialists. The Social Democrats, a relatively moderate bulwark on the left against the Communist menace, were gasping for air at 20.4 percent.

Goebbels ordered a top-secret analysis of what had gone wrong. With his elaborate propaganda operation reaching into every region and locality, he had what amounted to an intelligence and opinion-survey apparatus. When the reports came in, they revealed that Storm Trooper violence and hooliganism during the preceding months were the leading culprits in election setbacks. "A great portion of the electorate was offended by the rowdy behavior of the Storm Troopers, who became a genuine pestilence in the land following the elections of July 31," noted Nazi *gau* officials in Silesia. The image of an out-of-control party had cost the Nazis dearly with middle-class voters.[19] The party's rather dire financial condition, both regionally and nationally, also contributed to the Nazis' backslide. The analysis, entitled *Stimmungsbericht* (Morale Report) for internal purposes, reached the pessimistic conclusion that "we must not let it come to another election. The results could be unimaginable."

Among the Nazis, the mood was miserable. The election reversal was seen as the third slap in Hitler's face of 1932—following the lost presidential election in the spring and the August 13 rejection by Hindenburg. The charismatic halo had slipped. People were questioning the leader's judgment.

Goebbels took the election results especially hard. "Revolting, retching... We suffered a heavy setback," he wrote. "Now we face tough fighting ahead."[20]

47

SECRET RELATIONSHIP

I must now look after the girl. But that does not mean I intend to marry her.

—Adolf Hitler, November 1932

Hitler's frantic election campaigning had been interrupted—very briefly—by a telling interlude. In late 1932, his new girlfriend, Eva Braun, tried to kill herself.[1]

Eva Braun had quietly entered Hitler's life even before the 1931 suicide of his half niece Geli. Some have even speculated that Geli's awareness of another young woman enjoying Hitler's attention could have contributed to her decision to shoot herself.

In contrast to his proud public display of his attachment to Geli, Hitler never showed the outside world that he had a mistress named Eva. Born in 1912, educated in Catholic schools, and trained for retail work, Eva had in 1929 taken a job in Heinrich Hoffmann's Munich photography shop, where Hitler met her. Eva was seventeen; Hitler was forty. Though "feather-brained," more interested in movies and dance halls than theater and concerts, the young woman had what Hoffmann called a "chocolate-box type of prettiness."[2] Over time, Hitler found ways and reasons to spend time with her, dropping by Hoffmann's shop with small gifts and even inviting her along on group picnics in the Bavarian countryside—just as he had previously done with Geli.

While he clearly enjoyed Eva's company and became increasingly involved with her, Hitler was neither seriously in love nor very concerned with his new girlfriend's emotional state, especially during the busiest political year of his life. Always traveling in 1932, he had little time for her. Feeling neglected and complaining of loneliness, Eva finally wrote

Hitler a farewell note and, late at night on November 1, shot herself in the chest with her father's 6.35mm pistol. But Eva missed her heart and other vital organs. Her sister later claimed that Eva had been able to call the doctor herself.

Hitler was stunned. He rushed to Munich and took a huge bouquet to Eva in the hospital. According to Hoffmann's account, Hitler's chief concern, just as it had been when Geli died, was less his suffering girlfriend than his own political reputation. "Is the doctor a man who will hold his tongue?" he asked Hoffmann.

Mulling his options, Hitler remarked: "The girl did it for the love of me. But I have given her no cause which could possibly justify such a deed. Obviously, I must now look after the girl. But that does not mean I intend to marry her."

Hoffmann demurred. "No one could blame you for what Eva has done."

"Who do you think would believe that?" replied Hitler. "What guarantee is there that something of that kind might not occur again?"

Hitler consoled himself with the idea that Eva herself could be counted on to keep their relationship secret. "The great thing about Eva is that she is no political bluestocking," Hitler told Hoffmann. "I loathe politically minded women. The *chère amie* [girlfriend] of a politician must be quietly discreet."

After the hospital visit, Hitler immediately returned to Berlin, where he spoke to a packed Sports Palace that same night. But he made good on his vow to take care of Eva, moving her into his Munich apartment and, later, into his Obersalzberg house. From the day she shot herself until their joint suicide, in 1945, Hitler would show much more concern for Eva than he had in the past, sometimes calling her daily from Berlin even as he kept the relationship secret from the German people.

48

ETERNAL INTRIGUER

There are a great many intriguers at work.

— *British ambassador Sir Horace Rumbold, 1932*

Never has a great movement been victorious if it went down the path of compromise.

—*Adolf Hitler, December 1932*

Following the Nazis' loss of four percentage points in the November 6 election, a "chess match for power" unfolded, as Goebbels put it.[1] In the end, the moves and countermoves would leave German politics unsettled, volatile, and vulnerable to potential coup attempts from the left and right. The chess match would find Hitler checkmated and headed into the deepest crisis the Nazi Party had faced since the failed 1923 putsch attempt.

Chancellor Papen made the first move. To continue governing, he wanted Hitler as his enabler. Well aware that the Nazi Party, even wounded, was still Germany's largest, Papen on November 13 again urged Hitler to put national interest above party interest by joining him in forming a government.[2] But Hitler saw the offer as another trick to rope him in and humiliate him in the bargain, just as had happened in the summer. After waiting three days for dramatic effect, Hitler replied: "I am in no way inclined to experience a repeat of the events of August 13."[3] It was still all or nothing for Hitler.

That made it a dead end for Papen. After less than six months in office, the hapless aristocrat on November 17 tendered his resignation. At Hindenburg's request, Papen continued in a caretaker role, leaving the leadership question as muddy as ever. "Everything more or less depends on chance and the good or bad mood of four or five individuals," groused diarist Harry Kessler.[4] The unhappy count was referring to the confidants around the president—Papen, Schleicher, Meissner, and Oskar von Hindenburg—and to President Hindenburg himself, who counted above all others.

Hindenburg was worn down and tired. His closest advisers, including Papen, had counseled him to find a way to accept Hitler as a leader. The Nazi's political popularity could not be denied. Hindenburg had also just received a petition from nineteen leading bankers and businessmen, including Hjalmar Schacht, Fritz Thyssen, Kurt von Schröder, Wilhelm Keppler, and Count Eberhard von Kalckreuth, head of the country's largest agribusiness association. The signatories argued that since Hitler was leader of the largest nationalist group, the president should offer him the chancellorship.*

On November 19, the old general once again summoned the former private first class, Adolf Hitler, to his offices. Hitler arrived in an upbeat mood.[5] With Papen on ice, the Nazi leader felt his chance had finally come. The atmospherics were decidedly improved: the Old Gentleman no longer seemed to regard Hitler as a backwoods provincial who might serve only as postal minister. The meeting ended inconclusively but resumed two days later. In it, Hindenburg made a historic turnaround: he opened the door to the possibility of a Hitler-led government. Yet the president's offer was cloaked in a caveat: the Nazi party chief would have to assemble a cabinet that represented a parliamentary majority—something no German government had done since 1930. The president already knew that the headstrong Alfred Hugenberg was bitterly opposed to Hitler's ascension into the chancellor's chair. Without Hugenberg's German National People's Party, Hitler probably could not form a coalition with majority backing in parliament.

Hitler was again stymied. He would not accept the keys to the kingdom with conditions attached; he had no interest in a chancellorship tethered to a millstone of constant compromise with coalition partners. Hitler

* Though most of Germany's leading Ruhr region industrialists, except Thyssen, had declined to sign the petition, some of them signaled their silent support.

asked President Hindenburg for the right to rule with a minority cabinet under presidential decree, as Papen and Brüning had done. Alternatively, Hitler suggested that he form a government intent on building parliamentary support for a special enabling act—requiring two-thirds approval by the parliament—that would grant him authoritarian powers. Both Hitler's demands were summarily rejected in a letter from Otto Meissner, who cited President Hindenburg's ongoing qualms about a Hitler-led "single-party dictatorship." Hindenburg again humbled Hitler by justifying his position as the only way to remain true to his oath of office and to "his conscience."

Goebbels suspected that General von Schleicher was behind the new snub. "The eternal intriguer has won again—until such time as he is eaten by the revolution," wrote Goebbels.[6]

Another critical moment had come and gone. Offered the chancellor's chair—albeit with stringent limitations—Hitler had walked away, leaving his troops restless and puzzled. The endless jousting and backroom scheming were exhausting everyone's patience. Morale was crumbling among the Nazi rank and file; Nazi newspaper subscriptions were being canceled. Some Nazis were even defecting to the Communists.[7] Nazi Party membership was falling, and dues were often not being paid, reported Munich police intelligence.[8]

Gregor Strasser was especially frustrated by Hitler's mulish habit of letting the perfect stand in the way of the good. Through exposure to a wide range of non-Nazi groups and political activists, the ambitious Strasser had become a pragmatic Nazi; Hitler remained a militant fanatic.[9] Strasser consorted with members of an intellectual circle around Hans Zehrer, publisher of a neoconservative monthly called *Die Tat* (The Deed). Zehrer and his fellows advocated a broad nationalistic front that even embraced labor unions, pure anathema to Hitler's one-party fanaticism.

Strasser believed that a post like vice-chancellor, even with limited power, could be a springboard to full power. His opinion mattered. While Goebbels, Göring, Röhm, and Frick were more often in the headlines—and got more face time with Hitler—Strasser was widely respected inside the party and regarded as second only to Hitler. The national organization leader—Strasser's official title—traveled often to *gau* offices and even outlying chapters. The big Bavarian with the loud laugh had a strong internal network of supporters and devotees, including around one-third of the 196 Nazis elected to the Reichstag in November. Sixty to seventy Nazi parliamentarians might, in a pinch, follow Strasser rather than Hitler. They shared Strasser's view that the party would soon be in trouble if Hitler stuck to an uncompromising course and did not embrace alliances with other nationalistic forces.

Defense Minister von Schleicher, who knew everything, was aware of the turmoil among the Nazis. As a backstage player in Hindenburg's and Papen's negotiations with Hitler, he was privy to the unfolding crisis, step-by-step. Over time, he began putting out feelers about his own chances for taking over. At a December 1 meeting with President Hindenburg and the still caretaking Chancellor von Papen, Schleicher sensed a propitious moment to plant the notion that a cabinet headed by him might thread the needle and bring the Nazis aboard, thus thwarting Hitler's demand for full power.[10]

But the Old Gentleman spurned the offer. He had taken a personal liking to Papen, the polite plutocrat, and urged the lame-duck chancellor to try again to form a working cabinet. Hindenburg again promised Papen the powers of presidential rule by emergency decree—but he dramatically upped the ante. He offered to dissolve the Reichstag yet again but to delay new elections indefinitely. A blatant violation of the Weimar constitution—which mandated that elections be held within sixty days of a Reichstag dissolution—such a radical step would throw Germany into a full-blown constitutional crisis. The president's unexpected proposal put Papen in an untenable quandary. The surprise development also put Schleicher and Papen, the longtime friends and now rivals, at daggers drawn.

As the two men departed the presidential office, Schleicher sarcastically commented: "Little monk, little monk, you have chosen an arduous path." Schleicher's scornful jibe played on a famous line from history, allegedly uttered in 1521 to persecuted religious reformer Martin Luther as the bullheaded monk left the Diet of Worms, headed for internal exile. The remark stung Papen and sealed his break with Schleicher.[11]

Within a day, however, Papen felt the brunt of Schleicher's prediction. Convening his cabinet, the still sitting chancellor presented the president's radical offer to suspend parliament and elections indefinitely. Schleicher, as defense minister, quickly expressed opposition. Civil war might follow, he said, and the military would be unable to contain it. Schleicher summoned Lieutenant Colonel Eugen Ott, an officer whom he had commissioned to study the Reichswehr's readiness. Schleicher asked Ott if the German military, with only one hundred thousand men, could thwart a concerted internal uprising by Germany's assorted militant groups while defending the country's borders from possible foreign attack. Of special concern was the East Prussian frontier with Poland; radical Polish elements had already threatened intervention in Germany.[12]

Ott's response was that the Reichswehr, in its diminished state, could not possibly do both jobs. Disorder and breakdown were certain. (Schleicher may have ensured that Ott's analysis was given a negative slant for his own political reasons.) Schleicher added that the Prussian police, "undermined by [leftist] propaganda," could not be considered absolutely reliable.[13]

With his unique standing as both a political figure and a military man, Schleicher and his dramatic presentation in the cabinet meeting carried the day—and triggered Papen's undoing. To finance minister Count Lutz Schwerin von Krosigk (one of the cabinet barons), the war-game report made a "devastating impression."[14] All but one of the cabinet ministers opposed the continuation of a government led by Papen.

A stricken Chancellor von Papen went straight to President Hindenburg with the news of the cabinet's vote of no confidence. The president, too, was turned around by Schleicher's impossible-sounding two-front scenario. The weight of his years and the long struggle to save Germany left the president unable to resist the pressure that Schleicher had now built. "I am too old and have been through too much to accept the responsibility for a civil war," Hindenburg told Papen. "Our only hope is to let Schleicher try his luck." It had taken Schleicher only twenty-four hours to reverse fortunes from the previous day. His moment had come.

As the defrocked Papen stood to leave Hindenburg's office, "two great tears" rolled down the president's face. A few hours later Hindenburg sent

Papen a parting gift—a photograph of himself inscribed with the first line of a famous soldier's song about losing a brother in arms: *Ich hatt' einen Kameraden!* (I once had a comrade).[15] Despite their official separation, the two men would stay close. Hindenburg wanted Papen to continue living in his special quarters in the nearby interior ministry building.

Schleicher's long-running scheme to take power had reached fruition. On December 2, 1932, he was sworn in by President Hindenburg as the Weimar Republic's twelfth chancellor, forming its twentieth cabinet in fourteen years. To Hitler and the Nazis, Schleicher's leap into the chancellor's chair was just another annoying delay. "This is the Old Gentleman's last dodge," wrote Goebbels.[16] To foreign observers, the political carousel was shrouded in a fog of conspiratorial confusion. "There are a great many intriguers at work," was British ambassador Sir Horace Rumbold's slightly baffled dispatch to London.[17]

As Schleicher began contemplating his new cabinet, he pondered how to handle Hitler. Neutralizing the Nazi leader by giving him a piece of power had been among Schleicher's arguments while Papen was in office. Now he sent Lieutenant Colonel Ott to Weimar—where Hitler was campaigning for Nazi candidates in the crucial Thuringian state election. Ott's charge was to persuade Hitler to join his new cabinet or, at the least, indirectly support his government. Schleicher may, in fact, have had a hidden agenda: securing an obstinate rejection from Hitler, thus freeing the new chancellor to make cabinet choices without Hitler's involvement. Either way, Ott's blandishments to Hitler at the Hotel Elephant in Weimar were useless. Hitler harangued Ott for three hours, even arguing against Schleicher's acceptance of the job of chancellor in the first place, though it was already too late.

Hitler tried to put the best face on the unruly slide of political affairs and the Nazis' newly precarious standing. He told *Daily Express* correspondent Sefton Delmer that "not more than four months from now... our day will have arrived."[18] Such a prediction seemed pure fantasy. It sounded even worse when the Thuringian election returns came in on

December 4. Despite furious electioneering by Hitler, the Nazis had lost fully 40 percent of their support in the state compared to their parliamentary tally only three months before. To Hitler's enemies, the spectacular setback was proof of Hitler's now inexorable decline.

NIMBUS DESTROYED, trumpeted the *Berliner Tageblatt.*

Far more alarming for Hitler, the Thuringian vote confirmed fears among some Nazis, especially Gregor Strasser, that Hitler was damaging the Nazi movement with his headstrong demand for full power. Strasser's dismay hardened when Hitler spoke on December 5 to the Nazi delegation to the Reichstag, ordering them to take a hard line against the Schleicher cabinet, avoiding all temptations to cooperate. "Never has a great movement been victorious if it went down the path of compromise," Hitler rasped. Wilhelm Frick, the fawning leader of the Nazis' parliamentary caucus, rose to pledge his "unshakable and inviolable loyalty" to the Führer. But Strasser sat unmoved. When Goebbels looked at him, the propaganda boss saw a face "turned to stone."

Nineteen thirty-two was supposed to have been Hitler's year of triumph. Now it was turning into his year of disaster.

49

CRISIS

The year 1932 has been one long streak of bad luck. We just have to smash it to pieces.

—Joseph Goebbels, December 24, 1932

Four days after the Thuringian election, on the morning of December 8, 1932, Gregor Strasser sat down at a desk in Berlin's Hotel Excelsior. He composed a letter to "Herr Adolf Hitler, presently residing at the Hotel Kaiserhof, Berlin." The missive contained a bombshell: Strasser was resigning from the Reichstag; he was quitting all his offices in the Nazi Party; he was effectively leaving the movement. The man who had walked step-by-step with Hitler for more than ten years, the former military commander who had built and held together the burgeoning Nazi network during a decade of turmoil, the loyal paladin who had repeatedly proclaimed his fealty to the Führer—that man was quitting.

In his letter, Strasser excoriated Hitler's approach to gaining power. He denounced the Nazi chief's all-or-nothing attitude, his rigid rejection of coalition politics, and especially his disruptive political style. "The single-minded hope that chaos will produce the party's hour of destiny is, I believe, erroneous, dangerous, and not in the interests of Germany as a whole," wrote the angry Nazi. Strasser advocated the creation of a "great broad front" of like-minded people to create a "new-style state." In other words, he favored any coalition that might work, even if it meant joining Papen's cabinet. Strasser complained that the Storm Troopers' campaigns of violence—especially the constant clashes with Communists—had gone beyond all acceptable bounds: the "brutal confrontation with Marxism cannot and may not... stand at the center of the internal political task," he wrote.

Accusing Hitler of sabotaging him and his work in the eyes of other party leaders, Strasser announced that he would be departing Germany forthwith.[1]

Even as Hitler read Strasser's unsparing letter, at noon on the same day, Strasser was holding a farewell meeting in his Reichstag office with eight key gauleiters—his handpicked cadre of inspectors general who had carried out his will in all thirty-five Nazi *gaus* around the country. According to Schleswig-Holstein gauleiter Hinrich Lohse, Strasser dumbfounded this inner core of loyal lieutenants with his decision to resign. Several of "the toughest men in the party" were brought to the verge of tears. "[They] pleaded with him in stricken and choked voices . . . not to leave them."[2]

In a hoarse tone, Strasser told the men he believed the Führer's obstinacy was shaking the party's cohesion and threatening to destroy it. "Given the unheard-of stresses of our followers, our Storm Troopers, and our party comrades, we can't make them wait forever [to assume power] without their becoming impatient and disappointed and finally leaving the party." Strasser's main charge was that Hitler no longer had a clear idea of what the movement was. "In only one matter is he clear: he wants to be chancellor under any circumstances," said Strasser. Yet there was "no real prospect of reaching this goal in the foreseeable future."

Strasser then shocked the gauleiters with a radical proposal: he endorsed taking the "revolutionary path" to power if that would break Hitler's intractability. Proposing a violent overthrow of the German government was heresy, a stark repudiation of Hitler's decision eight years earlier to seek power only by the "legal path." With more than half a million uniformed Storm Troopers and SS men ready for action, said Strasser, a Nazi coup d'état would have a chance to succeed "even if it were bloody and faced serious resistance by state forces."

Surprise and panic swept through the Nazi world. Rumors reached Goebbels that Strasser was staging a palace coup inside the party.[3] Strasser's apostasy was an implicit call for rebellion, and Goebbels feared a mass defection to a banner that was now marching away from him and Hitler.[4] It could be the beginning of the party breakup that many feared over Hitler's obdurate stance. A movement torn between its violent impulses and its political maneuvering seemed to have reached a cracking point.

Two of Strasser's closest gauleiters hurried to the Hotel Kaiserhof to try to reason with Hitler. Instead, the Nazi chief summoned all eight gauleiters to his suite. Awaiting their arrival, he retreated into history. Rereading Mark Antony's speech about Caesar and Brutus in Shakespeare's *Julius Caesar,* Hitler seized on its famous appeal: "Friends, Romans, countrymen, lend me your ears.... Men have lost their reason." Clearly Hitler saw himself as Caesar and Strasser as Brutus, the one-time loyalist who in 44 BCE participated in the assassination of the Roman emperor. To Hitler, the men around Strasser had lost their reason.[5]

When the eight gauleiters arrived, Hitler flew into a two-hour effusion of rhetoric and persuasion. His speech to the men was a classic salvaging of a seemingly hopeless situation. As he had done at his 1924 treason trial, as he had done in the 1926 Bamberg meeting, as he had done after the disastrous 1928 election, an incited Hitler mounted a bravura performance of political and historical argumentation along with his customary melodramatic finale. Pacing up and down before the men—he kept them standing—Hitler took apart Strasser's arguments one by one. He insisted that compromising his principles by joining Chancellor Papen's cabinet would have made the collapse of the Nazi movement just "a matter of time."[6] Taking the illegal route to power through a coup d'état—as Strasser had proposed and as so many Storm Troopers wished to do—was suicide: Hitler would never lead the "flower of German manhood" into the machine guns of the police and the Reichswehr, as had happened in the 1923 putsch attempt. Rather than stage a self-destructive uprising, said Hitler, it was better to await the longed-for moment when he would be offered the chancellorship—"a day that is probably closer than we think." (Hitler's words must have been pure chutzpah; he could not have foreseen the unlikely events of the coming weeks.)

During his declamation, Hitler searched every face "as though wondering: are you still with me or have you gone over to the disloyal traitors?" recalled Lohse. In the charged atmosphere of his performance, Hitler doubled down: "If all of you intend to leave me, my life's work and my struggle have no further meaning. In that case I would have nothing more to keep me on this earth, and I will draw the consequences." Glancing at the bust of the deceased Geli Raubal that he kept on his hotel-room mantelpiece, Hitler added: "I only ask that my coffin and my body be covered with the flag that I created for the movement and as a symbol for the new Germany."

Hitler's melodramatic disquisition, with its suicide threat, worked; the gauleiters were won over. "He triumphed," recalled Lohse. To seal the gauleiters' return to the fold of loyalty, Hitler offered each man his signature handclasp and penetrating gaze.

The reconverted gauleiters' challenge was now to bring their revered Gregor Strasser back into the warm embrace of party comity. That evening, two of them tracked down Strasser having dinner at his regular restaurant; they begged him to reconsider his drastic action. But Strasser gruffly paid his check and departed with hardly a gesture of farewell. By the next morning he was headed for the Italian Alps.

The rupture was complete.

The Nazi Party was a construct unusually reliant on personalities and loyalty. Now it faced its worst identity crisis since the failed putsch of 1923. Despite his successful oration before the eight men in his hotel suite, Hitler was by no means certain that he could hold the entire party together. That evening he turned to the comfort of the Goebbelses' apartment, in Berlin's West End, to ruminate and lick his wounds.[7] Returning to the Kaiserhof in the middle of the night, he suddenly called Goebbels, Röhm, and Himmler to a 3:00 a.m. strategy meeting. When he arrived, Goebbels found Hitler poring over a copy of the next morning's *Tägliche Rundschau;* the newspaper's report on Strasser's sensational resignation depicted the apostate Nazi as the party's great man.

A fuming Hitler began tossing out ideas and orders for structural changes in the Nazi Party. He would liquidate the entire inspector general corps—the backbone of Strasser's power in the party. He would kill the so-called organizational department, the basis for Strasser's internal reach. He would place himself at the head of organizational matters—just as he had done when reining in the Storm Troopers after the Walter Stennes rebellion. In the dead of night, the four men began composing lists of Strasser sympathizers who would be purged from their posts or from the party altogether.

The morning newspapers made Strasser's defection the political buzz of the day. A PALACE REVOLUTION AGAINST HITLER, headlined the *Frankfurter Zeitung*.[8] In the *Vossische Zeitung*, Konrad Heiden wrote: "[Hitler] is still reaching for the brass ring, but the carousel has turned past the ring, and Hitler is grasping into thin air while his comrades are hopping off."[9]

Hitler sank again into a funk: if the party fell apart, he said, he would "end it all in three minutes" with a pistol.[10]

But within two days, Hitler responded to the crisis in his time-honored fashion—with frantic traveling and speech making. On December 10, he embarked on a nine-day, seven-city morale-boosting journey, with stops in Breslau, Dresden, Chemnitz, Leipzig, Berlin, Magdeburg, Halle, Hamburg, and Nuremberg. Because the year's nonstop campaigning had depleted the party treasury, Hitler no longer traveled by chartered plane but rather by car. Either way, he had to proceed: the fabric of the party had been rent by Strasser's defection and needed urgent attention.

Arriving at 10:30 p.m. in Breslau, the capital of Silesia, Hitler spoke until midnight to ten thousand Nazi functionaries. Speculations about the crumbling of the movement were "completely misplaced," he told the men. As always when pressed into desperation, Hitler reached for grandiose imagery and historic precedent, glorifying his failures while levering himself onto the tallest available pedestal. Unashamed to join the company of Germany's greatest heroes, Hitler invoked the memory of Frederick the Great facing down his enemies on Silesian soil during the Seven Years' War (1756–63). "Despite heavy and fateful losses, [Frederick] never even thought of capitulating," intoned Hitler, referencing his own current travails. "Distant Prussian history was not just about victories: it also included setbacks."[11] What mattered now was not holding on to power but continuing the struggle. For Hitler, struggle was the heart of the matter. Trying to recast the narrative of his missteps, Hitler told party leaders in Leipzig: "The true greatness of a statesman is shown not on the eve of victory but on the eve of reversals."[12]

By Christmastime, Hitler had completed his tour and collected pledges of loyalty across the country. The Nazi orator had thrown his persuasive passion into the breach of party dissension and come out ahead. Where Strasser's defection had exposed Hitler's glaring weaknesses—overweening megalomania, organizational dysfunction—the Nazi leader had replied with his strengths: oratorical fire, messianic conviction, and a promise of seeing the holy land in the near distance. He had tossed Strasser onto the dustbin of Nazi history. "Strasser has lost across the board," commented Goebbels with satisfaction.[13]

Yet while Hitler's display of moxie staved off dissolution of his movement, no one was quite sure where it was going. Many believed the enterprise had passed its peak and, through Hitler's stubbornness, missed its chance. In the larger scheme of German politics, Hitler appeared slated for a permanent outsider role. Though Papen was now out of office, the policies he had instituted to reverse Brüning's deflationary regime were having a tonic effect on the Depression-racked economy, weakening Hitler's apocalyptic appeal.

The past year's five election campaigns had been exhausting; Hitler had made 234 speeches and traveled tens of thousands of miles. His exertions, along with Goebbels's enormous propaganda campaigns, had depleted the Nazi Party treasury; Goebbels called the party finances "a monetary calamity."[14] Berliners joked that there were now more Storm Troopers with tin collection cups supposedly soliciting donations for Germany's annual winter aid drive than there were honest beggars on the streets of the city.

As 1932 ended, political analysts wrote off Hitler as a flash in the pan. The fearsome Nazi ascent of the past two years seemed to be fizzling. "The mighty Nazi assault on the democratic state has been denied," announced the *Frankfurter Zeitung* with finality.[15]

Even Hitler's biggest cheerleader, Goebbels, was glum: "The year 1932 has been one long streak of bad luck. We just have to smash it to pieces."[16]

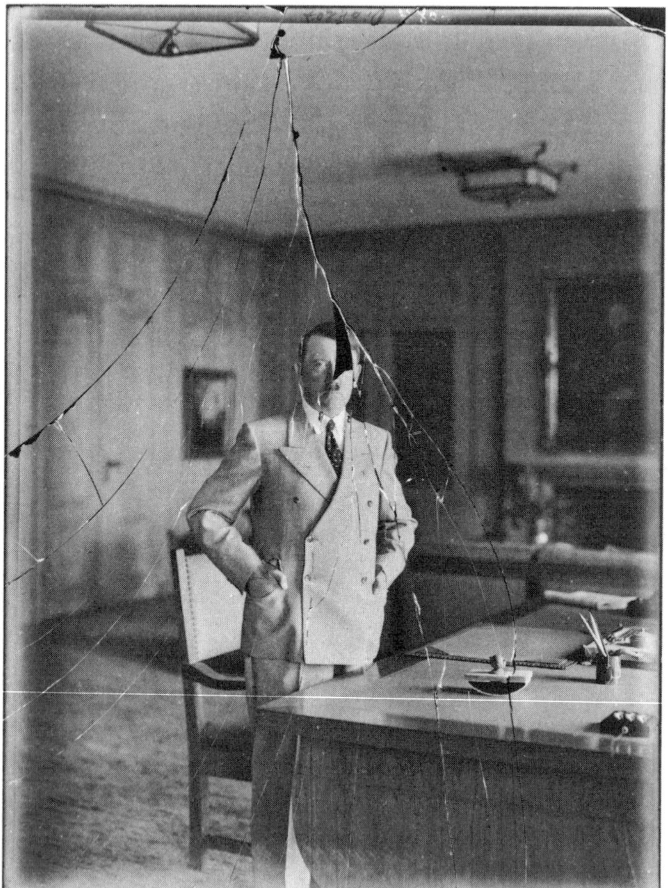

Part Five

ENDGAME

(1933)

People were walking around at lunchtime with spoons in their pockets because they could get a meal in exchange for a ration stamp.

—*Alois Pfaller, a former Young Communist League member*[1]

Many of us went hungry.

—*Storm Trooper*[2]

50

NEW YEAR'S RECKONING

The republic has been rescued.

—*Julius Elbau,* Vossische Zeitung *editor in chief*

This year belongs to us. I will guarantee you that in writing.

—*Adolf Hitler, January 1, 1933*

Hitler had holed up on the Obersalzberg. It was Christmastime, 1932, and Hitler had, as always, taken to the mountains. Ensconced among the snowdrifts and Alpine vistas of his retreat, Hitler was busily dictating his annual New Year's message to the Nazi Party. As he paced the rooms of his little lodge above Berchtesgaden, the Nazi leader shouted and revised and generally speechified to his diligent secretary. "His voice carries all the way over here to me," noted Joseph Goebbels, writing in his journal in a small inn across a meadow from Hitler's house.[1]

Braced by the clean air, freed from the journalistic slings and arrows of Germany's capital city, Hitler in the mountains regained his raw edge. He was bent on convincing the whole of the Nazi movement that rumors of his demise were decidedly premature. And he started by convincing his entourage.

When traveling, Hitler never liked to be alone. He required company and an audience, especially when in the Alps. This year's holiday gaggle included attorney Hans Frank, Saxony gauleiter Martin Mutschmann, and party official Robert Ley. Goebbels had traveled by overnight train from Berlin only to be borne the final stretch up the snowbound mountain in a pony cart (Goebbels came even though Magda was hospitalized in Berlin with a dangerous pregnancy). The photographer Heinrich

Hoffmann, almost always somewhere near Hitler these days, had journeyed from Munich.

On December 30, the group gathered to hear their chief read his New Year's declaration aloud. The statement would appear in all the Nazi newspapers the following day. A bombastic end-of-year reckoning, the long essay sounded like one of Hitler's arm-waving orations, bristling with denunciations of Bolshevists, Jews, and the German government. "Barbarism, human regression, barely imaginable suffering, and centuries' worth of lost progress" would be Germany's fate if it stayed on its present course, Hitler railed. "Bourgeois liberalism and international Marxism are the common enemies."[2]

Swinging back at the prevailing narrative of Nazi decline, Hitler declared 1932 a banner year in which historic victories had been achieved and the party had risen to become the strongest in Germany. The Nazi boss blasted the "Jewish press" that had been pronouncing him "dead" and a "thing of the past" ever since 1923, following his failed putsch. Defending his refusal of the vice-chancellorship in a Papen or Schleicher cabinet, Hitler argued that taking such a post would be political capitulation for a useless title with no power; it would plant the "seed of destruction" of the Nazi Party.

"Once [the movement] agrees to that," said Hitler, "it is snared."

"Hitler is smashing," scribbled Goebbels in his diary. "Radical in the extreme... That's the only way we can win."[3]

But Goebbels's real mood showed later: "Everybody is waiting for the new year. The old year was a total loss. Be done with it!"

At the stroke of midnight on New Year's Eve, amid celebrations and forced smiles, Goebbels shook Hitler's hand with a bravely hopeful statement: "I wish you power!"[4]

Nothing seemed less likely on the first day of 1933. The Nazi movement was destabilized: Gregor Strasser's defection three weeks earlier still reverberated, keeping everyone on edge. The Storm Troopers under Ernst Röhm were an uncertain factor. They could go rogue at any time, staging their own attack on the state. A breakup of the Nazi Party seemed plausible, with Hitler's future stymied. The political cognoscenti were sure that the Hitler juggernaut was over. "The republic has been rescued," wrote the *Vossische Zeitung* editor in chief, Julius Elbau, in a front-page essay.[5] Capturing the collective sigh of relief among the educated elites, the newspaper called the Nazi enterprise nothing more than "a giant conglomerate with feet of clay."

Yet Hitler believed more in himself than in anyone else's judgment of him. His life's imperative was the surmounting of any and all odds. Departing the Obersalzberg for Munich on New Year's Day, the Nazi chief was surprisingly upbeat. Along with Rudolf and Ilse Hess and Heinrich Hoffmann, Hitler attended the de rigueur social event of the day, a New Year's performance of Wagner's *Die Meistersinger von Nürnberg* at the National Court Theater, a high temple of culture.[6] The operagoers then went to a jovial New Year's soiree at Ernst Hanfstaengl's fashionable apartment. Hanfstaengl noted that the young Eva Braun—"well built, with blue eyes and a modest, diffident manner"—attended, though she did not arrive or leave with Hitler. Guests gathered around the capacious fireplace to hear a classic Hitlerian monologue on conductor Hans Knappertsbusch's interpretation of Wagner's opera, which the Nazi leader found wanting.

Positively surprising to Hanfstaengl was the fact that Hitler was in a "most benign mood." When taking his leave, he signed his host's guest book. Then, in a tone of suppressed excitement, the Nazi leader told Hanfstaengl: "This year belongs to us. I will guarantee you that in writing."[7]

Besides his manic conviction that he was destined to be Germany's savior, why was Hitler speaking so optimistically when everyone around him had long faces?

51

ASSIGNATION IN COLOGNE

[It was] the hour of the birth of the Third Reich.

—*Karl Dietrich Bracher, 1964*

My little Franz, you've committed another blunder.

—*Chancellor Kurt von Schleicher, January 1933*

In its short fourteen-year existence, the Weimar Republic had endured more than a dozen coup attempts, one period of bloody armed insurrection (in 1919 in Berlin), repeated threats of outright civil war, Hitler's brief uprising in Munich, and more than three hundred political murders. The country's economy, once roaring on the upswing and recovering from the First World War, had been devastated by the Great Depression. Now governing with the twentieth cabinet formed in those fourteen years, Kurt von Schleicher was the republic's twelfth chancellor. The country was exhausted.

Struggling to find a way out of the mess, Schleicher in early January of 1933 was attempting, without much success, to put together a new political coalition that could command wide support and make headway toward solving Germany's problems. He grappled with forming a "lateral coalition" of both left and right called a *Querfront*.[1] But the new chancellor was having trouble making the unmatched pieces of Germany's political puzzle fit together.

At the same time, another mysterious drama was unfolding. On the evening of January 3, Hitler and a small traveling party boarded a night train from Munich to Bonn, the small university town on the Rhine River just south of Cologne. No one but Hitler knew why they were journeying up the Rhine when their final destination was the tiny north German state of Lippe-Detmold. The Nazi chief planned to campaign in little Lippe's January 15 state election—normally an insignificant event but very handy for Hitler's current purpose of proving that the Nazi Party was not moribund. Bonn, however, was not on the direct route to Lippe. Why the detour?

The mystery deepened when Hitler's troupe arrived on January 4 in Bonn. After breakfast in the riverside Rheinhotel Dreesen—one of Hitler's favorite hostelries—the Nazi chief departed alone in a chauffeured car with drawn window curtains. Without revealing his business, Hitler ordered his men to meet him later in the afternoon on the other side of Cologne, twenty miles to the north.

Unbeknownst to his team, the Nazi chief's undisclosed destination was a deluxe villa in the leafy precincts of Cologne. He was headed for a clandestine meeting with former chancellor Franz von Papen. It was as unlikely a confab as could be imagined. For this secretive tête-á-tête, the two men had been brought together by a Cologne aristocrat, Baron Kurt von Schröder. A prominent banker and Hitler sympathizer, Schröder belonged to a small circle of business and economic advisers to the Nazi Party who were committed to boosting Hitler into some kind of governing responsibility. The banker also knew of Papen's boiling frustration over his dismissal from office by President Hindenburg—and his bitterness toward his former friend and successor, Kurt von Schleicher.

"Hate burned in Papen," recalled one political leader.[2]

In mid-December, at Berlin's Deutscher Herrenklub (German Gentlemen's Club), Schröder had heard Papen deliver a revenge-tinged talk defending his tenure as chancellor. In a chance conversation with Papen, Schröder broached the idea of a confidential sit-down with Hitler. The banker's timing was serendipitous. Papen was lusting for retribution and, if possible, a return to office. Hitler was seeking salvation from an inexorable decline. The two former adversaries might see reason to make common cause. Schröder brokered a secret meeting at his home.

The political assignation in Cologne began with a surprise. While Hitler had arrived at Schröder's villa late in the morning, entering unnoticed through a rear door, Papen was not so lucky. When the dapper ex-chancellor stepped from his taxi at the home's front entrance, a photographer suddenly emerged and took a picture. The secret meeting was a secret no more.

Hitler and Papen saw each other as convenient vehicles for their own agendas. Papen's goal was to turn the tables on Schleicher, reclaiming the chancellorship. His larger aim was to redeem his own reputation by creating an authoritarian government of nationalist conservatives that could lead Germany to economic and political stability. With Hitler and the thirteen million voters in his coalition, Papen believed, he could accomplish the deed. Papen's blithe calculation was that Hitler could be persuaded to bring his vast popular standing into a government led by a Chancellor Papen—with Hitler as vice-chancellor.

Hitler's goal was simpler: he wanted raw, pure, and complete power. He needed Papen to get past President Hindenburg, still the chief obstacle to the Nazi leader's goal of assuming the chancellorship. Hitler knew that if he could form a bond with Papen, he might crack the closed ring around the otherwise unreachable president.

Papen was still on exceptionally friendly terms with the Old Gentleman, who lived behind the protective wall of his inner circle, controlled by State Secretary Meissner and presidential son Oskar von Hindenburg. Since President Hindenburg had asked Papen—whom he now regarded almost as another son—to stay in Berlin as his informal adviser, the former chancellor enjoyed privileged entrée to the presidential suite. Papen's living quarters in the interior ministry gave him unique access to the president via a secluded route: through the parklike gardens behind the interior ministry, the presidential palace, and the chancellery. Known as the Ministerial Gardens, the four private parks were separately fenced off but had connecting gates. Passing unseen by the outside world through the trees and foliage, Papen could call on Germany's head of state by his back door almost anytime, and the press and the public were none the wiser.

When they sat down at 11:30 a.m. on January 4 in Baron von Schröder's private study, Hitler and Papen talked for two hours with only Schröder as a silent witness. Though Hitler had brought Rudolf Hess, Heinrich Himmler, and economic adviser Wilhelm Keppler along, they were not part of the closed meeting with Papen. In Schröder's account, the conversation began, not surprisingly, with a tirade by Hitler.[3] The Nazi leader

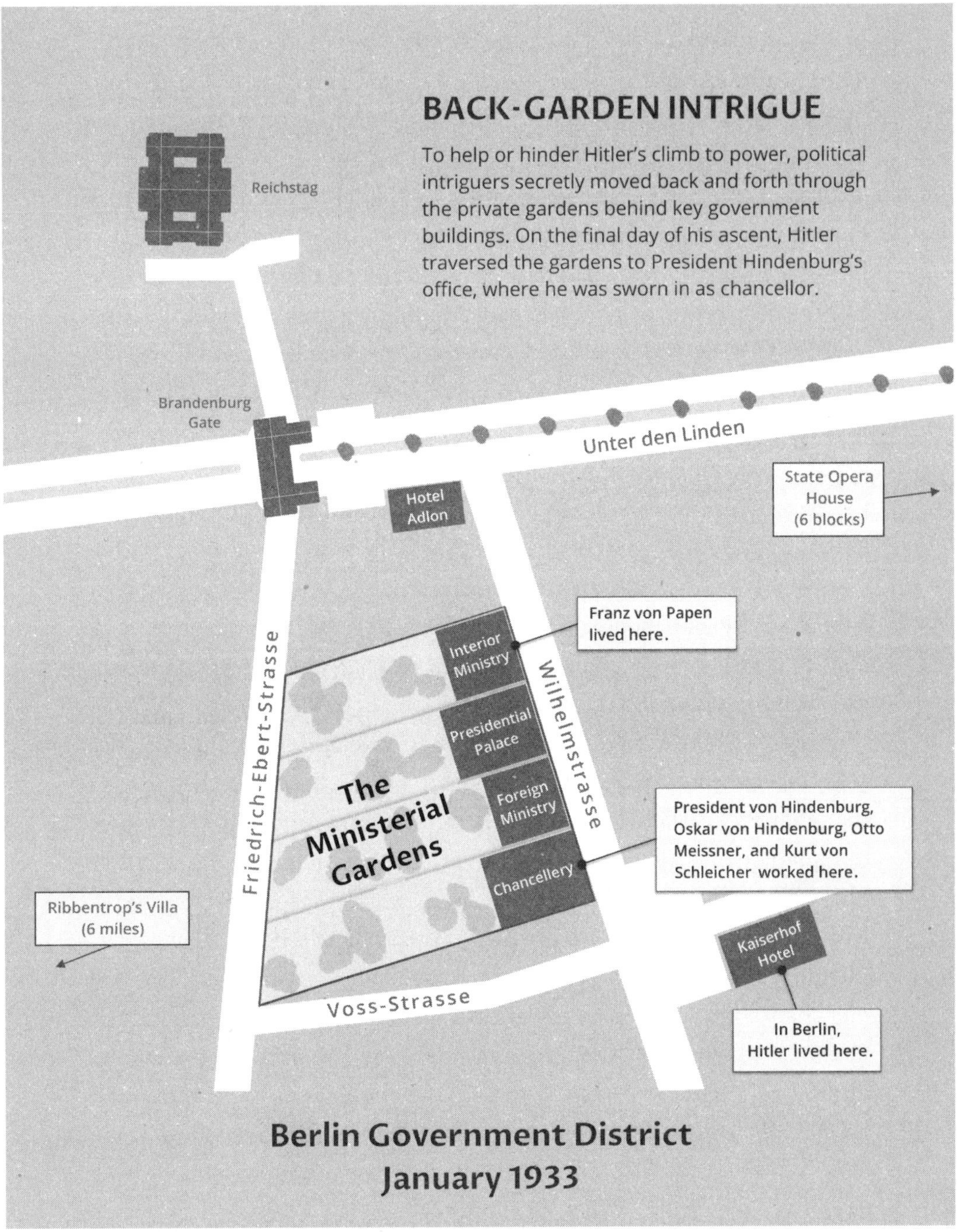
BACK-GARDEN INTRIGUE
To help or hinder Hitler's climb to power, political intriguers secretly moved back and forth through the private gardens behind key government buildings. On the final day of his ascent, Hitler traversed the gardens to President Hindenburg's office, where he was sworn in as chancellor.
Reichstag
Brandenburg Gate
Unter den Linden
Hotel Adlon
State Opera House (6 blocks)
Franz von Papen lived here.
Interior Ministry
Presidential Palace
Foreign Ministry
Chancellery
Wilhelmstrasse
Friedrich-Ebert-Strasse
The Ministerial Gardens
President von Hindenburg, Oskar von Hindenburg, Otto Meissner, and Kurt von Schleicher worked here.
Ribbentrop's Villa (6 miles)
Kaiserhof Hotel
Voss-Strasse
In Berlin, Hitler lived here.

Berlin Government District
January 1933

was still seething from the rebuff he received on August 13, 1932, from Hindenburg and Papen. He also vented his lingering anger over the death sentences, issued five months earlier, against Nazi Storm Troopers for the murder in Potempa, Silesia—though the legal penalties had long since been reduced.[4] Raising a long-settled issue and heaping abuse on his interlocutor was a familiar Hitler ploy.[5]

Papen soon guided the conversation to politics. He later claimed that he proposed a Schleicher-Hitler duumvirate—a government with two heads. Schröder remembered it as a Papen-Hitler duumvirate. Either way, Hitler rejected the idea out of hand. Making yet another speech, Hitler insisted that he was interested only in a government led by himself, though he would accept some of Papen's followers in his cabinet as long as they supported Hitler's policies, including the removal of all Social Democrats, Communists, and Jews from high positions in Germany.

The two men were far apart. But by the end of their meeting, they had agreed on the larger goal of replacing the Schleicher government with a new, highly nationalistic cabinet. Sticking points would be ironed out in later discussions. Though little had been decided, the sit-down had opened the door to a frontal assault on the existing order. It was, as a German historian later noted, "the hour of the birth of the Third Reich."[6]

Word of the two politicians' meeting soon leaked to Berlin's *Tägliche Rundschau,* the newspaper that was close to Chancellor Schleicher.[7] Papen thought that Schleicher found out about the planned meeting with Hitler by tapping Papen's phones.[8] Another version of events claimed that one of Hitler's bodyguards was bribed to report on the leader's whereabouts. More astonishing but also more likely is the tale of a Berlin dentist, Dr. Helmuth Elbrechter, whose patients included Chancellor Schleicher, former chancellor Brüning, and Nazi defector Gregor Strasser. Dr. Elbrechter is said to have heard about the upcoming meeting from a patient: he dispatched a Strasser supporter to take the photograph, then alerted the *Tägliche Rundschau.*[9] The newspaper stopped its presses to remake its January 5 front page with an amazingly accurate headline: HITLER AND PAPEN AGAINST SCHLEICHER.[10]

News of the Hitler-Papen huddle caused a political uproar. A stunned Chancellor Schleicher summoned Hans Zehrer, the editor of the *Tägliche*

Rundschau, to his office. Zehrer waited until the afternoon of January 5, when he received the photos of Papen stepping out of his taxi, before heeding Schleicher's call. As the newspaper editor laid the prints on Schleicher's desk, the chancellor sensed that Papen's outreach to Hitler meant only one thing—his former friend Franz von Papen was now his enemy.[11] Hitler, the fading Nazi drum major, was back in play. The tectonic plates had shifted again.[12]

Schleicher hurried to see President Hindenburg. The chancellor shared the news of Papen's intrigues, asking the president to discourage his protégé, the former chancellor, from interfering in politics. The anxious Schleicher overplayed his hand by entreating Hindenburg not to hold any meetings with Papen without Schleicher's presence. Schleicher's request was an unwelcome intrusion into the realm of personal relationships: the old president harrumphed and agreed to take his chancellor's demand under advisement—a brush-off.[13] Three days later, Hindenburg met with Papen without telling Schleicher. The president unofficially deputized the former chancellor, his newest confidant, to be his back-channel source of information on Hitler.[14] Completing his journey into duplicity, Papen called on Schleicher to assure him, straight-faced, that he was making no secret deals with Hitler.

By now Schleicher was in trouble with President Hindenburg. The hard-charging chancellor had committed the cardinal error of jumping into the controversy over *Osthilfe*—the Eastern Aid program, which would break up bankrupt Junker estates. Schleicher made matters easier for his enemies in other ways. At an off-the-record dinner with journalists on January 13, he contradicted his earlier positions, claiming he had no interest in forming a government that commanded a parliamentary majority, though he had said the opposite several days before. Schleicher's "lateral coalition" strategy was not working: his outreach to parts of the labor movement sparked consternation in the world of big business, which equated organized labor with socialism and maybe communism. Fears of Bolshevism flared up again, and Schleicher, the army general, was denounced in some circles as Marxist. He also drew the enmity of the powerful agrarian lobbies in the east, who opposed his land redistribution scheme. Clumsily floating the trial balloon of "underpinning" his administration by appointing the irascible Alfred

Hugenberg to the cabinet, Schleicher made matters worse by adding the inscrutable Gregor Strasser to his possible list of ministerial candidates—as a bluff to flush out Hitler.[15]

Schleicher became desperate enough to consider asking President Hindenburg for the most explosive option: dissolution of the Reichstag, with elections postponed beyond the constitutionally mandated sixty days. A formerly shrewd behind-the-scenes intriguer, Schleicher was proving to be an inept wielder of actual power.

Hitler was deeply suspicious of Schleicher's reported attempts to recruit Strasser. Indeed, Schleicher, in his creative imaginings, had conjured the notion of a new party, to be called the Social National Party. The party would be headed by Strasser, thus dividing the Nazi Party, especially through its Reichstag delegation. The Social Democratic newspaper, *Vorwärts,* printed a cartoon showing Schleicher examining pictures of both Hitler and Strasser, as though trying to choose between them.[16]

In mid-December Schleicher had tried to locate Strasser for a meeting—but Strasser had deserted Germany and landed in Rome. When he returned on December 28 to Berlin's Hotel Excelsior, the phone was ringing. It was Schleicher calling. The chancellor wanted to arrange an audience for Strasser with President Hindenburg to obtain the president's blessing should he bring Strasser into his government. Schleicher was trying to use Strasser as a wedge to move Hitler away from his demand for full power as chancellor.[17]

On the morning of January 6 Strasser appeared early at Schleicher's office. Unknown even to the chancellor's staff, the two men then slipped through the chancellery's private rear garden to reach Hindenburg's quarters. Schleicher left Strasser alone with the president for a get-acquainted chat. It was a success. The Old Gentleman took a liking to the tall, bald former First World War officer with the plainspoken manner. "The man makes an entirely different impression from this Hitler fellow," Hindenburg told Schleicher. "He is quite another type. I like him much better."[18]

News of Strasser's visit to the president soon leaked, leaving Hitler shaken.[19] But by now Hitler's own "secret" January 4 meeting with Papen in Cologne had come to dominate the political grapevine. People were sharing sundry theories of what really happened, while the actual players were dodging brickbats. Hitler and Papen announced that they had only discussed the possibility of a broad "nationalist unity front."[20]

Schleicher was being played by Papen, but he was too convinced of his own conspiratorial brilliance to notice. Over afternoon tea with the French ambassador, André François-Poncet, Schleicher dismissed Papen's undertaking with Hitler as "frivolous." Papen had blithely imagined that he could "pull off a master stroke and serve up Hitler to us on a platter," Schleicher told the ambassador. "Now Papen is embarrassed. I won't scold him. I'll just say to him, 'My little Franz, you've committed another blunder.'"[21]

To Hitler, the breach of secrecy about his meeting with Papen at the Cologne villa was an unintended godsend. The man who had been left for politically dead at year's end was back in the headlines. It now seemed unlikely that many Nazi Party members would follow Gregor Strasser into a new power arrangement with Schleicher. Slowly, Hitler began to regard the news of Strasser's reemergence more calmly. He had other moves in mind.

52

IMPALING A FLY

The Nazi Party must be in serious trouble if the great "Führer" himself is traveling to tiny villages.

— Lippische Landes-Zeitung, *January 1933*

Like all the large political parties, the Nazis ran slates in every legislative election in Germany's seventeen states. Like the national elections, the state elections determined legislative makeup and which party, or coalition of parties, would govern. The state elections occurred on varying schedules, sometimes staggered, sometimes clustered. In the winter of 1933, only one state election was scheduled—the one in little Lippe.

State elections in Germany could be important as harbingers of the national political mood. In big states such as Prussia and Bavaria, they could also be significant simply because of their size. The state elections in Lippe were neither. Slated for January 15, 1933, the balloting in the tiny former princely state—it had only 174,000 residents—was of zero interest or importance to the rest of Germany. Hitler decided to change that. If he could stir the political pot and put the Lilliputian election on the national map, it would serve nicely as a grandstand for his political comeback. "Lippe is the first opportunity to go from the defensive back on the offensive," Goebbels noted.[1] Hitler decided to throw the Nazi Party full tilt into the minuscule state race.

Just hours after his meeting with former chancellor Papen at Kurt von Schröder's villa in Cologne, Hitler began his campaign in Lippe. On the evening of January 4, he quietly took up quarters in a mansion at the bucolic estate of Baron Adolf von Oeynhausen; the location gave him easy access to every part of Lippe. The public never found out that Hitler was once again living in luxury while campaigning on everyone else's misery.

Goebbels's propaganda department laid out a dense timetable of seventeen Hitler speeches over the next eleven days. Other Nazi notables, including Frick, Göring, Prince August Wilhelm (Auwi), and Goebbels himself, would also campaign. To boost turnout to their rallies, the Nazi election machine would bring in trainloads of supporters from outside Lippe. The local *Lippische Landes-Zeitung* newspaper carped: "The Nazi Party must be in serious trouble if the great 'Führer' himself is traveling to tiny villages."[2]

Hitler, however, loved campaigning in Lippe. He lived well by day and worked hard by night. He rose late and lazed through the afternoons in the comfort that suited his nonconformist inclinations. Then he would rush around in his big Mercedes to evening rallies in large meeting halls, in small pubs, even in unheated tents on open fields.[3]

The region's history was ideal for the Führer's histrionic style. Lippe was the home of the darkly brooding Teutoburg Forest, site of a famous 175-foot-high statue atop a small mountain. The statue, known as the Hermann Monument, depicted a sword-bearing Hermann, also known as Arminius, the original German. In the year 9 CE, Hermann, chief of the Germanic Cherusci tribe, vanquished the seemingly unstoppable Roman legions that had marauded their way straight up the Rhine River, grabbing all the excellent river ports and hot-springs watering holes along the way. Nobody could halt the Romans—until Hermann's troops did in the Battle of the Teutoburg Forest. The victory began unifying scattered tribes by giving them a new sense of Germanness, or so goes the lore. Hitler used the monument site as a campaign backdrop on a day when the mountain was covered in fog and "felt so grand," recalled Goebbels.[4] The scene neatly fed into Hitler's narrative of mystical German strength and reemerging greatness.

By now, the Nazi propaganda blitz in Lippe was being widely watched. The attention paid off. On election day, January 15, the Nazis won a whopping plurality, capturing nearly 40 percent of the Lippe vote. Tiny though the total vote was (39,064 ballots for the Nazi Party), Hitler's rebound from only 6 percent in Lippe in the November 1932 election was nonetheless impressive. It was a morale booster inside the party—or at least the Nazi newspapers gave it that spin, proclaiming the Nazi Party back in the game. "The party is on the go again," noted Goebbels in his diary. "Now just hold steady. And get rid of defeatists."[5]

To others, Hitler's Lippe "victory" was meaningless as a barometer of the national political mood. Conditions in the little state, which the Nazis could easily flood with people and propaganda, were not replicable anywhere else. The *Berliner Tageblatt*'s editor, Theodor Wolff, dismissed Hitler's ballyhooed bounce in Lippe as the equivalent of "a fly impaled on the tip of his sword."[6]

Still, the Nazis had made their point: Hitler was not dead yet. Just as Papen had feared (in a conversation with a confidant), Hitler's good showing in Lippe could only harden the Nazi leader's demand for the highest political office in the land.[7]

Flush from his Lippe win, Hitler traveled the following day to Weimar. Fired up and spoiling for battle, Hitler—in a meeting of Nazi Party leaders—lashed out at the apostate Gregor Strasser. His goal was to finish off Strasser as a political factor whose lingering appeal to some Nazis was still unsettling the party. Finger-pointing and mutual recrimination characterized the weekend gathering before Hitler arrived, with some Nazis accusing others of being Strasser's coconspirators. Rudolf Hess repeatedly had to cool tempers and smooth ruffled feathers.[8] "Horrible accusations against Strasser," noted Goebbels. "His best friends are deserting him. [The Saxony gauleiter] calls him a Jew."

By the time Hitler spoke on Monday, January 16, the dissenters were silent. Nobody had ever dreamed of joining Strasser's protest; everyone had always been united shoulder to shoulder behind the Führer. Hitler only had to drive nails into Strasser's coffin. For three hours, the Nazi leader unloaded, crushing Strasser "in all the details," reported Goebbels. "People's eyes were opened. The case is now closed."[9]

Otto Strasser denounced Hitler's diatribe against Gregor Strasser as a "banishment court" in the manner of ancient Greek ostracism.[10] That did not end the symbolic burial of his brother. In Dresden, Nazi operatives removed the signage from a newly christened regional party headquarters. The words that came down were: GREGOR STRASSER HAUS.[11]

53

BERLIN NIGHTS

I'm afraid we just can't get around Hitler.

—*Oskar von Hindenburg, January 1933*

I have never seen him in such a state.

—*Joachim von Ribbentrop, January 1933*

The Lippe election was done, and Gregor Strasser's ghost was vanquished. Hitler could now resume his quest for a deal with Franz von Papen. Their political dance moved from Cologne to Berlin and would take place mostly in the home of a little-known wine merchant named Joachim von Ribbentrop.

The son of a failed military officer, a knockabout businessman who had worked in the United States and Canada before the First World War, Ribbentrop made his best career move when he married Annelies Henkell, the scion of Germany's Henkell winemaking family, famous purveyors of sparkling wine. Fluent in English and French, young Ribbentrop entered his father-in-law's business and built the family firm into an impressive international wine-marketing company.

The Champagne peddler had become a faux patrician: through the luck of a legal adoption by an elderly aristocratic aunt, Ribbentrop acquired the right to add the prefix *von* to his last name, signifying nobility. He soon had a fancy villa in Berlin's fashionable Dahlem neighborhood. He traveled in select circles, including in the Gentlemen's Club, where he rubbed elbows with well-met businessmen, officers, and diplomats. Among them was Papen. And while some members of the Berlin elite, such as the French ambassador, André François-Poncet, considered Ribbentrop a humorless blowhard who "only listened to himself," the self-made gentleman aspired to greater things than selling fancy wine.[1] He wanted to play at politics. He wanted to meet Hitler.

In August of 1932, Ribbentrop had traveled to Berchtesgaden, where he had been "very strongly" impressed by the Nazi leader and had quickly joined the Nazi Party. Now, in January of 1933, Ribbentrop saw himself as a natural power broker between Hitler and the ruling establishment. Like the banker Schröder in Cologne, Ribbentrop in Berlin had the seclusion of his comfortable mansion to offer for private meetings and secret negotiations.

The first clandestine meeting in Ribbentrop's home took place on January 10. Hitler had taken a day off from campaigning in Lippe. With the small gathering scheduled for late evening, Hitler used attendance at an opera—Verdi's *La Traviata*—as a cover for his plans. After the performance, the Nazi leader was quietly driven to Ribbentrop's Dahlem villa. Hitler's driver eased his car into the garage; Hitler crossed the lawn into a back door. Papen was already there. This time there was no photographer.

This first Berlin rendezvous ended inconclusively. A planned lunchtime follow-up the next day was abruptly canceled by Hitler. But after the Lippe election, the behind-the-scenes maneuvering picked up again. On January 17 Hitler met with Alfred Hugenberg, who counted politically as the de facto leader of Germany's bourgeois right, making him a prickly player in every discussion of power sharing. Though Hugenberg's German National People's Party had won only 8.3 percent in the last election, the blunt-spoken party leader was considered essential to any right-wing government of "nationalist concentration," as Papen liked to call it. Given his media empire, Hugenberg could make more trouble outside the tent than inside it.

Hitler and Hugenberg were natural enemies who nonetheless could not live without each other. Just as they were during their 1929 campaign against the Young Plan, just as they were at the ill-fated 1931 "national front" rally in Bad Harzburg, the two men at their Berlin meeting were like wary opponents in a cage, each aware that the other must survive. Hugenberg had put up with frequent insults and dismissals by Hitler, but the press baron still craved power; he had no choice but to seek rapprochement with the Nazi chief.

Hugenberg proposed to Hitler that they both join Schleicher's government—an option that Hitler immediately rejected. Hitler promised Hugenberg a ministerial post if he would support a Hitler-led cabinet. Hugenberg refused. He reminded Hitler that President Hindenburg had already twice declined to make the Nazi leader the head of a German government. Hitler scornfully dismissed Hindenburg as a dim old man with "a political vocabulary of eighty sentences."[2] The Hitler-Hugenberg conversation ended rancorously. Efforts to build an alternative government seemed stalled.

The following day, January 18, Hitler met again with Papen for lunch at Ribbentrop's villa. The men were joined by Heinrich Himmler and Ernst Röhm. Once again the discussion reached the familiar impasse: Hitler wanted to be chancellor, but so did Papen, who said that he could not overcome President Hindenburg's opposition to Hitler as government leader. Besides his visceral dislike of Hitler, Hindenburg believed the Nazi leader was too party-focused and did not have the entire German people's interests at heart. The president feared that Hitler would turn the government into a one-party dictatorship and might even raise the risk of war.

Easily affronted and fixated on his goal, Hitler declared that he saw no reason to continue the meetings. Papen's ploy to drive out Schleicher with a Papen-led government that somehow included Hitler was now dead in the water. Hitler's future was again uncertain.

Even without a photographer in the bushes, word of the negotiations in the Dahlem villa somehow leaked out. The *Vossische Zeitung* learned of the Papen-Hitler luncheon as soon as it happened and plastered it onto the front page of its late-afternoon edition. "[B]usy behind-the-scenes games" were afoot, reported the newspaper. "It's not easy to keep up with the swirl of negotiations and overtures that have taken place in recent days (with and without the public's knowledge)."[3]

But the negotiations were at a standstill: so Hitler went to the movies, taking Goebbels along. The two men saw a historical film called *The Rebel,* about a young Austrian who rose from humble origins to lead his compatriots to valiant resistance against the heaviest of odds, the Napoleonic occupation of Tyrol. Always rejecting compromise and firing up his followers with blistering rhetoric, the rebel was fanatically committed to his cause and would eventually die a martyr's death. Hitler came out of the film "all on fire," wrote Goebbels. The Nazi leader was so taken with the movie that he went to see it again the next night.[4]

Hitler's stubbornness and his confidence had now reached grandiose extremes. He was scheduled to speak the next day, January 20, to ten thousand party leaders in Berlin's Sports Palace. There, he cast himself as a lonely crusader.[5] Donning the mantle of Martin Luther, the Reformation leader, Hitler shouted to his followers: "Here I stand because I can do no other!" In borrowing Luther's putative assertion at his 1521 excommunication trial, Hitler was claiming he could not accept a lesser role than chancellor of Germany—any more than Luther could compromise with the pope in Rome.[6] Hitler also was stoking his followers for an ongoing long struggle—hardly the expectation of quick ascension to power.

With Papen's plot stalled and Hitler showing no signs of compromise, Ribbentrop the wine merchant cast about for ways to break the deadlock. The ambitious businessman came up with a cunning idea: how about trying to breach President Hindenburg's opposition to Hitler through his weak spot—his devotion to his son, Oskar von Hindenburg? Though considered a political nonentity, the forty-nine-year-old Oskar clearly had his father's ear. Diarist Harry Kessler considered both Hindenburgs beset by an inferiority complex, reporting that Oskar often harangued his father and the Old Gentleman responded with roars that could be heard out on the street.[7] Officially employed as the president's military adjutant, Colonel Hindenburg (after thirty years in the military, he was still not a general officer) served mainly as his father's helpmeet and personal adviser. Oskar and his family even lived with the widowed president in the presidential quarters. The Berlin joke was that Oskar's real title was "the not constitutionally stipulated presidential son."

If Oskar could be convinced of Hitler's suitability for the chancellorship, maybe talks would reopen.

Oskar von Hindenburg accepted the offer of a nocturnal assignation with Hitler and Papen at Ribbentrop's home on Sunday night, January 22. As cover, Oskar—accompanied by presidential adviser Otto Meissner—used an opera performance to sneak away for a political tryst. Attending Wagner's *Das Liebesverbot* at the State Opera House in Berlin, the two officials and their wives made sure they were seen and greeted by all and sundry during the opera's intermission. But when the lights went down for the second act, the two men quietly left their loge and slipped out a back door into the snowy night. On Unter den Linden, with their overcoat collars turned high, they furtively hailed a taxi. Checking the back window to make sure they were not being followed, Oskar von Hindenburg drew a crack from Meissner: "Not even in the movies are people so secretive!"

Exiting the cab several streets from Ribbentrop's villa to disguise their intentions, the two men at first had difficulty locating their destination on foot. But soon they were standing in the warmth of the Champagne merchant's living room sipping fine bubbly with Papen and Ribbentrop. Hitler, who arrived a few minutes later through the back door, drank his usual mineral water. After the chilled men had warmed up, Hitler turned to Hindenburg and asked, "Colonel, shall we chat alone for a bit in the other room?"[8]

Exactly what was said between Hitler and Oskar von Hindenburg during the ensuing two hours is unknown. It was long speculated that Hitler blackmailed the president's son by threatening to disclose embarrassing details about a financial irregularity: President Hindenburg had improperly deeded his Neudeck estate to his son to avoid inheritance taxes. But no evidence has emerged to support such accusations.

In his sit-down with the president's son, Hitler felt that he was operating from a position of strength. He had won Lippe and overcome the Strasser challenge. On that Sunday afternoon, he had also won a showdown with the Communist Party and Berlin's forces of order. A provocative Nazi demonstration by thirty-five thousand Storm Troopers in front of the Communist Party headquarters on Berlin's Bülowplatz had been sanctioned by the government; fourteen thousand policemen had been deployed to protect the Nazi demonstrators. Chancellor Schleicher had even banned a Communist counterdemonstration, throwing his administration's implied endorsement behind the Nazis. Schleicher had also quietly visited the demonstration, remarking on the columns of Storm Troopers marching past: "These guys would make outstanding soldiers." The chancellor was still nursing his hopes of integrating the Nazi militiamen into Germany's armed forces.

With things seeming to roll his way, Hitler apparently made a positive impression on Oskar von Hindenburg. Returning in a taxi to central Berlin, the president's son told Meissner with a sigh: "I'm afraid we just can't get around Hitler. He's offering so many concessions and making so many promises that it is hard to see how one can keep him out."[9]

Hitler was not so kind in his reaction to Hindenburg. "Young Oskar cut a rare image of stupidity," he told Goebbels.[10]

More important than Oskar von Hindenburg's lukewarm endorsement of Hitler was a stunning change of heart that same evening by Franz von Papen. Finally recognizing that German politics had careened down a path of paralysis, tying itself into a knot that could only be cut by drastic measures, the former chancellor decided to accept Hitler's demand that he, not Papen, become the next chancellor. To depose Schleicher and regain power, Papen was willing to take a back seat to the Nazi leader. Reversing his opening gambit of January 4, Papen said he would accept the vice-chancellorship in a Hitler-led cabinet. Papen's sole condition was that Hitler's cabinet include only two other Nazis—a concession Hitler had already made. Papen went a crucial step further: he promised to try to change President Hindenburg's mind about appointing Hitler to the top job.

Two forces drove Papen's surprisingly altered position. The first was the plotter's recognition that Hitler's insistence on becoming chancellor was not a negotiating ploy; it was an unalterable stance. Without conceding the chancellorship to Hitler, Papen realized, there was no way to move forward; the game was over. Hitler had shown a willingness to walk away from the deal; Papen had not.

The second impulse was Papen's self-induced belief that Hitler could be controlled from below by a sly vice-chancellor. So great was the former chancellor's desire for revenge against Schleicher that he was blinded to

Hitler's strengths. Papen's need to displace and replace Schleicher led him to make a deal with the devil without recognizing its dangers. The Westphalian aristocrat who had commanded cavalry in wartime and run the German government for five and a half months believed that, with his extensive connections in the German establishment, he could easily manipulate the former trench runner and unpromoted private from Austria.

"We've hired him," Papen would soon tell a fellow politician who doubted the wisdom of Papen's decision.[11] Papen did not realize that co-option was not an option.

Part of Papen's calculation rested on the Nazi leader's agreement to a mixed cabinet of ministers from other parties, all conservatives. Yet the two ministries that Hitler insisted upon were critical ones: the Reich ministry of the interior (for Frick) plus an unspecified cabinet position for Göring that would most likely include the position of Prussian state commissioner or Prussian minister of the interior. Either of those would hold power over Prussia's massive police apparatus. The Prussian police force was like an internal army: with fifty thousand men, it was half the size of the entire German military. The Prussian police could easily overpower the Social Democratic–controlled Berlin police force. But with seven other cabinet posts left open for other parties, Papen thought he could keep Hitler in check.

The first barrier to Hitler's accession to the chancellor's chair was now lowered; only the high wall of Hindenburg's opposition—and the low wall of Hugenberg's truculence—remained.

But General Kurt von Schleicher was not going willingly into the dark night.

After the clandestine nighttime meeting between Hitler and Oskar von Hindenburg at Ribbentrop's villa, chief of staff Meissner walked into his office at eight o'clock the next morning to find his secretary holding up the telephone receiver: "The chancellor wishes to speak with you."

"Was the stew tasty?" Chancellor Schleicher asked a surprised Meissner. Though regarded as a master negotiator and skillful schemer himself,

Meissner had now been outflanked by Schleicher, the ultimate conniver.[12] The chancellor already knew exactly what had gone on the night before at Ribbentrop's home, right down to the simple meal that had been served.[13]

Later that morning, Papen trekked into President Hindenburg's chambers. He was ready to inform the Old Gentleman of his change of heart; he now supported a Hitler-led cabinet. But Hindenburg was not ready for such a monumental shift; he remained opposed to naming Hitler to the job once held by Otto von Bismarck. After leaving the chancellery, Papen shared the news with Ribbentrop, who immediately went to tell Hitler. In her notes, Ribbentrop's wife, Annelies, wrote: "Hitler rejects everything."[14]

Stalemate.

Seeing no reason to stay in Berlin, Hitler angrily departed for Munich.

Negotiations were stalled. But Hitler's lieutenants were determined to regain momentum. Göring and Wilhelm Frick met with Papen for afternoon tea at Ribbentrop's villa. They pondered how to form a cabinet of nationalists that might appeal to President Hindenburg. The next day tea was served again at the Dahlem villa, but only to Oskar von Hindenburg and Ribbentrop. The younger Hindenburg agreed that a Hitler-led cabinet built around a "nationalist front"—a revived version of Hugenberg's Harzburg Front—might get a hearing from his father.

The following day Göring assembled a powwow in his Reichstag office; it included some members of Hugenberg's German National People's Party. The group's discussions continued later that evening in Oskar von Hindenburg's house in Potsdam, outside Berlin. The president's son was now fully on board with bringing Hitler to power. The men drafted a letter to Hugenberg.

Not originally part of Papen's scheme, Hugenberg suddenly became central to the plot. As the key nationalist leader after Hitler, Hugenberg the businessman appealed to Hindenburg's elitist leanings. With his background as one of Germany's top industrialists, Hugenberg seemed a natural candidate for the post of economic czar in a future cabinet. After decades of nibbling around the edges, Hugenberg was eager for a ministerial post.

Bringing the media mogul into the conspiracy was now key to building a nationalist cabinet that President Hindenburg would accept. Hitler agreed to return to Berlin. On Friday, January 27, Göring hosted a meeting between Hitler and Hugenberg in his Reichstag chambers. The two men were still at bitter odds with each other. Hugenberg flatly refused to join a Hitler-led government if the Nazi leader insisted on installing Göring as Prussian interior minister. Hugenberg also objected to Hitler's control over key jobs in the chancellery—chief of staff and press spokesman. Hugenberg the adamant was facing down Hitler the insistent. Furious, the Nazi chief broke off the discussions and threatened to depart Berlin again for Munich.

"I have never seen him in such a state," noted Ribbentrop.[15]

Göring and Ribbentrop barely succeeded in keeping Hitler from leaving town. Holed up in his Kaiserhof Hotel suite, the Nazi leader refused an invitation that evening to meet again with Papen at Ribbentrop's villa. He even rejected a proffered audience with President Hindenburg because he had already "said all there is to say to the field marshal," noted Ribbentrop.

Ribbentrop told Papen that evening about Hitler's vehemence; Papen's support for the Nazi leader only increased. Papen tried to allay some of Hitler's concerns by labeling Hugenberg a man of "secondary importance." As for Hugenberg's resistance to giving Göring control over the Prussian police, Papen argued that he would retain for himself the critical post of state commissioner for Prussia, tantamount to governor of the state. He could easily rein in Göring's excesses—or so Papen believed, and so he hoped to convince Hugenberg. By naming Göring *deputy* interior minister (under himself), Papen made the deal palatable to Hugenberg while actually giving the hard-hitting Nazi free rein over the vast police apparatus.[16]

To Ribbentrop—facilitator, keen observer, note taker, and Hitler promoter—the game had shifted. Papen, he believed, was now "absolutely certain that he must achieve Hitler's chancellorship at all costs. This recognition by Papen is, I believe, the turning point."[17]

Off in his Kaiserhof Hotel suite, Hitler kept quiet and waited.[18]

54

SCHLEICHER'S FALL

> I get sick just thinking about being governed again by these notorious nobodies and high-stakes speculators. . . . The whole business is a mixture of corruption, backstairs intrigue, and nepotism reminiscent of the worst days of absolutist monarchy.
>
> —*Count Harry Kessler, January 28, 1933*

Berlin churned with rumors of Chancellor Schleicher's impending fall and a revived Papen government. Among the literary types at the hoary Romanisches Café, in animated conversations among well-heeled patrons of the Adlon and Kaiserhof hotels, in chats among politicians at the Reichstag and along Wilhelmstrasse, Germany's uncertain political fate overshadowed all other topics. The heated journalistic grapevine—and the newspaper headlines—bruited about a Papen-Hugenberg cabinet in the making rather than a Papen-Hitler government. The fixation on the improbable pairing of Papen and Hugenberg seemed to many a prescription for popular upheaval or even civil war. After all, Papen had just five months earlier lost a no-confidence vote in parliament by a 91 percent margin. In the last election, Hugenberg's party had garnered less than 10 percent of the vote. Together these two losers would have an overwhelming majority of the German people against them.

How could such a government hold?

The German army was alarmed. It feared being drawn into the fracas to maintain order. Rushing to the chancellery to find out what was going on, the army chief of staff, General Kurt von Hammerstein, sat down for a private chat with Chancellor Schleicher. The chancellor confirmed to the general that he expected to be booted out of office by President Hindenburg within a couple of days.[1] Hammerstein proceeded to the presidential suite, where he painted a dire picture for Hindenburg. Civil war was certain, he said, if the president anointed a Papen-Hugenberg regime. Appointment of a government that commanded the support of no more than 7 percent of the German people—Hammerstein's estimate—would surely unleash a violent response from the Nazis and the Communists. The army would be called upon to quell the disorder in defense of an untenable regime—a job the military did not want, said the general.

It was a disappointing meeting. President Hindenburg rejected political advice from a military man, even his top general. A frustrated Hammerstein concluded that Hindenburg had not even understood the issue. "Hindenburg did not grasp my concern that the army could be misused," he said. "What would come next was totally unclear."

By now Hammerstein believed Hitler was the only possible next chancellor, and he told Schleicher so.

To a sideline observer such as Count Harry Kessler, it felt as though Germany was headed for a bleak future. "I get sick just thinking about being governed again by these notorious nobodies and high-stakes speculators," he noted. The entire political circus seemed to him like "a mixture of corruption, backstairs intrigue, and nepotism reminiscent of the worst days of absolutist monarchy."[2]

Despite President Hindenburg's promise to give Schleicher "full support" when the new chancellor took office in December, the president was now keeping Schleicher at arm's length. Even Otto Meissner and Oskar von Hindenburg had been plotting behind his back. For the first time in his political life, the consummate conspirator—Schleicher—had been outplayed at his own game. The once-bumbling Papen was bulldozing him off the field.

On Saturday, January 28, a blustery newspaper editorial argued that political machinations had reached such a boiling point that a "presidential crisis" might ensue if a Papen-Hugenberg cabinet were named. The incendiary commentary effectively conjured a palace coup against Hindenburg. Since the essay appeared in the *Tägliche Rundschau*—a newspaper believed to be under Schleicher's indirect control—it sounded like Schleicher's desperate last stand.

Schleicher was out of options. He and his cabinet were certain to face a no-confidence vote when the Reichstag reconvened on Tuesday, January 31. Schleicher decided to press Hindenburg one last time for an order to dissolve the Reichstag before it could vote him out of office. Schleicher summoned his cabinet at 11:30 a.m. on Saturday morning, informing them of his plan to approach the president again. At 12:15 p.m., he walked to Hindenburg's offices, on the other side of the chancellery. Within fifteen minutes, he was back in the cabinet room.

"It was like talking to a wall," Schleicher reported to his ministers.[3]

Schleicher's attempt to lead Germany was over. His cabinet's last official act was to approve half a billion marks for a public works program designed to alleviate Depression-driven unemployment. Nearly two million Germans—one-third of those on the jobless rolls—would find work in the coming six months. But Schleicher would no longer be around to get the credit.[4] The scheming general had been in office for fifty-seven days.

Within hours, President Hindenburg had summoned Papen to his chambers. For the third time in seven months, the president tasked the charming cavalryman from Westphalia with forming a government.

The news of Schleicher's downfall exploded onto the streets of Berlin in Saturday's late-afternoon newspapers. But the uproar was not about a possible Hitler ascension to power. The political establishment was exercised about the destabilizing impact of a new Papen government based on almost no popular support; there was little talk of a regime led by Hitler.[5] President Hindenburg's snubs of the Nazi leader in August and November of 1932 made a Hitler chancellorship seem unthinkable.

Hitler was now the least active player in the drama. Yet even while doing nothing—or entertaining his entourage with biting monologues over tea in the Kaiserhof Hotel lobby—he was the silent force driving all other political considerations. Wherever he was, he carried with him the unseen but weighty following of the eleven million Germans who had voted for his party in the last election. Nobody else had come close. Hitler's stubborn will, his insistence on all or nothing, his unpredictable temper, his erratic comings and goings—they made him an implacable player. All the churning in the Papen conspiracy turned on finding a way to put Hitler into power.

55

UNFATHOMABLE ASCENT

A small sense of horror crept through me.

— Count Lutz Schwerin von Krosigk, January 1933

In two months, we'll have pushed Hitler so far into a corner that he'll squeal.

— Franz von Papen, January 1933

Gentlemen, you can't keep the Reich president waiting any longer.

— Otto Meissner, January 1933

The first half of Franz von Papen's plan had come to pass: Schleicher was out. Now Papen could focus solely on the second part: closing the deal for a new government with Hitler as chancellor and himself as vice-chancellor. But loose ends lay everywhere. Hitler was balking at Hugenberg and vice versa. Other cabinet members had to be recruited for key posts such as defense and finance, probably including some holdovers from Schleicher's government.

On Sunday, January 29, Papen had a busy day ahead. It began with a shock. Receiving Hitler at 11:00 a.m. in his apartment at the interior ministry, Papen was stunned to hear the Nazi leader pose new conditions. Hitler said he would take the chancellorship only if President Hindenburg committed in advance to dissolving the Reichstag and holding new elections. All the prospective cabinet members, including Papen, would also have to agree to Hitler's new demand.

As Papen listened in near disbelief, Hitler added a second demand. The president and all cabinet members would have to agree in advance to support an "enabling act" that would give the new chancellor—Hitler—and his cabinet nearly unlimited executive powers. Such an act, which required parliamentary passage, would exceed even the occasional emergency decrees that Hindenburg had issued under Chancellors Brüning and Papen to stem political violence. It would grant Hitler sweeping authority to act without further parliamentary approval. Similar acts had been granted multiple times during the Weimar Republic—notably to Gustav Stresemann in 1923 so he could bring hyperinflation under control. But approving an enabling act for Hitler, with his extreme views and draconian plans, was a more drastic request.

That Alfred Hugenberg would fiercely object to Hitler's insistence on new elections was certain. Hugenberg's party was sure to fare poorly in another run against the Nazis, especially if Hitler were already in the bully pulpit of the chancellery. Yet Hugenberg was essential for President Hindenburg's approval of the new cabinet; the president wanted the crusty businessman as a brake on Hitler's excesses. With sinking spirits, Papen realized that Hitler's new demands could be a deal breaker. Dismayed and disarmed, the duplicitous former chancellor handled the new roadblock the old-fashioned way: he lied. Or at least he committed the sin of omission.

When Hugenberg arrived at Papen's apartment a few hours later, the former chancellor did not tell the media mogul about Hitler's new conditions. Instead of the truth, Papen offered goodies. Hugenberg's chief interest was in salvaging the German economy: Papen told the press baron that President Hindenburg wanted him to run all four key economic portfolios—the Reich ministries of economics and agriculture and the same two ministries in the Prussian government. Flattered by the president's offer and none the wiser about Hitler's stipulation of new elections, Hugenberg accepted.[1] With his hands on the levers of the economy and his high opinion of himself intact, Hugenberg may have believed that he would fast become the most powerful man in the cabinet, even with Hitler as chancellor.

"We're boxing Hitler in," said Hugenberg.[2]

An afternoon gathering in Papen's apartment turned rancorous as leaders of the Steel Helmet veterans' organization and other conservatives arrived. Their support was key to forming the new government. Steel

Helmet cocommander Theodor Duesterberg raised objections to the appointment of Hitler as chancellor; he regarded Hitler as a mendacious charlatan given to breaking his word. "If you get in bed with an anaconda, you can't complain later if you wake up with broken legs," he warned. He also told Hugenberg that if he made a pact with the devil, he would "one night have to flee through the ministry gardens in your underwear" to avoid arrest.[3] Another member of the conservative nobility, Ewald von Kleist-Schmenzin, challenged the wisdom of appointing the fanatical Nazi leader as Germany's chancellor. The serenely confident Papen insisted that the new cabinet, with a preponderance of conservatives not part of the Nazi Party, could easily control the noisy Nazi chief.

"In two months, we'll have pushed Hitler so far into a corner that he'll squeal," said Papen.[4]

After much back-and-forth, Duesterberg's cochief of the Steel Helmet association, Franz Seldte, agreed to join Hitler's cabinet as labor minister. The 250,000-strong ex-soldiers' league would be seen by President Hindenburg as a healthy counterweight to the Storm Troopers and the Communist Red Front paramilitary.

Meanwhile, Hitler realized that his surprise new conditions could be too great a demand for President Hindenburg. Over lunch at the Kaiserhof, he sought to mollify the Old Gentleman; he asked Ribbentrop to reassure the president that the new election he wanted would also be Germany's *last* election.[5]

The Berlin rumor mill now concluded that either a Papen-Hugenberg cabinet was forming or Adolf Hitler himself was coming to power. "No interruption of the constant secret negotiations" was in sight, noted the *Vossische Zeitung*.[6] Either way, prodemocracy Berliners wanted no part of it. A massive demonstration was called to protest the possibility of an authoritarian government. One hundred thousand people showed up Sunday afternoon in the Lustgarten, in front of the Royal Palace. The speeches and loudspeakers could probably be heard inside Papen's apartment, just nine blocks away, where he was negotiating cabinet arrangements. In the Tegel Forest, on the outskirts of Berlin, six thousand well-outfitted members of the Social Democratic Reichsbanner paramilitary held maneuvers. They claimed they would resist by force what they regarded as a fascist overthrow of the government.[7]

In his apartment, Papen ground on. In a phone conversation with Finance Minister Schwerin von Krosigk, Papen claimed that negotiations were proceeding well. Krosigk heard confirmation of Papen's claim from a colleague who had run into Otto Meissner that day at a riding tournament. Yet the finance minister remained unconvinced. He received an alarming bit of intelligence from Kurt von Plettenberg, another well-connected aristocrat who showed up at Krosigk's residence for a light supper. Plettenberg reported that deposed chancellor Schleicher and army chief of staff Hammerstein had decided that President Hindenburg was "no longer in full control of his mental faculties." The two generals were discussing a "presidential crisis," said Plettenberg. If Plettenberg's information was accurate, the military men were considering overthrowing the president.

Still ensconced in his defense ministry apartment, adjacent to the Landwehr Canal—just over a mile from Papen's apartment—Schleicher was trying to hold on to his secondary job as defense minister. Knowing that Papen was his implacable enemy, he began to promote Hitler's cause. He dispatched Hammerstein to a secret meeting with the Nazi leader in the stylish villa of Edwin Bechstein, the rich piano manufacturer, and his wife, Helene, the ardent Hitler supporter. Hammerstein's mission was to offer Hitler the military's support—possibly by force—to make him, not Papen, the next government chief.[8] The Nazi leader was noncommittal, but he disingenuously accepted Schleicher's offer to remain in the cabinet as defense minister, though he already knew that President Hindenburg, the old soldier, had reserved that choice for himself.

When Hammerstein returned to Schleicher's residence, a more inflammatory train of events was set in motion. Werner von Alvensleben, a former army officer and the well-connected executive secretary of the Gentlemen's Club, had showed up. The two generals asked Alvensleben to try to find out what was really going on. Why not pay a visit to Goebbels, who always seemed to know everything?

At Goebbels's apartment, in the West End, Alvensleben found both

Hitler and Göring at the dinner table. During their conversation, the garrulous Alvensleben casually commented that the German military was prepared to intervene if Papen's convoluted negotiations ended up with a Papen-Hugenberg cabinet—President Hindenburg's preferred choice. After all, Schleicher had already suggested mobilization of the Potsdam Reichswehr garrison, the largest military unit in the Berlin region.

Alvensleben's passing remark alarmed Hitler. Distrustful of Schleicher and of the military leadership, Hitler feared that his carefully negotiated ascension to power, so palpably close, might now be derailed by hasty military intervention. Hitler reached for his own armed might: the Storm Troopers. He ordered Berlin commander Helldorf to put six battalions of his men on full alert and even notified crypto-Nazis in the massive Berlin police force about a planned putsch.[9] He was ready to resist the German army if necessary.

The bruit of a coup d'état shot through the political grapevine and into the ears of the men around President Hindenburg. Otto Meissner was awakened by a phone call at two in the morning with the news that he himself might be arrested—within the hour. As though in a game of telephone, Alvensleben's ill-founded and worse-timed comment had gathered embellishments: President Hindenburg was to be detained, placed in a sealed train, and bundled off to house arrest on his own East Prussian estate; Oskar von Hindenburg would be held, too.

The idea that Schleicher might resort to a military putsch gained traction.[10] He was an aggrieved party: he had been unceremoniously relieved one day earlier of the office he had coveted for years, and he had just discovered that President Hindenburg intended to push him completely into the cold by firing him from his other job, minister of defense, thus ending his lifelong standing as a man of the military.

Schleicher had learned of the president's scheme from a telegram. In it, Hindenburg had summoned General Werner von Blomberg from meetings in Geneva to become Germany's next defense minister. An East Prussian aristocrat who was highly regarded in the military, Blomberg was also a bitter personal enemy of Schleicher. The ex-chancellor's network of informants was still intact; he soon had a purloined copy of the president's telegram—signed by Oskar von Hindenburg—on his desk.

President Hindenburg was exhausted by the political whirligig. Papen, Meissner, and even the president's own son, Oskar, urged the Old Gentleman to appoint Hitler the leader of a cabinet that would include only two other Nazis and seven non-Nazis. The rumors of an impending military putsch raised pressure for a speedy decision. One of Hindenburg's aristocratic neighbors in East Prussia—always influential with the president—argued that Hitler could easily be controlled by the military and the conservatives.[11]

There remained one caveat. Hindenburg still wanted to avert a government that could turn into one-party rule by Hitler. The president was not prepared to grant Hitler the luxury of a "presidential" cabinet that could govern by executive decree, as Chancellors Papen and Brüning had done. With a conservative cabinet of "nationalist unity" as his overriding goal, the president wanted Hitler to govern only through a "parliamentary" cabinet based on majority support in the Reichstag; Hitler's power would depend on keeping a broad coalition together.

Papen knew that Hitler would never accept such an arrangement. A parliament-based cabinet would restrain the Nazi leader; it could fall apart as soon as one party strongly disagreed with a policy Hitler promoted.

Desperate to keep his plot moving ahead, Papen decided to waltz around President Hindenburg's demand by leaving one cabinet post unfilled: minister of justice. Papen suggested to Hindenburg that negotiations were imminent with the Catholic Centre Party to fill the position, even though he knew that neither Hitler nor Hugenberg would accept the Centre Party in the cabinet (it was considered too centrist, coalition-prone, and not sufficiently nationalistic; as a participant in almost all the cabinets of the previous thirteen years, providing most of the chancellors, the party was tainted with the failures of the Weimar democracy).

Papen was President Hindenburg's most trusted political ally. Yet by leading the president to believe that a majority-based "parliamentary" cabinet would exist as soon as the Centre Party joined—a political impossibility—Papen was knowingly misleading the head of state.[12]

Credulous and unaware, the Old Gentleman was satisfied that Papen would be in the cabinet as deputy chancellor, keeping a watchful eye on Hitler.[13] "It seemed a natural precaution for him to take," recalled Papen, "once he had finally made up his mind to take the dreaded plunge of appointing Hitler as Chancellor."[14]

To Franz von Papen, the deal was done. The plot he had imagined in mid-December and set in motion in early January had reached fruition. On Sunday evening, January 29, Papen informed Hitler that "all obstacles had been removed." Hindenburg would expect the Nazi leader in the presidential suite at 11:00 a.m. on Monday.[15] Persistent rumblings of a possible Schleicher-led coup d'état gave urgency to promptly swearing in a new government.

But Papen's political package was not so neatly tied as he thought. Stray threads threatened to come unraveled; the whole bundle could split open. Even with an 11:00 a.m. oath-taking scheduled in President Hindenburg's offices, the final phase of Hitler's long march to power began to suggest low comedy, with potential cabinet members coming and going in the dark and telephone lines buzzing with misinformation and speculation.

"A feverish mood prevailed in Berlin among those in the know," recalled Duesterberg, correctly sensing that extremely bad times might be ahead. "Germany was in a kind of nightmare. What a [new] government or, more particularly, a 'Hitlerian system' would mean for the country was clear only to a very few people."[16]

The final herky-jerky act of the ascension drama began unfolding early Monday morning, January 30, on the platform at Berlin's Anhalter train station. There, General von Blomberg, Hindenburg's choice for defense minister, disembarked from the overnight train from Geneva and found two competing forces awaiting his arrival. Two officers from bitterly opposed camps wanted to pick him up. One was a major sent by Generals Hammerstein and Schleicher to whisk him straight to Schleicher's quarters in the defense ministry, thereby preventing him from being sworn in by President Hindenburg.

But the other man at the train station bore the name and the pull of presidential orders: Colonel Oskar von Hindenburg. Blomberg instinctively knew he should go with the president's son. Within minutes, the general took the oath of office as Germany's new defense minister. The act was a flagrant but breezy violation of the Weimar constitution, which stipulated that the president should only swear in ministers named by the chancellor. Yet at that moment, Germany was without a head of government.

In the Wild West atmosphere of the moment, there was no obvious way to stymie Hindenburg's high-handed constitutional breach. An outraged Schleicher could only fulminate. The now defrocked former defense minister called State Secretary Meissner to complain bitterly about a "constitutional violation."

Finance Minister Krosigk still did not know what was happening. An early-morning phone call from Schleicher's top aide, Erwin Planck, claimed that the cabinet deal with Hitler was off; the Nazi leader was probably headed for Munich. Planck said that Papen had been summoned to the president's office at 11:00 a.m., where he would no doubt be sworn in as chancellor.

Krosigk's phone rang again, and "things became even more puzzling," he recalled.[17] On the line was a member of President Hindenburg's staff. Would the finance minister kindly appear at the president's office before 11:30 a.m.? Now Krosigk assumed that he was about to be dragooned into joining a Papen cabinet—a prospect he bitterly opposed. He telephoned another cabinet member, Baron Konstantin von Neurath, the foreign minister. "We agreed not to be part of this... arrangement," Krosigk noted. He and Neurath were willing to serve only in a cabinet that included the Nazis. During a phone call with Papen, Krosigk was reassured that a Hitler-led cabinet was certain.

Arriving at the chancellery, Krosigk at first couldn't find a place to sit ("Every nook and cranny is filled," said the house porter). Soon, however, Krosigk found accommodation with Neurath in the work space of an official named Herr Doehle, who recounted the overnight uproar about a rumored putsch.

In the next room, Krosigk could hear Hitler, Papen, and Hugenberg in heated argument.

His furious efforts notwithstanding, Papen's deal was on the verge of falling apart. When Hugenberg, Seldte, and several others gathered at Papen's apartment early Monday morning, the former chancellor was in an agitated state.[18] Theodor Duesterberg had suddenly rejected the participation of his Steel Helmet coleader, Franz Seldte, in Hitler's cabinet (Seldte could not join the cabinet as a representative of the Steel Helmet association without Duesterberg's approval).

Already impatient, Papen was driven to the edge. The former chancellor reached for his last weapon of persuasion; he invoked the specter of a bloody coup d'état by repeating the rumor that the Potsdam garrison was mobilizing. "If the new cabinet is not installed by eleven o'clock, the army will march," he insisted. "We're threatened with a military dictatorship under Schleicher and Hammerstein."

Duesterberg was skeptical. Papen's source for the rumor was Oskar von Hindenburg. "I suggested we should slow down and check this out," noted Duesterberg.

"Then do it!" blurted Papen.

Hurrying three buildings up Wilhelmstrasse to the chancellery, Duesterberg found Oskar's office door blocked by a Reichswehr sergeant—"whether for his security or to stand guard over him, I couldn't tell," noted Duesterberg. The usually calm Colonel Hindenburg was stomping about and swearing. He denounced Schleicher as a traitor whom he would get back at someday. Duesterberg became convinced that Schleicher's threat of a military coup was real.

Upon returning to Papen's apartment, Duesterberg found that Hitler and Göring had arrived. Duesterberg avoided shaking their hands, a blatant breach of etiquette as well as a political statement: he still refused to endorse a Hitler chancellorship. Sensing trouble, Hitler crossed the room to approach Duesterberg with teary eyes and his most sincere tone of voice. As if drawing the Steel Helmet leader into the circle of the anointed, as he had done so often with his balky paladins, Hitler gazed into Duesterberg's eyes and offered apologies—his 1932 presidential campaign had caustically criticized Duesterberg for having a Jewish grandfather. "I deeply regret that my newspapers attacked and offended you," said Hitler. The Nazi leader was "very emotional and took my hand in both of his, the way one does among the bereaved after a funeral," recalled Duesterberg.[19] Göring followed Hitler's example, telling Duesterberg: "Now we have to stick together."

Taken aback, Duesterberg relented.

But Hugenberg did not. As the appointed time for the swearing-in of the new cabinet approached, Papen took the men on the rear-gardens trek toward President Hindenburg's offices. It was the same secluded route he had often taken for back-channel chats with the president. The group crossed the foreign ministry gardens, then passed through a back gate into the chancellery gardens. As they walked, fierce debate erupted. Hugenberg had just learned of Hitler's insistence on dissolving the Reichstag and holding new elections. When the group stepped inside chief of staff Meissner's ground-floor office in the chancellery, Hitler continued to insist that he must have a commitment to dissolution of the parliament and a new election before he would accept the chancellorship.

Hitler was now arguing fervently. He gave Hugenberg his "holy word of honor as a German man" that he would keep the new cabinet together no matter the outcome of the new balloting. Hitler promised the designated economics and agriculture minister that he would not lose his posts even though his party might lose votes in the election.

Hugenberg stood his stubborn ground.

Now began what Duesterberg remembered as "a downright comical besieging of Hugenberg. I attempted to stand by him, but Seldte, Hitler, Göring, and Papen brought all their persuasive powers to bear on Hugenberg. The whole show turned more and more dramatic. Papen said, rather pathetically, 'Herr Privy Councilor [Hugenberg], will the German unity that we've finally achieved be destroyed by your opposition? A German man [Hitler] has given you his word of honor with all of us as witnesses!'"[20]

Krosigk and Neurath, both designated to stay in their posts of finance minister and foreign minister, entered Meissner's office. The entire new cabinet was assembled, but in a standoff. As the new arrivals began pressuring Hugenberg to accept Hitler's demand for new elections, Meissner burst into the room. It was already fifteen minutes past 11:00 a.m., the expected hour of the oath-taking. Holding up his pocket watch, Meissner said, "Gentlemen, you can't keep the president waiting any longer. The time for the swearing-in has come." If the new cabinet did not show up immediately, implied Meissner, the president would walk away, and the deal would be off.

Alfred Hugenberg was now only a few steps away from gaining control of Germany's economic leadership. Laboring under a false rumor of armed revolution, feeling pressured not to keep an elderly gentleman waiting, and facing the persuasive power of all other members of the future cabinet, he gave in. He would support Hitler's demands. The impasse was broken.

Relieved and impatient, Otto Meissner led the assemblage up the stairs to the second floor, where Hindenburg awaited them. Papen took the lead, introducing each member of the coming cabinet to the president. Yet in the milling around, Krosigk suddenly dug in his heels. The designated finance minister's demand for a promise by Hitler to support responsible fiscal and monetary policies had not yet been given, he realized. Knowing his deal was, unbelievably, once again in danger of collapse, Papen sprang into action, pulling Hitler into the conversation. Krosigk murmured his queries and Hitler mumbled his assurances. One of the most improbable compacts in history, teetering on uncertainly until the very last minute, was finally done.

With the entire new government arrayed before him, Hindenburg began reading the oath. At 11:30 a.m., the old field marshal, stone-faced and grave, swore in Adolf Hitler, private first class, as chancellor of Germany. Looking Hindenburg in the eye and lying through his teeth, the Nazi boss promised to uphold the German constitution and even to reinstate regular parliamentary government after the coming elections.

Resigned and stoic, Hindenburg simply nodded. "Gentlemen, go with God!" he said, and left the room.

An elated Chancellor Hitler departed the chancellery for the short ride across the square to the Kaiserhof Hotel. Surrounded by a mob of wildly enthusiastic supporters, his car could barely make it to the hotel entrance. Hitler looked stunned by the moment. Once again, he spent part of the afternoon taking tea in the hotel lobby with his coterie of closest aides. Seven hours later, he stood in the window of his new office—and new home—saluting tens of thousands of torch-bearing Storm Troopers and Berliners streaming down Wilhelmstrasse. To many, Hitler seemed like a clean slate. He was the new start that Germany needed. For young Melita Maschmann, the Berlin teenager who watched the torchlight parade from a sidewalk, the coming "national community" had already acquired a "magical glow."[21]

But for Alfred Hugenberg, the whole business quickly seemed like a huge mistake. He told a friend on the following day that he already regretted making Hitler's final ascent possible: "Yesterday, I did the stupidest thing of my life. I joined forces with the greatest demagogue in world history."[22]

Hugenberg's insight was prophetic, but late. Thirteen years after entering political life, nearly ten years after his failed coup d'état, eight years after refounding the Nazi Party and starting over, Adolf Hitler was in power. The ascent was over. The rest could begin.

Epilogue

The Hindenburg camarilla thought they were using Hitler to gain mass support for their authoritarian concept. Hitler thought the opposite. He won. Within days of his ascension to power, the Nazi leader's reign broke over Germany with a fury. Hitler's goons began making good on their leader's long-standing promises of harsh treatment of Communists, Socialists, and Jews, rounding up, detaining, and beating perceived opponents.

After only four weeks in office, the new chancellor received an unimaginably potent political gift—the torching of the German Reichstag. An arson attack committed by a Dutch former Communist, the sensational Reichstag fire engulfed the hulking parliament's plenary chamber and the surrounding rooms, with flames shooting through its glass dome into the sky.[1] The conflagration was meant to trigger Nazi overreach and bring Germans to their political senses. The fire did, in fact, provoke fearsome Nazi repressions but did not cost Hitler any support. Instead, his extreme measures—designed to protect Germany from "Bolshevist takeover"—were endorsed by the parliament with the swift passage of the Reichstag Fire Decree and the Enabling Act of 1933. Both passed only with Nazi strong-arm tactics inside parliament, yet both were immediately signed by President Hindenburg.*

All Germans had been appalled by the destruction of their very symbol of government. Many feared exactly what Hitler warned against: an attempted Communist coup. Yet even with the Reichstag fire windfall—and with Social Democrats and Communists severely hampered in their

* The Reichstag fire was such a bonanza for Hitler that many suspected the Nazis might have set the blaze themselves. But years of investigation debunked any such scenario. The young Dutchman, Marinus van der Lubbe, who had confessed to the crime, was quickly tried and hanged. Historians no longer doubt that he committed the arson.

political campaigning—the Nazis were able to pull only 44 percent of the vote in a snap election held one week after the fire. Hitler's base was still less than half the electorate.

Despite the electoral shortfall, the new laws gave Hitler, Göring, and Himmler a free hand in suspending civil rights, habeas corpus, press freedoms, and other structures of a democratic order. Even the student body at Berlin's renowned university joined in the political tyranny. On the night of May 10, 1933, students staged a cultish book-burning in front of the State Opera House, a symbol of German high culture. Rushing to the raging bonfire, Goebbels egged them on.

It took one more year for Hitler to strip his own movement and other political forces of their potential to derail his onrushing train of authoritarian rule. On the nights of June 30–July 2, 1934, the Nazi leader instigated a massacre of his enemies and suspected doubters that left at least eighty-five and possibly several hundred people brutally murdered. Hitler's promise that "heads would roll" when he came to power was fulfilled. Among those slaughtered were two of the men who had been closest to the Nazi leader throughout his rise to power: Gregor Strasser and Ernst Röhm. Another was the man who had conspired in boosting Hitler into the highest ranks of government, former chancellor Kurt von Schleicher (along with his wife). Vice-chancellor Franz von Papen, still in Hitler's cabinet, was spared, but just barely. Though he had recently given a widely noted speech criticizing Hitler's regime, Papen was only pushed out of the government and dispatched to Austria as ambassador.

Hitler excused his acts of carnage as the necessary response to alleged reports that Röhm and his Storm Troopers had planned a putsch against the Nazi regime. Once again, parliament and President Hindenburg believed Hitler, endorsing his bloodbath as a necessary measure of protection for the nation. The sanguinary event became known in Germany as the Röhm-Putsch. To the rest of the world, it was the Night of the Long Knives. Either way, the bloodstained horror cleared the way for Hitler's coming excesses.

Unfettered, freed of restraints from many who foresaw Hitler's journey into darkness, the Nazi dictator could begin taking steps to implement the plans he had preached for more than a decade. And in time it all came to pass: the breaking of the shackles of the Treaty of Versailles; the shirking of First World War reparations payments; the reclaiming of lost bits of territory, such as the Saarland, on the other side of the Rhine River; the revitalization of Germany's economy; the brazen rebuilding of Germany's armed forces; the "coordination" of all news and information media on the Nazi Party line; the construction of concentration camps for perceived enemies, weaklings, and racial outliers.

Just as he had forecast in nearly seven hundred speeches over the span of eight years, in one unpublished and two published books, in articles and conversations and letters, Hitler embarked on the two life goals he had described so many times: war and extermination. And when they ultimately brought ruin and destruction to Germany, he succeeded in the act of reckoning that he had threatened for so long. On April 30, 1945, along with Eva Braun, whom he had married two days earlier, Hitler deserted the countrymen he had won, led to new heights, and finally driven into the abyss. He committed suicide.

ACKNOWLEDGMENTS

On a dreary fall day in 2016, Amber Paranick at the Library of Congress's Newspaper and Current Periodical Reading Room led me to a huge bound volume on a plain table. Gray-backed and broad, the massive book held the 1925 issues of Adolf Hitler's daily newspaper, the *Völkischer Beobachter.* Flipping it open, I confronted for the first time an original copy of Hitler's infamous broadsheet. With its wreathed swastika in the center of the masthead, the sight of this notorious relic gave me a shudder.

The newspaper's front page, dated February 26, 1925, bore a large headline that proclaimed Hitler's return to politics after a year in prison. APPEAL TO THE FORMER MEMBERS OF THE NATIONAL SOCIALIST GERMAN WORKERS' PARTY! it read, announcing a mass beer-hall rally for the following evening. That beer-hall speech marked the beginning of Hitler's comeback and climb to power. It also gave me the beginning of this book.

Librarians and archivists are the secret weapons of every history writer. Without Paranick and her helpful colleagues at the Library of Congress—including Bryan E. Cornell, in the Recorded Sound Reference Center—I would have had no chance of reconstructing the most consequential political crusade in history.

Especially crucial to my undertaking was the chief archivist of Munich's peerless Institut für Zeitgeschichte (Institute for Contemporary History), Dr. Klaus A. Lankheit. The institute is the preeminent center of research on Hitler and the Third Reich. With support from Lankheit and the assistant director, Esther-Julia Howell, I was put into the skilled hands of the center's digital copying expert, Heike Musculus. Frau Musculus, along with Marion Grossmann, patiently assisted my frenzied digging through the fifty-thousand-page accumulation of newspaper clippings and other records pertinent to Hitler's speech-ridden climb to power. Courtney Marie Burrell, a doctoral candidate in Munich, facilitated selection and delivery of the materials.

Simone Paulmichl, the institute's press chief, backed by the institute's directors, Andreas Wirsching and Magnus Brechtken, generously supported my work and introduced me to an exceptional resource, historian Albert A. Feiber. A coeditor of a powerful book, *Die tödliche Utopie*,* about Hitler's life at his Alpine retreat above the town of Berchtesgaden, Feiber graciously spent a day tramping through winter snows on the Obersalzberg with me to point out the precise spots where the Nazi politician lived, worked, and relaxed during his long months in the mountains.

It was here, Hitler later claimed, that he had made some of his most important decisions.

My grasp of a flood of research was immeasurably enhanced by the guidance of scholars who have devoted their professional lives to disentangling the tortured roots of the Nazi enterprise. Especially generous with time and shared knowledge was Othmar Plöckinger, an editor of the renowned 2016 critically annotated edition of *Mein Kampf.* The author of several groundbreaking works on Hitler, Plöckinger frequently guided me to useful material—and shared insights over a four-hour working dinner on the Mönchsberg overlooking his hometown of Salzburg, Austria. Equally hospitable was historian Roman Töppel, also an editor of the annotated *Mein Kampf.* Töppel led me to such surprising details as Hitler's apparent fantasy, in an obscure 1923 interview with a Catalonian newspaper, of exterminating all Germany's Jews in a single night.

In Munich, I was repeatedly aided by historian Paul Hoser, who had just uncovered newsmaking proof of Hitler's "courteous" nine-year relationship with a Jewish landlord. Hoser spent long hours with me at the Bavarian State Library and in his book-filled apartment discussing the shadings and shadows of Hitler's zigzag political journey. Professor Alan Steinweis, head of the Holocaust studies program at the University of Vermont, is equally at

* Volker Dahm, Albert A. Feiber, Hartmut Mehringer, and Horst Müller, *Die tödliche Utopie: Bilder, Texte, Dokumente, Daten zum Dritten Reich* (Munich and Berlin: Institut für Zeitgeschichte, Dokumentation Obersalzberg, 1999).

home in Munich, where he provided numerous research tips as well as excellent company. At the stunning new National Socialist Documentation Center (NS-Dokumentationszentrum), built on the site of Hitler's former Nazi Party headquarters (the Brown House), the director, Winfried Nerdinger, and Dr. Angela Hermann shared insights on the fraught politics of memory in the city that Hitler liked to call "the capital of the Nazi movement."

During travels to Hitler's favored venues north of Munich, I met in Nuremberg with Professor Peter Fleischmann, the state archive director and scholar who had made international headlines by uncovering medical proof, in a prison admissions ledger, that Hitler indeed had an undescended testicle, as had long been speculated. Fleischmann shared insights and warm hospitality, giving me a lengthy tour of Nuremberg's infamous Nazi Party parade grounds. In Bayreuth, I was received at the Richard Wagner Museum and home by its director, Sven Friedrich, and press chief, Christine Brömel, who provided pithy background on Hitler's close relations with the Wagner family. Across town, Peter Emmerich gave me an eye-opening tour of Wagner's Festival Theater, one of Hitler's favorite spots on earth, where only Wagner's operas are performed.

In Weimar, the celebrated home of German classicism, I quickly discovered the small city's importance as a home away from home for Hitler during his climbing years. Staying, as Hitler did, at the Hotel Elephant on Market Square, I was joined by journalist and author Claus Christian Malzahn, who invited me to a seminar he was holding at the nearby University of Jena, the site of Hitler's first attempt to intrude his rabid racism into German academe.

For help in using the incomparable online edition of Goebbels's diaries, I owe a special debt of gratitude to Louise Madore of the Walter de Gruyter Verlag. Thanks also to her colleagues Irene Butt, Ulrike Engel, and Julia Brauch.

Closer to home, I'm grateful for research guidance and support from Professor Jeffrey Herf, of the University of Maryland, and Professor Randall Bytwerk, at Calvin University. Thanks also to Georgetown University historian Anna von der Goltz, Professor Marc Morjé Howard, and his student Will Spach, who assisted in my research.

A singular callout goes to former *Time* correspondent Ann Blackman and her colleagues Melissa August and Bill Hooper for digging out all six *Time* cover stories on Hitler from 1931 to 1945. Friends who shared their deep knowledge, advice, and support include Gabor Steingart, Gregor Peter Schmitz, Michael S. Cullen, Jeremiah Riemer, Roger M. Williams, James Reston Jr., Laurence Latourette, and Jonathan M. Weisgall.

I am also indebted to the resourceful staffs at the Franklin D. Roosevelt Presidential Library, in Hyde Park, New York; the Hoover Institution Library and Archives, in Palo Alto, California; Georgetown University; American University; the United States Memorial Holocaust Museum Library and Archives; the German Historical Institute; and Howard University, in Washington, DC, where Niketha McKenzie, Adia Coleman, and Ruth Rasby were warmly helpful. At the National Archives in College Park, Maryland, invaluable assistance came from Richard Schneider, Nick Natanson, Kaitlyn Crain Enriquez, Kelsey Noel, and Ruth Beamon.

As a publishing project, this book owes its realization to my matchless agent, Gail Ross, and her colleague Dara Kaye, of the Ross Yoon Agency. The final product was immensely enhanced by the counsel of editor Phil Marino, assisted by Elizabeth Gassman, and the work of production editor Pamela Marshall, at Little, Brown. Superb historical research, fact-checking, diction improvements, and flawless copyediting were provided by Barbara Clark, an editor with an exceptionally fine ear and eye for language.

But none of it would have happened without the patient indulgence and editorial inspiration of my wife, Linda M. Harris, whose structural sense, historical curiosity, and feel for words made the work possible. To her I offer the deepest thanks.

A NOTE ON SOURCES

More than four hundred books, articles, and other resources cluttered my desk, my study, and my intellectual world as I wrote this book. But a pair of original sources stand out. These are designated by the two most frequent abbreviations in the endnotes: RSA and TBJG, Hitler's speeches and Goebbels's diaries respectively.

RSA stands for *Hitler. Reden, Schriften, Anordnungen: Februar 1925 bis Januar 1933*—Hitler's Speeches, Writings, Directives: February 1925 to January 1933.

TBJG stands for *Die Tagebücher von Joseph Goebbels*—The Diaries of Joseph Goebbels.

RSA

The RSA is a collection of the 692 speeches—some more than two hours long—that Hitler made during the eight years of his climb to power, 1925 to 1933. An indispensable road map of Hitler's improbable ascent, the twelve-book set is 5,172 pages long, plus a supplemental volume of maps, an index, and an addenda. The collection also includes the relatively few essays, editorials, and internal party directives issued by Hitler during this period. More interesting are the handful of interviews with foreign journalists that Hitler gave as he scrambled toward the top (the interviews with Anglo-American newspapers appear in English). The RSA collection even contains the full draft of *Hitlers Zweites Buch* (Hitler's Second Book), a two-hundred-page sequel to *Mein Kampf* that was never published in Hitler's lifetime.

Because Hitler was above all a man of words—hundreds of thousands, even millions of them, both spoken and written—his political journey is the spoken and written record he left behind, along with journalistic and political commentary on the noisy but seemingly quixotic undertaking.

This record is nowhere better presented than in the RSA. It is the product of nearly two decades of meticulous research by Munich's renowned Institut für Zeitgeschichte (Institute for Contemporary History). In reconstructing Hitler's speeches, the institute's researchers occasionally found surviving typescripts or transcripts, sometimes polished, that had sporadically appeared in the Nazi newspaper, *Völkischer Beobachter.* But the scholars relied above all on hundreds of laboriously collected newspaper stories from all over Germany, an especially rich source of reports on Hitler's rallies, since German reporters in that era typically knew shorthand and often made verbatim notes. One of the RSA's strengths is its detailed footnoting of these newspaper stories, giving the researcher an instant feel for how Hitler's long march was playing to various audiences.

Luckily, these primary sources—the newspaper clippings—are all still available in the institute's archives. They are gathered in a series of file drawers that were informally dubbed "Materialsammlung Reden Schriften Anordnungen" by archive director Klaus A. Lankheit during my 2017 research. Estimated at roughly fifty thousand pages, the source materials were then in the process of being digitally scanned. In my endnotes, I refer to items pulled from this resource as "Materialsammlung-RSA."

TBJG

This thirty-two-volume collection of Goebbels's diaries provides a contemporaneous insider's account of Hitler's rise and reign.

The roughly six thousand entries in Goebbels's diaries run to more than fifteen thousand pages. They can be self-serving, vengeful, and written with future publication in mind. Yet they are for the most part intimate, straight from the gut, and often sharply insightful. They capture the daily accretion of events, aggravations, disappointments, and successes during Hitler's rise, along with Goebbels's waxing and waning self-esteem as he rises and falls in Hitler's favor. Through the diaries, Goebbels became Hitler's Boswell, though he occasionally sounds more like a carping crow on Hitler's shoulder—as he frequently does throughout this book.

This definitive collection of Goebbels's massive diaries was also generated by arduous research at the Institute for Contemporary History. Historian Elke Fröhlich spent nearly a quarter of a century digging, assembling, and scrapping for access to the scattered remains of Goebbels's voluminous scribblings. Fröhlich's tenacious labors included heroic efforts to secure the only surviving glass-plate copies of key parts of the diaries from secretive, closed Moscow archives. Her final product—assisted by young scholars such as Angela Hermann—is an indispensable resource for any student of the still staggering Hitler story.

Luckily, the current publisher of Goebbels's diaries—Walter de Gruyter Verlag, in Berlin—offers a searchable online version that is nearly essential for modern research. *Die Tagebücher von Joseph Goebbels Online* was enormously useful to me in writing this book.

MA and AA

Leading German newspapers such as the *Vossische Zeitung, Berliner Tageblatt, Frankfurter Zeitung,* and others published two editions daily, except on Sundays and Mondays, when they published a single edition. The two daily editions—Tuesday through Saturday—are designated in the notes by the abbreviation MA, for *Morgenausgabe* (morning edition), and AA, for *Abendausgabe* (afternoon or evening edition). A story that appeared in one edition might well not appear in the other.

NOTES

Prologue

1. "1933-01-30-Deutscher Rundfunk: Hitler wird Reichskanzler (Teil 1)," at https://archive.org/details/19330130DeutscherRundfunkHitlerWirdReichskanzlerTeil15m10s; H. R. Knickerbocker Papers, Columbia University, quoted in Andrew Nagorski, *Hitlerland: American Eyewitnesses to the Nazi Rise to Power* (New York: Simon and Schuster, 2012), 104.
2. TBJG, January 31, 1933.
3. Melita Maschmann, *Account Rendered: A Dossier on My Former Self* (London: Abelard-Schuman, 1965), loc. 302, Kindle.
4. William Sheridan Allen, *The Nazi Seizure of Power: The Experience of a Single German Town 1922–1945,* rev. ed. (1965; repr., New York and London: Franklin Watts, 1984), xviii.
5. Hans Frank, *Im Angesicht des Galgens: Deutung Hitlers und seiner Zeit auf Grund eigener Erlebnisse und Erkenntnisse* (Munich and Gräfelfing: Friedrich Alfred Beck Verlag, 1953), 25.

Part One: Rebirth and Rebuilding (1925–1928)

1. Theodore Abel, *Why Hitler Came into Power* (1938; repr., Cambridge, MA: Harvard University Press, 1986), 123–24.
2. Detlev J. K. Peukert, *Jugend Zwischen Krieg und Krise: Lebenswelten von Arbeiterjungen in der Weimarer Republik* (Cologne: Bund Verlag, 1987), 149.

Chapter One: Backstory

1. Ian Kershaw, *Hitler,* vol. 1, *1889–1936: Hubris* (New York: W. W. Norton, 1998), 24.
2. Amos Elon, *The Pity of It All: A History of Jews in Germany, 1743–1933* (New York: Metropolitan Books, 2003), 339.
3. [Captain Karl Mayr], "I Was Hitler's Boss," *Current History* 1, no. 3 (November 1941), 193–99.
4. Ernst Deuerlein, "Hitlers Eintritt in die Politik und die Reichswehr," *Vierteljahrshefte für Zeitgeschichte* 7, no. 2 (1959), 200.
5. Adolf Hitler, *Mein Kampf: Zwei Bände in einem Band, Ungekürzte Ausgabe* (Munich: Zentralverlag der NSDAP, Franz Eher Nachfolger, 1943), 235. By 1943, the book was in its 855th printing.
6. Hitler, *Mein Kampf,* 238. Like so many of the tales in Hitler's autobiographical chronicle, this one may have only a weak basis in truth, as shown by historian Othmar Plöckinger in a careful study of available documents. Yet the story is the closest account available of the way Hitler made the leap into party politics and may comport loosely with the actual events. See Othmar Plöckinger, *Unter Soldaten und Agitatoren: Hitlers prägende Jahre im deutschen Militär 1918–1920* (Paderborn, Germany: Verlag Ferdinand Schöningh, 2013), 140–53.
7. RSA, Band I, Dok. 65, p. 154.
8. RSA, Band II, Teil 1, Dok. 159, p. 437.
9. Theodore Abel, *Why Hitler Came into Power* (1938; repr., Cambridge, MA: Harvard University Press, 1986), 4.

10. Friedrich Kroner, "Überreizte Nerven" [Overwrought nerves], *Berliner Illustrierte Zeitung,* August 26, 1923, quoted in *The Weimar Republic Sourcebook,* ed. Anton Kaes, Martin Jay, and Edward Dimendberg (Berkeley: University of California Press, 1994), 63–64.
11. As the putsch began, a nearly hysterical Hitler threatened to kill the Bavarian ruling triumvirate whom he was holding hostage—and shoot himself, too; he raised his Browning pistol to his head but did not fire it. A few minutes later, in front of three thousand people at the Bürgerbräukeller, Hitler declared: "Either the German revolution begins tonight, or we will all be dead by dawn!" Hours later, as the coup d'état unraveled, Hitler said to his coconspirators: "If this works out, fine. If not, we'll all hang ourselves." Two days later, as police surrounded Hitler and he reached for his gun, the Nazi leader shouted: "This is the end—I will never let those swine take me!" But Helene Hanfstaengl stayed his hand. Even during his first weeks at Landsberg Prison, Hitler tried to commit suicide by means of a hunger strike. The chief warden was about to begin force-feeding him with life-sustaining "synthetic nourishment" in the prison hospital when the Nazi leader was talked out of the strike by friends and the prison psychologist. By that time, Hitler had already begun to weaken, and he was emitting a repulsive "penetrating odor," according to a prison guard. See Franz Hemmrich, "Adolf Hitler in der Festung Landsberg," Institut für Zeitgeschichte, Munich, Archive ED 153; Archiv Manfred Deiler, pp. 9–15. See also Alois Maria Ott, "Aber plötzlich sprang Hitler auf..." *Bayern Kurier,* November 3, 1973.
12. John Toland, *Adolf Hitler* (New York: Doubleday, 1976), 1:190.

Chapter Two: Resurrection

1. RSA, Band I, Dok. 6, p. 20.
2. Kurt G. W. Ludecke, *I Knew Hitler: The Lost Testimony by a Survivor from the Night of the Long Knives* (1938; repr., Barnsley, UK: Pen & Sword, 2011), 177.
3. "Erledigung Hitlers," *Frankfurter Zeitung und Handelsblatt (Erstes Morgenblatt)* 70, no. 841 (November 11, 1925).
4. Police reports: Polizeidirektion München, Nr. VId 234/25, March 4, 1925; P.N.D. [Police Intelligence Service], Nr. 496. Newspaper articles: "Hitler enttäuscht seine Anhänger: 'Gefühl ist alles'—Eine theatralische Versöhnungsszene," *Berliner Tageblatt,* February 28, 1925. Cf. "Der Diktator Hitler," *Frankfurter Zeitung,* March 3, 1925, 1; "Die Hitler-Versammlung," *Augsburger Abendzeitung,* February 28, 1925; "Hitlers Wiedereintritt in das öfftentliche Leben," *Völkischer Kurier,* March 1, 1925; "Hitler aus seiner Festungstid.," *Völkische Zeitung,* February 28, 1925; "Eine Provokation der Staatsautorität," *Münchener Post,* February 28, 1925. All articles in Materialsammlung-RSA, Institut für Zeitgeschichte, Munich.
5. Karl Alexander von Müller, *Im Wandel einer Welt: Erinnerungen, Band Drei 1919–1932,* ed. Otto Alexander von Müller (Munich: Süddeutscher Verlag, 1966), 144–45, reprinted in Ernst Deuerlein, *Der Aufstieg der NSDAP in Augenzeugenberichten* (Munich: Deutscher Taschenbuch Verlag, 1974), 164–65.
6. "Der Diktator Hitler," *Frankfurter Zeitung,* March 3, 1925, 1.
7. RSA, Band I, Dok. 6, pp. 14–28.
8. Rudolf Heberle, *From Democracy to Nazism: A Regional Case Study on Political Parties in Germany* (1945; repr., New York: Grosset & Dunlap, 1970), 6.
9. Stefanie Fischer, *Ökonomisches Vertrauen und antisemitische Gewalt: Jüdische Viehhändler in Mittelfranken 1919–1939* (Göttingen: Wallstein Verlag, 2014), 129ff.
10. Nachum Tim Gidal, *Jews in Germany: From Roman Times to the Weimar Republic* (Cologne: Konemann, 1998), 24.

11. "Walther Rathenau, 'Höre Israel,'" Das Wilhelminische Kaiserreich und der Erste Weltkrieg (1890–1918), Deutsche Geschichte in Dokumenten und Bildern, Deutsches Historisches Museum, http://ghdi.ghi-dc.org/sub_document.cfm?document_id=717&language=german. Rathenau never denied his own Jewishness but considered himself "a German of Jewish origin" rather than a German Jew: "My people are the German people; my home is Germany; my faith is German faith, which stands above all denominations." See Walther Rathenau, *An Deutschlands Jugend* (Berlin: S. Fischer Verlag, 1918), 5.
12. Ludiger Heid, "Nur wenige fühlten sich ihnen verwandt: Die erste wissenschaftliche Darstellung dieses Aspekts der Geschichte der Juden und des Antisemitismus," *Die Zeit,* April 3, 1987, https://www.zeit.de/1987/15/nur-wenige-fuehlten-sich-ihnen-verwandt.
13. Tim Grady, *The German-Jewish Soldiers of the First World War in History and Memory* (Liverpool, UK: Liverpool University Press, 2011), Google Books; Amos Elon, *The Pity of It All: A History of Jews in Germany, 1743–1933* (New York: Metropolitan Books, 2003), 338.
14. RSA, Band I, Dok. 6, p. 20.
15. RSA, Band 1, Dok. 4, p. 8.

Chapter Three: Wagner's Ghost

1. Brigitte Hamann, *Winifred Wagner: A Life at the Heart of Hitler's Bayreuth* (New York: Harcourt, 2006), 58; Konrad Heiden, *The Führer* (Edison, NJ: Castle Books, 2002), 198; "Houston Stewart Chamberlain Letter to Hitler October 7, 1923," World Future Fund, http://www.worldfuturefund.org/wffmaster/Reading/Germany/Chamberlain.htm.
2. August Kubizek, *The Young Hitler I Knew: The Memoirs of Hitler's Childhood Friend* (1953; repr., Barnsley, UK: Greenhill Books, 2006), loc. 1237ff, Kindle.
3. Wolfram Pyta, *Hitler: Der Künstler als Politiker und Feldherr—Eine Herrschaftsanalyse* (Munich: Siedler Verlag, 2015), 63–79.
4. Hamann, *Winifred Wagner,* 105.
5. "Die Verfassung des Deutschen Reiches," Article 41, paragraph 1, http://www.documentarchiv.de/wr/wrv.html#DRITTER_ABSCHNITT02.

Chapter Four: Ebert to Hindenburg

1. Scheidemann's exact words have long been a matter of historical uncertainty. The version used here comes from Ernst Friedegg, an Austrian journalist who allegedly took them down verbatim and published them in 1919 in the *Deutscher Revolutionsalmanach.* Cf. Heinrich Winkler, "Doch, so war es!" *Die Zeit,* April 25, 2018; Manfred Jessen-Klingenberg, *Die Ausrufung der Republik durch Philipp Scheidemann am 9. November 1918,* in *Geschichte in Wissenschaft und Unterricht* 19 (1968), 653–54; *Philipp Scheidemann: Bericht über den 9. November 1918,* Deutsches Historisches Museum; Lothar Machtan, "Und nun geht nach Hause," *Die Zeit,* April 5, 2018, citing Ernst Drahn, *Deutsche Revolutions-Almanach für das Jahr 1919 über die Ereignisse des Jahres 1918,* https://www.zeit.de/2018/15/philipp-scheidemann-sozialdemokrat-republik-ausrufung-1918/komplettansicht.
2. This was Scheidemann's version of events. See Machtan, "Und nun geht nach Hause."
3. Count Harry Kessler, *Berlin in Lights: The Diaries of Count Harry Kessler (1918–1937)* (New York: Grove Press, 2000), 7–8.
4. John Maynard Keynes, *The Economic Consequences of the Peace* (New York: Harcourt, Brace, and Howe, 1920), Project Gutenberg, n.p.
5. RSA, Band I, Dok. 16, p. 47.
6. RSA, Band, I, Dok. 40, p. 73; "1925 German Presidential Election," *Wikipedia,* https://en.wikipedia.org/wiki/German_presidential_election_1925.

7. Ernst Hanfstaengl, *15 Jahre mit Hitler: Zwischen Weissem und Braunem Haus* (Munich: R. Piper & Co. Verlag, 1980), 180.
8. Ernst Deuerlein, *Der Aufstieg der NSDAP in Augenzeugenberichten* (Munich: Deutscher Taschenbuch Verlag, 1989), 249–50.
9. Andreas Dorpalen, *Hindenburg and the Weimar Republic* (Princeton, NJ: Princeton University Press, 1964), 254.
10. Kessler, *Berlin in Lights,* 267.
11. Edgar Ansel Mowrer, *Triumph and Turmoil: A Personal History of Our Time* (New York: Weybright and Talley, 1968), 164.

Chapter Five: Always on the Run

1. Rudolf Hess, *Briefe: 1908–1933* (Munich: Albert Langen / Georg Müller Verlag, 1987), 364.
2. Eberhard Jäckel and Axel Kuhn, eds., *Hitler: Sämtliche Aufzeichnungen, 1905–1924* (Stuttgart: Deutsche Verlagsanstalt, 1980), 771.
3. P.N.D. [Police Intelligence Service], No. 503, "Mitgliederversammlung der NSDAP, Sektion Haidhausen am 15.4.1925 im Hofbräukeller," Materialsammlung-RSA, Institut für Zeitgeschichte, Munich.
4. RSA, Band I, Dok. 72, p. 171.
5. RSA, Band I, Dok. 11, p. 37.
6. P.N.D. [Police Intelligence Service], No. 502, BayHStA, Abt. 1, Sonderabgabe I 1838, Materialsammlung-RSA, Institut für Zeitgeschichte, Munich.
7. Over the coming year, eight other states would place bans on Hitler's public speaking. See Albrecht Tyrell, *Führer befiehl... Selbstzeugnisse aus der "Kampfzeit" der NSDAP* (Düsseldorf: Droste Verlag, 1969), 107–8; "Reichsrat (Deutschland)," *Wikipedia,* https://de.wikipedia.org/wiki/Reichsrat_(Deutschland).
8. "Adolf Hitler in Weimar," *Frankfurter Zeitung,* March 25, 1925 (MA).

Chapter Six: *Mein Kampf*

1. The long-standing myth that Hitler dictated his book rather than typed it was convincingly refuted by Austrian historian Othmar Plöckinger in *Geschichte eines Buches: Adolf Hitlers "Mein Kampf" 1922–1945* (Munich: R. Oldenbourg Verlag, 2006), 146–53. The American provenance of the Remington typewriter (serial number NK 43 025) and the probability that it was a gift from Helene Bechstein comes from Florian Beierl and Othmar Plöckinger, "Neue Dokumente zu Hitlers Buch *Mein Kampf,*" *Vierteljahrshefte für Zeitgeschichte* 57, no. 2 (2009), 261–318.
2. Rudolf Hess, *Briefe: 1908–1933* (Munich: Albert Langen / Georg Müller Verlag, 1987), 349.
3. Adolf Hitler, *Mein Kampf: Zwei Bände in einem Band, Ungekürzte Ausgabe,* 851st–855th printing (Munich: Zentralverlag der NSDAP, Franz Eher Nachfolger, 1943), "Vorwort."
4. Adolf Hitler, *Hitler, Mein Kampf: Eine kritische Edition,* ed. Christian Hartmann, Thomas Vordermayer, Othmar Plöckinger, and Roman Töppel (Munich: Institut für Zeitgeschichte, 2016), 9. This historic two-volume work (1,966 pages) is a paragraph-by-paragraph deconstruction of Hitler's bloated manifesto. Upon its publication, in January of 2016, it became a bestseller in Germany.
5. Hitler, *Mein Kampf,* 311ff.
6. Hitler, *Mein Kampf,* 314.
7. Hitler, *Mein Kampf,* 311ff.
8. Houston Stewart Chamberlain, *Rasse und Persönlichkeit. Aufsätze von Houston Stewart Chamberlain* (Munich, F. Bruckmann, 1925), 73–74. This section draws extensively on a

comprehensive and incisive article by the historian Roman Töppel: "'Volk und Rasse': Hitler's Quellen auf der Spur," *Vierteljahrshefte für Zeitgeschichte* 64, no. 1 (2016), 1–36.

9. Peter G. J. Pulzer, *Die Entstehung des politischen Antisemitismus in Deutschland und Österreich 1867–1914* (Göttingen: Vandenhoeck & Ruprecht, 2004), 258.
10. Arthur de Gobineau, *The Inequality of Human Races,* trans. Adrian Collins (New York: G. P. Putnam's Sons, 1915).
11. Theodor Fritsch, ed., *Handbuch der Judenfrage. Eine Zusammenstellung des wichtigsten Materials zur Beurteilung des jüdischen Volkes* (1907; repr., Leipzig: Hammer-Verlag, 1933), 408.
12. RSA, Band IV, Teil 1, Dok. 32, p. 133.
13. Hitler, *Mein Kampf,* 148.
14. Hitler, *Mein Kampf,* 231–32.
15. Hitler, *Mein Kampf,* 252.
16. Hess, *Briefe,* 320.
17. Eberhard Jäckel and Axel Kuhn, eds., *Hitler: Sämtliche Aufzeichnungen, 1905–1924* (Stuttgart: Deutsche Verlagsanstalt, 1980), 1242.
18. Gerhard L. Weinberg, ed., *Hitler's Table Talk 1941–1944: His Private Conversations* (New York: Enigma Books, 2008), 218.
19. Plöckinger, *Geschichte,* 67.
20. Plöckinger, *Geschichte,* 72.
21. The Zugspitze is higher, at 9,718 feet, but it lies partially in Austria.
22. Konrad Heiden, *Adolf Hitler: Das Zeitalter der Verantwortungslosigkeit* (Zurich: Europa Verlag, 1936), 1:76–77.
23. Albert A. Feiber, "Der Obersalzberg," in *Die tödliche Utopie: Bilder, Texte, Dokumente, Daten zum Dritten Reich,* ed. Volker Dahm, Albert A. Feiber, Hartmut Mehringer, and Horst Müller (Munich-Berlin: Institut für Zeitgeschichte, Dokumentation Obersalzberg, 1999), 61.
24. Weinberg, *Hitler's Table Talk,* 217.
25. Plöckinger, *Geschichte,* 349–56, 405ff.
26. *Simplicissimus,* August 31, 1925.
27. *Abwehrblätter* 35, no. 19/20 (October 20, 1925), in Plöckinger, *Geschichte,* 304.
28. *Bayerisches Vaterland, Hamburgischer Correspondent, Neue Freie Presse* (Vienna), and *Frankfurter Zeitung,* in Plöckinger, *Geschichte,* 225–27.
29. Plöckinger, *Geschichte,* 159.
30. Eberhard Jäckel, *Hitlers Welanschauung: Entwurf einer Herrschaft* (Stuttgart: Deutsche Verlags-Anstalt, 1981), 7.
31. Victor Klemperer, *LTI: Notizbuch eines Philologen,* ed. Elke Fröhlich (Stuttgart: Reclam Verlag, 2010), 34.

Chapter Seven: Bayreuth

1. Gerhard L. Weinberg, ed., *Hitler's Table Talk 1941–1944: His Private Conversations* (New York: Enigma Books, 2008), 215.
2. Brigitte Hamann, *Winifred Wagner: A Life at the Heart of Hitler's Bayreuth* (New York: Harcourt, 2006), 108.
3. Adolf Hitler, *Monologe im Führerhauptquartier 1941–1944: Die Aufzeichnungen Heinrich Heims,* ed. Werner Jochmann (Hamburg: Albrecht Knaus, 1980), 308.
4. Hamann, *Winifred Wagner,* 109–10.
5. Rudolf Hess, letter to Emil Hamm, August 11, 1925, in Othmar Plöckinger, ed., *Quellen und Dokumente zur Geschichte von "Mein Kampf" 1924–1945* (Stuttgart: Franz Steiner Verlag, 2016), 105.

6. Othmar Plöckinger, *Geschichte eines Buches: Adolf Hitlers "Mein Kampf" 1922–1945* (Munich: R. Oldenbourg Verlag, 2006), 92.

Chapter Eight: Strasser and Goebbels

1. Konrad Heiden, *Geschichte des Nationalsozialismus: Die Karriere einer Idee* (Berlin: Rowohlt, 1932), 180.
2. Ian Kershaw, *Hitler,* vol. 1, *1889–1936: Hubris* (New York: W. W. Norton, 1998), 269.
3. Peter D. Stachura, *Gregor Strasser and the Rise of Nazism* (London: George Allen & Unwin, 1982), 41.
4. Stachura, *Gregor Strasser,* 46.
5. Jeremy Noakes and Geoffrey Pridham, eds., *Documents on Nazism: 1919–1945* (New York: Viking Press, 1974), 70.
6. Goebbels's voluminous diaries are an indispensable insider's account of the Nazi enterprise. The full set of thirty-two volumes and more than fifteen thousand pages is available only in German. See Joseph Goebbels, *Die Tagebücher von Joseph Goebbels: Sämtlich Fragmente,* ed. Elke Fröhlich (Munich: K. G. Saur Verlag, 2008), available in print and online from Walter de Gruyter Verlag, Berlin.
7. Joseph Goebbels, "Erinnerungsblätter," in Peter Longerich, *Goebbels: A Biography* (New York: Random House, 2015), loc. 610, Kindle.
8. Toby Thacker, *Joseph Goebbels: Life and Death* (New York: Palgrave Macmillan, 2009), 33–34.
9. Ralf Georg Reuth, *Goebbels,* trans. Krishna Winston (New York: Harcourt Brace, 1993), 62.
10. TBJG, July 14, 1925.
11. TBJG, November 6, 1925.
12. TBJG, November 23, 1925.
13. *Völkischer Beobachter* 174 (October 22, 1925), 1, in Albrecht Tyrell, *Führer befiehl... Selbstzeugnisse aus der "Kampfzeit" der NSDAP* (Düsseldorf: Droste Verlag, 1969), 118.
14. These included Max Erwin von Scheubner-Richter and Alfred Rosenberg.
15. Volker Ullrich, *Hitler: Ascent 1889–1939* (New York: Alfred A. Knopf, 2016), loc. 4454, Kindle.
16. Arbeitsgemeinschaft der nord- und westdeutschen Gaue.
17. Gregor Strasser, "Geleitwort: Nationalsozialistische Briefe," in Werner Jochmann, *Nationalsozialismus und Revolution: Ursprung und Geschichte der NSDAP in Hamburg 1922–1933, Dokumente* (Frankfurt-am-Main: Europäischer Verlagsanstalt, 1963), 218–19.
18. TBJG, August 21, 1925.
19. TBJG, October 2, 1925.
20. An English translation of the Twenty-Five Points can be read at https://avalon.law.yale.edu/imt/1708-ps.asp.
21. "The oft-mentioned Twenty-Five Points are not taken seriously as a program," wrote Konrad Heiden in 1932 on the first page of his history of the Nazi Party. See Heiden, *Geschichte,* 7.
22. Reinhard Kühnl, "Zur Programmatik der nationalsozialistischen Linken: Das Strasser-Programm von 1925/26," *Vierteljahrshefte für Zeitgeschichte* 14, no. 3 (1966), 324–33.
23. Kühnl, "Zur Programmatik," 332n57.

Chapter Nine: Bamberg Debacle

1. Werner Jochmann, *Nationalsozialismus und Revolution: Ursprung und Geschichte der NSDAP in Hamburg 1922–1933, Dokumente* (Frankfurt-am-Main: Europäischer Verlagsanstalt, 1963), 220.

2. Otto Strasser, *Hitler and I* (Boston: Houghton Mifflin, 1940), 86; Helmut Heiber, *Das Tagebuch von Joseph Goebbels 1925/26* (Stuttgart: Deutsche Verlags-Anstalt, 1961), 56n1.
3. TBJG, January 25, 1926.
4. Albrecht Tyrell, "Gottfried Feder and the NSDAP," in *The Shaping of the Nazi State,* ed. Peter D. Stachura (London: Croom Helm, 1978), 69.
5. William Sheridan Allen, ed. and trans., *The Infancy of Nazism: The Memoirs of Ex-Gauleiter Albert Krebs 1923–1933* (New York: New Viewpoints, 1976), 232.
6. Strasser, *Hitler and I,* 88.
7. Werner Jochmann, *Im Kampf um die Macht: Hitlers Rede vor dem Hamburger Nationalklub von 1919* (Frankfurt-am-Main: Europäische Verlagsanstalt, 1960), 21n12, citing Otto Strasser, *Hitler und ich* (Buenos Aires: Editorial Trenkelbach, 1940), 86ff.
8. RSA, Band I, Dok. 101, pp. 294–96.
9. Jochmann, *Im Kampf,* 21; TBJG, February 15, 1926. Robert Ley, a Rhineland Nazi, was not yet a "Municher," but he had never fully bought into Strasser's northern initiative. He would soon become one of Hitler's strongest supporters.
10. TBJG, February 25, 1926.
11. Among other things, Strasser never really gave up his underlying preference for socialism over brutal nationalism. *"We are Socialists,"* he wrote (in italics) in a long essay several months after the Bamberg meeting. National Socialists were "mortal enemies of the present capitalist economic system," he declared, complaining about wage injustice and the "immoral evaluation of individuals according to wealth and money instead of responsibility and achievement." See "Gedanken über Aufgaben der Zukunft," *NS-Briefe,* June 15, 1926, as "Thoughts About the Tasks of the Future," in Barbara Miller Lane and Leila J. Rupp, eds., *Nazi Ideology Before 1933: A Documentation* (Austin: University of Texas Press, 1978), 87–94.

Chapter Ten: Brutal Willpower

1. "Hitlers 'Sieg,'" *Bayerischer Kurier,* February 26, 1926, in Materialsammlung-RSA, Institut für Zeitgeschichte, Munich. Hitler was later forced by a lawsuit to make an apology; Esser spent two weeks in jail for the disruption.
2. RSA, Band II, Teil 1, Dok. 66, p. 116.
3. Albrecht Tyrell, *Führer befiehl... Selbstzeugnisse aus der "Kampfzeit" der NSDAP* (Düsseldorf: Droste Verlag, 1969), 145.
4. Werner Jochmann, *Im Kampf um die Macht: Hitlers Rede vor dem Hamburger Nationalklub von 1919* (Frankfurt-am-Main: Europäische Verlagsanstalt, 1960), 69–121; RSA, Band I, Dok. 103, pp. 297–330. Though Hitler's speech was before a closed meeting, the Nationalklub had commissioned a stenographer to take down his words. The original was destroyed during the Second World War, but copies were later recovered and verified.
5. Jochmann, *Im Kampf,* 61–62.
6. TBJG, April 13, 1926.

Chapter Eleven: Weimar Party Convention

1. TBJG, July 6, 1926.
2. Goebbels misidentified Senders as "Toni Sendler"—see TBJG, July 6, 1926; Hubert Reitterer, "Senders, Ernestine (Tini, Tiny)," in *Oesterreichisches Musiklexikon,* https://www.musiklexikon.ac.at/ml/musik_S/Senders_Ernestine.xml, accessed April 27, 2018; "Tini Senders Biography," IMDB, https://www.imdb.com/name/nm0784146/bio, accessed April 27, 2018; "Tini Senders 1874–1941," Cyranos, http://www.cyranos.ch/smsend-d.htm.

3. TBJG, July 6, 1926; Dietrich Orlow, *The Nazi Party 1919–1945: A Complete History* (Pittsburgh, PA: University of Pittsburgh Press, 1969–73), 52.
4. Erich Buhrow, "Tatsachenbericht der Reise von Danzig zum Weimarer Reichsparteitag 1926 von Erich W. Buhrow," NSDAP Hauptarchiv, Hoover Institution, reel 21.
5. Buhrow, "Tatsachenbericht."
6. RSA, Band II, Teil 1, Dok. 6, pp. 15–16.
7. RSA, Band II, Teil 1, Dok. 6, nn. 4–5, p. 16.
8. RSA, Band II, Teil 1, Dok. 7, pp. 17–25.
9. Walter Z. Laqueur, *Young Germany: A History of the German Youth Movement* (London: Routledge & Kegan Paul, 1962), 196–97.
10. The militia's full name was Reichsbanner Schwarz-Rot-Gold, or Reich Banner Black-Red-Gold, in honor of the German flag's colors during the Weimar Republic. While the Reichsbanner was originally founded by the Social Democratic Party, the Centre Party, and the German Democratic Party, it was overwhelmingly associated with the Social Democrats.
11. Sven Felix Kellerhoff, *Die NSDAP: Eine Partei und ihre Mitglieder* (Stuttgart: Klett-Cotta, 2017), 14.
12. "Nationalsozialistische Ausschreitungen," *Berliner Tageblatt*, July 5, 1926 (AA), 3.
13. Hitler denied that "Heil, Hitler!" was a direct copy of "Hail, Caesar!," asserting that the salutation derived from Martin Luther's 1521 trial at the Diet of Worms. See Gerhard L. Weinberg, ed., *Hitler's Table Talk 1941–1944: His Private Conversations* (New York: Enigma Books, 2008), 134.
14. RSA, Band II, Teil 1, n. 3, 17.
15. *Illustrierter Beobachter*, July 1926, 1.

Chapter Twelve: Conquering the World

1. Adolf Hitler, *Monologe im Führerhauptquartier 1941–1944: Die Aufzeichnungen Heinrich Heims*, ed. Werner Jochmann (Hamburg: Albrecht Knaus, 1980), 167.
2. TBJG, July 23–26, 1926.
3. Adolf Hitler, *Mein Kampf: Zwei Bände in einem Band, Ungekürzte Ausgabe*, 851st–855th printing (Munich: Zentralverlag der NSDAP, Franz Eher Nachfolger, 1943), 742.
4. Hitler, *Mein Kampf*, 152.
5. "German Territorial Losses, Treaty of Versailles, 1919," *Holocaust Encyclopedia*, US Holocaust Memorial Museum, https://encyclopedia.ushmm.org/content/en/map/german-territorial-losses-treaty-of-versailles-1919.
6. Eberhard Jäckel, *Hitlers Weltanschauung: Entwurf einer Herrschaft*, rev. ed. (Stuttgart: Deutsche Verlags-Anstalt, 1981), 42–43.
7. Hitler, *Mein Kampf*, 741.
8. There was nothing original about Hitler's thinking. As he did in almost all his bold and definitive statements, he was borrowing in this case without attribution from long-standing debates and writings. Even before the First World War, political discourse had been filled with assertions of Germany's need for more land. In 1906, jingoist writer Klaus Wagner claimed that "the great nation needs new territory... it must spread out over a foreign soil and must displace strangers with the power of the sword." Cited in Daniel Chauncey Brewer, *The Peril of the Republic: Are We Facing Revolution in the United States?* (New York: G. P. Putnam's Sons, 1922), 271 (https://play.google.com/books/reader?id=XW0qAAAAYAAJ&hl=en_US&pg=GBS.PP12). In 1912, Heinrich Class, founder of the pan-German movement, wrote that Germany needed "land for settlement of Germans, for

whom the Fatherland will have no more room one day because of overpopulation." See Heinrich Class [Daniel Frymann, pseud.], *Wenn ich der Kaiser wär: Politische Wahrheiten und Notwendigkeiten* (Leipzig, 1912), 5ff., accessed November 25, 2019, at http://germanhistorydocs.ghi-dc.org/pdf/eng/523_Shades%20of%20the%20Future_104.pdf. In 1926, just as Hitler was penning his second volume, writer Hans Grimm published a sensational 1,300-page novel entitled *Volk ohne Raum* (People Without Space), which sold more than one hundred thousand copies. Grimm's title phrase, "people without space," immediately entered the language as a popular trope. See Hans Grimm, *Volk ohne Raum* (Munich: A. Langen, 1926).

9. Ian Kershaw, *Hitler,* vol. 1, *1889–1936: Hubris* (New York: W. W. Norton, 1998), 289.
10. Hitler, *Mein Kampf,* 740.
11. Hitler, *Mein Kampf,* 742.
12. Hitler, *Mein Kampf,* 732.
13. Hitler, *Mein Kampf,* 772.
14. Kershaw, *Hitler,* 243.
15. Joachim Fest, *Hitler* (New York: Harcourt Brace Jovanovich, 1974), 252, 304 (facing photograph).

Chapter Thirteen: Falling in Love

1. Günter Peis, "Hitlers unbekannte Geliebte," *Der Stern,* July 13, 1959, 26ff.

Chapter Fourteen: Girding for Battle

1. Ernst Deuerlein, *Der Aufstieg der NSDAP in Augenzeugenberichten* (Munich: Deutscher Taschenbuch Verlag, 1989), 264–65.
2. Ian Kershaw, *Hitler,* vol. 1, *1889–1936: Hubris* (New York: W. W. Norton, 1998), 276.
3. Joachim Fest, *Hitler* (New York: Harcourt Brace Jovanovich, 1974), 243.
4. Deuerlein, *Der Aufstieg,* 264–65.
5. TBJG, July 30 and August 1, 1926.
6. Harry Graf Kessler, *Tagebücher, 1918–1937: Komplettausgabe* (Berlin: Insel Verlag, 1961; Prague: e-artnow, 2013), loc. 1378, Kindle.
7. TBJG, November 1, 1926.

Chapter Fifteen: Conquering Berlin

1. Joseph Goebbels, "Erkenntnis und Propaganda," *Signale der neuen Zeit. 25 ausgewählte Reden* (Munich: Zentralverlag der NSDAP, 1934), 28–52, at German Propaganda Archive, Calvin College, http://research.calvin.edu/german-propaganda-archive/goeb54.htm.
2. TBJG, November 11, 1926.
3. Ralf Georg Reuth, *Goebbels,* trans. Krishna Winston (New York: Harcourt Brace, 1993), 80.
4. Joseph Goebbels, "Gegen den Zerfall," Teil 2, *Kampf um Berlin* (Munich: Zentralverlag der NSDAP, Franz Eher Nachfolger, 1934), https://archive.org/details/Goebbels-Joseph-Kampf-um-Berlin/page/n0.
5. TBJG, January 12, 1927.
6. TBJG, November 15, 1926.
7. Bernhard Fulda, *Press and Politics in the Weimar Republic* (Oxford, UK: Oxford University Press, 2009), 17.
8. Reuth, *Goebbels,* 83–84.
9. TBJG, February 12, 1927.
10. "Der Terror der Nationalsozialisten," *Vossische Zeitung,* March 22, 1927 (MA), 5.

11. "Let's speak plainly," began the report. "Berlin is both 'red' and Jewish. Every political event and election prove it again and again. And it has to be this way because it is Jewish. The one complements the other: Marxism and the stock market were always brothers in arms. Aristotle said: 'The essence of all things is the number.' It's the same in Berlin: here people think only by the numbers." See Reinhold Muchow, "Spezialbericht über die Vorgänge auf dem Bahnhof Berlin-Lichterfelde-Ost am 20. März 1927," in Martin Broszat, "Die Anfänge der Berliner NSDAP 1926/27," *Vierteljahrshefte für Zeitgeschichte* 8, no. 1 (1960), 85–118.
12. TBJG, March 21, 1927.
13. Testimony of Goebbels on March 21, 1927, in Reuth, *Goebbels,* 85.
14. TBJG, March 23, 1927.
15. TBJG, March 22, 1927.
16. TBJG, March 24, 1927.
17. "Der 1. Mai in Berlin und im Reich," *Berliner Tageblatt,* May 2, 1927.
18. *Deutsche Allegemeine Zeitung,* May 2, 1927.
19. *Vorwärts,* May 2, 1927.
20. *Vossische Zeitung,* May 2, 1927, 3.
21. Reuth, *Goebbels,* 86.
22. "Völkischer Versammlungsterror: Blutige Ausschreitungen der Nationalsozialistischen-Rollkommandos: Ein Pfarrer und ein Redakteur schwer verletzt," *Vossische Zeitung,* May 5, 1927 (MA), 5.
23. TBJG, May 6, 1927.

Chapter Sixteen: Impending Catastrophe

1. Police report, Polizeidirektion München, in Ernst Deuerlein, *Der Aufstieg der NSDAP in Augenzeugenberichten* (Munich: Deutscher Taschenbuch Verlag, 1989), 269–75.
2. Henry Ashby Turner Jr., *German Big Business and the Rise of Hitler* (Oxford, UK: Oxford University Press, 1985), 51, 59, 95, 97.
3. Albert Speer, *Spandau: The Secret Diaries* (New York: Macmillan, 1976), 73.
4. Kirdorf's name was spelled with one *f.* TBJG, November 15, 1936.
5. Henry Ashby Turner Jr., "Emil Kirdorf and the Nazi Party," *Central European History* 1, no. 4 (December 1968), 324–44.
6. Excerpt from Kirdorf in Deuerlein, *Aufstieg,* 285–86.
7. Currency conversion by the CPI (Consumer Price Index) Inflation Calculator, at http://www.in2013dollars.com/us/inflation/1927?amount=23809, and from the Historical Dollar-to-Marks Currency Conversion Page, created by Harold Marcuse, professor of German history at the University of California, Santa Barbara: http://marcuse.faculty.history.ucsb.edu/projects/currency.htm#tables. There is debate over whether Kirdorf really made this contribution. The key evidence is Hitler's claim to Goebbels in 1936—see TBJG, November 15, 1936.
8. RSA, Band II, Teil 2, Dok. 174, pp. 501–9.

Chapter Seventeen: *The Attack*

1. Otto Strasser and Michael Stern, *Flight from Terror* (1943; repr., New York: AMS Press, 1981), 46.
2. TBJG, December 1, 1926.
3. TBJG, June 15, 1926.
4. Russel Lemmons, *Goebbels and Der Angriff* (Lexington: University Press of Kentucky, 1994), 24ff, in Peter Longerich, *Goebbels: A Biography* (New York: Random House, 2015), loc. 2252, Kindle.

5. Longerich, *Goebbels,* loc. 2271.
6. Joseph Goebbels, "Wir fordern," *Der Angriff,* July 25, 1927. Found in *Der Angriff, Aufsätze aus der Kampfzeit* (Munich: Zentralverlag der NSDAP, 1935), 18–19, accessed November 27, 2019, at German Propaganda Archive, Calvin University: https://research.calvin.edu/german-propaganda-archive/angrif05.htm.
7. RSA, Band III, Teil 1, Dok. 63, p. 346.
8. Bjoern Weigel, "Bernhard Weiss," in Wolfgang Benz, ed., *Handbuch des Antisemitismus: Judenfeindschaft in Geschichte und Gegenwart* (Munich: De Gruyter Saur, 2008–2015), 2:880–82.
9. Paul Grossman, "Bernhard Weiss: True Life Crime Fighter Done in by Gangsters," *criminal element,* January 12, 2012, at https://www.criminalelement.com/bernhard-weiss-true-life-crime-fighter-done-in-by-gangsters/.

Chapter Eighteen: Altering the Unalterable

1. Ernst Deuerlein, *Der Aufstieg der NSDAP in Augenzeugenberichten* (Munich: Deutscher Taschenbuch Verlag, 1989), 287ff.
2. RSA, Band II, Teil 2, Dok. 203, pp. 570–82.
3. "Das 25-Punkte-Programm des NSDAP (vom 24. Februar 1920)," at http://www.documentarchiv.de/wr/1920/nsdap-programm.html.
4. RSA, Band III, Teil 1, Dok. 50, pp. 236–40.

Chapter Nineteen: Rock Bottom

1. Peter D. Stachura, "Der kritische Wendepunkt? Die NSDAP und die Reichstagswahlen vom 20. Mai 1928," *Vierteljahrshefte für Zeitgeschichte* 26, no. 1 (1978), 81.
2. Stachura, "Der kritische Wendepunkt?," 79.
3. Auszug aus dem Lagebericht Berlin Nr. 128 vom 20.II.29, 156–57 (Excerpt from the Berlin Situation Report no. 128, of February 20, 1929, filed by Munich Police Department, May 23, 1929), Materialsammlung-RSA, Institut für Zeitgeschichte, Munich.
4. Stachura, "Der kritische Wendepunkt?," 81 (note citing BA, Akte NS 26/1524).
5. RSA, Band II, Teil 2, Dok. 250, p. 766.
6. RSA, Band II, Teil 2, Dok. 230, p. 660.
7. Milan Hauner, *Hitler: A Chronology of His Life and Time,* 2nd rev. ed. (London: Palgrave Macmillan, 2008), 60 (note citing *Völkischer Beobachter,* January 20, 1928).
8. Peter Jelavic, "Modernity, Civic Identity, and Metropolitan Entertainment: Vaudeville, Cabaret, and Revue in Berlin, 1900–1933," in *Berlin: Culture and Metropolis,* ed. Charles W. Haxthausen and Heidrun Suhr (Minneapolis: University of Minnesota Press, 1990), 108.
9. Benjamin Carter Hett, *The Death of Democracy: Hitler's Rise to Power and the Downfall of the Weimar Republic* (New York: Henry Holt, 2018), 80.
10. Otto Friedrich, *Before the Deluge: A Portrait of Berlin in the 1920s* (New York: Harper & Row, 1972), 11.
11. Christopher Isherwood, *Christopher and His Kind: 1929–1939* (New York: Farrar, Straus and Giroux, 2013), accessed at https://books.google.com/books?id=YX3WAAAAQBAJ&pg=PT34&dq=christopher+and+his+kind+cosy+corner&hl=en&sa=X&ved=0ahUKEwivu6fhuZPiAhVCJKwKHcBnCa0Q6AEIKDAA#v=onepage&q=christopher%20and%20his%20kind%20cosy%20corner&f=false
12. Mel Gordon, *Voluptuous Panic: The Erotic World of Weimar Berlin* (Los Angeles: Feral House, 2000), 93ff.
13. Gordon, *Voluptuous Panic,* v.

14. Alex De Jonge, *The Weimar Chronicle: Prelude to Hitler* (New York: New American Library, 1978), 175.
15. Count Harry Kessler, *Berlin in Lights: The Diaries of Count Harry Kessler (1918–1937)* (New York: Grove Press, 2000), 390.
16. Sebastian Haffner, *Defying Hitler: A Memoir,* trans. Oliver Pretzel (New York: Farrar, Straus and Giroux, 2000), 77.
17. Weather mentioned in "Les élections allemandes," *Le Petit Parisien,* May 21, 1928, 1.
18. "Frankreichs Urteil über die Wahlen," *Vossische Zeitung,* May 22, 1928 (MA), 3.
19. TBJG, May 21, 1928.
20. Stachura, "Der kritische Wendepunkt?" 81, citing *Der Angriff,* May 30, 1928.
21. Kurt G. W. Ludecke, *I Knew Hitler: The Story of a Nazi Who Escaped the Blood Purge* (London: Jarrolds Publishers, 1938), 129.
22. Ernst Deuerlein, *Der Aufstieg der NSDAP in Augenzeugenberichten* (Munich: Deutscher Taschenbuch Verlag, 1989), 294.
23. Adolf Hitler, *Mein Kampf: Zwei Bände in einem Band, Ungekürzte Ausgabe,* 851st–855th printing (Munich: Zentralverlag der NSDAP, Franz Eher Nachfolger, 1943), 544.

Part Two: Reset (1928–1929)

1. Theodore Abel, *Why Hitler Came into Power* (1938; repr., Cambridge, MA: Harvard University Press, 1986), 125.
2. Detlev J. K. Peukert, *Jugend Zwischen Krieg und Krise: Lebenswelten von Arbeiterjungen in der Weimarer Republik* (Cologne: Bund Verlag, 1987), 120.

Chapter Twenty: Hitler's Second Book

1. Kurt G. W. Ludecke, *I Knew Hitler: The Story of a Nazi Who Escaped the Blood Purge* (London: Jarrolds Publishers, 1938), loc. 9207, Kindle.
2. David Pietrusza, *1932: The Rise of Hitler and FDR; Two Tales of Politics, Betrayal, and Unlikely Destiny* (Guilford, CT: Lyons Press, 2015), 44.
3. Adolf Hitler, *Hitler's Second Book: The Unpublished Sequel to Mein Kampf,* ed. Gerhard L. Weinberg (New York: Enigma Books, 2003), xiv–xv, cited in Albert Speer, *Spandauer Tagebücher* (Frankfurt-am-Main: Ullstein Verlag, 1975), 533; Albert Speer, *Erinnerungen* (Berlin: Propyläen Verlag, 1969), 100; Gerhard L. Weinberg, "Hitler's Editor Tells All," *The Guardian,* https://www.theguardian.com/double-take/2016/dec/08/hitler-editor-gerhard-weinberg-second-book-manuscript.
4. Gerhard L. Weinberg, ed., *Hitler's Table Talk 1941–1944: His Private Conversations* (New York: Enigma Books, 2008), 557–59.
5. Adolf Hitler, *Hitlers Zweites Buch: Ein Dokument aus dem Jahr 1928,* ed. Gerhard L. Weinberg, Quellen und Darstellungen zur Zeitgeschichte (Sources and Representations of Contemporary History) 7 (Stuttgart: Deutsche Verlags-Anstalt, 1961), 26, 31, at https://ia902506.us.archive.org/18/items/HitlersZweitesBuch19281961/Hitlers-zweites-Buch-1928%261961.pdf.
6. Hitler, *Hitlers Zweites Buch.* The complete book is also printed in RSA, Band II A, under the title "Aussenpolitische Standortbestimmung nach der Reichstagswahl." It is available in English as Gerhard L. Weinberg, *Hitler's Second Book: The Unpublished Sequel to Mein Kampf,* trans. Krista Smith (New York: Enigma, 2003).

   Hitler's "second book" was long a mystery. Kept secret and hidden in a safe at Nazi Party headquarters, the book was not published in Hitler's lifetime. Its very existence was unknown in the postwar period. Only vague hints in Hitler's preserved conversations and in one secretary's memoirs led Munich's Institut für Zeitgeschichte (Institute for Contemporary History) to ask historian Gerhard L. Weinberg to search for such a document (RSA, Band II A, Einleitung, pp. xi–xxv). In 1958, Weinberg unearthed Hitler's unpublished manuscript among captured German documents stored in Alexandria, Virginia. The German-American scholar published it in 1961 in German as *Hitlers Zweites Buch* in cooperation with the Institut für Zeitgeschichte. An unauthorized English edition called *Hitler's Secret Book* soon followed, but it was considered a bowdlerized version of the original; one scholar derided it as a "burlesque imitation" and a poor translation (see Oron J. Hale, *Journal of Central European Affairs* 22 [1962], 240–42). Finally, in 2003, Weinberg published the highly regarded English edition entitled *Hitler's Second Book.*

Written in 1928, the "second book" was in fact the third volume of Hitler's long-running political manifesto, starting with the first volume of *Mein Kampf,* composed in prison in 1924. After 1930, *Mein Kampf*'s first two volumes were normally published as a single book, hence the label "second book" for the newly discovered manuscript.

7. RSA, Band I, p. xix; RSA, Band II A, pp. vi–212. The Immigration Act marked the high point of scientific racism in American eugenics, according to Jonathan Peter Spiro, in *Defending the Master Race: Conservation, Eugenics, and the Legacy of Madison Grant* (Burlington: University of Vermont Press, 2009), 328.
8. Hitler, *Hitler's Second Book,* 112.
9. Spiro, *Defending the Master Race,* 150.
10. Madison Grant, *The Passing of the Great Race, or The Racial Basis of European History* (New York: Charles Scribner's Sons, 1916), 109.
11. Grant, *The Passing,* 57; Madison Grant, *Der Untergang der grossen Rasse: die Rassen als Grundlage der Geschichte Europas* (Munich: J. F. Lehmann, 1925).
12. Sometimes Hitler referred to the "elementary" or "eternal" laws of nature. See Adolf Hitler, *Mein Kampf: Zwei Bände in einem Band, Ungekürzte Ausgabe,* 851st–855th printing (Munich: Zentralverlag der NSDAP, Franz Eher Nachfolger, 1943), 311, 316; RSA, Band I, Dok. 57, p. 130; and throughout the RSA under "Naturgesetz." See also Grant, *The Passing,* 18.
13. Stefan Kühl, *The Nazi Connection: Eugenics, American Racism, and German National Socialism* (New York: Oxford University Press, 1994), 85.
14. Hitler, *Hitler's Second Book,* xxv.
15. Hitler, *Hitler's Second Book,* 90.

Chapter Twenty-One: Taking Stock

1. Hitler in fact lived only seventeen more years. See the letter to Dr. Artur Dinter in Albrecht Tyrell, *Führer befiehl. . . Selbstzeugnisse aus der "Kampfzeit" der NSDAP* (Düsseldorf: Droste Verlag, 1969), 203–5; RSA, Band II, Teil 1, Dok. 4, p. 23.
2. RSA, Band III, Teil 1, Dok. 13, pp. 35–48.
3. Peter D. Stachura, *Gregor Strasser and the Rise of Nazism* (London: George Allen & Unwin, 1982), 64.
4. Stachura, *Gregor Strasser,* 68–69.
5. Ernst Deuerlein, *Der Aufstieg der NSDAP in Augenzeugenberichten* (Munich: Deutscher Taschenbuch Verlag, 1989), 293–94.
6. Stachura, *Gregor Strasser,* 69.
7. Tyrell, *Führer befiehl,* 255–57.
8. Adolf Hitler, *Mein Kampf: Zwei Bände in einem Band, Ungekürzte Ausgabe,* 851st–855th printing (Munich: Zentralverlag der NSDAP, Franz Eher Nachfolger, 1943), 544.
9. Peter Longerich, *Goebbels: A Biography* (New York: Random House, 2015), loc. 2636, Kindle.

10. TBJG, October 1, 1928.
11. TBJG, October 4, 1928.
12. "1928, Sportpalast: Hitlers erste elektroakustisch verstärkte Massenansprache," Medien stimmen.de, https://www.medienstimmen.de/chronik/1926-1930/1928-sportpalast-hitlers-erste-elektroakustisch-verstaerkte-massenansprache/.
13. RSA, Band III, Teil 1, Dok. 50, pp. 236–40.
14. Ian Kershaw, *Hitler*, vol. 1, *1889–1936: Hubris* (New York: W. W. Norton, 1998), 304.
15. TBJG, November 17, 1928.
16. Rudolf Hess, *Briefe: 1908–1933* (Munich: Albert Langen / Georg Müller Verlag, 1987), 394–96.
17. Deuerlein, *Der Aufstieg*, 296.

Chapter Twenty-Two: 1929

1. RSA, Band III, Teil 2, Dok. 3, p. 25; translation from Gordon W. Prange, ed., *Hitler's Words* (Washington, DC: American Council on Public Affairs, 1944), 1, in Milan Hauner, *Hitler: A Chronology of His Life and Time*, 2nd rev. ed. (London: Palgrave Macmillan, 2008), 63.
2. RSA, Band III, Teil 2, Dok. 6, pp. 45–71.
3. "Der Jude und das deutsche Weib," *Illustrierter Beobachter* 2, no. 4 (February 28, 1927), 44.
4. Thomas Wiles Arafe Jr., *The Development and Character of the Nazi Political Machine, 1928–1930, and the NSDAP Electoral Breakthrough* (dissertation, Louisiana State University, 1976), 189–93, http://digitalcommons.lsu.edu/cgi/viewcontent.cgi?article=3908&context=gradschool_disstheses.
5. Arafe, *The Development and Character*, 4.
6. Ian Kershaw, *Hitler*, vol. 1, *1889–1936: Hubris* (New York: W. W. Norton, 1998), 308.
7. RSA, Band III, Teil 2, Dok. 58, p. 310.
8. TBJG, May 2, 1929.
9. Christopher Isherwood, *The Berlin Stories* (New York: New Directions, 1945), xii.
10. Alex De Jonge, *The Weimar Chronicle: Prelude to Hitler* (New York: New American Library, 1978), 125.
11. *Ums täglich Brot—Hunger in Waldenburg* (later released in English as *The Shadow of a Mine*), https://www.youtube.com/watch?v=y-pHGVBo-XQ.

Chapter Twenty-Three: Alfred Hugenberg

1. Woodruff D. Smith, *The Ideological Origins of Nazi Imperialism* (New York: Oxford University Press, 1989), 184.
2. Milan Hauner, *Hitler: A Chronology of His Life and Time*, 2nd rev. ed. (London: Palgrave Macmillan, 2008), 64–65.
3. RSA, Band III, Teil 2, Dok. 88, p. 411.
4. Anna von der Goltz, *Hindenburg: Power, Myth, and the Rise of the Nazis* (Oxford, UK: Oxford University Press, 2009), 140.

Chapter Twenty-Four: Conquering Nuremberg

1. RSA, Band III, Teil 2, Dok. 61, p. 334.
2. Hans Christian Täubrich, "Reichsparteitage der NSDAP, 1923–1938," Historisches Lexikon Bayerns, https://www.historisches-lexikon-bayerns.de/Lexikon/Reichsparteitage_der_NSDAP,_1923-1938. This is a useful web-based resource maintained by the Bavarian State Library.

3. See the documentary film *Der Nürnberger Parteitag der Nationalsozialistischen Deutschen Arbeiterpartei, 1.–4. August 1929*. The film can be viewed at http://www.archiv-akh.de/filme/1291#1.
4. RSA, Band III, Teil 3, Dok. 92, n. 23, p. 363.
5. Sefton Delmer, *Trail Sinister: An Autobiography, Volume One* (London: Secker & Warburg, 1961), 143.
6. TBJG, August 3, 1929; TBJG, August 5, 1929.
7. TBJG, August 2, 1929.
8. TBJG, August 3, 1929.
9. Nazi Party memorandum, March 1, 1929; "Richtlinien," RSA, Band III, Teil 2, Dok. 60, pp. 313ff.
10. The film was entitled *Der Nürnberger Parteitag*.
11. TBJG, August 3, 1929.
12. "Hold Hitlerites Guilty," *New York Times*, August 25, 1929.
13. *Fränkische Tagespost*, August 5, 1929, in RSA, Band III, Teil 2, Dok. 65, n. 3, p. 355.
14. RSA, Band III, Teil 2, Dok. 65, pp. 354–55.
15. "Hold Hitlerites Guilty."
16. *Vossische Zeitung*, August 6, 1929 (AA).

Chapter Twenty-Five: Cataclysm

1. Louis P. Lochner, *Always the Unexpected: A Book of Reminiscences* (New York: Macmillan, 1956), 129, 135–36.
2. Edgar Ansel Mowrer, *Triumph and Turmoil: A Personal History of Our Time* (New York: Weybright and Talley, 1968), 68.
3. Mowrer, *Triumph and Turmoil*, 168.
4. Lochner, *Always the Unexpected*, 201.

Part Three: Turning Point (1930–1931)

1. Theodore Abel, *Why Hitler Came into Power* (1938; repr., Cambridge, MA: Harvard University Press, 1986), 126–27.
2. Abel, *Why Hitler Came into Power*.

Chapter Twenty-Six: Fondness for Fighting

1. A copy of the letter was shared with a researcher on the condition that the overseas German's name be withheld from publication. See Fritz Dickmann, "Die Regierungsbildung in Thüringen als Modell der Machtergreifung: Ein Brief Hitlers aus dem Jahre 1930," *Vierteljahrshefte für Zeitgeschichte* 14, no. 4 (1966), 454–64; RSA, Band III, Teil 3, Dok. 11, pp. 59–64.
2. Ernst Deuerlein, *Der Aufstieg der NSDAP in Augenzeugenberichten* (Munich: Deutscher Taschenbuch Verlag, 1989), 305–6.
3. The two economic crises are linked in Karl Dietrich Bracher, *The German Dictatorship: The Origins, Structure, and Consequences of National Socialism* (New York: Praeger, 1970), 16.
4. Dickmann, "Die Regierungsbildung," 456.
5. RSA, Band III, Teil 3, p. 60.
6. RSA, Band III, Teil 3, Dok. 11, pp. 61–62; Dickmann, "Die Regierungsbildung," 454–65.
7. TBJG, April 4, 1930.
8. *Völkischer Beobachter*, April 29, 1930, in Albrecht Tyrell, *Führer befiehl... Selbstzeugnisse aus der "Kampfzeit" der NSDAP* (Düsseldorf: Droste Verlag, 1969), 331–32.

9. Otto Strasser, *Hitler and I* (Boston: Houghton Mifflin, 1940), 94ff.
10. Reverend Bernard Strasser, "Gregor and Otto Strasser: A Footnote to the History of Nazi Germany," typescript, August 27, 1974, Hoover Institution Archives, Stanford University, 8–9.
11. TBJG, May 22, 1930.

Chapter Twenty-Seven: A Black Day

1. "Allgemeine Wetterlage," *Vossische Zeitung*, March 26, 1930, 11.
2. *Frankfurter Zeitung*, March 28, 1930, in Heinrich August Winkler, *Weimar 1918–1933: Die Geschichte der ersten deutschen Demokratie* (Munich: C. H. Beck, 2018), 372.
3. TBJG, January 24, 1932; Philip Metcalfe, *1933* (New York: Permanent Press, 1988), loc. 1223, Kindle.
4. Louis P. Lochner, *Always the Unexpected: A Book of Reminiscences* (New York: Macmillan, 1956), 202; Bernard V. Burke, *Ambassador Frederic Sackett and the Collapse of the Weimar Republic, 1930–1933: The United States and Hitler's Rise to Power* (New York: Cambridge University Press, 1994), 53–55.
5. Hans Mommsen, *Aufstieg und Untergang der Republik von Weimar 1918–1933* (Berlin: Ullstein Verlag, 1989), 645–49.
6. Adolf Hitler, *Hitler, Mein Kampf: Eine kritische Edition*, ed. Christian Hartmann, Thomas Vordermayer, Othmar Plöckinger, and Roman Töppel (Munich: Institut für Zeitgeschichte, 2016), 18.
7. By 1945, *Mein Kampf* would go through more than eleven hundred printings, be translated into eighteen languages, and sell more than twelve million copies. The book made Hitler a rich man and underpinned the fortunes of the Franz Eher Nachfolger publishing house, run by Max Amann.
8. For "civil servants and salaried employees," see Volker Ullrich, *Hitler: Ascent 1889–1939* (New York: Alfred A. Knopf, 2016), loc. 5287, Kindle; James K. Pollock Jr., "The German Reichstag Elections of 1930," *American Political Science Review* 24, no. 4 (November 1930), 989–95.
9. TBJG, July 18, 1930.
10. TBJG, July 18, 1930.
11. David Clay Large, *Berlin* (New York: Basic Books, 2000), 235–37.

Chapter Twenty-Eight: Two Months That Changed the World

1. "Ten Commandments of the Storm Troopers," attributed to Stuttgart Sturmführer Max Bücherl, in appendix C of Thomas Wiles Arafe Jr., *The Development and Character of the Nazi Political Machine, 1928–1930, and the NSDAP Electoral Breakthrough* (dissertation, Louisiana State University, 1976), 293, http://digitalcommons.lsu.edu/cgi/viewcontent.cgi?article=3908&context=gradschool_disstheses, citing HA reel 58, folder 1401 (1928), "Berichte der Staatspolizei Württemberg zur politischen Lage, Aus der NSDAP" (Württemberg state police reports on the political situation, from the National Socialist German Workers' Party), *Geheim*, December 12, 1928.
2. Adolf Hitler, "An der Wende des deutschen Schicksals," *Illustrierter Beobachter*, August 2, 1930, RSA, III, 3, Dok. 80, p. 293ff.
3. Emphasis in original transcript. RSA, III, 3, Dok. 76, p. 280.
4. This typology is well presented in Benjamin Carter Hett, *The Death of Democracy: Hitler's Rise to Power and the Downfall of the Weimar Republic* (New York: Henry Holt, 2018), xvii–xix, 67–68.
5. RSA, Band III, Teil 3, Dok. 76, p. 275ff.

6. "Wahlparole," *Vossische Zeitung,* July 18, 1930 (AA), 1.
7. Daniel Mühlenfeld, "'Wie ich National-Sozialist wurde': Biographische Selbstzeugnisse Mülheimer Nationalsozialisten in der Theodore-Abel-Collection," *Mülheimer Jahrbuch* 74 (2019), 266–80.
8. William Sheridan Allen, *The Nazi Seizure of Power: The Experience of a Single German Town 1922–1945,* rev. ed. (1965; repr., New York and London: Franklin Watts, 1984), 32.
9. Karl Dietrich Bracher, *The German Dictatorship: The Origins, Structure, and Consequences of National Socialism* (New York: Praeger, 1970), 150, cited in Arafe, *The Development and Character,* 262.
10. Thomas Childers, "Nazis," *Washington Post,* October 22, 2017, B3.
11. Theodore Abel, *Why Hitler Came into Power* (1938; repr., Cambridge, MA: Harvard University Press, 1986), 175–76.
12. Turlach O Broin, "Mail-Order Demagogues: The NSDAP School for Speakers, 1928–34," *Journal of Contemporary History* 51, no. 4 (2016), 724.
13. O Broin, "Mail-Order Demagogues," 715–737.
14. "Since the beginning of time, the power that unleashed the great political and religious avalanches has been the magical force of the spoken word," he wrote. See Adolf Hitler, *Mein Kampf: Zwei Bände in einem Band, Ungekürzte Ausgabe,* 851st–855th printing (Munich: Zentralverlag der NSDAP, Franz Eher Nachfolger, 1943), 116.
15. O Broin, "Mail-Order Demagogues," 715–37.
16. Adolf Hitler, "My Terms to the World," *Sunday Express,* September 28, 1930.
17. Prop[aganda] Rundschreiben Nr. 16 of Gau Gross-Berlin, NSDAP Hauptarchiv, August 5, 1930, reel 70, folder 1529.
18. Hett, *The Death of Democracy,* illustrations, 138–39.
19. German Propaganda Archive, Calvin College, http://www.bytwerk.com/gpa/posters/snake1.jpg.
20. Arafe, *The Development and Character,* 159, note citing Hitler, *Mein Kampf,* 180.
21. Only around three million radios were then licensed in a nation of sixty-two million.
22. Arafe, *The Development and Character,* 145–46, note citing *Völkischer Beobachter,* August 29, 1930, 3.
23. Arafe, *The Development and Character,* 163.
24. Childers, "Nazis."
25. Z. A. B. Zeman, *Nazi Propaganda* (New York: Oxford University Press, 1964), 18, cited in Arafe, *The Development and Character,* 201.
26. Walter Z. Laqueur, *Young Germany: History of the German Youth Movement* (New York: Basic Books, 1962), chapter 19.
27. Mühlenfeld, "'Wie ich National-Sozialist wurde,'" 271–74.
28. Arafe, *The Development and Character,* appendix C, 293, note citing HA reel 58, folder 1401 (1928), "Berichte der Staatspolizei Württemberg zur politischen Lage, Aus der NSDAP; Geheim, 12.12.28" (Württemberg State Police Reports on the National Socialist German Workers' Party, *Secret,* December 12, 1928).
29. *Mein Arbeitstag, Mein Wochenende: 150 Berichte von Textilarbeiterinnen,* ed. Deutscher Textilarbeiterverband (Berlin: Textilpraxis Verlag, 1930), 187–89, in Anton Kaes, Martin Jay, and Edward Dimendberg, eds., *The Weimar Republic Sourcebook* (Berkeley: University of California Press, 1994), 208–10.
30. Abel, *Why Hitler Came into Power,* 142.
31. Gustav Heinsch, "Lebenslauf!," Theodore Fred Abel papers, Hoover Institution, https://digitalcollections.hoover.org/objects/58336; Abel, *Why Hitler Came into Power,* 242.

32. Arafe, *The Development and Character*, 173–74.
33. Detlef Mühlberger, *The Social Bases of Nazism 1919–1933*, New Studies in Economic and Social History 48 (Cambridge, UK: Cambridge University Press, 2003), 5.
34. Arafe, *The Development and Character*, 178.
35. Arafe, *The Development and Character*, 179.
36. "German Election (1920–1930)," British Pathé, April 13, 2014, https://www.youtube.com/watch?v=lw7qJmaSXc0.

Chapter Twenty-Nine: Hitler on the Hustings

1. Rudolf Hess, *Briefe: 1908–1933* (Munich: Albert Langen / Georg Müller Verlag, 1987), 406.
2. RSA, Band III, Teil 3, pp. 275–14; Guido Enderis, "Fascists Make Big Gains in Germany, Communists Also Increase Strength as Moderates Drop in Reich Election," *New York Times*, September 15, 1930, 1.
3. *Das Höchste Kreisblatt*, RSA, III, 3, Dok. 81, n. 1, p. 295.
4. Speech in Frankfurt, August 3, 1930, RSA, III, 3, Dok. 81, pp. 295ff.
5. *Vossische Zeitung*, August 4, 1930.
6. Speech in Cologne, August 18, 1930, RSA, III, 3, Dok. 90, pp. 342ff.
7. Edgar Ansel Mowrer, *Triumph and Turmoil: A Personal History of Our Time* (New York: Weybright and Talley, 1968), 208.
8. Speech in Munich, August 12, 1930, RSA, III, 3, Dok. 87, pp. 323ff.
9. *Essener Anzeiger*, August 16, 1930, in RSA, III, 3, Dok. 88, n. 2, p. 336.
10. *Vossische Zeitung*, August 16, 1930.
11. *Vossische Zeitung*, August 12, 1930.
12. TBJG, August 24, 1930.
13. Peter Longerich, *Goebbels: A Biography* (New York: Random House, 2015), loc. 3362, Kindle; TBJG, September 1, 1930.
14. Ian Kershaw, *Hitler*, vol. 1, *1889–1936: Hubris* (New York: W. W. Norton, 1998), 347–48.
15. RSA, Band III, Teil 3, Dok. 100, pp. 378ff.
16. Kershaw, *Hitler*, 346–47.
17. TBJG, September 1, 1930.

Chapter Thirty: Turning Point

1. Speech in Berlin, September 10, 1930, RSA, Band III, Teil 3, Dok. 110, pp. 408ff.
2. TBJG, September 11, 1930.
3. Richard J. Evans, *The Coming of the Third Reich* (London: Allen Lane, 2003), 269–70.
4. Sefton Delmer, *Trail Sinister: An Autobiography, Volume One* (London: Secker & Warburg, 1961), 90.
5. Guido Enderis, "Fascists Make Big Gains in Germany, Communists Also Increase Strength as Moderates Drop in Reich Election," *New York Times*, September 15, 1930, 1–2.
6. TBJG, September 14, 1930.
7. Guido Enderis, "Moderate Coalition Looked for in Reich," *New York Times*, September 12, 1930, 1.
8. Ernst Deuerlein, *Der Aufstieg der NSDAP in Augenzeugenberichten* (Munich: Deutscher Taschenbuch Verlag, 1989), 313.
9. Bernd Sösemann, ed., *Theodor Wolff: Der Journalist. Berichte und Leitartikel* (Düsseldorf, n.p., 1993), 273 (dated September 14, 1930), cited in Volker Ullrich, *Hitler: Ascent 1889–1939* (New York: Alfred A. Knopf, 2016), loc. 20264, Kindle.

10. "L'Allemagne votera aujourd'hui avec plus de passion que d'habitude," *Le Petit Parisien,* September 14, 1930, 1.
11. Henry de Korab, "L'Allemagne a élu hier le Reichstag," *Le Matin,* September 15, 1930, 1.
12. Adolf Hitler, *Monologe im Führerhauptquartier 1941–1944: Die Aufzeichnungen Heinrich Heims,* ed. Werner Jochmann (Hamburg: Albrecht Knaus, 1980), 170.
13. TBJG, September 16, 1930.
14. "1930 German Federal Election," *Wikipedia,* https://en.wikipedia.org/wiki/German_federal_election,_1930.
15. Ullrich, *Hitler,* loc. 5373, Kindle, cited in Jürgen W. Falter, *Hitlers Wähler* (Munich: C. H. Beck, 1991), 98ff, 366ff.
16. William Sheridan Allen, *The Nazi Seizure of Power: The Experience of a Single German Town 1922–1945,* rev. ed. (1965; repr., New York and London: Franklin Watts, 1984), 86.
17. Allen, *The Nazi Seizure of Power,* 84–85.
18. Allen, *The Nazi Seizure of Power,* 78.
19. Joseph V. Fuller, ed., "Papers Relating to the Foreign Relations of the United States, 1930, Volume III" (Washington, DC: Government Printing Office, 1945), document 49.
20. Karl Dietrich Bracher, *Die Auflösung der Weimarer Republik: Eine Studie zum Problem des Machtverfalls in der Demokratie,* Schriften des Instituts für politische Wissenschaft 4 (Stuttgart and Düsseldorf: Ring Verlag, 1955), 425n70.
21. Count Harry Kessler, *Berlin in Lights: The Diaries of Count Harry Kessler (1918–1937)* (New York: Grove Press, 2000), 396.
22. Deuerlein, *Der Aufstieg,* 318–19.
23. Ullrich, *Hitler,* note citing Carl von Ossietzky, *Sämtliche Schriften* (Reinbek, Germany: Rohwolt, 1994), 5:447, 453, 455.
24. Ullrich, *Hitler,* loc. 5391, Kindle, note citing Victor Klemperer, *Leben sammeln, nicht fragen wozu und warum: Tagebücher 1925–1932,* ed. Walter Nowojski (Berlin: Aufbau Verlag, 1996), 659.
25. Ernst Toller, "Reichskanzler Hitler," *Die Weltbühne,* October 7, 1930, in Ullrich, *Hitler,* loc. 5545, Kindle.
26. Falter, *Hitlers Wähler;* Thomas Childers, "Who, Indeed, Did Vote for Hitler?," *Central European History* 17, no. 1 (March 1984), 45–53.
27. Thomas Childers, "Foreword, 1986," in Theodore Abel, *Why Hitler Came into Power* (1938; repr., Cambridge, MA: Harvard University Press, 1986), xiii–xx.
28. Columbia University sociologist Theodore Abel's 1934 study is a unique primary source. With Nazi Party cooperation, he was able to solicit 683 personal histories from rank-and-file party members about their reasons for joining the movement before Hitler took power in 1933. To stimulate participation, Abel structured his research as an essay contest, offering cash prizes for "the most detailed and trustworthy accounts." Despite the inherent weakness of the method—the participants were all committed Nazis and knew their essays might be read by party officials—the Abel collection is a rare touchstone of the sentiments of early Nazi Party supporters. The 581 surviving original essays—typed or handwritten—are archived at the Hoover Institution at Stanford University as part of the Theodore Abel papers. The essays are accessible online at https://oac.cdlib.org/view?docId=tf3489n5vz;developer=local;style=oac4;doc.view=items. Fortunately for researchers, the first printed compendium of the essays appeared in 2018: Wieland Giebel, *Warum ich Nazi wurde: Biogramme früher Nationalsozialisten* (Berlin: Berlin Story Verlag, 2018). See Abel, *Why Hitler Came into Power.* Detailed and revealing analysis of Abel's data is in Peter H. Merkl, *Political Violence Under the Swastika: 581 Early Nazis* (Princeton, NJ: Princeton University Press,

1975), 32–33. Cf. Ian Kershaw, *Hitler,* vol. 1, *1889–1936: Hubris* (New York: W. W. Norton, 1998), 332ff.

29. Gustav Heinsch personal history, Theodore Abel Papers, Hoover Institution Library and Archives, https://digitalcollections.hoover.org/objects/58336/span-classqueryhlgustavspan-span-classqueryhlhe?ctx=de92f43f-9927-4e24-ae34-e820cd8cc8fd&idx=0.
30. Abel, *Why Hitler Came into Power,* 212.
31. Abel, *Why Hitler Came into Power,* 139.
32. Hermann Jung, personal history, in Theodore Abel papers, Nazi Biograms, Hoover Institution Library and Archives.
33. Merkl, *Political Violence,* 668.
34. Enderis, "Fascists Make Big Gains."
35. "Hitler et son parti l'emportent," *Le Figaro,* September 15, 1930.
36. Guido Enderis, "Moderates Shape Coalition to Hold Power in Germany," *New York Times,* September 16, 1930, 1.
37. "Le 'Graf Zeppelin' à Genève," *Le Petit Parisien,* September 15, 1930, 3.
38. Some historians have attributed the failure of Germany's first effort at democracy to the "lack of synchronization between the economic, social, and political spheres." See David Blackbourn and Geoff Eley, *The Peculiarities of German History: Bourgeois Society and Politics in Nineteenth-Century Germany* (Oxford, UK: Oxford University Press, 1984), 7. Cf. Ralf Dahrendorf, *Society and Democracy in Germany* (New York: Doubleday, 1967).
39. Deuerlein, *Der Aufstieg,* 318–20.
40. Deuerlein, *Der Aufstieg,* 322–23. Partly translated from German back into English. Full original unavailable.
41. "Hitler's Special Talk to *The Daily Mail,*" *Daily Mail,* September 27, 1930.
42. Viscount Rothermere, "My Hitler Article and Its Critics," *Daily Mail,* October 2, 1930.
43. Adolf Hitler, "My Terms to the World," *Sunday Express,* September 28, 1930.
44. *Jüdisch-liberale Zeitung,* September 17, 1930, http://sammlungen.ub.uni-frankfurt.de/cm/periodical/pageview/2621338.
45. Ullrich, *Hitler,* loc. 5391, Kindle, cited in Thea Sternheim, *Tagebücher 1903–1971,* ed. Thomas Ehrsam and Regula Wyss, vol. 2, *1925–1936* (Göttingen: Wallstein Verlag, 2002), 296 (entry for September 15, 1930), 298 (entry for September 20, 1930).
46. Bella Fromm, *Blood and Banquets: A Berlin Social Diary* (New York: Birch Lane Press, 1990), 98.
47. Fromm, *Blood and Banquets,* 27.
48. Kershaw, *Hitler,* 335.
49. Jewish Telegraph Agency, *New York Times,* September 19, 1930, 9.

Chapter Thirty-One: Hearts and Minds

1. RSA, Band III, Teil 3, Dok. 116, pp. 420ff.
2. Ernst Deuerlein, *Der Aufstieg der NSDAP in Augenzeugenberichten* (Munich: Deutscher Taschenbuch Verlag, 1989), 340–41.
3. Henry Ashby Turner Jr., *German Big Business and the Rise of Hitler* (Oxford, UK: Oxford University Press, 1985), 130.
4. Rudolf Hess, *Briefe: 1908–1933* (Munich: Albert Langen / Georg Müller Verlag, 1987), 405.
5. Various newspapers. For appearance of the court building, see "Reichsgericht," *Wikipedia,* at https://en.wikipedia.org/wiki/Reichsgericht.

6. Hans Frank, *Im Angesicht des Galgens: Deutung Hitlers und seiner Zeit auf Grund eigener Erlebnisse und Erkenntnisse* (Munich: Friedrich Alfred Beck Verlag, 1953), 83.
7. "Zeugenaussage vor dem IV. Strafsenat des Reichsgerichts in Leipzig," RSA, Band III, Teil 3, Dok. 123, pp. 434–51.
8. Deuerlein, *Der Aufstieg,* 339; Anthony Read, *The Devil's Disciples: Hitler's Inner Circle* (New York: W. W. Norton, 2003), 202–3.
9. Guido Enderis, "Hitler Would Scrap Versailles Treaty and Use Guillotine," *New York Times,* September 26, 1930; RSA, Band III, Teil 3, Dok. 123, pp. 441–42.
10. Volker Ullrich, *Hitler: Ascent 1889–1939* (New York: Alfred A. Knopf, 2016), loc. 27043, Kindle.
11. Carl von Ossietzky, "Der Prozess der Offiziere," *Die Weltbühne,* October 1, 1930, 501.
12. "Hitler Hysterics Cause Slump," *Daily Herald* (London), September 26, 1930, 1.
13. Enderis, "Hitler Would Scrap Versailles."
14. TBJG, September 26, 1930.
15. Deuerlein, *Der Aufstieg,* 342.
16. Heinrich August Winkler, *Weimar 1918–1933: Die Geschichte der ersten deutschen Demokratie* (Munich: C. H. Beck, 2018), 393.
17. Ian Kershaw, *Hitler,* vol. 1, *1889–1936: Hubris* (New York: W. W. Norton, 1998), 339, note citing Heinrich Brüning, *Memoiren 1918–1934* (Munich: Deutsche Verlags-Anstalt, 1970), 1:207.
18. "Conquest of Russia One Aim of Hitler," *New York Times,* September 29, 1930.
19. Bernard V. Burke, *Ambassador Frederic Sackett and the Collapse of the Weimar Republic, 1930–1933: The United States and Hitler's Rise to Power* (New York: Cambridge University Press, 1994), 91–92.
20. Deuerlein, *Der Aufstieg,* 342–43.
21. "Der erste Tag," *Vossische Zeitung,* October 14, 1931 (MA), 2.
22. Alexander von Stenbock, "Menschen vor zerbrochenen Scheiben," *Vossische Zeitung,* October 14, 1930 (AA).
23. *Le Matin,* October 14, 1930, 1.
24. "Hitlerites in Riots, Stone Jewish Shops as Reichstag Opens," *New York Times,* October 14, 1930, 1.
25. Harry Graf Kessler, *Tagebücher, 1918–1937: Komplettausgabe* (Berlin: Insel Verlag, 1961; Prague: e-artnow, 2013), loc. 10013, Kindle (entry for October 13, 1930).
26. Harald Sandner, *Hitler: Das Itinerar; Aufenthaltsorte und Reisen von 1889 bis 1945* (Berlin: Berlin Story Verlag, 2016), 792.
27. Interview with International News Service, RSA, Band IV, Teil 1, Dok. 7, p. 19.
28. Deuerlein, *Der Aufstieg,* 323.
29. TBJG, October 18, 1930.
30. Manfred Görtemaker, *Thomas Mann und die Politik* (Frankfurt: Fischer Verlag, 2005), 61.
31. Dietrich Orlow, *The Nazi Party 1919–1945: A Complete History* (Pittsburgh, PA: University of Pittsburgh Press, 1969–73), 188–89.
32. Deuerlein, *Der Aufstieg,* 345, 366.
33. Richard J. Evans, *The Coming of the Third Reich* (London: Allen Lane, 2003), illustration 17.
34. *Vossische Zeitung,* December 5, 1930.
35. "Mit Stinkbomben und weissen Mäusen," *Berliner Volks-Zeitung,* December 6, 1930 (MA).
36. David Clay Large, *Berlin* (New York: Basic Books, 2000), 239, citing Leni Riefenstahl, *A Memoir* (New York: Picador, 1995), 62.
37. TBJG, December 9, 1930.

Chapter Thirty-Two: Waiting for Hitler

1. TBJG, March 6, 1931.
2. Hjalmar Schacht, *My First Seventy-Six Years* (London: Allan Wingate, 1955), 279.
3. Schacht, *My First,* 280.
4. Hans Hubert Hofmann, *Der Hitlerputsch: Krisenjahre deutscher Geschichte 1920–1924* (Munich: Nymphenburger Verlagshandlung, 1961), 284ff.
5. *Vossische Zeitung,* February 10, 1931 (MA).
6. David Pietrusza, *1932: The Rise of Hitler and FDR; Two Tales of Politics, Betrayal, and Unlikely Destiny* (Guilford, CT: Lyons Press, 2015), 73.
7. *Vossische Zeitung,* March 28, 1931 (AA).
8. *Vossische Zeitung,* March 28, 1931 (AA).
9. *Vossische Zeitung,* March 28, 1931, (AA), 3.
10. Peter Longerich, *Goebbels: A Biography* (New York: Random House, 2015), loc. 3564, Kindle.
11. TBJG, March 26, 1931.
12. TBJG, March 29, 1931.
13. Italics in original. RSA, Band IV, Teil 1, Dok. 61, pp. 206ff.
14. Volker Ullrich, *Hitler: Ascent 1889–1939* (New York: Alfred A. Knopf, 2016), loc. 5676, Kindle, citing Peter Longerich, *Die braunen Bataillone* (Munich: C. H. Beck, 1989), 81ff, 115ff.
15. RSA, Band IV, Teil 1, Dok. 59, p. 200.
16. RSA, Band IV, Teil 1, Dok. 68, pp. 229–30.
17. RSA, Band IV, Teil 1, Dok. 68, pp. 229–30.

Chapter Thirty-Three: Open Revolt

1. Ian Kershaw, *Hitler,* vol. 1, *1889–1936: Hubris* (New York: W. W. Norton, 1998), 349.
2. TBJG, April 2, 1931.
3. Kershaw, *Hitler,* 142; Adolf Hitler, *Mein Kampf: Zwei Bände in einem Band, Ungekürzte Ausgabe,* 851st–855th printing (Munich: Zentralverlag der NSDAP, Franz Eher Nachfolger, 1943), 658ff.
4. "Führerkrise im Hitler-Lager" and "Wer nicht pariert," *Vossische Zeitung,* April 2, 1931 (MA), 1.
5. "Nationalsozialisten Berlins!," in "Germany—NSDAP—Gauleitung Berlin. Files of the Stennes Case (1931)," Hoover Institution Archive, box 2.
6. "S.A. Kameraden!," in "Germany—NSDAP—Gauleitung Berlin. Files of the Stennes Case (1931)," Hoover Institution Archive, box 2.
7. "Rebels Break Away from Hitler Ranks," *New York Times,* April 3, 1931.
8. TBJG, April 2, 1931.
9. TBJG, April 4, 1931.
10. RSA, Band IV, Teil 1, Dok. 79, pp. 246ff.
11. RSA, Band IV, Teil 1, Dok. 80, pp. 248ff.
12. RSA, Band IV, Teil 1, Dok. 93, p. 291.
13. Kershaw, *Hitler,* 350, note citing Peter Longerich, *Die braunen Bataillone* (Munich: C. H. Beck, 1989), 111.
14. Walter Galenson and Arnold Zellner, "International Comparison of Unemployment Rates," in *The Measurement and Behavior of Unemployment* (Cambridge, MA: National Bureau of Economic Research, 1957), 455.
15. "Reich Dictatorship Urged as Brüning Leaves for London," *New York Times,* June 4, 1931, 1.

16. David Pietrusza, *1932: The Rise of Hitler and FDR; Two Tales of Politics, Betrayal, and Unlikely Destiny* (Guilford, CT: Lyons Press, 2015), 74.
17. Louis P. Lochner, *Always the Unexpected: A Book of Reminiscences* (New York: Macmillan, 1956), 179.
18. "13. Juli 1931—Deutschland erlebt die erste Banken-Krise," WDR, https://www1.wdr.de/stichtag/stichtag5686.html, accessed January 2, 2018; Paul Bruppacher, *Adolf Hitler und die Geschichte der NSDAP Teil 1: 1889 bis 1937* (Norderstedt, Germany: Books on Demand, 2014), 242.
19. Harold James, "The Causes of the German Banking Crisis of 1931," *Economic History Review* 37, no. 1 (1984), 68–87; Fabian Lindner, "In Today's Debt Crisis, Germany Is the US of 1931," *The Guardian*, November 24, 2011.
20. Sefton Delmer, *Trail Sinister: An Autobiography, Volume One* (London: Secker & Warburg, 1961), 128.
21. Eugene Davidson, *The Making of Adolf Hitler: The Birth and Rise of Nazism* (New York: Macmillan, 1977), photographs 314–15.
22. Theodore Abel, *Why Hitler Came into Power* (1938; repr., Cambridge, MA: Harvard University Press, 1986), 218.
23. Volker Ullrich, *Hitler: Ascent 1889–1939* (New York: Alfred A. Knopf, 2016), loc. 5902, Kindle, citing Jürgen Falter, Thomas Lindenberger, and Siegfried Schumann, *Wahlen und Abstimmungen in der Weimarer Republik. Materialien zum Wahlverhalten 1919–1933* (Munich: C. H. Beck, 1986), 100, 94, 95.
24. Ullrich, *Hitler*, loc. 5908, Kindle.
25. *Vossische Zeitung*, April 9, 1931.
26. Guido Enderis, "Prussian Plebiscite Fails by 3,500,000; 13 Die in Berlin Riot," *New York Times*, August 10, 1931.
27. TBJG, August 10, 1931.
28. *New York Times*, July 20, 1935.
29. Ullrich, *Hitler*, loc. 5923, Kindle.
30. Police report in RSA, Band IV, Teil 2, Dok. 31, n. 16, p. 106.

Chapter Thirty-Four: Hitler and Women

1. "Report of Dr. Sauer," September 28, 1931, Bavarian State Archives, cited in Ron Rosenbaum, *Explaining Hitler: The Search for the Origins of His Evil* (New York: HarperPerennial, 1999), 103. Italics added and translation improved.
2. Edgar Ansel Mowrer, *Triumph and Turmoil: A Personal History of Our Time* (New York: Weybright and Talley, 1968), 208.
3. Ernst Hanfstaengl, *Hitler: The Memoir of a Nazi Insider Who Turned Against the Führer* (New York: Arcade Publishing, 2011), loc. 406–80, Kindle.
4. Christa Schroeder, *He Was My Chief: The Memoirs of Adolf Hitler's Secretary* (London: Frontline Books, 2009), 126.
5. Schroeder, *He Was My Chief*, 133.
6. Robert G. L. Waite, *The Psychopathic God Adolf Hitler* (New York: Basic Books, 1977), 276.
7. Otto Wagener, *Hitler—Memoirs of a Confidant*, ed. Henry Ashby Turner Jr. (New Haven, CT: Yale University Press, 1985), 33.
8. Professor Fleischmann's 552-page book deals not only with the admissions ledger but also with the more than 350 visitors' cards that were issued for Hitler's callers while he was behind bars. On the question of which testicle Hitler was missing, the Russian doctors had in 1945 written that the dead dictator's *left* testicle "could not be found in the scrotum or in

the inguinal canal, nor in the small pelvis." (See Lev A. Bezyminski, *The Death of Adolf Hitler: Unknown Documents from Soviet Archives* [New York: Harcourt, Brace & World, 1968], 114.) By contrast, the Landsberg Prison doctor had written in 1923 that Hitler was missing his *right* gonad. In the ledger, the doctor had first written "left-sided," then had crossed out "left" and written "right" just above it, correcting himself. He seemed certain enough. A facsimile of the entry can be seen on page 407 of Fleischmann's book, entry number 45 (miswritten as 48). See Peter Fleischmann, *Hitler als Häftling in Landsberg am Lech 1923/24* (Neustadt an der Aisch: Verlag Ph. C. W. Schmidt, 2015), 9ff, 18, 44, 72, 407, 416–17.

Chapter Thirty-Five: Geli

1. Ernst Hanfstaengl, *Hitler: The Memoir of a Nazi Insider Who Turned Against the Führer* (New York: Arcade Publishing, 2011), 164; Anton Joachimsthaler, *Hitlers Liste: Ein Dokument persönlicher Beziehungen* (Munich: F. A. Herbig, 2003), 313–14.
2. Joachim Fest, *Hitler* (New York: Harcourt Brace Jovanovich, 1974), 254.
3. Anna Maria Sigmund, *Des Führers bester Freund: Adolf Hitler, seine Nichte Geli Raubal und der "Ehrenarier" Emil Maurice—eine Dreiecksbeziehung* (Munich: Wilhelm Heyne Verlag, 2003), 61.
4. Ilse Hess recorded interview with John Toland, April 21, 1971, John Toland papers, Library of Congress Recorded Sound Reference Center, Library of Congress, RWE 1761, RWE 1791.
5. Heinrich Hoffmann, *Hitler Was My Friend: The Memoirs of Hitler's Photographer* (Barnsley, UK: Frontline Books, 2011), 148.
6. Alexander Historical Auctions, View 37, Lot 597, description at bottom, accessed December 11, 2017. *Spiegel Online,* on April 13, 2016, reported that the picnic was held on the way to Bayreuth for the music festival.
7. Henriette von Schirach, *Frauen um Hitler: Nach Materialien von Henriette von Schirach* (Munich: F. A. Herbig, 1983), 55–59.
8. Hanfstaengl, *Hitler,* 162.
9. Hoffmann, *Hitler Was My Friend,* 148.
10. Ernst Hanfstaengl, in *Hitler Source-Book,* by Walter C. Langer, 891 (963 in PDF online, accessed December 12, 2017, at https://ia801307.us.archive.org/11/items/OSSHitlerSourcebook/OSS%20Hitler%20Sourcebook.pdf). Also available at https://archive.org/details/OSSHitlerSourcebook/page/n2. Langer's sourcebook is a 1,019-page collection of interviews and research about Hitler compiled in 1943 for the Office of Strategic Services, the forerunner to the Central Intelligence Agency (collaborators on the project were Henry A. Murray, Ernst Kris, and Bertam D. Lewin). From the research, Langer, a psycholanalyst, wrote a confidential 176-page profile of Hitler called *A Psychological Analysis of Adolph [sic] Hitler: His Life and Legend* (Washington, DC: M. O. Branch, Office of Strategic Services, n.d.), available at https://www.cia.gov/library/readingroom/docs/CIA-RDP78-02646R000600240001-5.pdf.

    In his report, Langer posited deviant tendencies in Hitler, including masochism, femininity, and coprophagia—the desire to be defecated or urinated upon. The psychoanalyst's sole source for this last assertion was former Nazi Otto Strasser, then exiled in Canada. Strasser was a bitter enemy of Hitler whose brother, Gregor, had been murdered by Hitler's men in 1934. In his 1943 interview with Langer, Otto Strasser claimed that Geli Raubal—Hitler's deceased half niece and alleged lover—told him that Hitler demanded perverse sexual favors (*Source-Book,* 919 [991 in PDF file]). Langer's report was declassified in 1968 and published in lightly revised form in 1972. Langer lent credence to Strasser's story, claiming Hitler's coprophagic tendencies supported a diagnosis of masochism, showing that he "despises himself" and felt a need to "degrade himself." While the claim of coprophagic preferences was never confirmed by other evidence, and Strasser's reliability has long been called into question, Langer's book helped fuel decades of speculation about sexual deviation as the root of Hitler's genocidal megalomania. See Walter C. Langer, *The Mind of Adolf Hitler* (New York: Basic Books, 1972), 174–75.

11. Joachimsthaler, *Hitlers Liste,* 323.
12. John Toland, *Adolf Hitler* (New York: Doubleday, 1976), loc. 5058–59, Kindle; Ilse Hess interview with John Toland, RWE 1761.
13. Volker Ullrich, *Hitler: Ascent 1889–1939* (New York: Alfred A. Knopf, 2016), loc. 6438, Kindle.
14. Schirach, *Frauen um Hitler,* 67.
15. Ronald Hayman, *Hitler and Geli* (New York: Bloomsbury, 1997), 163.
16. This version of events came from the testimony of Frau Winter and her husband. But Ronald Hayman reports two other versions of the way the door was forced open. Ilse Hess claimed that her husband, Rudolf Hess, broke down the door. Maria Reichert said that Nazi officials Max Amann and Franz X. Schwartz, summoned to the apartment, called a locksmith. All three versions have persisted in the literature. See Hayman, *Hitler and Geli,* 184.
17. Sigmund, *Des Führers bester Freund,* 170; medical examiner's report, Hayman, *Hitler and Geli,* 166.
18. According to police doctor Müller, in Hayman, *Hitler and Geli,* 164.
19. Hoffmann, *Hitler Was My Friend,* 153.
20. Hayman, *Hitler and Geli,* 189.
21. Hans Frank, *Im Angesicht des Galgens: Deutung Hitlers und seiner Zeit auf Grund eigener Erlebnisse und Erkenntnisse* (Munich: Friedrich Alfred Beck Verlag, 1953), 97–98.
22. Hoffmann, *Hitler Was My Friend,* 156–57.
23. *Münchener Post,* September 21, 1931.
24. Frank, *Im Angesicht,* 98.
25. Joachimsthaler, *Hitlers Liste,* 35; Otto Wagener, *Hitler aus nächster Nähe: Aufzeichnungen eines Vertrauten 1929–1932,* ed. H. A. Turner Jr. (Frankfurt-am-Main: Ullstein Verlag, 1978), 358, accessed June 30, 2018, at https://ia600805.us.archive.org/34/items/Wagener1978HitlerAusNchsterNNhe/Wagener%201978%20-%20Hitler%20aus%20n%C3%A4chster%20N%C3%A4he.pdf.
26. Wagener, *Hitler,* 375–78.
27. Peter Longerich, *Goebbels: A Biography* (New York: Random House, 2015), loc. 3860–94, Kindle.

Chapter Thirty-Six: Hindenburg, Hugenberg, and Harzburg

1. Harold Callender, "Herr Hitler Replies to Some Fundamental Questions," *New York Times,* December 20, 1931, 5 (139 in TimesMachine version).
2. Volker Ullrich, *Hitler: Ascent 1889–1939* (New York: Alfred A. Knopf, 2016), loc. 5979, Kindle, citing Heinrich Brüning, *Memoiren 1918–1934* (Munich: Deutsche Verlags-Anstalt, 1970), 391.
3. TBJG, October 12, 1931.
4. Karl Dietrich Bracher, *Die Auflösung der Weimarer Republik: Eine Studie zum Problem des Machtverfalls in der Demokratie,* Schriften des Instituts für politische Wissenschaft 4 (Stuttgart and Düsseldorf: Ring Verlag, 1955), 408.

5. Alan Bullock, *Hitler: A Study in Tyranny* (Old Saybrook, CT: Konecky & Konecky, 1962), 189.

Chapter Thirty-Seven: Boxheim and the American Media

1. "Wie die SA-Leute 'Regieren' sollten: Das hochverräterische Dokument der hessischen Nationalsozialisten," *Vossische Zeitung,* November 26, 1931, 4; Ernst Deuerlein, *Der Aufstieg der NSDAP in Augenzeugenberichten* (Munich: Deutscher Taschenbuch Verlag, 1989), 361–63.
2. "Reichsanwalt gegen Hitlerführer," *Vossische Zeitung,* November 26, 1931 (MA), 1.
3. Carl Misch, "Das Boxheimer Dokument," *Vossische Zeitung,* November 26, 1931 (MA), 1–2.
4. "L'agitation raciste en Allemagne," *Le Temps,* December 7, 1931.
5. "Allemagne: Le projet de 'putsch' hitlerien," *Le Temps,* November 29, 1931, 2.
6. RSA, Band IV, Teil 2, Dok. 90, p. 255.
7. *Le Temps,* November 29, 1931.
8. Richard J. Evans, *The Coming of the Third Reich* (London: Allen Lane, 2003), 274.
9. "Adolf Hitler: Right Goes Hand in Hand with Might," *Time,* December 21, 1931.
10. "Three Against Hitler," *Time,* December 21, 1931, 19.
11. Ernst Hanfstaengl, *15 Jahre mit Hitler: Zwischen Weissem und Braunem Haus* (Munich: R. Piper & Co. Verlag, 1980), 256–59.
12. Guido Enderis, "Hitler Backs Debts, Bars Reparations; Sees Victory Soon," *New York Times,* December 5, 1931, 1; "Herr Hitler's Policy," *The Times* (London), December 5, 1931, in RSA, Band IV, Teil 2, Dok. 83, pp. 231–32. The Nazi Party claimed membership of eight hundred thousand.
13. The slogan "God punish England!" (*Gott strafe England!*) came from German-Jewish poet Ernst Lissauer (1882–1937). At the outbreak of the First World War, in 1914, Lissauer composed a poem called "Hymn of Hate Towards England" (*Hassgesang gegen England*). See Richard Millington and Roger Smith, "'A Few Bars of the Hymn of Hate': The Reception of Ernst Lissauer's 'Haßgesang gegen England' in German and English," *Studies in Twentieth & Twenty-First Century Literature* 41, no. 2 (2017), at https://newprairiepress.org/sttcl/vol41/iss2/5/.
14. "News agencies were the easiest way to influence hundreds, or even thousands, of newspapers around the world." See Heidi J. S. Tworek, *News from Germany: The Competition to Control World Communications, 1900–1945,* Harvard Historical Studies 190 (Cambridge, MA: Harvard University Press, 2019), 4.
15. RSA, Band IV, Teil 2, Dok. 90, p. 254.
16. "Hitler's Voice to Be Heard Here Tonight as He Speaks in Berlin," *New York Times,* December 11, 1931, 11; "Hitler strebt nach dem Mikrophon," *Vossische Zeitung,* December 12, 1931 (MA), 2; RSA, Band IV, Teil 2, Dok. 91, p. 256; also n. 2, p. 256.
17. "Hitler an Hearst: Ersatz für die nichtgehaltene Rede," *Vossische Zeitung,* December 12, 1931 (AA), 1; RSA, Band IV, Teil 2, Dok. 91, n. 2, p. 256.
18. "'Nazis' Would Assure Nordic Dominance, Sterilize Some Races, Ban Miscegenation," *New York Times,* December 8, 1931, 1.
19. "Constructive Rule Pledged by Hitler," *New York Times,* December 8, 1931, 6.
20. "Adolf Hitler," *Time.* The other *Time* cover stories appeared in 1933, 1936, 1939, 1941, and 1945. Special thanks to *Time* researchers Melissa August and Bill Hooper and to former *Time* correspondent Ann Blackman.
21. Bella Fromm, *Blood and Banquets: A Berlin Social Diary* (New York: Birch Lane Press, 1990), 41–42.

22. Max Wallace, *The American Axis: Henry Ford, Charles Lindbergh, and the Rise of the Third Reich* (New York: St. Martin's Press, 2003), 1–2.
23. Dorothy Thompson, *"I Saw Hitler!"* (New York: Farrar & Rinehart, 1932), 13–14.
24. Thompson, *"I Saw Hitler!,"* 12.
25. Thompson, *"I Saw Hitler!,"* 31.
26. The Nazis hated Thompson's report. In 1934, she became the first American journalist expelled by the Nazis.

Part Four: Grasping for Power (1932)

1. Theodore Abel, *Why Hitler Came into Power* (1938; repr., Cambridge, MA: Harvard University Press, 1986), 88.

Chapter Thirty-Eight: A Floating Political Game

1. Unemployment averaged 29.9 percent in 1932: RSA, Band V, Teil 1, Dok. 40, p. 63, n. 9. Alpha History, in an article entitled "The Great Depression in Germany," says German industrial production was at 58 percent of its 1928 level: http://alphahistory.com/weimarrepublic/great-depression/; "5,666,000 Germans Are Jobless; Year-End Total Sets a Record," *New York Times,* January 8, 1932; Henry Ashby Turner Jr., *German Big Business and the Rise of Hitler* (Oxford, UK: Oxford University Press, 1985), 204.
2. T. R. Ybarra, "Triumvirs of Germany's Destiny," *New York Times,* December 6, 1931, 133.
3. "Hindenburg on Radio Warns on Burdening Reich Too Heavily," *New York Times,* January 1, 1932, 1.
4. H. R. Knickerbocker, *The German Crisis* (New York: Farrar & Rinehart, 1932), 9. Cf. the collection of documents assembled by John L. Heineman, professor emeritus at Boston College, about the collapse of the Weimar Republic at https://www2.bc.edu/john-heineman/Collapse.html.
5. TBJG, January 1, 1932.
6. Police report, Abeteilung I.A., P.K.D., "Bericht über den Verlauf der am 4. Januar 1932 im Konzerthaus Clou stattgefundenen öffentlichen Versammlung der Standarte 6 der SA der NSDAP," Materialsammlung-RSA, Institut für Zeitgeschichte, Munich.
7. Konrad Heiden, *The Führer* (Edison, NJ: Castle Books, 2002), 342.
8. Ian Kershaw, *Hitler,* vol. 1, *1889–1936: Hubris* (New York: W. W. Norton, 1998), 361; Volker Ullrich, *Hitler: Ascent 1889–1939* (New York: Alfred A. Knopf, 2016), loc. 29888n17, Kindle.
9. *Die Rote Fahne,* January 27, 1932.
10. A detailed discussion of this famous event is in Turner, *German Big Business,* 204–19. The speech and extensive footnotes can be found in RSA, Band IV, Teil 3, Dok. 15, pp. 74–110.
11. Ironically, some of the most important heavy-industry tycoons stayed away, including Gustav Krupp von Bohlen und Halbach, Dr. Carl Duisberg, Paul Reusch, and Fritz Springorum. The speech's text and other details are in RSA, Band IV, Teil 3, Dok. 15, pp. 74ff.
12. Otto Dietrich, *Zwölf Jahre mit Hitler* (Munich: Isar Verlag, 1955), 185ff, in Turner, *German Big Business,* 216.
13. TBJG, January 10, 1932.
14. Dietrich Orlow, *Weimar Prussia, 1925–1933: The Illusion of Strength* (Pittsburgh, PA: University of Pittsburgh Press, 1991), 189; Christopher Clark, *Iron Kingdom: The Rise and Downfall of Prussia, 1600–1947* (Cambridge, MA: Harvard University Press, 2006), 651.
15. *Völkischer Beobachter,* Sonder-Nummer 22, Februar 1932, Materialsammlung-RSA, Institut für Zeitgeschichte, Munich.

16. Sefton Delmer, *Trail Sinister: An Autobiography, Volume One* (London: Secker & Warburg, 1961), 146.
17. TBJG, February 23, 1932.
18. Andreas Dorpalen, *Hindenburg and the Weimar Republic* (Princeton, NJ: Princeton University Press, 1964), 256.

Chapter Thirty-Nine: Running for President

1. *Schlesische Zeitung*, March 4, 1932 (AA), cited in RSA, Band IV, Teil 3, Dok. 34, p. 166, n. 1.
2. Andreas Dorpalen, *Hindenburg and the Weimar Republic* (Princeton, NJ: Princeton University Press, 1964), 284.
3. "Der Passionsweg," *Vossische Zeitung*, March 7, 1932 (AA), 1; RSA, Band IV, Teil 3, Dok. 34, p. 170.
4. See the fundamental thesis of Fritz Stern in his book *The Politics of Cultural Despair: A Study in the Rise of the Germanic Ideology* (Berkeley: University of California Press, 1961).
5. Harold Callender, "20,000 Hail Hitler at Frankfurt Talk," *New York Times*, March 7, 1932, 8.
6. William Sheridan Allen, ed. and trans., *The Infancy of Nazism: The Memoirs of Ex-Gauleiter Albert Krebs 1923–1933* (New York: New Viewpoints, 1976), 163–65.
7. The speech, including the sound of Hindenburg's fist banging on his desk, can be heard at https://www.youtube.com/watch?v=ExP4DNx6Rxs. The full printed text is at "Rundfunk-Ansprache des Reichspräsidenten von Hindenburg vom 10. März 1932 an das deutsche Volk," *Deutsche Reichsgeschichte in Dokumenten 1931–1934*, in the Internet Archive: https://archive.org/stream/DeutscheReichsgeschichteInDokumenten1931-1934/DeutscheReichsgeschichteInDokumenten1931-1934_djvu.txt.
8. Heinrich August Winkler, *Weimar 1918–1933: Die Geschichte der ersten deutschen Demokratie* (Munich: C. H. Beck, 2018), 448; Eugene Davidson, *The Making of Adolf Hitler: The Birth and Rise of Nazism* (New York: Macmillan, 1977), 313.
9. Winkler, *Weimar*, 447.
10. Reichsbanner Schwarz-Rot-Gold, Bund Aktiver Demokraten E.V., https://reichsbanner.de/reichsbanner-geschichte/kampf-um-die-republik/eiserne-front/.
11. RSA, Band IV, Teil 3, Dok. 6, p. 28, n. 6.
12. RSA, Band IV, Teil 3, Dok. 39, pp. 190–91. Hindenburg was eighty-four years old, not eighty-five.

Chapter Forty: Certain of Victory

1. *Sozialistische Arbeiter Zeitung*, Berlin, March 12, 1932, at http://library.fes.de/breslau/sozialistische-arbeiterzeitung/pdf/1932/1932-061.pdf.
2. RSA, Band IV, Teil 3, Dok. 44, p. 204, n. 1.
3. "Five Obtain Places on German Ballot," *New York Times*, March 4, 1932, 11.
4. Hitler interview with H. R. Knickerbocker in the *New York Evening Post*, March 12, 1932, in RSA, Band IV, Teil 3, Dok. 46, p. 219.
5. TBJG, March 2, 1932.
6. TBJG, March 13, 1932.
7. John Toland interview with Gerdy Troost, November 5, 1971, John Toland papers, Motion Picture, Broadcasting, and Recorded Sound Division, Library of Congress, RWE 1716 B2, RWE 1729-1730 A.

8. Toland interview with Gerdy Troost, Library of Congress, RWE 1793 A1.
9. RSA, Band IV, Teil 3, Dok. 47, pp. 223–25.
10. TBJG, March 14, 1932.
11. *Vossische Zeitung*, March 14, 1932.

Chapter Forty-One: Hitler over Germany

1. Count Harry Kessler, *Berlin in Lights: The Diaries of Count Harry Kessler (1918–1937)* (New York: Grove Press, 2000), 412.
2. Anna von der Goltz, *Hindenburg: Power, Myth, and the Rise of the Nazis* (Oxford, UK: Oxford University Press, 2009), 157–66.
3. Ian Kershaw, *Hitler*, vol. 1, *1889–1936: Hubris* (New York: W. W. Norton, 1998), 363n299.
4. RSA, Band V, Teil 1, Dok. 3, pp. 16ff.
5. Crowd estimates from two different newspapers ranged from forty-five thousand to ninety thousand. RSA, Band V, Teil 1, Dok. 6, p. 19, n. 1.
6. Hans Baur, *I Was Hitler's Pilot: The Memoirs of Hans Baur* (Barnsley, UK: Frontline Books, 2013), loc. 469, Kindle.
7. "Hitler im Flug," *Vossische Zeitung* (MA), April 5, 1932, 3.
8. "Hitler Gets Women's Cheers," *New York Times*, April 5, 1932; RSA, Band V, Teil 1, Dok. 7, p. 20, n. 1.
9. RSA, Band V, Teil 1, Dok. 7, p. 21, n. 5.
10. "Werbung im Schafspelz," *Vossische Zeitung*, April 5, 1932 (AA), 2.
11. RSA, Band V, Teil 1, Dok. 7, p. 20, n. 1.
12. Baur, *I Was Hitler's Pilot*, loc. 478, Kindle.
13. *Völkischer Beobachter*, May 3, 1932.
14. Sefton Delmer, *Trail Sinister: An Autobiography, Volume One* (London: Secker & Warburg, 1961), 15–21, 141ff.
15. Sefton Delmer, "Hitler and the Crown Prince," *Daily Express*, April 6, 1932, 1. After the Second World War broke out, Delmer became a propagandist for Britain.
16. Volker Ullrich, *Hitler: Ascent 1889–1939* (New York: Alfred A. Knopf, 2016), loc. 6973–78, Kindle.
17. The writers were later identified as Joseph Stettner and Korbinian Rutz in Thomas Weber, *Hitler's First War: Adolf Hitler, the Men of the List Regiment, and the First World War* (Oxford, UK: Oxford University Press, 2010), 99–106, 282–83.
18. "Ist Hitler reinrassig?," *Bayr.* [illegible]*ztg.*, 79, April 7, 1932, in Materialsammlung-RSA, Institut für Zeitgeschichte, Munich.
19. TBJG, April 11, 1932.
20. RSA, Band V, Teil 1, Dok. 33, p. 51, n. 2.
21. RSA, Band V, Teil 1, Dok. 33, pp. 51ff.

Chapter Forty-Two: Groundswell

1. RSA, Band V, Teil 1, Dok. 40, p. 64.
2. RSA, Band V, Teil 1, Dok. 37, p. 57.
3. RSA, Band V, Teil 1, Dok. 35, p. 54, n. 3.
4. "Der Freistaat Preussen: Landtagswahl 1932," accessed February 12, 2018, at http://www.gonschior.de/weimar/Preussen/LT4.html.
5. TBJG, April 25, 1932.

Chapter Forty-Three: Intrigue and Betrayal

1. Karl Dietrich Bracher, *Die Auflösung der Weimarer Republik: Eine Studie zum Problem des Machtverfalls in der Demokratie,* Schriften des Instituts für politische Wissenschaft 4 (Stuttgart and Düsseldorf: Ring Verlag, 1955), 481.
2. Joachim Fest, *Hitler* (New York: Harcourt Brace Jovanovich, 1974), 334.
3. TBJG, March 12, 1932.
4. Hitler was already claiming that the Storm Troopers numbered four hundred thousand, but they reached that strength only in June of 1932. RSA, Band V, Teil 1, Dok. 35, p. 54, n. 3.
5. Bracher, *Die Auflösung,* 481–90.
6. Bracher, *Die Auflösung,* 485n16.
7. Gordon A. Craig, *Germany: 1866–1945* (Oxford, UK: Oxford University Press, 1978), 535.
8. Benjamin Carter Hett, *The Death of Democracy: Hitler's Rise to Power and the Downfall of the Weimar Republic* (New York: Henry Holt, 2018), 85.
9. Bracher, *Die Auflösung,* 487.
10. Hett, *The Death of Democracy,* 136.
11. Such machinations to appease the seemingly unstoppable Nazi juggernaut were proof to later historians, such as Heinrich August Winkler, that high-ranking members of the German judiciary and civil service "had already accepted the inevitable victory of the Nazi Party well before Hitler's final seizure of power." See Heinrich August Winkler, *Der Weg in die Katastrophe. Arbeiter und Arbeiterbewegung in der Weimarer Republik 1930–1933,* Geschichte der Arbeiter und der Arbeiterbewegung in Deutschland seit dem Ende des 18. Jahrhunderts (History of workers and the labor movement in Germany since the end of the eighteenth century) 11 (Bonn: Verlag J. H. W. Dietz Nachf., 1990), 449, in https://de.wikipedia.org/wiki/Boxheimer_Dokumente#cite_note-32.
12. Bracher, *Die Auflösung,* 481n2.
13. Bracher, *Die Auflösung,* 488.
14. Hett, *The Death of Democracy,* 140–41.
15. Volker Ullrich, *Hitler: Ascent 1889–1939* (New York: Alfred A. Knopf, 2016), loc. 7046, Kindle.
16. TBJG, May 9, 1932.
17. TBJG, May 13, 1932.
18. Bracher, *Die Auflösung,* 524–25.
19. Bracher, *Die Auflösung,* 514.
20. Hett, *The Death of Democracy,* 144, citing Heinrich Brüning, *Memoiren 1918–1934* (Munich: Deutsche Verlags-Anstalt, 1970), 600.
21. TBJG, May 31, 1932.

Chapter Forty-Four: High-Water Mark

1. André François-Poncet, *The Fateful Years: Memoirs of a French Ambassador in Berlin, 1931–1938* (New York: Harcourt, Brace, 1949), 23.
2. Karl Dietrich Bracher, *Die Auflösung der Weimarer Republik: Eine Studie zum Problem des Machtverfalls in der Demokratie,* Schriften des Instituts für politische Wissenschaft 4 (Stuttgart and Düsseldorf: Ring Verlag, 1955), 519n179.
3. Archiv der sozialen Demokratie, Staatsstreich in Preussen, accessed February 2018, at https://www.fes.de/archiv/adsd_neu/inhalt/stichwort/preussenschlag.htm.
4. "Hat Hitler Mongolenblut?," *Der gerade Weg,* July 23, 1932, 1.
5. The Socialists filed a suit in the Supreme Court that would be decided in their favor in October but would not restore them to power.

6. "Die drei grossen Deutschlandfahrten des Führers (März und April 1932)," *Der National-sozialist,* undated, in Materialsammlung-RSA, Institut für Zeitgeschichte, Munich.
7. Theodore Abel, *Why Hitler Came into Power* (1938; repr., Cambridge, MA: Harvard University Press, 1986), 299.
8. Abel, *Why Hitler Came into Power,* 298.
9. Hans Baur, *I Was Hitler's Pilot: The Memoirs of Hans Baur* (Barnsley, UK: Frontline Books, 2013), loc. 490–511, Kindle.
10. "Hitler spricht vor Dreiβigtausend!," *Göttinger Tageblatt,* July 22, 1932, 8.
11. "Die grosse Pleite," *Volksblatt für Göttingen und Südhannover,* July 22, 1932.
12. Baur, *I Was Hitler's Pilot,* loc. 512–23, Kindle.
13. Some political scientists cast doubt on the impact of Hitler's campaigning on his actual vote share, suggesting voter behavior was driven mainly by economic and social conditions. See Peter Selb and Simon Munzert, "Examining a Most Likely Case for Strong Campaign Effects: Hitler's Speeches and the Rise of the Nazi Party, 1927–1933," *American Political Science Review* 112, no. 4 (November 2018), 1050–66.
14. TBJG, August 1, 1932.

Chapter Forty-Five: At the Gates of Power

1. TBJG, August 9, 1932.
2. TBJG, August 7, 1932.
3. Volker Ullrich, *Hitler: Ascent 1889–1939* (New York: Alfred A. Knopf, 2016), loc. 7343, Kindle, citing notes by Meissner dated August 11, 1932; Walther Hubatsch, *Hindenburg und der Staat: Aus den Papieren des Generalfeldmarschalls und Reichspräsidenten von 1878 bis 1934* (Göttingen: Musterschmidt, 1966), 335–38 (quotation on 336).
4. Ian Kershaw, *Hitler,* vol. 1, *1889–1936: Hubris* (New York: W. W. Norton, 1998), 371, citing Thilo Vogelsang, "Dokumentation: Zur Politik Schleichers gegenüber der NSDAP 1932," *Vierteljahrshefte für Zeitgeschichte* 6 (1958), 86–118 (particularly 89).
5. TBJG, August 13, 1932.
6. Kershaw, *Hitler,* 367.
7. Franz von Papen, *Der Wahrheit eine Gasse* (Munich: P. List, 1952), 222ff.
8. TBJG, August 14, 1932.
9. RSA, Band V, Teil 2, Dok. 167, p. 300, nn. 3, 5, 6.
10. *The Trial of the Major War Criminals Before the International Military Tribunal, Nuremberg: November 14, 1945–October 1, 1946* (published at Nuremberg, 1948) 32:150, at https://www.loc.gov/rr/frd/Military_Law/pdf/NT_Vol-XXXII.pdf.
11. Ullrich, *Hitler,* loc. 7380, Kindle, citing a memorandum from Meissner dated August 13, 1932; first printed in Thilo Vogelsang, *Reichswehr, Staat und NSDAP* (Stuttgart: Deutsche Verlags-Anstalt, 1962), 479ff.
12. Jewish Telegraphic Agency, August 3, 1934, accessed February 2018, at https://www.jta.org/1934/08/03/archive/jews-placed-trust-in-von-hindenburg; "Jews Placed Trust in von Hindenburg," *Jewish Daily Bulletin,* August 3, 1934: 4.
13. Ernst Deuerlein, *Der Aufstieg der NSDAP in Augenzeugenberichten* (Munich: Deutscher Taschenbuch Verlag, 1989), 398.
14. Franz von Papen, *Memoirs* (London: Andre Deutsch, 1952), 197.
15. Letter of Wilhelm Keppler to Baron von Schröder, December 26, 1932, in Thilo Vogelsang, "Dokumentation: Zur Politik Schleichers gegenüber der NSDAP 1932," *Vierteljahrshefte für Zeitgeschichte* 6, no. 1 (1958), 86.

16. Esau was the son of Isaac: see Genesis 25:19–34. Also see Milan Hauner, *Hitler: A Chronology of His Life and Time,* 2nd rev. ed. (London: Palgrave Macmillan, 2008), 83. The interview in the *Rheinisch-Westfälische Zeitung* was conducted, possibly with embellishments, by Otto Dietrich, Hitler's domestic press chief, who was the son-in-law of the newspaper's publisher. RSA, Band V, Teil 1, Dok. 169, p. 304, n. 1.
17. TBJG, August 14, 1932.
18. TBJG, August 14, 1932.
19. RSA, Band V, Teil 1, Dok. 172, p. 314.
20. "Die mutmasslichen Urheber des Anschlages auf die Kieler Synagoge verhaftet," *Das Jüdische Echo* 34 (1932), 270.
21. Andrew Nagorski, *Hitlerland: American Eyewitnesses to the Nazi Rise to Power* (New York: Simon and Schuster, 2012), 88, citing Hans von Kaltenborn, *Fifty Fabulous Years, 1900–1950: A Personal Review* (New York: G. P. Putnam's Sons, 1950), 188.
22. Nagorski, *Hitlerland,* 86–88.
23. Nagorski, *Hitlerland,* 88, citing Kaltenborn, *Fifty Fabulous Years,* 186.

Chapter Forty-Six: Falling Comet

1. Alois Maria Ott, letter to Werner Maser, December 12, 1973, from Institut für Zeitgeschichte, Munich; Archive ED 699/42.
2. "Ausbreitung des Nationalsozialistischen Guerillakrieges in Deutschland," *Das Jüdische Echo* 34 (1932), 270.
3. "German Men and Women!," Central Association of German Citizens of the Jewish Faith, Hamburg, April 1932, in Anton Kaes, Martin Jay, and Edward Dimendberg, eds., *The Weimar Republic Sourcebook* (Berkeley: University of California Press, 1994), 272–75.
4. Thomas Childers and Eugene Weiss, "Voters and Violence: Political Violence and the Limits of National Socialist Mass Mobilization," *German Studies Review* 13, no. 3 (October 1990), 483–84.
5. RSA, Band V, Teil 1, Dok. 174, p. 317.
6. Ian Kershaw, *Hitler,* vol. 1, *1889–1936: Hubris* (New York: W. W. Norton, 1998), 382.
7. Joseph Goebbels, *Vom Kaiserhof zur Reichskanzlei: Eine historische Darstellung in Tagebuchblättern* (Munich: Zentral-Verlag der NSDAP, Franz-Eher Nachfolger, 1934), 159.
8. "Reichstag Is Calm; Will Ask Hindenburg to Let It Continue," *New York Times,* August 31, 1932, 1.
9. TBJG, September 28, 1932.
10. TBJG, October 16, 1932.
11. RSA, Band V, Teil 2, Dok. 193, p. 363.
12. RSA, Band V, Teil 2, Dok. 10, p. 21, n. 1.
13. Werner Jochmann, *Nationalsozialismus und Revolution: Ursprung und Geschichte der NSDAP in Hamburg 1922–1933, Dokumente* (Frankfurt-am-Main: Europäischer Verlagsanstalt, 1963), 414–17.
14. RSA, Band V, Teil 2, Dok. 25, pp. 82ff.
15. RSA, Band V, Teil 2, Dok. 10, p. 21, n. 1; Kershaw, *Hitler,* 389.
16. Volker Ullrich, *Hitler: Ascent 1889–1939* (New York: Alfred A. Knopf, 2016), loc. 7609, citing Konrad Heiden, *Adolf Hitler: Das Zeitalter der Verantwortungslosigkeit* (Zurich: Europa Verlag, 1936), 302.
17. William Sheridan Allen, *The Nazi Seizure of Power: The Experience of a Single German Town 1922–1945,* rev. ed. (1965; repr., New York and London: Franklin Watts, 1984), 136.
18. "Ohne Mehrheit," *Vossische Zeitung,* November 7, 1932, 1.

19. Thomas Childers, "The Limits of National Socialist Mobilisation: The Elections of 6 November 1932 and the Fragmentation of the Nazi Constituency," in *The Formation of the Nazi Constituency 1919–1933,* ed. Thomas Childers (London: Croom Helm, 1986), 234–55; Childers and Weiss, "Voters and Violence," 488.
20. TBJG, November 7, 1932.

Chapter Forty-Seven: Secret Relationship

1. Some versions of this story date the alleged suicide attempt earlier in 1932. See Heike B. Görtemaker, *Eva Braun: Leben mit Hitler* (Munich: C. H. Beck, 2010), 59–62, citing Eva's sister Ilse, as reported in Nerin B. Gun, *Eva Braun: Hitler's Mistress* (New York: Meredith Press, 1968), 65.
2. Heinrich Hoffmann, *Hitler Was My Friend: The Memoirs of Hitler's Photographer* (Barnsley, UK: Frontline Books, 2011), 159ff.

Chapter Forty-Eight: Eternal Intriguer

1. Joseph Goebbels, *Vom Kaiserhof zur Reichskanzlei: Eine historische Darstellung in Tagebuchblättern* (Munich: Zentral-Verlag der NSDAP, Franz-Eher Nachfolger, 1934), 207.
2. RSA, Band V, Teil 2, Dok. 65, p. 188, n. 1.
3. RSA, Band V, Teil 2, Dok. 65, p. 190.
4. Harry Graf Kessler, *Tagebücher, 1918–1937: Komplettausgabe* (Berlin: Insel Verlag, 1961; Prague: e-artnow, 2013), 9:531 (entry for November 19, 1932).
5. TBJG, November 19, 1932.
6. TBJG, November 25, 1932. Goebbels's venomous comment was prophetic. On June 30, 1934, Schleicher and his wife were murdered by one of Hitler's hit squads during the Night of the Long Knives.
7. Peter D. Stachura, *Gregor Strasser and the Rise of Nazism* (London: George Allen & Unwin, 1982), 105.
8. Munich police report, December 30, 1932, HA 70/1511, in Geoffrey Pridham, *Hitler's Rise to Power: The Nazi Movement in Bavaria, 1923–33* (London: Hart-Davis, MacGibbon, 1973; Sydney, Australia: Endeavour Press, 2016), loc. 62806n842, Kindle.
9. Stachura, *Gregor Strasser,* 114.
10. Henry Ashby Turner Jr., "The Myth of Chancellor Von Schleicher's Querfront Strategy," *Central European History* 41, no. 4 (December 2008), 673–81; Paul Betts, Maiken Umbach, and Ken Ledford, "Imagining Germany from Abroad: The View from Britain and the United States; a Joint Preface," *German History* 26, no. 4 (October 2008), 455–56.
11. Franz von Papen, *Memoirs* (London: Andre Deutsch, 1952), 327–28. The famous line was supposedly spoken by Georg von Frundsberg (1473–1528), a leader of Landsknecht foot soldiers: "Mönchlein, Mönchlein, du gehst einen schweren Gang!"
12. Papen, *Memoirs,* 332–33.
13. *The Trial of the Major War Criminals Before the International Military Tribunal, Nuremberg: November 14, 1945–October 1, 1946* (published at Nuremberg, 1948) 32:150, at https://www.loc.gov/rr/frd/Military_Law/pdf/NT_Vol-XXXII.pdf.
14. Volker Ullrich, *Hitler: Ascent 1889–1939* (New York: Alfred A. Knopf, 2016), loc. 7803, Kindle, citing Schwerin von Krosigk's diary notes on the cabinet meeting of December 2, 1932.
15. Papen, *Memoirs,* 334–36.
16. TBJG, December 2, 1932.
17. Random sheet, 186, Materialsammlung-RSA, Institut für Zeitgeschichte, Munich.
18. RSA, Band V, Teil 2, Dok. 73, p. 213.

Chapter Forty-Nine: Crisis

1. The extant letter may be only the first draft that Strasser wrote but is considered historically reliable. It is reprinted in English in Peter D. Stachura, *Gregor Strasser and the Rise of Nazism* (London: George Allen & Unwin, 1982), 113–14, and in German and English in Peter Stachura, "Der Fall Strasser," in *The Shaping of the Nazi State,* ed. Peter D. Stachura (London: Croom Helm, 1978), 113–15. Though he resigned from Nazi Party leadership, Strasser did not in fact vacate his Reichstag seat for another three months, despite the intention expressed in his letter. He also kept his membership in the rank and file of the party, though he never again participated in any party activities. As a Nazi, he was finished. As history would soon show, he had become a dead man walking.
2. The content of Strasser's and Hitler's remarks during this showdown is based primarily on the postwar recollections of Hinrich Lohse, former Nazi gauleiter of Schleswig-Holstein. See Hinrich Lohse, "Der Fall Strasser," Institut für Zeitgeschichte, Munich; Archive ZS 265, Band 1, 23ff.
3. TBJG, December 9, 1932.
4. While one-third of the Nazi Reichstag delegation may have been loyal to Strasser, claims that Chancellor Schleicher secretly offered Strasser the vice-chancellorship to split off the "Strasser wing" have not stood up to historical scrutiny. See Volker Ullrich, *Hitler: Ascent 1889–1939* (New York: Alfred A. Knopf, 2016), loc. 7818, Kindle; Peter Longerich, *Goebbels: A Biography* (New York: Random House, 2015), 194ff.
5. This would have been in character. Hitler admired and cited Shakespeare, especially *Julius Caesar.* See Ullrich, *Hitler,* loc. 21401n265, Kindle, citing Martin Broszat's note on meeting with Otto Wagener, February 5, 1960; Institut für Zeitgeschichte, Munich; Archive ZS 1732.
6. See Lohse, "Der Fall Strasser," and other references in RSA, Band V, Teil 2, Dok. 87, p. 252, n. 5.
7. TBJG, December 9, 1932.
8. RSA, Band V, Teil 2, Dok. 89, p. 256, n. 13.
9. Konrad Heiden, "Schach oder matt? Gregor Strassers Rebellion," *Vossische Zeitung,* December 10, 1932 (MA), 1–2.
10. TBJG, December 9, 1932.
11. RSA, Band V, Teil 2, Dok. 89, pp. 253ff.
12. RSA, Band V, Teil 2, Dok. 92, pp. 259ff.
13. TBJG, December 12, 1932.
14. Joseph Goebbels, *Vom Kaiserhof zur Reichskanzlei: Eine historische Darstellung in Tagebuchblättern* (Munich: Zentral-Verlag der NSDAP, Franz Eher Nachfolger, 1934), 227–29 (December 21–23, 1932).
15. "Ein Jahr deutscher Politik," *Frankfurter Zeitung,* January 1, 1933, in RSA, Band V, Teil 2, Dok. 107, n. 52, pp. 307–8.
16. TBJG, December 24, 1932.

Part Five: Endgame (1933)

1. From interview on "Different Lenses of the Great Depression" (video), https://differentlensesofthegreatdepression.weebly.com/germany1.html.
2. Theodore Abel, *Why Hitler Came into Power* (1938; repr., Cambridge, MA: Harvard University Press, 1986), 91.

Chapter Fifty: New Year's Reckoning

1. TBJG, December 30, 1932.
2. RSA, Band V, Teil 2, Dok. 107, pp. 297ff.

3. TBJG, December 29 and 31, 1932.
4. TBJG, January 1, 1933.
5. *Vossische Zeitung,* January 1, 1933, pp. 1–2.
6. Heike B. Görtemaker, *Eva Braun: Leben mit Hitler* (Munich: C. H. Beck, 2010), 59–62.
7. Ernst Hanfstaengl, *Hitler: The Memoir of a Nazi Insider Who Turned Against the Führer* (New York: Arcade Publishing, 2011), loc. 3021, Kindle.

Chapter Fifty-One: Assignation in Cologne

1. The origin of the widely used term *Querfront* (lateral coalition) to describe Schleicher's strategy is in dispute. See Henry Ashby Turner Jr., "The Myth of Chancellor von Schleicher's *Querfront* Strategy," *Central European History* 41, no. 4 (December 2008), 673–81. But historians still use the term; see Benjamin Carter Hett, *The Death of Democracy: Hitler's Rise to Power and the Downfall of the Weimar Republic* (New York: Henry Holt, 2018), 164.
2. Theodor Duesterberg, in "Die Regierungsbildung am 30. Januar 1933," April 27, 1946, Institut für Zeitgeschichte, Munich; Archive, ZS 1700, 1.
3. This narrative is largely based on Schröder's account, produced in 1946 for the International Military Court in Nuremberg, in Ernst Deuerlein, *Der Aufstieg der NSDAP in Augenzeugenberichten* (Munich: Deutscher Taschenbuch Verlag, 1989), 411–14. Cf. Franz von Papen, *Memoirs* (London: Andre Deutsch, 1952), 227ff; Karl Dietrich Bracher, *Die Auflösung der Weimarer Republik: Eine Studie zum Problem des Machtverfalls in der Demokratie,* Schriften des Instituts für politische Wissenschaft 4 (Stuttgart and Düsseldorf: Ring Verlag, 1955), 686ff.
4. Papen, *Memoirs,* 227–28.
5. Andreas Dorpalen, *Hindenburg and the Weimar Republic* (Princeton, NJ: Princeton University Press, 1964), 410.
6. Bracher, *Die Auflösung,* 691. This narrative is based in part on Bracher's account, 686ff.
7. Dorpalen, *Hindenburg,* 415–16.
8. Papen, *Memoirs,* 231.
9. Elbrechter, a former Nazi fellow traveler and supporter of Goebbels, had become close to Strasser as well as Schleicher. He also functioned as a part-time journalist, contributing to the publications of the *Tat* Circle. See Udo Kissenkoetter, *Gregor Strasser und die NSDAP* (Stuttgart: Deutsche Verlags-Anstalt, 1978), 28–29, 111–12, 127–29, 205–7.
10. Henry Ashby Turner Jr., *Hitler's Thirty Days to Power: January 1933* (Reading, MA: Addison-Wesley, 1996), 47.
11. Hans Otto Meissner and Harry Wilde, *Die Machtergreifung: Ein Bericht über die Technik des Nationalsozialistischen Staatsstreichs* (Stuttgart: J. G. Cotta'sche Buchhandlung, 1958), 156; Bracher, *Die Auflösung,* 694–95.
12. Turner, *Hitler's Thirty Days,* 45.
13. Papen, *Memoirs,* 248.
14. Turner, *Hitler's Thirty Days,* 52.
15. Turner, *Hitler's Thirty Days,* 89–90.
16. Turner, *Hitler's Thirty Days,* illustrations, 66–67.
17. Turner, *Hitler's Thirty Days,* 85.
18. Meissner and Wilde, *Die Machtergreifung,* 151.
19. TBJG, January 13, 1933.
20. Turner, *Hitler's Thirty Days,* 48.
21. Turner, *Hitler's Thirty Days,* 50.

Chapter Fifty-Two: Impaling a Fly

1. Volker Ullrich, *Hitler: Ascent 1889–1939* (New York: Alfred A. Knopf, 2016), loc. 8191, Kindle.
2. Ullrich, *Hitler,* loc. 8198, Kindle.
3. Otto Dietrich, *With Hitler on the Road to Power: Personal Experiences with My Leader* (London: n.p., 1934), 63–64.
4. TBJG, January 13, 1933.
5. TBJG, January 16, 1933.
6. Henry Ashby Turner Jr., *Hitler's Thirty Days to Power: January 1933* (Reading, MA: Addison-Wesley, 1996), 65.
7. Joachim von Ribbentrop, *The Ribbentrop Memoirs* (London: Weidenfeld and Nicolson, 1953), 22n1.
8. RSA, Band V, Teil 2, Dok. 140, p. 370, n. 1.
9. TBJG, January 17, 1933.
10. "Scherbengericht über Gregor Strasser," *Vossische Zeitung,* January 25, 1933 (AA), 1.
11. *Frankfurter Zeitung,* 2. Morgenblatt, January 29, 1933, in Wieland Eschenhagen, ed., *Die "Machtergreifung": Tagebuch einer Wende nach Presseberichten vom 1. Januar bis 6. März 1933* (Darmstadt: Luchterhand, 1982), 77.

Chapter Fifty-Three: Berlin Nights

1. Alan Bullock, introduction to *The Ribbentrop Memoirs* by Joachim von Ribbentrop (London: Weidenfeld and Nicolson, 1953), x.
2. Henry Ashby Turner Jr., *Hitler's Thirty Days to Power: January 1933* (Reading, MA: Addison-Wesley, 1996), 71.
3. "Papen-Hitler-Schleicher," *Vossische Zeitung,* January 18, 1933 (AA), 1.
4. TBJG, January 19, 1933; Turner, *Hitler's Thirty Days,* 78.
5. RSA, Band V, Teil 2, Dok. 143, pp. 375ff.
6. Though subsequently disputed by scholars, it was widely believed in the 1930s that Martin Luther had said, "Here I stand. I can do no other." RSA, Band V, Teil 2, Dok. 143, p. 382.
7. Count Harry Kessler, *Berlin in Lights: The Diaries of Count Harry Kessler (1918–1937)* (New York: Grove Press, 2000), 469.
8. Hans Otto Meissner and Harry Wilde, *Die Machtergreifung: Ein Bericht über die Technik des Nationalsozialistischen Staatsstreichs* (Stuttgart: J. G. Cotta'sche Buchhandlung, 1958), 161ff; Turner, *Hitler's Thirty Days,* 111–12.
9. Meissner and Wilde, *Die Machtergreifung,* 163.
10. TBJG, January 25, 1933.
11. Ian Kershaw, *Hitler,* vol. 1, *1889–1936: Hubris* (New York: W. W. Norton, 1998), 421, citing Lutz Graf Schwerin von Krosigk, *Es geschah in Deutschland* (Tübingen and Stuttgart: Wunderlich-Verlag, 1952), 147.
12. Theodor Duesterberg described Meissner as a *Verhandlungskünstler*—a deal-making artist. See Theodor Duesterberg, "Die Regierungsbildung am 30. Januar 1933," April 27, 1946, Institut für Zeitgeschichte, Munich; Archive, ZS 1700, 1.
13. Meissner und Wilde, *Die Machtergreifung,* 164.
14. *The Ribbentrop Memoirs,* 23.
15. *The Ribbentrop Memoirs,* 24.
16. Kershaw, *Hitler,* 420.
17. *The Ribbentrop Memoirs,* 25.
18. "[Hitler] ist abwartend," TBJG, January 28, 1933.

Chapter Fifty-Four: Schleicher's Fall

1. "Niederschrift des Generalobersten Kurt v. Hammerstein," in Karl Dietrich Bracher, *Die Auflösung der Weimarer Republik: Eine Studie zum Problem des Machtverfalls in der Demokratie,* Schriften des Instituts für politische Wissenschaft 4 (Stuttgart and Düsseldorf: Ring Verlag, 1955), 733–34.
2. Harry Graf Kessler, *Tagebücher, 1918–1937: Komplettausgabe* (Berlin: Insel Verlag, 1961; Prague: e-artnow, 2013), loc. 10075, Kindle (January 28, 1933).
3. Volker Ullrich, *Hitler: Ascent 1889–1939* (New York: Alfred A. Knopf, 2016), loc. 8366, Kindle, citing Anton Golecki, ed., *Das Kabinett von Schleicher 1932–33,* Akten der Reichskanzlei 10 (Boppard am Rhein, Germany: Boldt Verlag, 1986), 317.
4. Henry Ashby Turner Jr., *Hitler's Thirty Days to Power: January 1933* (Reading, MA: Addison-Wesley, 1996), 133.
5. Turner, *Hitler's Thirty Days,* 42.

Chapter Fifty-Five: Unfathomable Ascent

1. In his diary, Reinhold Quaatz, a close adviser to Hugenberg, noted the press baron's desperation, per Larry Eugene Jones, "'The Greatest Stupidity of My Life': Alfred Hugenberg and the Formation of the Hitler Cabinet, January 1933," *Journal of Contemporary History* 27, no. 1 (January 1992), 63–87.
2. Gerhard Ritter, *Carl Goerdeler und die Widerstandsbewegung* (Stuttgart: Deutsche Verlags-Anstalt, 1954), 60; Theodor Duesterberg, "Die Regierungsbildung am 30. Januar 1933," April 27, 1946, Institut für Zeitgeschichte, Munich; Archive, ZS 1700, 1.
3. Henry Ashby Turner Jr., *Hitler's Thirty Days to Power: January 1933* (Reading, MA: Addison-Wesley, 1996), 147; Duesterberg, "Die Regierungsbildung," 2.
4. Ian Kershaw, *Hitler,* vol. 1, *1889–1936: Hubris* (New York: W. W. Norton, 1998), 724, citing Bodo Scheurig, *Ewald von Kleist-Schmenzin. Ein Konservativer gegen Hitler* (Frankfurt-am-Main: 1994), 121; Turner, *Hitler's Thirty Days,* 147, citing Ewald von Kleist-Schmenzin, "Die letzte Möglichkeit," *Politische Studien* 10 (1959), 92.
5. Joachim von Ribbentrop, *The Ribbentrop Memoirs* (London: Weidenfeld and Nicolson, 1953), 26.
6. "Verhandlungen mit Hitler," *Vossische Zeitung,* January 29, 1933 (MA), 1.
7. "Republicans Hold Huge Berlin Rally," *New York Times,* January 30, 1933, 5.
8. Turner, *Hitler's Thirty Days,* 148–49.
9. Turner, *Hitler's Thirty Days,* 149–50.
10. In fact, Schleicher and Hammerstein may never have seriously considered a putsch. Werner von Alvensleben had spontaneously made the whole thing up "for effect"—or so he told his brother later. But on the last weekend of January in 1933, nobody in Berlin knew that. Franz von Papen, *Memoirs* (London: Andre Deutsch, 1952), 248–49.
11. Turner, *Hitler's Thirty Days,* 143.
12. Turner, *Hitler's Thirty Days,* 150–51.
13. The title was changed from vice-chancellor to deputy chancellor to give the office added weight. In fact, it made no difference.
14. Papen, *Memoirs,* 241.
15. *The Ribbentrop Memoirs,* 26.
16. Duesterberg, "Die Regierungsbildung," 1.
17. "Tagebuchaufzeichnung des Reichsfinanzministers über Vorgänge in Berlin am 29. und 30. Januar 1933 und die Bildung des Kabinetts Hitler, Nr. 79," at http://www.bundesarchiv.de/aktenreichskanzlei/1919-1933/10014/vsc/vsc1p/kap1_2/para2_79.html.

18. Duesterberg, "Die Regierungsbildung," 2–3.
19. Duesterberg, "Die Regierungsbildung," 2–3.
20. Duesterberg, "Die Regierungsbildung," 3.
21. Melita Maschmann, *Account Rendered: A Dossier on My Former Self* (London: Abelard-Schuman, 1965), 10.
22. Ritter, *Carl Goerdeler*, 60.

Epilogue

1. Michael S. Cullen, *Der Reichstag: Parliament Denkmal Symbol* (Berlin: be.bra Verlag, 1995), 242.

BIBLIOGRAPHY

Newspapers and Magazines

Bayerischer Kurier
Berliner Tageblatt
Deutsche Allgemeine Zeitung
Deutsche Presse
Essener Anzeiger
Frankfurter Zeitung
Fränkische Tagespost
Grossdeutsche Zeitung
Jüdische Echo
Jüdisch-liberale Zeitung
München-Augsburger-Abendzeitung
Münchener Post
Münchener Zeitung
Münchner Neueste Nachrichten
Neue Freie Presse, Vienna
Neues Münchener Tagblatt
Süddeutsche Zeitung
Völkischer Beobachter
Völkischer Kurier
Vorwärts
Vossische Zeitung

Fliegende Blätter
Illustrierter Beobachter
Kladderadatsch
Simplicissimus
Vierteljahrshefte für Zeitgeschichte

Le Figaro, Paris
Le Petit Parisien, Paris
Le Temps, Paris
New York Times
The Times, London

Books, Articles, and Websites

Abel, Theodore. Theodore Fred Abel papers, Hoover Institution, Stanford University, Online Archive of California.

———. *Why Hitler Came into Power.* Cambridge, MA: Harvard University Press, 1986. Originally published in 1938 by Prentice-Hall (New York).

Allen, William Sheridan, ed. *The Infancy of Nazism: The Memoirs of Ex-Gauleiter Albert Krebs, 1923–1933.* New York: New Viewpoints, 1976.

———. *The Nazi Seizure of Power: The Experience of a Single German Town, 1922–1945.* Rev. ed. New York and London: Franklin Watts, 1984.

Arafe, Thomas Wiles, Jr. *The Development and Character of the Nazi Political Machine, 1928–1930, and the NSDAP Electoral Breakthrough.* Dissertation: Louisiana State University, LSU Digital Commons, 1976.

Aust, Stefan. *Hitlers erster Feind: Der Kampf des Konrad Heiden.* Reinbek, Germany: Rowohlt, 2016.

Baur, Hans. *I Was Hitler's Pilot: The Memoirs of Hans Baur.* Barnsley, UK: Frontline Books, 1958, 2003.

Baynes, N. H., ed. *Speeches of Adolf Hitler: Early Speeches, 1922–1924, and Other Selections.* New York: Howard Fertig, 2006.

Beierl, Florian, and Othmar Plöckinger. "Neue Dokumente zu Hitlers Buch *Mein Kampf.*" *Vierteljahrshefte für Zeitgeschichte* 57, no. 2 (2009): 261–79.

Benz, Wolfgang. *Die 101 wichtigsten Fragen: Das Dritte Reich.* Munich: C. H. Beck, 2006.

———, ed. *Handbuch des Antisemitismus: Judenfeindschaft in Geschichte und Gegenwart.* Munich: De Gruyter Saur, 2008–2015.

Blackbourn, David, and Geoff Eley. *The Peculiarities of German History: Bourgeois Society and Politics in Nineteenth-Century Germany.* Oxford, UK: Oxford University Press, 1984.

Bracher, Karl Dietrich. *Die Auflösung der Weimarer Republik: Eine Studie zum Problem des Machtverfalls in der Demokratie.* Stuttgart and Düsseldorf: Ring Verlag, 1957.

———. *The German Dictatorship: The Origins, Structure, and Consequences of National Socialism.* London: Penguin Books, 1970.

Broszat, Martin, and Norbert Frei, eds. *Das dritte Reich: Chronik, Ereignisse, Zusammenhänge.* Munich: Piper Verlag, 1989.

———. *Hitler and the Collapse of Weimar Germany.* Leamington Spa, UK: Berg, 1987.

———. Note on meeting with Otto Wagener, February 5, 1960. Munich: Institut für Zeitgeschichte, Archive ZS 1732.

Brüning, Heinrich. *Memoiren 1918–1934.* 2 vols. Munich: Deutsche Verlags-Anstalt, 1970.

Bullock, Alan. *Hitler: A Study in Tyranny.* Rev. ed. Old Saybrook, CT: Konecky & Konecky, 1962.

Burke, Bernard V. *Ambassador Frederic Sackett and the Collapse of the Weimar Republic, 1930–1933: The United States and Hitler's Rise to Power.* New York: Cambridge University Press, 1994.

Burleigh, Michael. *The Third Reich: A New History.* New York: Hill and Wang, 2000.

Bytwerk, Randall L., ed. *Landmark Speeches of National Socialism.* College Station: Texas A&M University Press, 2008.

———. "Nazi and East German Propaganda Guide Page." Calvin University. https://research.calvin.edu/german-propaganda-archive/.

Cassirer, Ernst. *The Myth of the State.* New Haven, CT: Yale University Press, 1946.

Chamberlain, Houston Stewart. *Foundations of the Nineteenth Century.* Trans. John Lees. Elibron Classics, 2005. Originally published as *Grundlagen des neunzehnten Jahrhunderts.* Munich: F. Bruckmann Verlag, 1899.

———. *Rasse und Persönlichkeit. Aufsätze von Houston Stewart Chamberlain.* Munich: F. Bruckmann Verlag, 1925.

Childers, Thomas. *The Nazi Voter: The Social Foundations of Fascism in Germany, 1919–1933.* Chapel Hill: University of North Carolina Press, 1983.

Citizens' Association to Research Landsberg's Contemporary History. "Landsberg im 20. Jahrhundert." http://www.buergervereinigung-landsberg.de/gedenkstaette/landsberg.htm.

Clark, Christopher. *Iron Kingdom: The Rise and Downfall of Prussia, 1600–1947.* Cambridge, MA: Harvard University Press, 2006.

Class, Heinrich. "If I Were Kaiser." Excerpt, Internet Archive.

——— [Daniel Frymann, pseud.]. *Wenn ich der Kaiser wär . . . : Politische Wahrheiten und Notwendigkeiten.* Leipzig: Deitrich, 1914.

Craig, Gordon, A. *The Germans.* New York: Meridian, 1983.

———. *Germany 1866–1945.* Oxford, UK: Oxford University Press, 1978.

Cullen, Michael S. *Der Reichstag.* Berlin: be.bra Verlag, 1995.

Dahm, Volker, Albert A. Feiber, Hartmut Mehringer, and Horst Möller, eds. *Die tödliche Utopie: Bilder, Texte, Dokumente, Daten zum Dritten Reich.* Munich-Berlin: Institut für Zeitgeschichte, 2003.

Dahrendorf, Ralf. *Society and Democracy in Germany.* New York: Doubleday, 1967.

Davidson, Eugene. *The Making of Adolf Hitler: The Birth and Rise of Nazism.* New York: Macmillan, 1977.

Deak, Istvan. *Weimar Germany's Left-Wing Intellectuals: A Political History of the Weltbühne and Its Circle.* Berkeley: University of California Press, 1968.

Deiler, Manfred. Archiv Manfred Deiler.

De Jonge, Alex. *The Weimar Chronicle: Prelude to Hitler.* New York: New American Library, 1978.

Delmer, Sefton. *Trail Sinister: An Autobiography, Volume One.* London: Secker & Warburg, 1961.

Deuerlein, Ernst. *Der Aufstieg der NSDAP in Augenzeugenberichten.* Munich: Deutscher Taschenbuch Verlag, 1974.

———. *Hitler: Eine politische Biographie.* Munich: List Verlag, 1959.

———. "Hitlers Eintritt in die Politik und die Reichswehr: Dokumentation." *Vierteljahrshefte für Zeitgeschichte* 7, no. 2 (1959).

Dietrich, Otto. *The Hitler I Knew: Memoirs of the Third Reich's Press Chief.* New York: Skyhorse Publishing, 2010.

———. *Zwölf Jahre mit Hitler.* Munich: Isar Verlag, 1955.

Domarus, Max. *The Essential Hitler: Speeches and Commentary.* Edited by Patrick Romane. Wauconda, IL: Bolchazy-Carducci, 2007.

Dorpalen, Andreas. *Hindenburg and the Weimar Republic.* Princeton, NJ: Princeton University Press, 1964.

Drexler, Anton. *My Political Awakening: From the Journal of a German Socialist Worker.* Lincoln, NE: RJG Enterprises, 2009.

Duesterberg, Theodor. "Die Regierungsbildung am 30. Januar 1933." Munich: Institut für Zeitgeschichte, Archive, ZS 1700, April 27, 1946.

Elon, Amos. *The Pity of It All: A History of Jews in Germany, 1743–1933.* New York: Metropolitan Books, 2003.

Eschenhagen, Wieland, ed. *Die "Machtergreifung": Tagebuch einer Wende nach Presseberichten vom 1. Januar bis 6. März 1933.* Darmstadt: Luchterhand, 1982.

Esser, Hermann. Documents (postwar interviews). Institut für Zeitgeschichte, ED 561/5-3.

Evans, Richard J. *The Coming of the Third Reich.* New York: Penguin Press, 2004.

Eyck, Erich. *A History of the Weimar Republic.* Vol. 2, *From the Locarno Conference to Hitler's Seizure of Power.* Cambridge, MA: Harvard University Press, 1964.

Falter, Jürgen. *Hitlers Wähler.* Munich: C. H. Beck, 1991.

Fest, Joachim. *The Face of the Third Reich: Portraits of the Nazi Leadership.* New York: Da Capo Press, 1999.

———. *Hitler.* New York: Harcourt, Brace, Jovanovich, 1973.

Fischer, Stefanie. *Ökonomisches Vertrauen und antisemitische Gewalt: Jüdische Viehhändler in Mittelfranken 1919–1939.* Göttingen: Wallstein Verlag, 2014.

Fleischmann, Peter, ed. *Hitler als Häftling in Landsberg am Lech, 1923/24.* Neustadt an der Aisch: Verlag Ph. C. W. Schmidt, 2015.

François-Poncet, André. *The Fateful Years: Memoirs of a French Ambassador in Berlin, 1931–1938.* New York: Harcourt, Brace, 1949.

Frank, Hans. *Im Angesicht des Galgens: Deutung Hitlers und seiner Zeit auf Grund eigener Erlebnisse und Erkenntnisse. Geschrieben im Nürnberger Justizgefängnis.* Munich: Friedrich Alfred Beck Verlag, 1953.

Frank, Niklas. *In the Shadow of the Reich.* New York: Alfred A. Knopf, 1991.

Friedrich, Otto. *Before the Deluge: A Portrait of Berlin in the 1920s.* New York: Harper & Row, 1972.

Fritsch, Theodor, ed. *Handbuch der Judenfrage. Eine Zusammenstellung des wichtigsten Materials zur Beurteilung des jüdischen Volkes.* Leipzig: Hammer-Verlag, 1933.

Fritsche, Peter. *Germans into Nazis.* Cambridge, MA: Harvard University Press, 1998.

Fromm, Bella. *Blood and Banquets: A Berlin Social Diary.* New York: Birch Lane Press, 1990.

Fulda, Bernhard. *Press and Politics in the Weimar Republic.* Oxford, UK: Oxford University Press, 2009.

Fuller, Joseph V., ed. "Papers Relating to the Foreign Relations of the United States, 1930, Volume III." Washington, DC: Government Printing Office, 1945.

Galenson, Walter, and Arnold Zellner. "International Comparison of Unemployment Rates." *The Measurement and Behavior of Unemployment.* Cambridge, MA: National Bureau of Economic Research, 1947.

Gassert, Philipp, and Daniel S. Mattern. *The Hitler Library: A Bibliography.* Westport, CT: Greenwood Press, 2001.

Gerlich, Fritz. *Ein Publizist gegen Hitler: Briefe und Akten 1930–1934.* Paderborn, Germany: Verlag Ferdinand Schöningh, 2010.

Gilbert, G. M. *Nuremberg Diary.* New York: Signet, 1947.

Gillessen, Günther. *Auf verlorenem Posten: Die Frankfurter Zeitung im Dritten Reich.* Munich: Siedler Verlag, 1986.

Goebbels, Joseph. *Die Tagebücher von Joseph Goebbels: sämtliche Fragmente.* Edited by Elke Fröhlich. Munich: K. G. Saur, 1987–2008. Published by the Institut für Zeitgeschichte in cooperation with the Federal German Archive, this is the only definitive version of Goebbels's diaries. Fifteen thousand pages in thirty-two volumes are now available in print and online from Walter de Gruyter Verlag, Berlin, which owns Saur.

———. *Die zweite Revolution: Briefe an Zeitgenossen.* Zwickau: Streiter-Verlag, 1926[?].

———."Erkenntnis und Propaganda." *Signale der neuen Zeit. 25 ausgewählte Reden.* Munich: Zentralverlag der NSDAP, Franz Eher Nachfolger, 1934.

———. *Kampf um Berlin.* Munich: Zentralverlag der NSDAP, Franz Eher Nachfolger, 1934.

———. *Vom Kaiserhof zur Reichskanzlei: Eine historische Darstellung in Tagebuchblättern.* Munich: Zentralverlag der NSDAP, Franz Eher Nachfolger, 1934.

Goldensohn, Leon, ed. *Nuremberg Interviews: An American Psychiatrist's Conversations with the Defendants and Witnesses.* New York: Alfred A. Knopf, 2004.

Goltz, Anna von der. *Hindenburg: Power, Myth, and the Rise of the Nazis.* Oxford, UK: Oxford University Press, 2009.

Gordon, Mel. *Voluptuous Panic: The Erotic World of Weimar Berlin.* Los Angeles: Feral House, 2008.

Görtemaker, Heike B. *Eva Braun: Leben mit Hitler.* Munich: C. H. Beck, 2010.

———. *Eva Braun: Life with Hitler.* New York: Alfred A. Knopf, 2011.

Görtemaker, Manfred. *Thomas Mann und die Politik.* Frankfurt: Fischer Verlag, 2005.

Grady, Tim. *The German-Jewish Soldiers of the First World War in History and Memory.* Liverpool, UK: Liverpool University Press, 2011.

Grant, Madison. *Der Untergang der grossen Rasse: Die Rassen als Grundlage der Geschichte Europas.* Munich: J. F. Lehmann, 1925.

———. *The Passing of the Great Race, or The Racial Basis of European History.* New York: Charles Scribner's Sons, 1916.

Grill, Johnpeter Horst. "The Nazi Party's Rural Propaganda Before 1928." *Central European History* 15, no. 2 (June 1982): 149–85.

Gun, Nerin B. *Eva Braun: Hitler's Mistress.* New York: Meredith Press, 1968.

Haffner, Sebastian. *Defying Hitler: A Memoir.* Translated by Oliver Pretzel. New York: Farrar, Straus and Giroux, 2000.

———. *Geschichte eines Deutschen. Die Erinnerungen, 1914–1933.* Stuttgart: Deutsche Verlags-Anstalt, 2001.

———. *The Meaning of Hitler.* Cambridge, MA: Harvard University Press, 1983.

Hamann, Brigitte. *Hitler's Vienna: A Dictator's Apprenticeship.* Oxford, UK: Oxford University Press, 1999.

———. *Winifred Wagner: A Life at the Heart of Hitler's Bayreuth.* New York: Harcourt, 2006.

Hanfstaengl, Ernst. *15 Jahre mit Hitler: Zwischen Weissem und Braunem Haus.* Munich: R. Piper & Co. Verlag, 1980.

———. *Hitler: The Memoir of a Nazi Insider Who Turned Against the Führer.* New York: Arcade Publishng, 2011.

———. "I Was Hitler's Closest Friend." *Cosmopolitan,* March 1943: 43.

Hansen, Ron. *Hitler's Niece.* New York: HarperCollins, 1999.

Hauner, Milan. *Hitler: A Chronology of His Life and Time.* New York: Milan Hauner, 1983.

Hayman, Ronald. *Hitler and Geli.* New York: Bloomsbury, 1997.

Heberle, Rudolf. *From Democracy to Nazism: A Regional Case Study on Political Parties in Germany.* New York: Grosset & Dunlap, 1970.

Heiden, Konrad. *Adolf Hitler: Das Zeitalter der Verantwortungslosigkeit.* Vol. 1. Zürich: Europa Verlag, 1936.

———. *The Führer.* Edison, NJ: Castle Books, 2002 (from editions of 1934–1939).

Heinz, Grete, and Agnes F. Peterson, comps. *NSDAP Hauptarchiv: Guide to the Hoover Institution Microfilm Collection.* Stanford CA: Hoover Institution Press, 1964.

Hemmrich, Franz. "Adolf Hitler in der Festung Landsberg." Handwritten. Institut für Zeitgeschichte, ED 153; Archiv Manfred Deiler.

Hess, Rudolf. *Briefe 1908–1933: Herausgegeben von Wolf Rüdiger Hess.* Munich: Georg Müller Verlag, 1987.

Hett, Benjamin Carter. *The Death of Democracy: Hitler's Rise to Power and the Downfall of the Weimar Republic.* New York: Henry Holt, 2018.

Historisches Lexikon Bayerns. http://www.historisches-lexikon-bayerns.de/artikel/artikel_44472.

Hitler, Adolf. *Hitler, Mein Kampf: Eine kritische Edition.* Edited by Christian Hartmann, Thomas Vordermayer, Othmar Plöckinger, and Roman Töppel. Munich: Institute für Zeitgeschichte, 2016.

———. *Hitler. Reden, Schriften, Anordnungen. Februar 1925 bis Januar 1933.* Edited by Institut für Zeitgeschichte. 6 vols. plus supplementary volume (13 books, 5,427 pages). Munich: De Gruyter Saur, 1991–2003.

———. *Hitler. Reden, Schriften, Anordnungen. Februar 1925 bis Januar 1933.* Materialsammlung, Institut für Zeitgeschichte, Munich. This "materials collection" is the trove of supporting documents that underlie the six volumes of Hitler's 692 speeches along with his writings, orders, and interviews. Estimated at fifty thousand pages, the "materials collection" very usefully includes countless newspaper accounts of Hitler's travels and addresses.

———. *Hitler's Secret Conversations, 1941–1944*, with an introductory essay by H. R. Trevor-Roper. New York: Farrar, Straus and Young, 1953.

———. *Mein Kampf: Zwei Bände in einem Band, Ungekürzte Ausgabe.* 851st–855th printing. Munich: Zentralverlag der NSDAP, Franz Eher Nachfolger, 1943.

———. *Mein Kampf* (English edition). Translated by Ralph Manheim, with an introduction by Konrad Heiden. Boston: Houghton Mifflin, 1943.

———. *Monologe im Führerhauptquartier 1941–1944: Die Aufzeichnungen Heinrich Heims herausgegeben von Werner Jochmann.* Hamburg: Albrecht Knaus, 1980.

Hitler über Deutschland. Film documenting Hitler's third 1932 airborne election campaign. Bundesarchiv, Benutzungsmedien Film Online.

Hitler über Deutschland. Book of photographs produced by Heinrich Hoffmann, partially viewable at "Hitler Over Germany" on Randall Bytwerk's German Propaganda Archive at Calvin University. https://research.calvin.edu/german-propaganda-archive/hitler3.htm.

Hoegner, Wilhelm. *Die verratene Republik: Deutsche Geschichte, 1919–1933.* Munich: Nymphenburger Verlagshandlung, 1979.

———. *Hitler und Kahr: Die bayerischen Napoleonsgrössen von 1923: Ein im Untersuchungsausschuss des Bayerischen Landtags aufgedeckter Justizskandal, Teil I und Teil II.* Munich: Landesausschuss der S.P.D. in Bayern, 1928.

Hoffmann, Heinrich. *The Hitler Nobody Knows.* Lincoln, NE: Preuss Publishing, 2006.

———. *Hitler Was My Friend: The Memoirs of Hitler's Photographer.* London: Frontline Books, 2011.

Hofmann, Hans Hubert. *Der Hitlerputsch: Krisenjahre deutscher Geschichte 1920–1924.* Munich: Nymphenburger Verlagshandlung, 1961.

Hoser, Paul. *Die politischen, wirtschaftlichen und sozialen Hintergründe der Münchner Tagespresse zwischen 1914 und 1934.* Europäische Hochschulschriften Reihe III, Bd. 447, 2 Bde. Frankfurt am Main: 1990 (zugl. Diss. München 1988).

———. "Nationalsozialistische Deutsche Arbeiterpartei (NSDAP), 1920–1923/1925–1945." Historisches Lexikon Bayerns.

———. "Thierschstraße 41. Der Untermieter Hitler, sein jüdischer Hausherr und ein Restitutionsproblem." *Vierteljahrshefte für Zeitgeschichte* (A) 65 (2017): 131–61.

Hubatsch, Walther. *Hindenburg und der Staat: Aus den Papieren des Generalfeldmarschalls und Reichspräsidenten von 1878 bis 1934.* Göttingen: Musterschmidt, 1966.

Irving, David. *Göring: A Biography.* New York: William Morrow, 1989.

Isherwood, Christopher. *The Berlin Stories.* New York: New Directions, 1945.

———. *Christopher and His Kind: 1929–1939.* London: Eyre Methuen, 1977.

———. *Goodbye to Berlin.* London: Folio Society, 1975.

Jablonsky, David. *The Nazi Party in Dissolution: Hitler and the Verbotzeit 1923–1925*. London: Frank Cass, 1989.

Jäckel, Eberhard, and Axel Kuhn, eds. *Hitler: Sämtliche Aufzeichnungen, 1905–1924*. Stuttgart: Deutsche Verlags-Anstalt, 1980.

———. *Hitlers Weltanschauung: Entwurf einer Herrschaft*. Expanded and revised ed. Stuttgart: Deutsche Verlags-Anstalt, 1981.

Jelavic, Peter. "Modernity, Civic Identity, and Metropolitan Entertainment: Vaudeville, Cabaret, and Revue in Berlin, 1900–1933." In *Berlin: Culture and Metropolis*, edited by Charles W. Haxthausen and Heidrun Suhr. Minneapolis: University of Minnesota Press, 1990.

Joachimsthaler, Anton. *Hitlers Liste: Ein Dokument persönlicher Beziehungen*. Munich: F. A. Herbig, 2003.

Jochmann, Werner. *Im Kampf um die Macht: Hitlers Rede vor dem Hamburger Nationalklub von 1919*. Frankfurt am Main: Europäische Verlagsanstalt, 1960.

———. *Nationalsozialismus und Revolution: Ursprung und Geschichte der NSDAP in Hamburg, 1922–1933. Dokumente*. Frankfurt-am-Main: Europäische Verlagsanstalt, 1963.

Jones, Larry Eugene. "Die Tage vor Hitlers Machtübernahme." *Vierteljahrshefte für Zeitgeschichte* 37, no. 4 (1989): 759–74.

———. "'The Greatest Stupidity of My Life': Alfred Hugenberg and the Formation of the Hitler Cabinet, January 1933." *Journal of Contemporary History* 27, no. 1 (January 1992).

Junge, Traudl. *Until the Final Hour: Hitler's Last Secretary*. London: Weidenfeld and Nicolson, 2003.

Kaes, Anton, Martin Jay, and Edward Dimendberg, eds. *The Weimar Republic Sourcebook*. Berkeley: University of California Press, 1994.

Kaltenborn, Hans von. *Fifty Fabulous Years, 1900–1950: A Personal Review*. New York: Putnam, 1950.

Kellerhoff, Sven Felix. *Die NSDAP: Eine Partei und ihre Mitglieder*. Stuttgart: Klett-Cotta, 2017.

———. *Mein Kampf: Die Karriere eines Buches*. Stuttgart: Klett-Cotta, 2015.

Kershaw, Ian. *Hitler*. Vol. 1, *1889–1936: Hubris*. New York: W. W. Norton, 1998.

———. *The "Hitler Myth" Image and Reality in the Third Reich*. Oxford, UK: Oxford University Press, 1980.

Kessler, Harry. *Berlin in Lights: The Diaries of Count Harry Kessler (1918–1937)*. New York: Grove Press, 2000.

———. *In the Twenties: The Diaries of Harry Kessler*. With an introduction by Otto Friedrich. New York: Holt, Rinehart and Winston, 1971.

———. *Tagebücher, 1918–1937: Komplettausgabe*. Berlin: Insel Verlag, 1961; Prague: e-artnow, 2013.

Kissenkoetter, Udo. *Gregor Strasser und die NSDAP*. Stuttgart: Deutsche Verlags-Anstalt, 1978.

Klemperer, Victor. *I Will Bear Witness 1933–1941: A Diary of the Nazi Years*. Translated by Martin Chalmers. New York: Modern Library, 1999.

———. *Leben sammeln, nicht fragen wozu und warum: Tagebücher*. Vol. 1, *1918–1924*. Vol. 2, *1925–1932*. Berlin: Aufbau-Verlag, 1996.

———. *LTI. Notizbuch eines Philologen*. Edited by Elke Fröhlich. Stuttgart: Reclam Verlag, 2010.

Knickerbocker, H. R. *The German Crisis*. New York: Farrar & Rinehart, 1932.

Knowlton, James, and Truett Cates, trans. *Forever in the Shadow of Hitler? Original Documents of the Historikerstreit, the Controversy Concerning the Singularity of the Holocaust*. Atlantic Highlands, NJ: Humanities Press, 1993.

Kubizek, August. *The Young Hitler I Knew: The Memoirs of Hitler's Childhood Friend.* London: Greenhill Books, 2006.

Kühnl, Reinhard. "Zur Programmatik der nationalsozialistischen Linken: Das Strasser Programm von 1925/26," *Vierteljahrshefte für Zeitgeschichte,* Jg. 14 (1966), Heft 3.

Lane, Barbara Miller, and Leila J. Rupp, eds. *Nazi Ideology Before 1933: A Documentation.* Austin: University of Texas Press, 1978.

Langer, Walter C. *Hitler Source-Book.* National Archives. https://ia801307.us.archive.org/11/items/OSSHitlerSourcebook/OSS%20Hitler%20Sourcebook.pdf. Also available at https://archive.org/details/OSSHitlerSourcebook/page/n2.

———. *The Mind of Adolf Hitler.* London: Pan Books, 1973.

Laqueur, Walter Z. *Young Germany: A History of the German Youth Movement.* London: Routledge & Kegan Paul, 1962.

Large, David Clay. *Berlin.* New York: Basic Books, 2000.

———. *Where Ghosts Walked: Munich's Road to the Third Reich.* New York: W. W. Norton, 1997.

Larson, Erik. *In the Garden of Beasts: Love, Terror, and an American Family in Hitler's Berlin.* New York: Crown, 2011.

Leber, Julius. *Ein Mann geht seinen Weg.* Berlin: Mosaik-Verlag, 1952.

Lochner, Louis P. *Always the Unexpected: A Book of Reminiscences.* New York: Macmillan, 1956.

Lohse, Hinrich. "Der Fall Strasser." Munich: Institut für Zeitgeschichte, Archive ZS 265, Band 1.

Longerich, Peter. *Goebbels: A Biography.* New York: Random House, 2015.

Ludecke, Kurt G. W. *I Knew Hitler: The Lost Testimony by a Survivor from the Night of the Long Knives.* Barnsley, UK: Pen & Sword, 2013.

Maschmann, Melita. *Account Rendered: A Dossier on My Former Self.* London: Abelard-Schuman, 1965.

Maser, Werner. *Adolf Hitler, Mein Kampf: Der Fahrplan eines Welteroberers: Geschichte, Auszüge, Kommentare.* Esslingen, Germany: Bechtle Verlag, 1974.

———. *Der Sturm auf die Republik: Frühgeschichte der NSDAP.* Stuttgart: Deutsche Verlags-Anstalt, 1973.

———, ed. *Hitler's Letters and Notes.* New York: Bantam, 1976.

———. *Hitlers Mein Kampf: Entstehung, Aufbau, Stil, Änderungen, Quellen, Quellenwert, kommentierte Auszüge.* Munich: Bechtle Verlag, 1966.

[Mayr, Captain Karl]. "I Was Hitler's Boss." *Current History* 1, no. 3 (November 1941): 193–99.

Meissner, Hans Otto, and Harry Wilde. *Die Machtergreifung: Ein Bericht über die Technik des nationalsozialistischen Staatsstreichs.* Stuttgart: J. G. Cotta'sche Buchhandlung Nachfolger, 1958.

Merkl, Peter H. *The Making of a Stormtrooper.* Princeton, NJ: Princeton University Press, 1980.

———. *Political Violence Under the Swastika: 581 Early Nazis.* Princeton, NJ: Princeton University Press, 1975.

Mommsen, Hans. *Aufstieg und Untergang der Republik von Weimar 1918–1933.* Berlin: Ullstein Verlag, 1989.

———. *The Rise and Fall of Weimar Democracy.* Chapel Hill: University of North Carolina Press, 1989.

Mosse, George L. *Confronting History: A Memoir.* Madison: University of Wisconsin Press, 2000.

———. *Nazi Culture: Intellectual, Cultural, and Social Life in the Third Reich.* New York: Grosset & Dunlap, 1966.

Mowrer, Edgar Ansel. *Triumph and Turmoil: A Personal History of Our Time.* New York: Weybright and Talley, 1968.

Mühlberger, Detlef. *The Social Bases of Nazism*. Cambridge, UK: Cambridge University Press, 2003.

Müller, Karl Alexander von. *Im Wandel einer Welt, Erinnerungen, 1919–1932*. Munich: Süddeutscher Verlag, 1966.

———. *Mars und Venus: Erinnerungen 1914–1919*. Stuttgart: Verlag Gustav Klippert, 1954.

Nagorski, Andrew. *Hitlerland: American Eyewitnesses to the Nazi Rise to Power*. New York: Simon & Schuster, 2012.

Nicholls, A. J. *Weimar and the Rise of Hitler*. 4th ed. New York: St. Martin's Press, 2000.

Niewyk, Donald L. *The Jews in Weimar Germany*. Baton Rouge and London: Louisiana State University Press, 1980.

Noakes, Jeremy, and Geoffrey Pridham, eds. *Nazism: A History in Documents and Eyewitness Accounts 1919–1945; Volume 1, The Nazi Party, State and Society 1919–1939*. New York: Schocken Books, 1983.

NSDAP Hauptarchiv. Hoover Institution, Stanford University. Also available on microfilm in several other archives and through interlibrary loan. This is a somewhat haphazard collection of an estimated four hundred thousand surviving documents from the Nazi Party's main archive.

O Broin, Turlach. "Mail-Order Demagogues: The NSDAP School for Speakers, 1928–34." *Journal of Contemporary History* 51, no. 4 (2016).

Orlow, Dietrich. *The History of the Nazi Party*. Vol. 1, *1919–33*. London: David & Charles, 1969.

———. *The History of the Nazi Party*. Vol. 2, *1933–1945*. Pittsburgh, PA: University of Pittsburgh Press, 1973.

———. *Weimar Prussia, 1925–1933: The Illusion of Strength*. Pittsburgh, PA: University of Pittsburgh Press, 1991.

Ott, Alois Marie. "Aber plötzlich sprang Hitler auf..." *Bayern Kurier*, November 3, 1973.

Papen, Franz von. *Der Wahrheit eine Gasse*. Munich: P. List, 1952.

Peis, Günter. "Hitlers unbekannte Geliebte." *Der Stern*, July 13, 1959.

Peukert, Detlev J. K. *Jugend zwischen Krieg und Krise: Lebenswelten von Arbeiterjungen in der Weimarer Republik*. Cologne: Bund Verlag, 1987.

———. *The Weimar Republic: The Crisis of Classical Modernity*. New York: Hill and Wang, 1987.

Pietrusza, David. *1932: The Rise of Hitler and FDR; Two Tales of Politics, Betrayal, and Unlikely Destiny*. Guilford, CT: Lyons Press, 2016.

Plöckinger, Othmar. *Geschichte eines Buches: Adolf Hitlers "Mein Kampf" 1922–1945*. Munich: R. Oldenbourg Verlag, 2006.

———, ed. *Quellen und Dokumente zur Geschichte von "Mein Kampf" 1924–1945*. Stuttgart: Franz Steiner Verlag, 2016.

———. *Reden um die Macht? Wirkung und Strategie der Reden Adolf Hitlers im Wahlkampf zu den Reichstagswahlen am 6. November 1932*. Vienna: Passagen, 1999.

———, ed. *Schlüsseldokumente zur internationalen Rezeption von "Mein Kampf."* Stuttgart: Franz Steiner Verlag, 2016.

———, ed. *Sprache zwishcen Politik, Ideologie und Geschichtsschreibung: Analysen historischer und aktueller Übersetzungen von "Mein Kampf."* Stuttgart: Franz Steiner Verlag, 2019.

———. *Unter Soldaten und Agitatoren: Hitlers prägende Jahre im deutschen Militär, 1918–1920*. Paderborn, Germany: Ferdinand Schöningh, 2013.

Prange, Gordon W. *Hitler's Speeches and the United States*. New York: Oxford University Press, 1941.

Pridham, Geoffrey. *Hitler's Rise to Power: The Nazi Movement in Bavaria, 1923–33*. London: Hart-Davis, MacGibbon, 1973. Sydney, Australia: Endeavour Press, 2016.

Pulzer, Peter G. J. *Die Entstehung des politischen Antisemitismus in Deutschland und Österreich 1867–1914*. Göttingen: Vandenhoeck & Ruprecht, 2004.

———. *The Rise of Anti-Semitism in Germany and Austria*. New York: John Wiley and Sons, 1964.

Pyta, Wolfram. *Hitler: Der Künstler als Politiker und Feldherr: Eine Herrschaftsanalyse*. Munich: Siedler Verlag, 2015.

Read, Anthony. *The Devil's Disciples: Hitler's Inner Circle*. New York: W. W. Norton, 2004.

Redles, David. *Hitler's Millennial Reich: Apocalyptic Belief and the Search for Salvation*. New York: New York University Press, 2005.

Remarque, Erich Maria. *All Quiet on the Western Front*. New York: Fawcett Crest, 1987.

———. *Erich Maria Remarque's* All Quiet on the Western Front. Bloom's Guides, edited by Harold Bloom. New York: Chelsea House, 2008.

Reuth, Ralf Georg. *Goebbels*. Translated by Krishna Winston. New York: Harcourt Brace, 1993.

Rhodes, Richard. *Masters of Death: The SS-Einsatzgruppen and the Invention of the Holocaust*. New York: Alfred A. Knopf, 2002.

Ribbentrop, Joachim von. *The Ribbentrop Memoirs*. With an introduction by Alan Bullock. London: Weidenfeld and Nicolson, 1953.

Ritter, Gerhard. *Carl Goerdeler und die deutsche Widerstandsbewegung*. Stuttgart: Deutsche Verlags-Anstalt, 1954.

Rosenbaum, Ron. *Explaining Hitler: The Search for the Origins of His Evil*. New York: Harper-Perennial, 1999.

Rosenberg, Alfred. *Memoirs of Alfred Rosenberg*. With commentaries by Serge Lang and Eric Posselt. Chicago: Ziff-Davis, 1949.

———. *The Myth of the Twentieth Century: An Evaluation of the Spiritual-Intellectual Confrontations of Our Age*. Torrance, CA: Noontide Press, 1982. Originally published in Germany in 1930.

Ryback, Timothy W. *Hitler's Private Library: The Books That Shaped His Life*. New York: Alfred A. Knopf, 2008.

Sales, Raoul de Roussy de, ed. *Adolf Hitler: My New Order*. New York: Reynal & Hitchcock, 1941.

Sandner, Harald. *Hitler: Das Itinerar: Aufenthaltsorte und Reisen von 1889 bis 1945*. Berlin: Berlin Story Verlag, 2016.

Sauerwein, Jules. *30 ans à la une*. Paris: Plon, 1962.

Schacht, Hjalmar. *My First Seventy-Six Years*. London: Allan Wingate, 1955.

Schirach, Henriette von. *Frauen um Hitler: Nach Materialien von Henriette von Schirach*. Munich: F. A. Herbig, 1983.

Schroeder, Christa. *He Was My Chief: The Memoirs of Adolf Hitler's Secretary*. London: Frontline Books, 2009.

Shirer, William L. *The Rise and Fall of the Third Reich: A History of Nazi Germany*. New York: Simon and Schuster, 1960.

Sigmund, Anna Maria. *Des Führers bester Freund: Hitler, seine Nichte Geli Raubal und der "Ehrenarier" Emil Maurice—eine Dreiecksbeziehung*. Munich: Wilhelm Heyne Verlag, 2005.

———. *Women of the Third Reich*. Richmond Hill, Ontario: NDE Publishing, 2000.

Smith, Woodruff D. *The Ideological Origins of Nazi Imperialism*. New York: Oxford University Press, 1989.

Snyder, Louis L. *Encyclopedia of the Third Reich*. New York: Paragon House, 1989.

Sommer, Karl. *Beiträge zur bayerischen und deutschen Geschichte in der Zeit von 1910–1933.* Munich: Self-published by the heirs, 1981 (Bayerische Staatsbibliothek).

Sösemann, Bernd. *Das Ende der Weimarer Republik in der Kritik demokratischer Publizisten.* Berlin: Colloquium Verlag, 1976.

Speer, Albert. *Erinnerungen.* Berlin: Propyläen Verlag, 1969.

———. *Spandau: The Secret Diaries.* New York: Macmillan, 1976.

Spiro, Jonathan Peter. *Defending the Master Race: Conservation, Eugenics, and the Legacy of Madison Grant.* Burlington: University of Vermont Press, 2009.

Stachura, Peter D. "Der kritische Wendepunkt? Die NSDAP und die Reichstagswahlen vom 20. Mai 1928." *Vierteljahrshefte für Zeitgeschichte* 26, no. 1 (1978): 81.

———. *Gregor Strasser and the Rise of Nazism.* London: George Allen & Unwin, 1982.

———, ed. *The Shaping of the Nazi State.* London: Croom Helm, 1978.

Steinweis, Alan E. *Studying the Jew: Scholarly Anti-Semitism in Nazi Germany.* Cambridge, MA: Harvard University Press, 2006.

Stern, Fritz. *Einstein's German World.* Princeton, NJ: Princeton University Press, 1999.

———. *The Politics of Cultural Despair: A Study in the Rise of the Germanic Ideology.* Berkeley: University of California Press, 1961.

Strasser, Reverend Bernard. "Gregor and Otto Strasser: A Footnote to the History of Nazi Germany." Hoover Institution Archives, Stanford University, August 27, 1974.

Strasser, Gregor. "Gedanken über Aufgaben der Zukunft." *NS-Briefe,* June 15, 1926. Translated as "Thoughts About the Tasks of the Future." In Barbara Miller Lane and Leila J. Rupp, eds., *Nazi Ideology Before 1933: A Documentation.* Austin: University of Texas Press, 1978.

Strasser, Otto, and Michael Stern. *Flight from Terror.* New York: AMS Press, 1981.

———. *Hitler and I.* Boston: Houghton Mifflin, 1940.

Tagebuchaufzeichnung des Reichsfinanzministers über Vorgänge in Berlin am 29. und 30. Januar 1933 und die Bildung des Kabinetts Hitler, Nr. 79. http://www.bundesarchiv.de/aktenreichskanzlei/1919-1933/10014/vsc/vsc1p/kap1_2/para2_79.html.

Thacker, Toby. *Joseph Goebbels: Life and Death.* New York: Palgrave Macmillan, 2009.

Thompson, Dorothy. *"I Saw Hitler!"* New York: Farrar & Rinehart, 1932.

Toland, John. *Adolf Hitler.* 2 vols. New York: Doubleday, 1976.

———. *Hitler: The Pictorial Documentary of His Life.* New York: Ballantine, 1976.

———. John Toland papers, Library of Congress. These include audio recordings of interviews that Toland conducted for his Hitler biography with such surviving figures as Ernst Hanfstaengl, Helene Hanfstaengl Niemeyer, Ilse Hess, Gerdy Troost, and Albert Speer. Papers related to Toland's Hitler research are held at the Franklin D. Roosevelt Presidential Library, in Hyde Park, New York.

Töppel, Roman. "'Volk und Rasse': Hitler's Quellen auf der Spur." *Vierteljahrshefte für Zeitgeschichte* 64, no. 1 (2016).

Trevor-Roper, H. R. *The Last Days of Hitler.* New York: Macmillan, 1947.

The Trial of the Major War Criminals Before the International Military Tribunal, Nuremberg: November 14, 1945–October 1, 1946. Vol. 32. Published at Nuremberg, 1948. https://www.loc.gov/rr/frd/Military_Law/pdf/NT_Vol-XXXII.pdf.

Turner, Henry Ashby, Jr. *German Big Business and the Rise of Hitler.* New York: Oxford University Press, 1985.

———. *Hitler's Thirty Days to Power: January 1933.* Reading, MA: Addison-Wesley, 1996.

Tworek, Heidi J. S. *News from Germany: The Competition to Control World Communications, 1900–1945.* Harvard Historical Studies 190. Cambridge, MA: Harvard University Press, 2019.

Tyrell, Albrecht. *Führer befiehl... Selbstzeugnisse aus der "Kampfzeit" der NSDAP.* Düsseldorf: Droste Verlag, 1969.

Ullrich, Volker. *Adolf Hitler.* Vol. 1, *Die Jahre des Aufstiegs 1889–1939.* Frankfurt-am-Main: S. Fischer Verlag, 2013.

———. *Hitler: Ascent 1889–1939.* New York: Alfred A. Knopf, 2016.

"Von guter Selbstzucht und Beherrschung." *Der Spiegel,* April 17, 1989.

Wagener, Otto. *Hitler aus nächster Nähe: Aufzeichnungen eines Vertrauten 1929 –1932.* Edited by H. A. Turner, Jr. Frankfurt-am-Main: Ullstein Verlag, 1978.

———. *Hitler—Memoirs of a Confidant.* Edited by Henry Ashby Turner, Jr. New Haven, CT: Yale University Press, 1985.

Waite, Robert, G. L. *The Psychopathic God Adolf Hitler.* New York: Basic Books, 1977.

Wallace, Max. *The American Axis: Henry Ford, Charles Lindbergh, and the Rise of The Third Reich.* New York: St. Martin's Press, 2003.

Weber, Thomas. *Becoming Hitler: The Making of a Nazi.* New York: Basic Books, 2017.

———. *Hitler's First War: Adolf Hitler, the Men of the List Regiment, and the First World War.* Oxford, UK: Oxford University Press, 2010.

Weinberg, Gerhard L. *Germany, Hitler, and World War II.* Cambridge, UK: Cambridge University Press, 1995.

———, ed. *Hitler's Second Book: The Unpublished Sequel to Mein Kampf by Adolf Hitler.* New York: Enigma Books, 2003.

———, ed. *Hitler's Table Talk 1941–1944: His Private Conversations.* New York: Enigma Books, 2008.

Wheeler-Bennett, John W. *The Nemesis of Power: The German Army in Politics, 1918–1945.* London: Macmillan, 1956.

Winkler, Heinrich August. *Der Weg in die Katastrophe. Arbeiter und Arbeiterbewegung in der Weimarer Republik 1930–1933.* Bonn: Verlag J. H. W. Dietz Nachf., 1990.

———. *Germany: The Long Road West.* Vol. 1, *1789–1933.* Translated by Alexander J. Sager. Oxford, UK: Oxford University Press, 2006.

———. *Weimar: Die Geschichte der ersten deutschen Demokratie.* Munich: C. H. Beck, 1993.

Wucher, Albert. *Die Fahne Hoch: Das Ende der Republik and Hitlers Machtübernahme.* Munich: Süddeutscher Verlag, 1963.

Xammar, Eugeni. *Das Schlangenei. Berichte aus dem Deutschland der Inflationsjahre 1922–1924.* Berlin: Berenberg Verlag, 2007.

Zehnpfennig, Barbara. *Adolf Hitler: Mein Kampf: Weltanschauung und Programm: Studienkommentar.* Munich: Wilhelm Fink, 2011.

———. "Ein Buch mit Geschichte, ein Buch der Geschichte: Hitlers 'Mein Kampf.'" *Aus Politik und Zeitgeschichte,* Bundeszentrale für politische Bildung, 2015.

INDEX

Note: Italic page numbers refer to illustrations. "Photo insert" refers to photographic insert section.

ABOUT THE AUTHOR

Journalist and author Peter Ross Range has written about war, politics, international affairs, and history. A specialist in Germany, he served as *Time* correspondent in Germany and Vietnam and as White House correspondent for *U.S. News & World Report.* He has reported extensively for the *New York Times, National Geographic,* the *London Sunday Times Magazine,* and *Playboy.* He has been an Institute of Politics Fellow at Harvard's Kennedy School of Government, a Guest Scholar at the Woodrow Wilson International Center in Washington, and a Distinguished International Fellow at the University of North Carolina. He lives in Washington, D.C.